D1112177

PRINCIPLES OF EDUCATIONAL AND PSYCHOLOGICAL MEASUREMENT

PRINCIPLES OF EDUCATIONAL AND PSYCHOLOGICAL MEASUREMENT

A Book of Selected Readings

EDITED BY

WILLIAM A. MEHRENS

ROBERT L. EBEL

MICHIGAN STATE UNIVERSITY

RAND McNALLY & COMPANY

CHICAGO, ILLINOIS

RAND McNALLY EDUCATION SERIES

B. OTHANEL SMITH, Advisory Editor

Printed in U.S.A. by Rand McNally & Company
Library of Congress Catalogue Card Number: 67-14694

PREFACE

The editors of this text believe that a comprehensive grasp of the principles of measurement can be accomplished through a study of some of the classical articles on measurement that have been published in the last thirty years. While good libraries should have most of the articles, they ordinarily have only one copy. For this reason, professors are reluctant to assign them as required reading. In addition, most of these articles are ones which every specialist in measurement should have in his personal library.

This book is designed to be useful in both undergraduate and graduate courses in the principles of measurement. It can serve as a supplementary text for any except the most elementary course. It can also serve as the main text in advanced seminars in measurement. The articles vary in levels of difficulty, but even the more difficult articles can be understood by almost any reader at a level that will make them useful.

The selection of articles to be used in this book was a difficult task. It is relatively easy to justify the merit of the articles included; a harder task is to justify the exclusion of many other worthwhile articles. In general, the selection was based on the following criteria: (1) The impact of the article: This was judged by the effect of the article on measurement and evaluation practices as well as the degree of reference to it in subsequent theoretical literature. (2) The author: An attempt was made to use articles by many different authors. While some authors have several articles in the book, most have only one. (3) Length of the article: Shorter articles were, in general, given preference. Outstanding longer articles of appropriate content are mentioned in the introductory comments and listed in the suggested readings. (4) Copyright date: If several articles covered essentially the same content, the most recent one was chosen. There are several articles included that may be considered to be relatively old, but they are not dated. These articles are essential background reading for many of the more recent publications that are, in essence, building on the foundations established by the older classics. To understand more recent articles without this background would be difficult.

The present collection includes 37 articles divided into five units: (1) Measurement Theory and Scaling, (2) Norms, (3) Reliability, (4) Validity, and (5) Item Analysis and Selection. All five units deal with the theory and philosophy of testing. No experimental studies of specific tests are included, since articles of this type, in general, have little impact on the principles of measurement.

The introduction to each article or group of articles points out its implications and relates it to other articles in the collection. Additional readings on the topic are provided in the introduction and in the list which follows every unit.

Obviously, the major contributions in an edited book are those of the authors. We extend our thanks to these authors and to their publishers who so graciously gave permission for use of their materials.

W. A. M.
R. L. E.

East Lansing, Michigan
1967

TABLE OF CONTENTS

PRINCIPLES OF EDUCATIONAL AND PSYCHOLOGICAL MEASUREMENT

Unit One:

MEASUREMENT THEORY AND SCALING

INTRODUCTION

1. Stevens, S. S., *On the Theory of Scales of Measurement*
2. Burke, Cletus J., *Additive Scales and Statistics*
3. Senders, Virginia L., *A Comment on Burke's Additive Scales and Statistics*
4. Baker, Bela O., Hardyck, Curtis D., and Petrinovich, Lewis F., *Weak Measurements* Vs. *Strong Statistics: An Empirical Critique of S. S. Stevens' Proscriptions on Statistics*

The first four articles in this unit relate to the theory of scales of measurement. The first article by Stevens is one of the classic articles on the classification of scales of measurement. Understanding this article is basic to the understanding of the three that follow.

An issue that has been much debated by test specialists is whether or not we can use statistical techniques that require interval data when we, in fact, probably have only measured on an ordinal scale. The articles by Burke, Senders, and Baker *et al.* discuss this problem. Other sources you may wish to consult are listed in the suggested readings at the end of this unit. Coombs (1950, 1964) has long been an advocate of the weak measurement theory. He has consistently taken the position that we rarely obtain interval measurement in psychology but often obtain more than just ordinal data, and suggests a more complete classification that includes an "ordered metric" scale. This scale not only gives us more descriptive information but also allows us to use correctly more powerful statistical tests than those appropriate to ordinal data. The references mentioned are only a sample of his extensive writings.

1. On the Theory of Scales of Measurement

S. S. STEVENS

For seven years a committee of the British Association for the Advancement of Science debated the problem of measurement. Appointed in 1932 to represent Section A (Mathematical and Physical Sciences) and Section J (Psychology), the committee was instructed

Stevens, S. S. On the theory of scales of measurement. *Science*, 1946, *103*, 677–680. Reprinted with the permission of the publisher and author.

to consider and report upon the possibility of "quantitative estimates of sensory events"—meaning simply: Is it possible to measure human sensation? Deliberation led only to disagreement, mainly about what is meant by the term measurement. An interim report in 1938 found one member complaining that his colleagues "came out by that same door as they went in," and in order to have another try at agreement, the committee begged to be continued for another year.

For its final report (1940) the committee chose a common bone for its contentions, directing its arguments at a concrete example of a sensory scale. This was the Sone scale of loudness (S. S. Stevens and H. Davis. *Hearing*. New York: Wiley, 1938), which purports to measure the subjective magnitude of an auditory sensation against a scale having the formal properties of other basic scales, such as those used to measure length and weight. Again the 19 members of the committee came out by the routes they entered, and their views ranged widely between two extremes. One member submitted "that any law purporting to express a quantitative relation between sensation intensity and stimulus intensity is not merely false but is in fact meaningless unless and until a meaning can be given to the concept of addition as applied to sensation" (Final Report, p. 245).

It is plain from this and from other statements by the committee that the real issue is the meaning of measurement. This, to be sure, is a semantic issue, but one susceptible of orderly discussion. Perhaps agreement can better be achieved if we recognize that measurement exists in a variety of forms and that scales of measurement fall into certain definite classes. These classes are determined both by the empirical operations invoked in the process of "measuring" and by the formal (mathematical) properties of the scales. Furthermore—and this is of great concern to several of the sciences—the statistical manipulations that can legitimately be applied to empirical data depend upon the type of scale against which the data are ordered.

A CLASSIFICATION OF SCALES OF MEASUREMENT

Paraphrasing N. R. Campbell (Final Report, p. 340), we may say that measurement, in the broadest sense, is defined as the assignment of numerals to objects or events according to rules. The fact that numerals can be assigned under different rules leads to different kinds of scales and different kinds of measurement. The problem then becomes that of making explicit (a) the various rules for the assignment of numerals, (b) the mathematical properties (or group structure) of the resulting scales, and (c) the statistical operations applicable to measurements made with each type of scale.

Scales are possible in the first place only because there is a certain isomorphism between what we can do with the aspects of objects and the properties of the numeral series. In dealing with the aspects of objects we invoke empirical operations for determining equality (classifying), for rank-ordering, and for determining when differences and when ratios between the aspects of objects are equal. The conventional series of numerals yields to analogous operations: We can identify the members of a numeral series and classify them. We know their order as given by convention. We can determine equal differences, as $8 - 6 = 4 - 2$, and equal ratios, as $8/4 = 6/3$. The isomorphism between these properties of the numeral series and certain empirical operations which we perform with objects permits the use of the series as a *model* to represent aspects of the empirical world.

The type of scale achieved depends upon the character of the basic empirical operations performed. These operations are limited ordinarily by the nature of the thing being scaled and by our choice of procedures, but, once selected, the operations determine that there will eventuate one or another of the scales listed in Table 1.[1]

TABLE 1

Scale	Basic Empirical Operations	Mathematical Group Structure	Permissible Statistics (invariantive)
NOMINAL	Determination of equality	*Permutation group* $x' = f(x)$ $f(x)$ means any one-to-one substitution	Number of cases Mode Contingency correlation
ORDINAL	Determination of greater or less	*Isotonic group* $x' = f(x)$ $f(x)$ means any monotonic increasing function	Median Percentiles
INTERVAL	Determination of equality of intervals or differences	*General linear group* $x' = ax + b$	Mean Standard deviation Rank-order correlation Product-moment correlation
RATIO	Determination of equality of ratios	*Similarity group* $x' = ax$	Coefficient of variation

The decision to discard the scale names commonly encountered in writings on measurement is based on the ambiguity of such terms as "intensive" and "extensive." Both ordinal and interval scales have at

[1] A classification essentially equivalent to that contained in this table was presented before the International Congress for the Unity of Science, September 1941. The writer is indebted to the late Prof. G. D. Birkoff for a stimulating discussion which led to the completion of the table in essentially its present form.

times been called intensive, and both interval and ratio scales have sometimes been labeled extensive.

It will be noted that the column listing the basic operations needed to create each type of scale is cumulative: to an operation listed opposite a particular scale must be added all those operations preceding it. Thus, an interval scale can be erected only provided we have an operation for determining equality of intervals, for determining greater or less, and for determining equality (not greater and not less). To these operations must be added a method for ascertaining equality of ratios if a ratio scale is to be achieved.

In the column which records the group structure of each scale are listed the mathematical transformations which leave the scale-form invariant. Thus, any numeral, x, on a scale can be replaced by another numeral, x', where x' is the function of x listed in this column. Each mathematical group in the column is contained in the group immediately above it.

The last column presents examples of the type of statistical operations appropriate to each scale. This column is cumulative in that *all* statistics listed are admissible for data scaled against a ratio scale. The criterion for the appropriateness of a statistic is *invariance* under the transformations in Column 3. Thus, the case that stands at the median (mid-point) of a distribution maintains its position under all transformations which preserve order (isotonic group), but an item located at the mean remains at the mean only under transformations as restricted as those of the linear group. The ratio expressed by the coefficient of variation remains invariant only under the similarity transformation (multiplication by a constant). (The rank-order correlation coefficient is usually deemed appropriate to an ordinal scale, but actually this statistic assumes equal intervals between successive ranks and therefore calls for an interval scale.)

Let us now consider each scale in turn.

NOMINAL SCALE

The *nominal scale* represents the most unrestricted assignment of numerals. The numerals are used only as labels or type numbers, and words or letters would serve as well. Two types of nominal assignments are sometimes distinguished, as illustrated (a) by the 'numbering' of football players for the identification of the individuals, and (b) by the 'numbering' of types or classes, where each member of a class is assigned the same numeral. Actually, the first is a special case of the second, for when we label our football players we are dealing with unit classes of one member each. Since the purpose is just as well served when any two designating numerals are interchanged, this scale form remains invariant under the general substitution or permutation group (sometimes called the symmetric group of transformations). The only statistic relevant to nominal scales of Type A is the number of cases, e.g. the number of players assigned numerals. But once classes containing several individuals have been formed (Type B), we can determine the most numerous class (the mode), and under certain conditions we can test, by the contingency methods, hypotheses regarding the distribution of cases among the classes.

The nominal scale is a primitive form, and quite naturally there are many who will urge that it is absurd to attribute to this process of assigning numerals the dignity implied by the term measurement. Certainly there can be no quarrel with this objection, for the naming of things is an arbitrary business. However we christen it, the use of numerals as names for classes is an example of the "assignment of numerals according to rule." The rule is: Do not assign the same numeral to different classes or different numerals to the same class. Beyond that, anything goes with the nominal scale.

ORDINAL SCALE

The *ordinal scale* arises from the operation of rank-ordering. Since any 'order-preserving' transformation will leave the scale form invariant, this scale has the structure of what may be called the isotonic or order-preserving group. A classic example of an ordinal scale is the scale of hardness of minerals. Other instances are found among scales of intelligence, personality traits, grade or quality of leather, etc.

As a matter of fact, most of the scales used widely and effectively by psychologists are ordinal scales. In the strictest propriety the ordinary statistics involving means and standard deviations ought not to be used with these scales, for these statistics imply a knowledge of something more than the relative rank-order of data. On the other hand, for this 'illegal' statisticizing there can be invoked a kind of pragmatic sanction: In numerous instances it leads to fruitful results. While the outlawing of this procedure would probably serve no good purpose, it is proper to point out that means and standard deviations computed on an ordinal scale are in error to the extent that the successive intervals on the scale are unequal in size. When only the rank-order of data is known, we should proceed cautiously with our statistics, and especially with the conclusions we draw from them.

Even in applying those statistics that are normally appropriate for ordinal scales, we sometimes find rigor compromised. Thus, although it is indicated in Table 1 that percentile measures may be applied to rank-ordered data, it should be pointed out that the customary procedure of assigning a value to a percentile by interpolating linearly within a class interval is, in all strictness, wholly out of bounds. Likewise, it is not strictly proper to determine the mid-point of a class interval by linear interpolation, because the linearity of an ordinal scale is precisely the property which is open to question.

INTERVAL SCALE

With the *interval scale* we come to a form that is "quantitative" in the ordinary sense of the word. Almost all the usual statistical measures are applicable here, unless they are the kinds that imply a knowledge of a 'true' zero point. The zero point on an interval scale is a matter of convention or convenience, as is shown by the fact that the scale form remains invariant when a constant is added.

This point is illustrated by our two scales of temperature, Centigrade and Fahrenheit. Equal intervals of temperature are scaled off by noting equal volumes of expansion; an arbitrary zero is agreed upon for each scale; and a numerical value on one of the scales is transformed into a value on the other by means of an equation of the form $x' = ax + b$. Our scales of time offer a similar example. Dates on one calendar are transformed to those on another by way of this same equation. On these scales, of course, it is meaningless to say that one value is twice or some other proportion greater than another.

Periods of time, however, can be measured on ratio scales and one period may be correctly defined as double another. The same is probably true of temperature measured on the so-called Absolute Scale.

Most psychological measurement aspires to create interval scales, and it sometimes succeeds. The problem usually is to devise operations for equalizing the units of the scales—a problem not always easy of solution but one for which there are several possible modes of attack. Only occasionally is there concern for the location of a 'true' zero point, because the human attributes measured by psychologists usually exist in a positive degree that is large compared with the range of its variation. In this respect these attributes are analogous to temperature as it is encountered in everyday life. Intelligence, for example, is usefully assessed on ordinal scales which try to approximate interval scales, and it is not necessary to define what zero intelligence would mean.

RATIO SCALE

Ratio scales are those most commonly encountered in physics and are possible only when there exist operations for determining all four relations: equality, rank-order, equality of intervals, and equality of ratios. Once such a scale is erected, its numerical values can be transformed (as from inches to feet) only by multiplying each value by a constant. An absolute zero is always implied, even though the zero value on some scales (e.g. Absolute Temperature) may never be produced. All types of statistical measures are applicable to ratio scales, and only with these scales may we properly indulge in logarithmic transformations such as are involved in the use of decibels.

Foremost among the ratio scales is the scale of number itself—cardinal number—the scale we use when we count such things as eggs, pennies, and apples. This scale of the numerosity of aggregates is so basic and so common that it is ordinarily not even mentioned in discussions of measurement.

It is conventional in physics to distinguish between two types of ratio scales: *fundamental* and *derived*. Fundamental scales are represented by length, weight, and electrical resistance, whereas derived scales are represented by density, force, and elasticity.

These latter are *derived* magnitudes in the sense that they are mathematical functions of certain fundamental magnitudes. They are actually more numerous in physics than are the fundamental magnitudes, which are commonly held to be basic because they satisfy the criterion of *additivity*. Weights, lengths, and resistances can be added in the physical sense, but this important empirical fact is generally accorded more prominence in the theory of measurement than it deserves. The so-called fundamental scales are important instances of ratio scales, but they are only instances. As a matter of fact, it can be demonstrated that the fundamental scales could be set up even if the physical operation of addition were ruled out as impossible of performance. Given three balances, for example, each having the proper construction, a set of standard weights could be manufactured without it ever being necessary to place two weights in the same scale pan at the same time. The procedure is too long to describe in these pages, but its feasibility is mentioned here simply to suggest that physical addition, even though it is sometimes possible, is not necessarily the basis of all measurement. Too much measuring goes on where resort can never be had to the process of laying things end-to-end or of piling them up in a heap.

Ratio scales of psychological magnitudes are rare but not entirely unknown. The Sone scale discussed by the British committee is an example founded on a deliberate attempt to have human observers judge the loudness ratios of pairs of tones. The judgment of equal intervals had long been established as a legitimate method, and with the work on sensory ratios, started independently in several laboratories, the final step was taken to assign numerals to sensations of loudness in such a way that relations among the sensations are reflected by the ordinary arithmetical relations in the numeral series. As in all measurement, there are limits imposed by error and variability, but within these limits the Sone scale ought properly to be classed as a ratio scale.

To the British committee, then, we may venture to suggest by way of conclusion that the most liberal and useful definition of measurement is, as one of its members advised, "the assignment of numerals to things so as to represent facts and conventions about them." The problem as to what is and is not measurement then reduces to the simple question: What are the rules, if any, under which numerals are assigned? If we can point to a consistent set of rules, we are obviously concerned with measurement of some sort, and we can then proceed to the more interesting question as to the kind of measurement it is. In most cases a formulation of the rules of assignment discloses directly the kind of measurement and hence the kind of scale involved. If there remains any ambiguity, we may seek the final and definitive answer in the mathematical group-structure of the scale form: In what ways can we transform its values and still have it serve all the functions previously fulfilled? We know that the values of all scales can be multiplied by a constant, which changes the size of the unit. If, in addition, a constant can be added (or a new zero point chosen), it is proof positive that we are not concerned with a ratio scale. Then, if the purpose of the scale is still served when its values are squared or cubed, it is not even an interval scale. And finally, if any two values may be interchanged at will, the ordinal scale is ruled out and the nominal scale is the sole remaining possibility.

This proposed solution to the semantic problem is not meant to imply that all scales belonging to the same mathematical group are equally precise or accurate or useful or "fundamental." Measurement is never better than the empirical operations by which it is carried out, and operations range from bad to good. Any particular scale, sensory or physical, may be objected to on the grounds of bias, low precision, restricted generality, and other factors, but the objector should remember that these are relative and practical matters and that no scale used by mortals is perfectly free of their taint.

2. Additive Scales and Statistics

CLETUS J. BURKE

Psychological measurements do not possess the simple properties of the scales obtained for those basic dimensions of physics which have been designated as "fundamental magnitudes." The implications of this

---

Burke, C. J. Additive scales and statistics. *Psychological Review*, 1953, *60*, 73–75. Reprinted with the permission of the publisher and author.

statement for quantitative psychology have been extensively studied and discussed with varying evaluations and recommendations. Frequently the recommendations have been such as to alter statistical practices, had they been followed.

Certain writers, notably Boring (2) and Stevens (6), have maintained that such statistical concepts as the sample mean and standard deviation presuppose, at the very least, a scale of equivalent units of some kind, thus casting doubt on the theoretical validity of extensive reliance on the *t* test, analysis of variance, and other statistical techniques widely used with psychological data. The resulting distrust of such widely used procedures has prompted Comrey (4) to seek their justification outside the strict limits of the traditional logic of measurement.

It is the purpose of the present paper to analyze this issue and to show that the use of the sample mean and standard deviation does no violence upon the data, whatever the properties of the measurement scale. Thus, the use of the usual statistical tests is limited only by the well-known statistical restrictions.

The argument to be given can be conducted from the axioms of probability and the axiomatic basis of measurement, but such detailed treatment would be merely pretentious, since the results which are necessary to establish the basic point are familiar to almost all psychologists.

THE NATURE OF MEASUREMENT SCALES

(The term "object" as used below should not be restricted to its usual meaning of "physical object"; rather it is to be interpreted with sufficient breadth to give the statements throughout this section meaning for psychological as well as physical measurement provided that the axioms can be satisfied.)

Objects which can be ordered on the basis of a pair of (physical, psychological, or other) relations are said to define a "dimension." For such objects there are two relations, objectual equality and objectual less-than-ness and the objects and relations satisfy the axioms of order reproduced by Comrey (4). Each object can be tagged with a number so that the numbers will satisfy a corresponding set of axioms. Thus there is a correspondence between the two systems:

(A) [Objects, objectual equality, objectual less-than-ness.]
(B) [Numbers, numerical equality, numerical less-than-ness.]

For some objects and relations, a further step is possible. An operation for combining the objects, "objectual addition," can be found such that the system:

(C) [Objects, objectual equality, objectual less-than-ness, objectual addition]

satisfies four additional axioms of combination (Comrey [4]). When this is the case the objects can be tagged with numbers so that the system:

(D) [Numbers, numerical equality, numerical less-than-ness, numerical addition]

satisfies four corresponding additional axioms of combination. Thus, in this case, there is a correspondence between (C) and (D).

When the systems (C) and (D) exist and correspond, we say that the objects define an "extensive dimension" and the numbers an "additive scale." In this case, of course, the systems (A) and (B) also exist and correspond.

When the systems (A) and (B) exist and correspond, but the systems (C) and (D) do not, we say that the objects define an "intensive dimension" and the numbers a "rank-order scale."

These matters are discussed in great detail by Campbell (3) and, more adequately for psychologists, by Bergmann and Spence (1). Pertinent information is presented in papers by Comrey (4) and Gulliksen (5). For our purposes, it is important to note only that the classification of a scale as additive depends upon the presence or absence of a certain correspondence, expressed in sets of axioms, between the numbers of the scale and the objects to which they refer—with, of course, appropriate ordering relations and combinative operations for each.

THE NATURE OF STATISTICS

Statistical methods serve two major functions for psychologists.

a. They are used to summarize the salient features of individual sets of data.

b. They are used to test for differences between different experimental groups.

We shall discuss the second function in some detail, restricting our discussion to the simple case in which two groups are compared. In the typical psychological experiment the operations performed by the experimenter yield two or more sets of numbers. (In fact, unless the data exist in numerical form, means and standard deviations cannot be computed and the data are irrelevant for the present discussion.) It is obvious that two experimental groups will be judged alike or different in a given respect according as the collections of numbers classifying them in this respect are judged to be alike or different. It should be emphasized that we are here comparing the two sets of numbers *as numbers* and nothing else about them matters until after the statistical test has been made. The application of statistical techniques reflects merely our recognition of the unreliability of the small sets of numbers we have obtained and our unwillingness to perform the experiment again and again to determine whether the direction of the difference between our groups is reliable. We conceptualize a larger set of numbers, the statistical population, from which the sets of numbers we have obtained are two small samples, and inquire into the likelihood of two samples as disparate as we have observed arising from the given population. In answering this question, we often use the sample means and standard deviations as indices of important aspects of our collections of numbers. No interpretation other than this indicial one is intended. Means and standard deviations are used because they can always be computed, since numbers can always be added, subtracted, multiplied, and divided, and because means and standard deviations, conceived of merely as the results of operations with numbers, behave in certain lawful statistical ways.

In summary, the statistical technique begins and ends with the numbers and with statements about them. The psychological interpretation given to the experiment does take cognizance of the origin of the numbers but this is irrelevant for the statistical test as such.

Obviously, the same argument applies directly to the first function of statistics as well. The statement "The mean of these scores is 121" conveys in general the same kind of information as the statement "The median of these scores is 122."

The objection that a well-established unit is necessary before the mean and standard deviation can be computed since their value is altered by a change in the absolute value of the scores (Comrey [4]) loses cogency when one notices that the mean and median will be affected in precisely the same way by adding a given number to each number in the sample and that the standard deviation and the interquartile range will be changed in the same way by multiplying each number in the sample by a given number.

AN EXAMPLE

To establish the point in another way, we consider an example of a statistical test based on an additive measure. Suppose that we are presented with two sticks, A and B, of apparently equal lengths, fixed on opposite sides of a room, and asked which is longer. We measure them and obtain a larger number for A. The two numbers, however, are nearly the same and we decide to repeat the measurement "just to make sure." On this occasion, we obtain a larger value for B. We proceed until we have 100 measurements on each stick and wish to answer the question without taking further measurements.

There are two collections of 100 numbers each, one for stick A and one for stick B. We test the hypothesis that they differ only through the unreliability of the measurements. A moment's reflection will show that we are not at all concerned with the additive nature of the scale for length. In adding the 100 numbers to obtain a mean for the measurements on stick A, we treat them as numbers and as nothing else. We make no interpretations whatever about adding 100 sticks together —there are only two sticks. Moreover, our interpretation by means of the t test is unaffected by the choice of length units we have made, provided that the units are the same for the two sticks.

It is seen that the comparison of the sets of measurements on the two sticks differs in no essential way from the comparison of two sets of IQ's.

SUMMARY AND CONCLUSIONS

We have noted that: (*a*) The properties of a scale of measurement involve correspondences between sets of axioms about objects and numbers, with appropriate relations and operations. (*b*) Statistical methods begin and end with numbers.

From (*a*) and (*b*), we have deduced that the properties of a set of numbers as a measurement scale should have no effect upon the choice of statistical techniques for representing and interpreting the numbers.

REFERENCES

1. Bergmann, G., & Spence, K. W. Logic of psychophysical measurement. *Psychol. Rev.*, 1944, **51**, 1–24.
2. Boring, E. G. The logic of the normal law of error in mental measurement. *Amer. J. Psychol.*, 1920, **31**, 1–33.
3. Campbell, N. R. *Physics, the elements*. London: Cambridge Univer. Press, 1920.
4. Comrey, A. L. An operational approach to some problems in psychological measurement. *Psychol. Rev.*, 1950, **57**, 217–228.
5. Gulliksen, H. Paired comparisons and the logic of measurement. *Psychol. Rev.*, 1946, **53**, 199–213.
6. Stevens, S. S. On the theory of scales of measurement. *Science*, 1946, **103**, 677–680.

3. A Comment on Burke's Additive Scales and Statistics

VIRGINIA L. SENDERS

Burke, in a recent article (1), states that "statistical technique begins and ends with numbers and with statements about them." Therefore, he concludes, "the properties of a set of numbers *as a measurement scale* should have no effect upon the choice of statistical techniques for representing and interpreting the numbers." Again, referring to statistical interpretation, Burke states that "the use of the sample mean and standard deviation does no violence upon the data, *whatever the properties of the measurement scale*. Thus, the use of the usual statistical tests is limited only by the well-known statistical restrictions" (italics mine).

Some rather unfortunate implications follow from Burke's position. When numbers have been assigned to objects according to some stated rules these numbers can indeed by manipulated in any way we desire. But once the manipulations have been completed and the tests made, a dilemma arises. If we have performed operations on the numbers which we could not perform on the objects, we must choose between two interpretive procedures. We must either assume that (*a*) what is true of the numbers is also true of the objects, or (*b*) what is true of the numbers is not necessarily true of the objects.

The first assumption leads to all sorts of difficulties, which have been adequately described by Campbell (2), Stevens (4), Reese (3), and others. These difficulties may be illustrated, in oversimplified form, by two examples, one numerical and one geometric.

Suppose we have a measurement scale which has ordinal but not interval or additive properties. Such a yardstick is illustrated below:

1 2 3 4 5

An object is measured by laying it against this yardstick in the usual way. We are given two pairs of objects, A and B, whose lengths are:

3

3 A

and

1

5 B.

The numbers assigned to the objects total 6 in both cases, but inspec-

Senders, Virginia L. A comment on Burke's additive scales and statistics. *Psychological Review,* 1953, *60,* 423–424. Reprinted with the permission of the publisher and author.

tion will reveal that the additions of the objects will give a longer line in case A than in case B.

Thus the statement that *there is no difference between the sums of the numbers used to represent length in the two cases* is correct, but strongly suggests the erroneous conclusion that if the two summed lines were laid side by side, no difference could be discerned between them.

The absurdity of possible conclusions may also be revealed by a numerical example. Suppose families are grouped according to income on a scale where the number 5 means "very rich" and number 1, "very poor." The actual income intervals, however, are unequal, as follows:

Number	*Income limits*	*Midpoint*
5	$5,000–$1,000,000	$502,500
4	3,000– 5,000	4,000
3	2,000– 3,000	2,500
2	1,000– 2,000	1,500
1	0– 1,000	500

In town A all the families have incomes which fall in class 3, while in town B half the families have incomes in class 5, and half, incomes in class 1. Both towns will have a *mean* of 3 if we consider only the numbers assigned to the categories, but it is evident that town B, with a mean income of $251,000 is richer than town A with a mean income of $2,500.

If we accept conclusion *b*, on the other hand, we are in an even more ridiculous position. Though our statistical procedures may have been perfectly justified and our interpretations correct when considered strictly in relation to the *numbers,* we can make no interpretation about the properties of the objects to which the numbers have been assigned. As psychologists, we can draw no conclusions about responses, organisms, or behavior, but only about numbers.

Since psychologists are presumably more interested in the behavior they describe with numbers than in the numbers themselves, they will learn more if their statistical techniques correspond with the properties of the set of numbers as a measurement scale than if these properties "have no effect upon the choice of statistical techniques for representing and interpreting the numbers."

REFERENCES

1. Burke, C. J. Additive scales and statistics. *Psychol. Rev.,* 1953, **60**, 73–75.
2. Campbell, N. R., *et al.* Final report. *Advanc. Sci.,* 1940, No. 2, 331–349.
3. Reese, T. W. The application of the theory of physical measurement to the measurement of psychological magnitudes, with three experimental examples. *Psychol. Monogr.,* 1943, **55**, No. 3 (Whole No. 251).
4. Stevens, S. S. Mathematics, measurement, and psychophysics. In S. S. Stevens (Ed.), *Handbook of experimental psychology.* New York: Wiley, 1951. Pp. 1–49.

4. Weak Measurements Vs. Strong Statistics: An Empirical Critique of S. S. Stevens' Proscriptions on Statistics[1, 2]

BELA O. BAKER
CURTIS D. HARDYCK
LEWIS F. PETRINOVICH

The disagreement between those who belong to what Lubin (1962) called the "school of 'weak measurement' theorists" and those who belong to what might be called the school of "strong statistics" has persisted for a number of years with little apparent change of attitude on either side. Stevens, as the leading spokesman for the weak measurement school, has asserted (1951) and reasserted (1959, 1960) the view that measurement scales are models of object relationships and, for the most part, rather poor models which can lead one far astray from the truth if the scores they yield are added when they should only be counted. At least two current statistics texts intended for psychologists (Senders, 1958; Siegel, 1956) present this view as gospel.

Opposing this view, an assortment of statistically minded psychologists—e.g., Lord (1953), Burke (1953), Anderson (1961), McNemar (1962), and Hays (1963) have argued that statistics apply to numbers rather than to things and that the formal properties of measurement scales, as such, should have no influence on the choice of statistics.

Baker, Bela O., Hardyck, Curtis D., and Petrinovich, Lewis F. Weak measurements vs. strong statistics: An empirical critique of S. S. Stevens' proscriptions on statistics. *Educational and Psychological Measurement*, 1966, *26*, 291–309. Reprinted with the permission of the publisher and authors.

[1] This research was supported by research grants from the National Institutes of Health, U.S. Public Health Service (MH 07310) and the Research Committee, University of California Medical Center. Preliminary work was accomplished by a grant of free computer time by the Computer Center, University of California, Berkeley.

[2] We are grateful to Professor Jack Block, Professor Quinn McNemar, and Miss Mary Epling for their many helpful suggestions throughout this study. We are also indebted to Mrs. Eleanor Krasnow who developed and tested the computer programs used in this study.

Savage (1957), a statistician, has supported this point of view, stating: "I know of no reason to limit statistical procedures to those involving arithmetic operations consistent with the scale properties of the observed quantities." In other words, a statistical test answers the question it is designed to answer whether measurement is weak or strong.

In his widely cited discussion of measurement, Stevens (1951) distinguished four classes of scales: Nominal, ordinal, interval, and ratio, and specified the arithmetic operations (and hence the statistics) which are permissible for each scale. Nominal scales consist simply of class names and can be treated only by counting operations and frequency statistics. Ordinal scales are developed by demonstrating that some objects have more of a particular quality than do other objects and representing numerically this order among objects. Lacking units, the numbers of an ordinal scale cannot be added, subtracted, multiplied, or divided, but they can be treated by order statistics such as the median or the rank-order correlation. Interval scales represent equal increments in the magnitudes of an object property by equal numerical increments. An increase of one unit in any region of an interval scale represents the same increment in the object property as does an increase of one unit in any other region of the scale. Scores from interval scales can be added and subtracted and hence such statistics as the mean, the standard deviation, and the product-moment correlation can be used. Ratio scales add a true zero point to equal intervals and can be multiplied, divided, and treated by subtle statistics which are of little concern to most psychologists.

Although Stevens develops his rationale for relating measurements and statistics almost exclusively in terms of descriptive statistics, he introduces the issue of hypothesis testing somewhat obliquely in his discussions of invariance of results under scale transformations (1951, 1959). He says, "The basic principle is this: Having measured a set of items by making numerical assignments in accordance with a set of rules, we are free to change the assignments by whatever group of transformations will preserve the empirical information in the scale. These transformations, depending on which group they belong to, will upset some statistical measures and leave others unaffected (1959, p. 30)."

If parametric significance tests, such as t or F are used, the permissible transformations are linear. Only then will invariant results be found in comparing groups. An implication of this point of view, which is not made explicit by Stevens, is that if a scale is viewed as a model of object relationships, then any scale transformation is a transformation of those relationships. Hence the problem of invariance of results under scale transformations raises the following question: Can we make correct decisions about the nature of reality if we disregard the nature of the measurement scale when we apply statistical tests?

This aspect of Stevens' position has apparently been ignored by many of his critics. Anderson (1961) dismisses out of hand any restriction on the uses of *t* arising from the nature of the measurements to which it is applied but discusses the question of invariance of results under scale transformations seriously and at length before concluding that: "The practical problems of invariance or generality of results far transcend measurement scale typology" (p. 316).

The aspects of the problem as related to descriptive and inferential statistics are as follows: The problem for descriptive statistics as presented by Stevens (1951, 1959, 1960) concerns the relationship of the value of a particular statistic computed on obtained measurements to the value of the same statistic computed under conditions of perfect measurement. The argument is that the farther the measurement model departs from the underlying properties of the objects being measured, the less accurate the statistics. In other words, this aspect is concerned with precision of measurement.

In making statistical inferences, however, the issue is whether one will arrive at the same probability estimates from different types of measurement scales. Given the condition that a measurement scale may be a very poor model indeed of the properties of the objects under study, the question of the effect of the scale on the sampling distribution of a statistic remains unanswered. Where hypothesis testing is the issue, the appropriate question is: Do statistics computed on measures which are inaccurate descriptions of reality distribute differently than the same statistics computed under conditions of perfect measurement? If not, then a research worker who has nothing better than an ordinal scale to work with may have to face the problem of more precise measurement for descriptive purposes, but at least the probability decisions he may make from his ordinal measurements will not be inappropriate for parametric statistical models.

In view of the importance of the issue raised by Stevens for users of statistics, it is surprising, as Lubin (1962) notes, that so few detailed discussions of the problem are available. If Stevens is correct, then psychologists should be disturbed about the state of their research literature. Since it can be safely asserted that most measurements in psychology yield scales which are somewhere between ordinal and interval scales, many psychologists may have been propagating fiction when they have made statistical inferences based on significance tests inappropriate to anything less than interval measurements. If Stevens' position is correct, it should be emphasized more intensively; if it is incorrect, something should be done to alleviate the lingering feelings of guilt that plague research workers who deliberately use statistics such as *t* on weak measurements.

A test of the issue would seem to require a comparison of the sampling distribution of a statistic computed under conditions of "perfect" measurement with the sampling distribution of the same statistic based on imperfect measurements. Since it is not possible to obtain such "perfect" measurements, this comparison is manifestly impossible. As noted above, however, Stevens has suggested that the main issue is that of invariance of results when measurement scales are transformed. Cast in these terms, the problem can be examined empirically. All that is required is that the sampling distribution of a statistic based on one set of scores be compared with the sampling distribution of the same statistic based on scores which are not "permissible" transformations of the first set. If Stevens is right, these sampling distributions should differ in some important way. If they do not, then the nature of the measurement scale is, within potentially determinable limits, an irrelevant consideration when one chooses an hypothesis testing statistics. . . .

[The authors next describe in detail their methodology. In essence, they constructed non-linear transformations of the unit-interval scores and used a computer to generate random samples of this transformed data. They analyzed their results by comparing distributions of *t* with the theoretical distributions for the appropriate degrees of freedom. Their results led to the following conclusions and recommendations.]

In reviewing the results presented so far, the following generalizations seem warranted:

1. The percentage of *t*'s reaching the theoretical 5 per cent and 1 per cent levels of significance is not seriously affected by the use of non-equal interval measurements.[4]

2. To the extent that there is any influence of the scale transformation on the percentage of *t's* reaching theoretical significance levels, the influence is more marked when intervals in one broad region of a scale are larger than intervals in another region of the scale than it is when interval sizes vary randomly.

3. If an investigator has a measuring instrument which produces either an interval scale or an ordinal scale with randomly varied interval sizes, he can safely use *t* for statistical decisions under all circumstances examined in this study. The single exception is that *t* should not be used to do a one tailed test when samples of unequal size have been drawn from a badly skewed population.

[4] It is possible that the effects of the scale transformations used in this study are actually due to change in the shape of the distributions which the different transformations produced. However, if this is the case, the arguments presented regarding the insignificant effects of the nature of measurement scales on probability statements are strengthened even more.

4. If a measurement scale deviates from reality in such a fashion that the magnitude of trait differences represented by intervals at the extremes of the scale may be greater than those represented by equal-appearing intervals in the middle of the scale (T_{16-25}), it seems reasonably safe to use *t*. Unequal sample sizes can even be used if the population is symmetrical, but the proscriptions against using one-tailed tests for unequal sample sizes from exponential populations still apply.

5. If the scale is of the kind represented by the relationship between C and T_{26-35} (in which inequality of units is present in one-half of the distribution only), it is still safe to use *t*, with a somewhat stricter limitation on the use of one-tailed tests. This arises from the finding that for all population distributions these transformations yielded skewed distributions of *t* when unequal sample sizes were used.

6. As a maximally conservative empirical set of rules for using *t*, the following restrictions would seem to be sufficient to compensate for almost any violation of assumptions investigated up to this time:

   a. Have equal sample sizes.

   b. Use a two-tailed test.

7. Returning to the question as originally formulated: Do statistics computed on a measurement scale which is at best a poor fit to reality distribute differently than the same statistics computed under conditions of perfect measurement? The answer is a firm "no," provided that the conditions of equal sample sizes and two-tailed tests are met. The research worker who has nothing better than an ordinal scale to work with may have an extremely poor fit to reality, but at least he will not be led into making incorrect probability estimates if he observes a few simple precautions.

As a final step, a different sort of analysis will be cited. The previous results and discussion related to one aspect of the measurement problem as posed by Stevens (1951); a second aspect remains. This concerns the accuracy of the descriptive statistics when the measurement model is a poor fit. Stevens has presented his point of view almost exclusively in terms of descriptive statistics and has tended to use illustrations from descriptive statistics to support his arguments. In the last analysis, this would seem to raise an epistemological question, since it is concerned with the relationship of measurement to a true value which cannot be known. However, evidence as to the correctness or incorrectness of the point of view can be examined from the data of the present study, even though the results are of no help in solving the problems faced by an experimenter who is wondering how to evaluate the validity and the precision of his measuring instrument.

The question of the accuracy of representation can be evaluated by defining the unit interval criterion *t* values as true measures and the values calculated on the various transformations as those obtained on a measurement model which misrepresents reality. Then the degree of relationship between the values of *t* calculated on specific samples for C and the values calculated on T_{1-35} can be obtained. This is a correlational question and the results are reported in Table 4.

TABLE 4. Mean[a] Correlation Coefficients and Standard Errors of Estimate for the Prediction of t's Based on Transformed Scores from t's Based on Criterion Unit-interval Scores

Population Distribution		NA = NB = 5 Mean r (1)	NA = NB = 5 Mean $S_{y \cdot x}$ (2)	NA = NB = 15 Mean r (3)	NA = NB = 15 Mean $S_{y \cdot x}$ (4)	NA = 5, NB = 15 Mean r (5)	NA = 5, NB = 15 Mean $S_{y \cdot x}$ (6)
N:	T_{1-5}	.997	.089	.997	.082	.997	.084
	T_{6-10}	.996	.111	.995	.100	.995	.104
	T_{11-15}	.992	.146	.991	.138	.991	.142
	T_{16-20}	.975	.244	.966	.265	.970	.260
	T_{21-25}	.968	.271	.964	.274	.966	.278
	T_{26-30}	.935	.401	.933	.380	.933	.386
	T_{31-35}	.914	.462	.911	.434	.912	.439
R:	T_{1-5}	.999	.056	.988	.048	.999	.033
	T_{6-10}	.996	.094	.996	.081	.996	.084
	T_{11-15}	.994	.117	.994	.088	.988	.104
	T_{16-20}	.973	.256	.973	.231	.973	.233
	T_{21-25}	.973	.258	.975	.227	.976	.225
	T_{26-30}	.948	.368	.943	.339	.944	.348
	T_{31-35}	.927	.430	.922	.394	.924	.404
E:	T_{1-5}	.994	.121	.993	.113	.992	.117
	T_{6-10}	.992	.138	.992	.126	.992	.129
	T_{11-15}	.984	.199	.985	.181	.983	.189
	T_{16-20}	.970	.283	.946	.342	.951	.324
	T_{21-25}	.963	.313	.953	.314	.954	.309
	T_{26-30}	.981	.218	.930	.382	.940	.325
	T_{31-35}	.966	.288	.885	.483	.922	.405

[a] Median values do not differ until the third decimal place for the majority of transformations

Columns (1), (3), and (5) contain for each of the distributions the correlations between values of *t* for each set of transformations and the corresponding values of *t* for the criterion. The correlations are impressively high. However, because of the broad range of values in the *t* distribution, the standard errors of estimate in columns (2), (4), and (6) are more informative statistics.

Several points can be noted in connection with Table 4: There is a regular progression in the size of the standard errors of estimate across the sets of transformations used, such that they are smallest for T_{1-15}, and largest for T_{26-35}. These standard errors also become larger as the magnitude of variations in interval size increases, but this is less striking than the differences among types of transformations. Variations in sample sizes and in the shape of the population distribution do not seem to have much influence on the standard errors of estimate; consequently these results seem to show a specific influence of scale transformations on the values of *t*. The correspondence between values of *t* based on the criterion unit interval scores and values of *t* based on transformations decreases regularly and dramatically—from standard errors of estimate on the order of .08 to standard errors of estimate on the order of .45—as the departure from linear transformations becomes more extreme. Here, then, is a finding consistent with Stevens' expectations: The value of *t* determined for a comparison of samples of non-interval scores does tend to be different from the value of *t* based on interval scores for the same samples and the discrepancy tends to become greater as the departure from equal intervals is more marked.

In conclusion, the views presented by Stevens (1951, 1959, 1960) and by advocates of his position such as Senders (1958), Siegel (1956), and Stake (1960) state that, when one uses *t*, the measurement model should have equal intervals representing linear transformations of the magnitudes of the characteristics being measured, or the statistic will be "upset." This view may be correct if one considers single specific determinations of a statistic in a descriptive sense—this seems to be the significance of the standard errors of estimate reported in Table 4—but it is incorrect when applied to the problem of statistical inference.

The present findings indicate that strong statistics such as the *t* test are more than adequate to cope with weak measurements—and, with some minor reservations, probabilities estimated from the *t* distribution are little affected by the kind of measurement scale used.

REFERENCES

Anderson, N. H. Scales and Statistics: Parametric and Nonparametric. *Psychological Bulletin,* 1961, 58, 305–316.

Boneau, C. A. The Effects of Violations of Assumptions Underlying the *t* Test. *Psychological Bulletin,* 1960, 57, 49–64.

Burke, C. J. Additive Scales and Statistics. *Psychological Review,* 1953, 60, 73–75.

Hays, W. L. *Statistics for Psychologists.* New York: Holt, Rinehart and Winston, 1963.

Lord, F. M. On the Statistical Treatment of Football Numbers. *American Psychologist,* 1953, 8, 750–751.

Lubin, A. Statistics. In *Annual Review of Psychology*. Palo Alto, Calif.: Stanford University Press, 1962.

McNemar, Q. *Psychological Statistics,* 3rd ed. New York: Wiley, 1962.

Norton, D. W. An Empirical Investigation of Some Effects of Non-Normality and Heterogeneity on the F-Distribution. Unpublished Doctoral Dissertation, State University of Iowa, 1952. Cited in E. F. Lindquist, *Design and Analysis of Experiments in Psychology and Education.* Boston: Houghton-Mifflin, 1953.

RAND Corporation. *A Million Random Digits.* New York: The Free Press of Glencoe, 1955.

Savage, I. R. Non-parametric Statistics. *Journal of the American Statistical Association,* 1957, 52, 331–344.

Senders, V. L. *Measurement and Statistics.* London: Oxford University Press, 1958.

Siegel, S. *Nonparametric Statistics.* New York: McGraw-Hill, 1956.

Stake, R. E. Review of *Elementary Statistics* by P. G. Hoel. *Educational and Psychological Measurement,* 1960, 20, 871–873.

Stevens, S. S. Mathematics, Measurement and Psychophysics. In S. S. Stevens (Ed.), *Handbook of Experimental Psychology.* New York: Wiley, 1951.

Stevens, S. S. Measurement, Psychophysics and Utility. In Churchman, G. W., and Ratoosh, P. (Eds.), *Measurement: Definitions and Theories.* New York: Wiley, 1959.

Stevens, S. S. Review of *Statistical Theory* by Lancelot Hogben. *Contemporary Psychology,* 1960, 5, 273–276.

5. Rational Hypotheses in the Construction of Tests

ROBERT M. W. TRAVERS

There are two approaches in test construction: (1) the scientific, rational, or theoretical approach, and (2) the technical or empirical approach. While no test constructor is likely to use one approach to the exclusion of the other, the relative emphasis varies considerably. Travers does a fine job discussing the pros and cons of each type of approach. One point which should be called to the reader's attention is the *absolute* necessity for the cross-validation of any scale constructed primarily through an empirical procedure. Cureton (1950) has written an interesting article showing the dangers of not cross validating empirically constructed tests.

Travers concludes his article by suggesting that test constructors have, in the past, been more technically than scientifically oriented and that this has been the reason for what he calls ". . . the rather meager advances made

---

Travers, R. M. W. Rational hypotheses in the construction of tests. *Educational and Psychological Measurement,* 1951, *11,* 128–137. Reprinted with the permission of the publisher and author.

in many areas of psychological measurement. . . ." This is a point that you may wish to challenge. If we can empirically construct tests that allow us to predict behavior, will not examination of the contents of these tests provide us with information from which we can build theories of behavior? That is, must the theory of behavior precede the test or will an *ex post facto* analysis of the empirically built test provide us with an understanding of behavior? The answer to the question is equivocal.

Travers' article was originally published in 1951, but the topic is still timely. Although construct validation has received considerable attention since the first publication of the *Technical Recommendations* (1954), the theoretical basis for many tests is still rather weak. *If* a more balanced approach is desirable, this might be accomplished by training psychometrists more thoroughly in philosophy of science and the role of theory in psychology.

Most of the work undertaken at the present time on the construction of tests is for the purpose of developing instruments useful in connection with some practical problem. Few psychological or educational tests are built for the purpose of testing some hypothesis of broad scientific significance. This trend toward the development of tests as tools for the technician rather than as scientific instruments for the research worker has had important effects on the methodology of test construction. The technician has developed techniques of his own which are somewhat different from those commonly adopted by the scientist. While one is tempted to contrast these techniques as the empirical versus the rational, or in terms of one of the other dualisms of philosophy, it seems better for the purpose of this discussion to refer to them simply as that of the technician and that of the scientist.

In the construction of tests, the scientist and the technician start from a common point of agreement, namely, that it is in nearly all cases unjustifiable to assume that a test measures what it is supposed to measure. There are exceptions to this, but they are few. The scientist and the technician also agree that since there is no certainty that a particular type of test will measure a specified variable it is necessary to set up hypotheses concerning the kind of test that will measure the given variable. Hypothesis formation is agreed upon to be an essential step, but the process is fundamentally different for the scientist than for the technician. For the scientist, hypothesis formation is the crucial and usually the most difficult step in his entire working procedure and one which calls for genius and originality. For him, the problem is to set up hypotheses which are rational, that is to say, which are consistent with established facts or with previous observations. It is the rationality of the scientist's hypotheses that distinguish his work from that of the technician whose usual procedure is to operate more on a hit-or-miss basis and to find out what will work.

THE TECHNICIAN'S APPROACH

The difference in the two methods of approach may be illustrated by some examples. The technician's approach is well illustrated by the *Strong Vocational Interest Blank* which covers, in a fairly comprehensive way, likes and dislikes for various types of work, for school subjects, for amusements, for activities, and for peculiarities of people. In addition, it contains sections in which the individual compares his interest in two activities or rates his characteristic behavior in various situations. The items seem to have been selected largely on the criterion of comprehensiveness rather than on any other. They were gathered together on the basis of the rather vague hypothesis that if a long enough list of preferences was prepared then surely some of them would discriminate between certain given groups. This kind of hypothesis is entirely different from the kind made by the scientist when he formulates one consistent with all known facts. The technician's approach is commonly characterized by trying various procedures until one is found which will work.

Strong (7) himself states that his instrument was not based on any series of carefully thought-out series of rational hypotheses and in the following quotation seems to imply that this is an advantage:

> It is well to recognize that the development of a scale for measuring an occupational interest is not based on any prior theorizing. The scale is based upon the differences in interests of men in one occupation and of men generally. The raw score obtained by an individual is the sum of the weights he earns on such a scale. The weights are not expressive of anyone's theories but are statistically derived from the data. (p. 76)

What Strong is saying is that he did not use the rational method of the scientist in developing his instrument but used a method of blind exploration. In the case of the *Strong Vocational Interest Blank* there can be no doubt that the procedure produced a useful instrument. The objections to the try-all-and-see-what-works method is not that it fails to produce an instrument of value. Also, the apparent ridiculous nature of the scale that is sometimes thus produced is not the most serious criticism that can be leveled against it. One is reminded in this connection of an example cited by Allport (1, p. 329) in which, in a certain scale, the children who gave the response word "green" to a stimulus word "grass" received a score of plus six for "loyalty to the gang." Although Allport cites this as an example of the misuse of statistics, the present writer believes that he is incorrect in that contention since scales which illustrate such phenomena are mainly a result of a failure to initiate the test-construction process with the formulation of rational hypotheses.

Before the basic weaknesses in the approach of the technician can be considered, it is necessary to study some other examples of hypotheses used in the construction of tests.

It is not possible to group tests into those that have been based on a rational hypothesis and those that have not, since it is more a question of the degree of rationality involved. Strong's basic hypothesis in the selection of his items cannot be described as completely lacking in rationality for it contains a small element of rationality. Hypotheses used in the selection of test items vary in the degree to which they are rational. For example, in the case of the *Minnesota Multiphasic Personality Inventory* the items were selected from a domain similar to the one in which it was desired to make measurements.

> The individual items were formulated partly on the basis of previous clinical experience. Mainly, however, the items were supplied from several psychiatric examination direction forms, from various textbooks of psychiatry, from certain of the directions for case taking in medicine and neurology, and from earlier published scales of personal and social attitudes. (5, p. 249).

There is, however, implicit in the procedure of Hathaway and McKinley, the idea of creating a "rather large reservoir of items from which various scales might be constructed." This reiterates the technique of selecting the items for a given scale by trying out a large number of items in the hope that some will provide useful discriminations.

It is not only in personality measurement that the technician's approach is commonly encountered. The reader can recall the case of one of the most widely used batteries of achievement tests at the elementary-school level in which the final selection of the items for each section was based on whether they demonstrated growth over the school year (3). This has been a common practice in the construction of achievement tests for the elementary-school level because some school administrators have been concerned with a variable of administrative significance called *grade level* and whatever shows an increasing score from one grade level to the next is hypothesized to measure it. What has happened in this case is that, since test items selected on the basis of educational and psychological criteria do not produce a satisfactory scale, other procedures have to be adopted in the final selection of items in order that the test may meet certain necessary metrical requirements. How this procedure affects the interpretation of scores derived from such an instrument still needs to be studied. The problem of the effect of these procedures, which reject items which do not belong to a given metric, on the meaningfulness of measures has been discussed at length in recent literature with respect to attitude measurement. However, there has been little discussion of this same problem in the area of measuring achievement, although until this matter is properly explored, techniques for measuring achievement will be characteristically those of the technician.

THE RATIONAL HYPOTHESIS APPROACH

It is of interest to compare the approach used in constructing the *Strong Vocational Interest Blank* and the *Minnesota Multiphasic Personality Schedule* with that used by Binet and Simon (2) in the development of their intelligence scale. The contrast is marked. These latter investigators exercised the greatest care in selecting or excluding items from their scale. Criteria for the initial selection of items were carefully drawn up and each item included could be rationally justified as appropriate. The items in each part of the scale were rationally hypothesized as belonging there. The validation procedure was a matter of demonstrating that the original hypothesis was sound, and not a process of separating from a miscellaneous group of items the ones that happened to show a given discrimination. While Binet and Simon borrowed extensively from other assessment instruments of the time and particularly from a questionnaire of two fellow physicians, Dr. Blin and Dr. Damaye, they did not, like so many modern test technicians, throw everything they could find into the preliminary form of their test in the hope that some of the items would have certain statistical properties. The method of Binet and Simon was rigorously scientific throughout and one from which many modern test technicians could profit. In addition, they were careful in identifying the assumptions on which their scale was based, noting, for example, that, since intellectual units could not be superimposed, equality of units could never be assumed. At no time in their entire procedure was there any attempt to try out material in the hope that some of it would yield scores which correlated with a criterion.

A more recent example of a rationally planned test is found in a project undertaken by the American Institute for Research under the direction of Dr. John Flanagan (4). The purpose of this project was to develop an instrument for the selection of research personnel. The initial step undertaken was to observe and enumerate the adequate and inadequate behaviors of research personnel. On this basis, critical requirements were established which formed the basis of the test plan. The construction of the test involved the development of test problems which would permit the applicant for a research position to show either the adequate or inadequate behaviors which had been previously listed. This procedure is in marked contrast with that of trying out masses of items in the hope that some might "work."

Unfortunately, the field of achievement testing has been dominated largely by the technician's approach, except possibly in the area of reading. It has been largely through the influence of Ralph Tyler and his students that any attempts have been made in education to break away from the technician's approach. In the latter approach the first step is to define achievement in terms of identifiable behaviors. The second step is to hypothesize on a rational basis the types of problem situation which will permit the identifiable behavior to appear or not to appear. Items are never included in a test on the basis of the vague hope that the score on the particular item will be correlated with the score on the test as a whole. On the contrary, the procedure is rational and every effort is made to identify the variable that is being measured. This is in contrast to the technician's approach which aims at finding a measure of some kind which does not have to have any meaning but which has to meet the sole standard of being correlated with a specified variable. Much work still needs to be done in developing more adequate techniques of defining educational objectives and for determining the degree to which behaviors manifest in test situations correspond to behaviors listed in the definition of objectives.

THE ADVANTAGES OF EACH OF THE TWO APPROACHES

From the point of view of utility, immediate and ultimate, both of the approaches to the construction of tests have merits and disadvantages. What has been referred to as the technician's approach has the outstanding advantage of producing an instrument of possible practical value in a short space of time. The approach which involves the establishment of rational hypotheses is tedious and usually requires a much longer time for the development of a useful instrument.

The advantage of the technician's approach is seen in a recent study by Pedersen (6) in which a paper-and-pencil test of supervisory ability was developed. When the test was scored on the basis of keys prepared prior to "validation," the validity was found to be 0.2 and 0.1. However, when an "empirical" key was developed on the basis of the degree to which the items predicted the criterion, validity coefficients of 0.5 and greater were achieved. What this means is that the hypothesis on which the original test was built was unsound. While the scientist in such a situation would have immediately prepared revised hypotheses, the technician does not need to do so. The result is that while the technician produces a useful instrument, he adds little to scientific knowledge since he avoids the problem of setting up and testing rational hypotheses. The technician can even start with misinformation and produce a useful device but he is usually as misinformed at the end of the process as he was at the beginning. The approach is consistent with the philosophy of an industrial society in which greater value is placed on the capacity to perform than on understanding. The technician's approach, because it builds a test instrument by following a set of rules which eliminate largely the need for thought, has certain dangers attached to it which need to be more clearly recognized. Consider, for example, a hypothetical case of a large industrial concern employing many young scientists. Some of these scientists are later placed in high administrative positions while some continue to do research. Suppose that the personnel department in this concern decided to develop an instrument which would discriminate between those newly-appointed scientists who would be likely to be promoted to high-level administrative work and those who would stay in research. The purpose of this instrument was to be able to select a greater number of those who could be promoted later to high administrative positions. In this situation, the test technicians followed the procedure of drawing up a biographical inventory which was administered to the group of scientists who had been promoted to high-level administrative positions and to a group who had been with the company an equal length of time but who had remained in research. It was found that quite a large number of the biographical items discriminated between the two groups, and by assigning proper weights to these items it was possible to develop a scoring system for the inventory which could be applied to new applicants for research positions. On this basis it became possible to select a larger number of scientists who had scores nearer to the administrators than to the research workers. Let us suppose that this scale was used over a period of years and studies indicated that it did predict with considerable accuracy those who would acquire administrative positions and that, therefore, it was decided to publish the scale under the title of *Scale of Administrative Ability*. The scale was also shown to be correlated with the ratings given these administrators by the top officials of the concern. This scale became widely used and was praised extensively by executives and was on its way to becoming a publishing success when a psychologist examined it with some care and observed that the responses which were given high loadings had no apparent relationship to success in an administrative capacity. For example, a person was given credit on the Administrative Scale for having a rural background, for coming from a family of skilled craftsmen, for *not* coming from a family that earned a living in a retail business in a large city. The scale bore little relationship to the purposes for which it was built, but as the technicians said, "it worked." The item weights were nonsensical but in view of the fact that the scale had been shown to have selective value, the scale and the procedure for building it seemed to be defensible. Many technicians felt justified in concluding that it was just additional evidence to show that the only way to build a measuring instrument is to try out large numbers of items, for who can tell which items will work?

However, this does not end the fable, for the scientist who noted the peculiar nature of the discriminating items in the scale went on to study the conditions under which the scale had been built and "validated." He soon discovered that the management of the manufacturing concern was strongly anti-semitic and excluded from promotions to high positions those who were Jewish in origin. Occasionally, it happened that a research worker who was Jewish was given an administrative post and when this happened the chances were that because of prejudice he would be given a low rating for administrative effectiveness.

The scale which the test technicians developed by a blind statistical method merely discriminated between a Jewish and a non-Jewish background and emphasized the sociological factors associated with this variable. When the scale was used in other places it would tend to exclude from positions those who came from Jewish homes. It would, in effect, be a device which perpetuated a wholly unjustifiable prejudice.

One cannot help wondering how often instruments built by test technicians do just this kind of thing. The technician's approach may have consequences such as these, though in general it does not. However, it is a basically dangerous technique. Similar examples of the dangers of this technique may be found in other fields. In contrast, the scientific approach to the construction of tests not only produces instruments of more certain value but also advances knowledge in a systematic way. Since the first step is to establish rational hypotheses concerning the form and type of instrument that will measure the domain of behavior that it is desired to measure, it is necessary to review and study all the available information on the problem. Unless this is done, hypotheses set up cannot be considered to be rational. Sometimes it is necessary to gather information before rational hypotheses can be established, but in any case the hypotheses established must be based firmly on previous knowledge and be consistent with known facts. After the measuring instrument has been built on this basis, the original hypotheses are tested by administering the test to selected groups. This process is sometimes called the validation procedure but in the method of science it is just a process of testing rational hypotheses. In a similar way, the common procedure of making item analyses against internal or external criteria should be a process of testing rational hypotheses.

SUMMARY AND IMPLICATIONS

In this article a distinction has been drawn between the scientific method of constructing tests and the procedures commonly adopted by technicians. It has been pointed out that these methods differ not only in procedural matters but in their consequences. The one method extends knowledge and aims at producing understanding. The other method is limited to the production of a useful measuring device which is often much less useful than it appears to be on the surface. At the present time these differences between the two approaches remain largely unrecognized despite their important consequences. The present writer feels that the rather meager advances made in many areas of psychological measurement during the last 20 years are mainly a consequence of the fact that these areas are staffed mainly by technicians interested in producing useful instruments and not by scientists interested in expanding knowledge.

REFERENCES

1. Allport, Gordon W. *Personality—A Psychological Interpretation.* New York: Henry Holt and Company, 1937.
2. Binet, Alfred, and Simon, Theophile. "Methodes Nouvelles Pour le Diagnotic Du Niveau Intellectuel Des Normaux." *L'Année Psychologique,* XI(1905), 191–244.
3. Buros, Oscar K. "Criticisms of Commonly Used Methods of Validating Achievement Test Items." *Proceedings of the 1948 Invitational Conference on Testing Problems.* Princeton: Educational Testing Service, 1949.
4. Flanagan, John C. "Critical Requirements for Research Personnel." *A Study of Observed Behaviors of Personnel in Research Laboratories.* American Institute for Research, 1949.
5. Hathaway, S. R. and McKinley, J. C. "A Multiphasic Personality Schedule (Minnesota): I. Construction of the Schedule." *Journal of Psychology,* X(1940), 249–254.
6. Pedersen, Ruth. "Development of a Paper-and-Pencil Test of Supervisory Judgment." *American Psychologist,* IV(1949), 277–278.
7. Strong, Edward K. *Vocational Interests of Men and Women.* Stanford, Calif.: Stanford Univ. Press, 1943.

6. The Normal Curve and the Attenuation Paradox in Test Theory

LLOYD G. HUMPHREYS[1]

The following article was written primarily as a response to Loevinger's (1951) paper on the attenuation paradox. The student may wish to read her article as well as one written by Lord (1955), but it is not necessary to do so to understand the Humphreys article.

Humphreys prefers to use the statistics appropriate for rank-order, point distributions. The articles by Burke, Senders, and Baker *et al.* should help one evaluate the importance of using this type of statistic.

Humphreys also suggests priorities of test construction decisions. He suggests, among other things, that one should not always try to maximize test reliability since it is a function of homogeneity as well as item reliability. The readings in the reliability section of this book should help the reader take a position concerning this.

The appearance of Loevinger's paper (2) on the attenuation paradox in test theory was the precipitating factor in the writing of this note.[2] In reacting to her development of the paradox (supposed lack of monotonic relationship between reliability and validity) certain biases concerning test theory and test statistics which the writer has held for several years were crystallized.

Bias Number One. Let's forget our fixation on the normal curve in test theory.

Bias Number Two. Let's use statistics appropriate for rank-order, point distributions.

In support of these biases the following two arguments are offered:

1. Test score distributions *are* rank-order, point distributions. The underlying trait may or may not be continuously and normally distrib-

---

Humphreys, L. G. The normal curve and the attenuation paradox in test theory. *Psychological Bulletin*, 1956, *53*, 472–476. Reprinted with the permission of the publisher and author.

[1] Visiting professor, University of Illinois, fall semester, 1955; on leave from Personnel Research Laboratory, Air Force Personnel and Training Research Center. This article is based in part on work done under ARDC Project No. 7702 in support of the research and development program of the Air Force Personnel and Training Research Center, Lackland Air Force Base, Texas. Permission is granted for reproduction, translation, publication, use, and disposal in whole or in part by or for the United States Government.

[2] The writer is indebted to Drs. Robert Travers, John Leiman, and John Schmid, Jr., for critical reading of this manuscript.

uted, but such speculation is of no import. Psychological tests furnish rank-order information only and, furthermore, we have few prospects of obtaining devices of any other type. Criteria, on the other hand, may occasionally be continuously distributed and certain of these distributions may be normal, but criteria also are more frequently in the form of tests, ratings, rankings, pass-fail, and other point distributions.

2. If no assumption is made concerning the shape of the criterion distribution in the work of Loevinger (2), Brogden (1), and Tucker (4), there is no paradox. For example, if all items in a test have difficulty values of .5 and if all intercorrelations of items are equal, the relationships contained in Table 1 between number of items, item reliability, or level or interitem correlations, and validity of total scores are obtained. It is seen that the relationship between reliability and validity *is* monotonic.

TABLE 1. Validity as a Monotonic Function of Reliability

Item Inter. r	Item Validity	Test Validity			
		9 Items	18 Items	45 Items	90 Items
1/9	$\sqrt{1/9}$	.73	.83	.92	.96
2/9	$\sqrt{2/9}$	.85	.91	.96	.98
3/9	$\sqrt{3/9}$	.90	.95	.98	.99
4/9	$\sqrt{4/9}$	.94	.97	.99	.993
5/9	$\sqrt{5/9}$	.96	.98	.991	.996
6/9	$\sqrt{6/9}$	.97	.99	.994	.997
7/9	$\sqrt{7/9}$	.98	.994	.997	.998
8/9	$\sqrt{8/9}$	.993	.997	.999	.999

Discussion. In obtaining the above results the same assumption about item validity made by preceding writers was used, i.e., each item except for errors of measurement is a true measure of the criterion. This means that the validity of an item is the square root of its reliability. In the present case reliability is indicated by the phi coefficient between items in the test, and the validity is a point biserial between the item and "true" score. The values in the table are those obtained by applying the usual formula for the correlation of sums. Please note that here and elsewhere, when the term "correlation" is used, a product-moment correlation is assumed.

The reader may have difficulty visualizing the shapes of these criterion distributions since the definition of true is tied to the concept of infinity. The amount of error isn't great in any derivation, however, if one substitutes a large number for infinity.[3] One thousand items will give results reasonably comparable to infinity—ten thousand would be eminently safe—and the shape of the distribution can actually be worked out. Suffice to say, however, that a criterion distribution, as defined for Table 1, will not be normal when all items have difficulty values of .5 unless item intercorrelations are zero. For the same item difficulty specifications the distribution becomes rectangular when item correlations reach ⅓ and becomes increasingly U shaped as item correlations increase from ⅓ to 1.00.

The importance of the assumption concerning normality of criterion distribution is made clear in Table 2. This table was constructed by first assuming certain item reliabilities stated in terms of the tetrachoric

TABLE 2. Comparison of Item Validities With and Without the Assumption of Criterion Distribution Normality

Item Reliabilities		Item Validities		Comparison Values
r_{tet}	Phi	$\sqrt{r_{tet}}$, or r_{bis}	$\sqrt{phi}$, or r_{pbis}	r_{pbis} computed from r_{bis}
10	063	316	251	251
20	128	447	358	358
30	194	548	440	438
40	262	632	512	506
50	333	707	577	566
60	410	775	640	620
70	493	837	702	669
80	590	894	768	716
90	713	949	844	759

correlation. These values are in Column 1. Column 2 contains the corresponding phi coefficients for the same items. Column 3 contains the item validities, stated as continuous biserials, when the criterion is assumed to be a true, normally distributed measure of the function measured by the item. Values in Column 3 are comparable to item validities used previously by Brogden and Loevinger. Column 4 also contains item validities, stated as point biserials, but the criterion is assumed to be the sum of an infinite number of items, of a given level

[3] The mathematician, H. T. Davis, made this suggestion in principle in a class at Indiana University in 1935–36. He stated that if mathematicians substituted a "very large number" for infinity in their calculations they would not obtain significantly different answers and their assumptions would have operational meaning. This suggestion seems peculiarly appropriate for test theory. For the latter theory the number does not need to be nearly as large as Dr. Davis envisioned.

of reliability, whose distribution takes the shape dictated by their intercorrelations. Column 5 also contains point biserials, but these were computed from the continuous biserials in Column 3, which were based on an assumed normal distribution, by multiplying each by the expression $z/\sqrt{pq}$. Comparison of Columns 4 and 5 shows how the assumption of normality attenuates item validities with the error becoming progressively larger with higher validities.

Similar tables can readily be computed for other levels of item difficulty. Again, there is no paradox, but the criterion distributions are skewed as well as flat when item intercorrelations are greater than zero. The assumption of a normal distribution of the criterion is not compatible with the mechanics of adding test items together.

The problem is more complex if item difficulties vary. Item reliability can no longer be estimated from the intercorrelations of the items in the test, but must be defined as correlation with a comparable item in another test. The comparable item must measure the same function *and* must have the same mean and variance. Intercorrelations of items having different means and variances, but otherwise measuring the same function equally reliably, will be lower than the products of the square roots of their reliabilities.

With items distributed in difficulty there is again no paradox, however, since spread of item difficulties will also affect the shape of the criterion distribution. Variance of item difficulties forces scores toward the center of the distribution and thus counters the effect of item intercorrelations.

It is still possible to argue that a paradox is involved since classical test theory does not allow for the flexibility in shape of distribution required in order for the classical formulas to be applicable. The locus of the paradox can, however, be more precisely stated. In order for the relationship between validity and reliability to hold, one cannot keep constant both the form of the criterion distribution and the distribution of difficulties of the test items.

Conclusion for test construction. The test technician should proceed with the job of test construction without making obeisance to the normal curve. His decisions should be made in sequential fashion from most to least important. The shape of his test score distribution is a decision made late in the sequence and his desires about shape of distribution should not lead to reversals of earlier, more important decisions. It should also be noted that all of his decisions are made with a particular group of examinees in mind, since the level and range of their ability are crucial factors in the writing and selection of test items.

The first step in test construction is to draw up specifications for the test. Decisions made at this stage should not be changed, unconsciously, by later statistical computations of the sort used in item analysis, measures of test reliability, and measures of test homogeneity. Blind application of statistical procedures may change the nature of the test.

For example, the test may be designed to predict a particular complex criterion. Items will then be included in numbers such that their weight in the total score will be optimum for the purpose. Selection of items on the basis of correlation of items against total test score would obviously be inappropriate. A Kuder-Richardson homogeneity coefficient would also be inappropriate for the test as a whole.

One may also be interested in measuring a psychological "trait." In this case the tendency is to think of the problem in terms of the homogeneity of the items on the grounds that a heterogeneous test by definition cannot measure a unitary trait. If homogeneity is defined as level of item intercorrelations, however, there is again the possibility of error in the blind following of statistical indices. Let us suppose that a mechanical information test is desired. The following are possible examples of such tests in descending order of item intercorrelations (difficulty level of items being held constant): (*a*) Information about the crosscut saw and its use; (*b*) Information about saws and their uses; (*c*) Information about woodworking tools and their uses; (*d*) Information about tools and their uses in woodworking, plumbing, metal working, automotive repairing, etc.

For many purposes test *d* may be most desirable, though its homogeneity as defined above is lower than for the other tests in the series. This means that the test specifications must indicate how broadly this test should be defined. Even a fairly broad test may be relatively homogeneous, however, in that the items in the test may still be more like each other than items in other tests in the same battery (3).

High item reliability is always desired. Nothing is gained from low item reliabilities. The reader must remember, however, that item reliability is defined as the correlation with another comparable item, and is not estimated from correlations with all other items in the test. Hence there is no contradiction between the present advice to achieve high item reliability and that given above which was to select a desired degree of homogeneity. The test constructor should, therefore, as his next step, write the most reliable items he possibly can for the function he wants to measure. By necessity, though not from choice, item reliabilities will often be quite low because reliable measurement in many areas is difficult.

One cannot be as dogmatic about high test reliability as about high item reliability. Test reliability is a function of item reliabilities *and* item intercorrelations; i.e., test reliability is in part a function of homogeneity. High test reliability can be achieved by narrowing the focus of the test and attaining high homogeneity. Care must be exercised in item selection, therefore, not to confuse item reliability and homogeneity and thereby change the function measured by the test. The test technician must maintain his original specifications in spite of temptations to increase test reliability.

The next decision concerns the shape of the distribution of test scores desired. Depending on the purpose of the test, the desired distribution may be normal, platykurtic, skewed, or U shaped. For a general purpose test the writer submits that a rectangular distribution is most useful since this distribution most accurately represents the information furnished by a psychological test. That is, the rank-ordering of persons is accomplished equally well in all parts of the range when the distribution is rectangular. This means that reliability of discrimination is maximized over all.

The desired shape is achieved or, more commonly approached by controlling the difficulty levels of the test items. Item difficulties alone are manipulated because previous decisions have fixed the general level of item intercorrelations that are possible. With high item intercorrelations, a constant level of item difficulty will produce a U-shaped distribution. As the variance of item difficulty increases, the peaks of the U-shaped distribution will converge to the center of the distribution.

The reader should be warned that some of the shapes of test score distributions are highly theoretical in terms of the characteristics of items available for most measurement purposes. One practical outcome, however, is to question the decision made automatically by most test constructors to vary the difficulty levels of the items in the test. With low item intercorrelations of the sort obtained in most aptitude tests only by careful selection of the most reliable items at a constant level of difficulty can a rectangular distribution be approached.

SUMMARY

1. The attenuation paradox in test theory is a result of the assumption made by previous writers of a continuous normal distribution of the criterion.

2. There is no paradox if the criterion distributions can assume any shape. If this is considered *ipso facto* paradoxical, then the locus of the paradox is in one's inability to hold constant both the shape of the criterion distribution and the distribution of item difficulties.

3. The pervasive use of the assumption of continuous normal distributions in test theory and test statistics is questioned on grounds that test data are in the form of rank-order, point distributions.

4. The test technician should make decisions in constructing a test in a particular sequence. This sequence is as follows:

a. Outline his test specifications. This will specify the desired degree of homogeneity (level of item intercorrelations) wanted in the test. High homogeneity is not necessarily desirable.

b. Write the most reliable items possible to measure the desired function or functions. Items of low reliability are never desired.

c. Do not always try to maximize test reliability, since the latter is a function both of item reliability and homogeneity. The desired degree of homogeneity should be maintained even if item-test correlations are low.

d. Select the form of the raw score distribution of test scores desired. This can be any form, though a rectangular distribution is recommended for a general purpose test.

e. Strive to obtain the desired form of distribution by varying item difficulties only. Previous and more important decisions have fixed the level of item intercorrelations which is the other determiner of shape of distribution.

REFERENCES

1. Brogden, H. E. Variations in test validity with variation in the distribution of item difficulties, number of items, and degree of their intercorrelation. *Psychometrika,* 1946, **11**, 197–214.
2. Loevinger, Jane. The attenuation paradox in test theory. *Psychol. Bull.,* 1954, **51**, 493–504.
3. Loevinger, Jane, Gleser, Goldine C., & DuBois, P. H. Maximizing the discriminating power of a multiple score test. *Psychometrika,* 1953, **18**, 309–317.
4. Tucker, L. R. Maximum validity of a test with equivalent items. *Psychometrika,* 1946, **11**, 1–13.

7. Problems in Mental Test Theory Arising from Errors of Measurement

FREDERIC M. LORD

Most students of test theory can define a true score and describe its relation to an observed score and an error of measurement. Many can suggest how a true score may be estimated, and can explain why the appropriate estimate is not the same when the score of a single examinee is considered in isolation as when it is considered as one of a particular set of scores. Some may be aware that it is more reasonable to assume a binomial than a normal distribution for errors of measurement. A few may know that satisfactory statistical solutions to problems like those listed below probably exist, but have not yet been fully developed and tested.

—The problem of estimating the frequency distribution of true scores
—The problem of testing the hypothesis that two tests both measure the same psychological dimension
—The problem of measuring true change over time.

But there remain many who do not know, and cannot do all of these things as well as Lord. For them this article should be interesting and instructive.

Several unsolved basic problems of mental test theory, arising from the presence of errors of measurement in the test scores, are discussed. The inadequacies of the classical model, with its normally and independently distributed errors, are pointed out. Two newer stochastic models, available for dealing with these problems, are described. It is observed that the proportion of test questions answered correctly by the examinee is by itself usually not a satisfactory estimate of the corresponding population proportion. Methods for estimating such population proportions are considered. Such methods are required in order (i) to determine whether or not two tests measure the same dimension, (ii) to measure changes in the characteristics of the examinees.

The psychometrician frequently wonders why modern statistical theory fails to provide ready-made, satisfactory statistical methods for answering certain rather basic questions that he would like to ask. Perhaps the professional statistician is also puzzled as to why the psychometrician thinks he has so many exceptional problems. Or, going further, the statistician may feel some doubt in his mind as to whether the psychometrician's problems are of a statistical nature at all. Are test scores really numerical measurements to which the usual arithmetical operations can usefully be applied, or should they be considered merely as nonmetric symbols which have few if any of the more useful properties of the number system?

Lord, F. M. Problems in mental test theory arising from errors of measurement. *Journal of the American Statistical Association*, 1959, *54*, 472–479. Reprinted with the permission of the publisher and author.

The plan of the present article is simply to outline a few very basic problems of mental test theory that seem to be well within the present grasp of modern statistics, but that have not yet been completely solved and cozily packaged. The selection of problems for discussion is dictated by the writer's interests—it is restricted to certain basic problems arising from the existence in almost all test scores of substantial errors of measurement. The purpose is not primarily to expound, but to stimulate interest in and active development of the statistical theory and methods needed in this area of mental test theory.

There follows first of all a section discussing the meaning and utility of the notions "true score" and "error of measurement" (these notions should be more acceptable to most statisticians than they are to many psychologists). The next two sections outline two usable statistical models for the relationships between actual scores, true scores, and errors of measurement. The fourth and fifth sections discuss some possible approaches to the basic problems of estimating the examinees' true scores. The last two sections outline two important practical problems, the solution of which requires the making of inferences about true scores.

1. THE "TRUE SCORE" AND THE ERROR OF MEASUREMENT

A mental test is a collection of tasks; the examinee's performance on these is taken as an index of his standing along some psychological dimension. A conveniently noncontroversial example is a test of spelling ability. Conventionally, the examiner chooses *n* words from the dictionary, requires the examinees to spell each of them, and uses the number (or proportion) of words spelled correctly by the examinee as his test score, representing, in some useful sense, his spelling ability. (It is probable that theoretically better indices of "spelling ability" could be devised, but this is outside the scope of the present discussion.)

Many equally satisfactory sets of *n* words could be chosen by the examiner to constitute a test of spelling ability. Such equally satisfactory sets will be called "parallel tests."

The basic trouble appears in the fact that an examinee's score will usually be found to fluctuate considerably from one parallel test to another, if more than one is administered. The psychologist cannot usefully consider that each parallel test represents a new psychological dimension—there simply would be too many dimensions for practical scientific investigation. Hence, he must say that his main interest lies in whatever it is that these parallel tests all have in common.

This leads directly to the useful concept of the examinee's "true score," which is frequently defined as the average of the scores that the examinee would make on all possible parallel tests if he did not change during the testing process. In the case of the spelling test, the true score might, by this definition, be the proportion of the words in the dictionary (or in some selected list) that the examinee knows how to spell. The error of measurement (e_a) is, by definition, merely the difference between the examinee's actual score (t_a) and his true score (τ_a):

(τ_a):
$$e_a = t_a - \tau_a.$$

The reader is referred to Gulliksen [3, chs. 2–5] for a basic treatment of true scores and errors of measurement and to various texts [3, chs. 6–10, 14–16; 2, chs. 13–14; 13, ch. 12] for an exposition of methods in current use for dealing with some of the psychometric problems caused by the errors of measurement.

The basic task of mental test theory must of necessity be to use the observed test scores in order to draw inferences about true scores. Since the observed scores differ from the true scores only because of errors of measurement, the psychologist can be interested in the observed scores only insofar as they provide information about true scores. This fact is not always as apparent as it should be, since tests are commonly used for selection purposes, and it is usually sufficient for practical purposes in such cases simply to select those examinees having the highest observed scores. There are other important practical uses of tests, on the other hand, that do require methods for making inferences about true scores; two of these will be described in the two last sections.

2. THE ASSUMPTION OF NORMALLY AND INDEPENDENTLY DISTRIBUTED ERRORS

Problems of mental test theory can be of professional interest to statisticians only when the errors of measurement have been conceptualized as stochastic variables. Two ways in which this may be done will be mentioned here.

A classical assumption is that each error of measurement is distributed normally, with zero mean, independently of true score. Thus, the conditional distribution of the observed score of examinee *a* for given true score is

$$f(t_a \mid \tau_a) = N(\tau_a, \sigma^2),$$

where the expression on the right is the usual one denoting a normal distribution with mean τ_a and a fixed variance σ^2 independent of *a*.

σ^2 is also the variance of the errors of measurement. Under certain circumstances a good estimate of σ^2 can be obtained by administering two parallel forms of the same test to the same group of examinees. (The correlation coefficient between two parallel test forms in such circumstances is the important statistic known as the *test reliability.*) In cases where the necessary assumptions are not met, there frequently are other, reasonably satisfactory procedures available for estimating the variance of the errors of measurement [3, chs. 15, 16]. Hereafter, then, the variance of the errors of measurement will be considered as a given quantity, known within a satisfactory approximation.

The assumption that each error is distributed $N(O, \sigma^2)$ independently of true score is probably quite adequate for many purposes. However, it is clear that these assumptions can not be met when the true score, expressed as a proportion of the number of items in the test, is near zero or near one. If n is the number of test items, *and* τ_a/n is some small number like .01, it is intuitively obvious, in view of the fact that the observed test score can never be negative, that the distribution of the errors of measurement will in all probability be skew, and that the standard deviation of this distribution will surely be less than if the true score were not so near to zero.

3. THE ITEM-SAMPLING MODEL FOR ERRORS OF MEASUREMENT

There is another way of thinking about errors of measurement that avoids this difficulty. As suggested before, it is almost always possible to imagine a large pool of test items from which many tests could be built, each of which would be considered an equally satisfactory substitute for the test actually administered. This pool constitutes a population of items which may be thought of as classified into strata on all relevant characteristics, such as item content, item difficulty, item discriminating power, and so forth. A whole series of parallel tests may be produced by drawing stratified random samples of items from this population (this is the essential feature of the Kuder-Richardson definition of "rationally equivalent" tests [5]). The examinee's true score may be thought of as the average of the scores that he would obtain on all such samples of items. This definition of parallelism provides a stochastic process that gives rise to the errors of measurement.[1]

The situation can be simplified by ignoring the stratification and assuming the test items to be selected by simple random sampling [7]. There is experimental evidence (e.g., [1]) to show that the approximations introduced by ignoring the stratification are not too large in many cases. If, as is commonly the case, the test items are scored either zero

[1] This model has recently been developed by the author in "The Joint Cumulants of True Values and Errors of Measurement," *Annals of Mathematical Statistics*, in press; and in "Inferences About True Scores from Parallel Test Forms," *Educational and Psychological Measurement*, in press.

or one, it is seen that the conditional distribution of test score for given true score is a binomial distribution:

$$f(t_a \mid \tau_a) = n^{-n} \binom{n}{t_a} \tau_a^{t_a} (n - \tau_a)^{n-t_a}$$

It is worth noting that in this formula, although the errors of measurement are uncorrelated with true score, the shape of the distribution of the errors of measurement is definitely dependent on the true score.

4. ESTIMATION OF AN EXAMINEE'S TRUE SCORE

Given either of the foregoing assumptions about the nature of the conditional distribution of observed score for fixed true score, it should be possible to use any set of observed scores to make inferences about the corresponding true scores. To start out with, for either of the conditional distributions already mentioned, the observed score is itself a sufficient statistic for estimating the true score.

In spite of this fact, the observed score is *not* an appropriate estimate of true score in most practical situations. In a typical situation an entire group of examinees is tested—for example, all the freshmen at Princeton University, or all the applicants for medical colleges throughout the country. When a distribution of observed test scores is available, there is one piece of information about each individual tested that was not taken into account when the observed test score was described as a sufficient statistic for estimating true score: there is the additional information that each individual is a member of the group. It may be known, for example, that he is a freshman at Princeton University and not a four-year-old child, or a poodle dog, or a man from Mars.

This information has a very real effect on the making of inferences regarding true scores. If the first 999 students in the sample display a bell-shaped frequency distribution of observed test scores, it will be extremely surprising if the next student in the sample turns up with an observed test score six standard deviations above the group mean. To take a less extreme example, it will be mildly surprising if his score is a mere two standard deviations above the group mean. This surprise has a clear, logical consequence when it comes to inferring the true score of the student whose observed score is very high for his group: the most plausible inference is that the error of measurement for this student was probably positive, and hence his true score is probably somewhat closer to the mean than his observed score.

The conclusion is that whenever a homogeneous group of examinees has been tested (a group which could, perhaps, be considered as a random sample from some hypothetical population), then there is available some information that was not taken into account when the observed score was described as a sufficient statistic for estimating the true score. When this additional information is taken into account, it must be concluded that whenever the observed score of an examinee is above the mean of his group, the best estimate of his true score must be somewhat less than his obtained score; and similarly whenever the observed score of the examinee is below the mean of his group, then the best estimate of his true score will be somewhat higher than his obtained score.

Note that this is not a case where the estimate of a parameter is modified because of *a priori* information about the frequency distribution of that parameter. Instead, it is a case where the sample itself provides information about the frequency distribution of the parameter to be estimated. If the sample distribution is bell-shaped, this clearly indicates that the true-score distribution in the group tested is not rectangular, for example. The situation is very similar to one recently treated in several articles in the statistical literature [4, 9, 10, 11].

In current psychometric theory, the only standard procedure for estimating true scores is by means of a regression equation:

$$\hat{\tau}_a - \mu_r = \beta_{rt}(t_a - \mu_t),$$

where μ is a group mean and β_{rt} is the ordinary regression coefficient of true score on observed score [8]. There is usually no difficulty in obtaining reasonably good estimates of the means and of β_{rt} from sample data. This equation would therefore be reasonably satisfactory if the regression of true score on observed score were known to be linear. While a good approximation to linearity may hold in most practical situations, one can easily imagine situations where linearity would not even be approximated—for example, a situation where the true-score distribution is actually dichotomous (the reader may wish to examine this case for himself). Hence this equation does not provide a theoretically satisfactory estimate. Some method that does not require the assumption of linearity needs to be worked out.

5. ESTIMATING THE FREQUENCY DISTRIBUTION OF TRUE SCORES

A problem closely related to the foregoing is the problem of estimating the shape of the frequency distribution of true scores for a group of examinees. (In fact, if the shape of this frequency distribution can be estimated, then the shape of the regression of true scores on observed scores can also be estimated, and a method for estimating true scores from observed scores by means of a curvilinear regression equation will have been found; or, even better, the true scores can be estimated by some sort of empirical Bayes procedure.) As a first step, it is necessary to know if the frequency distribution of obtained scores for examinee a, $f(t_a|\tau_a)$, is independent of the corresponding distribution for examinee b, $f(t_b|\tau_b)$. Under the classical theory with normally and identically distributed errors, these two distributions are clearly independent. They are also independent under the model that pictures the errors of measurement as arising from stratified random sampling of items, but in this case there is no convenient formula for the frequency distributions available. Under the model that assumes simple random sampling of items, there is a convenient formula for these frequency distributions (given in section 3), and they are almost, although not quite, independent.

Assuming independence, the distribution of observed scores is equal to the integral of the distribution of true scores times the conditional distribution of observed scores:

$$f(t) = \int_{-\infty}^{\infty} g(\tau) f(t|\tau)\, d\tau.$$

This is an integral equation that can be solved to determine the shape of the distribution of true scores once the form of the other two distributions is given. To the writer's best knowledge, this approach has not yet been tried out in psychometric work, although it appears to be very useful in the solution of certain very similar problems in astronomy [12].

6. THE HYPOTHESIS THAT TWO TESTS BOTH MEASURE THE SAME PSYCHOLOGICAL DIMENSION

Actually, there is very little in mental test theory on the problem of inferring the shape of the distribution of true scores for a group of examinees. It would seem that this is a problem that must be dealt with before mental test theory can go much further. Its solution may be basic to that of a rather important practical problem—that of determining whether two tests measure the same thing. Psychologists are continually publishing new tests of all varieties, but do two published tests purporting to measure the same dimension actually do so? Do two given tests of intelligence really measure the same thing? We have no adequate statistical test of this hypothesis. We are in the position of a scientist who continually builds measuring instruments but cannot tell whether two instruments are measuring the same or different physical properties!

If the true scores on two tests have a perfect curvilinear correlation, then the two tests can be said to be measuring the same characteristic. There is available a satisfactory method for estimating the size of the correlation between the true scores on two different tests only when their relationship can be assumed to be linear [3, pp. 101–4; 2, pp. 400–2; 13, pp. 299–301]. The assumption that the true scores of two tests have a linear relationship may often be plausible when the tests are at about the same difficulty level, but it is not even plausible when the tests are at distinctly different difficulty levels.

The problem here can be formulated in terms of estimating the bivariate frequency distribution of two true scores. For two tests, the bivariate distribution of observed scores is equal to the double integral of the bivariate distribution of true scores multiplied by the two conditional distributions of observed scores:

$$f(t_1, t_2) = \int_{-\infty}^{\infty} \int_{-\infty}^{\infty} g(\tau_1, \tau_2) f_1(t_1 | \tau_1) f_2(t_2 | \tau_2) \, d\tau_1 d\tau_2.$$

To determine whether two tests measure the same thing, it is necessary to test the hypothesis that τ_1 and τ_2 are really functionally related rather than stochastically related. It should be possible to develop a statistical test of this hypothesis from the foregoing equation.

7. THE MEASUREMENT OF CHANGE

Another situation where a consideration of true scores becomes quite important and where satisfactory methods are at present available only for the linear case is in the measurement of change. Suppose two parallel tests (t_1 and t_2) have been given to the same examinees on two separate occasions. It is desired to estimate the true "gain" or change $(\tau_{2a} - \tau_{1a})$ in each examinee during the time elapsed. Now, in the simple case where there has been only one testing, the actual observed scores will rank the examinees in the same rank order as would the best estimates of the true scores. It has been customary to assume, by analogy, that when two parallel tests have been given, the observed gains $(t_{2a} - t_{1a})$ rank the examinees in the same rank order as would the best estimates of the true gains. There is actually no such convenient relationship [6]. As a result, this is a case where the problem of the estimation of true values becomes of direct practical importance in the use and interpretation of mental test scores.

It is seen to be logically necessary to compare the observed bivariate distribution of t_1 and t_2 with the distribution that would have been found if these two parallel tests had been administered virtually simultaneously. The latter distribution can sometimes be approximated experimentally, or it can be inferred theoretically from an acceptable statistical model for the relation between true scores and errors of measurement. Any difference between (a) the bivariate distribution of t_1 and t_2 observed when the two tests are separated by a time interval (and perhaps by some experimental treatment) and (b) the distribution that would have been found if no time had elapsed—any such difference must logically be due to changes in true scores rather than to mere errors of measurement. In this way, it should be possible to make inferences about the true change in each individual examinee. Practical methods for doing this have not as yet been worked out in detail.

Sometimes a question is raised as to whether the test-score metric is sufficiently meaningful so that it is of some use to make inferences about gains or losses. Suppose that t_1 and t_2 each consists of a random sample of 100 words from the large Webster's Dictionary. If it is estimated that a student's true score has increased by five points during the school year, this means that it is estimated that he can now spell five percent more of the words in the dictionary correctly than he could a year ago. Correspondingly, if the estimate of a student's true gain is negative, this means that it is estimated that he can now spell fewer words in the big Webster than he could a year ago. Stated in these terms, the utility of the estimates should be obvious.

REFERENCES

1. Cronbach, Lee J., "Coefficient Alpha and the Internal Structure of Tests," *Psychometrika,* 16 (1951), 309–12.
2. Guilford, J. P., *Psychometric Methods.* New York: McGraw-Hill, 1954.
3. Gulliksen, Harold, *Theory of Mental Tests.* New York: Wiley, 1950.
4. Johns, M. V., Jr., "Non-parametric Empirical Bayes Procedures," *Annals of Mathematical Statistics,* 28 (1957), 649–69.
5. Kuder, G. F. and Richardson, M. W., "The Theory of Estimation of Test Reliability," *Psychometrika,* 2 (1937), 151–60.
6. Lord, Frederic M., "The Measurement of Growth," *Educational and Psychological Measurement,* 16 (1956), 421–37.
7. Lord, Frederic M., "Statistical Inferences About True Scores," *Psychometrika,* 24 (1959), 1–17.
8. Peters, Charles C. and Van Voorhis, Walter R., *Statistical Procedures and Their Mathematical Bases.* New York: McGraw-Hill, 1940, eq. 125.
9. Robbins, Herbert, "Asymptotically Subminimax Solutions of Compound Statistical Decision Problems," *Proceedings of the Second Berkeley Symposium on Mathematical Statistics and Probability.* University of California Press, 1951, 131–48.
10. Robbins, Herbert, "An Empirical Bayes Approach to Statistics," *Proceedings of the Third Berkeley Symposium on Mathematical Statistics and Probability.* University of California Press, 1956, 157–63.
11. Steinhaus, H., "The Problem of Estimation," *Annals of Mathematical Statistics,* 28 (1957), 633–48.
12. Trumpler, Robert J. and Weaver, Harold F., *Statistical Astronomy.* University of California Press, 1953.
13. Walker, Helen M. and Lev, Joseph, *Statistical Inference.* New York: Henry Holt, 1953.

UNIT ONE: MEASUREMENT THEORY AND SCALING ADDITIONAL READINGS

American Psychological Association. Technical Recommendations for Psychological Tests and Diagnostic Techniques. Published as a supplement to *Pychological Bulletin,* 1954, *51*:2.

Bereiter, C. E. How may units of measurement be safely ignored? *Journal of Educational Measurement,* 1964, *1,* 19–22.

Coombs, C. H. Psychological scaling without a unit of measurement. *Psychological Review,* 1950, *57,* 145–158.

Coombs, C. H. *A Theory of Data.* New York: Wiley, 1964, 585 pp.

Coombs, C. H., Raiffa, H., and Thrall, R. M. Some views on mathematical models and measurement theory. *Psychological Review,* 1954, *61,* 132–144.

Cureton, E. E. Validity, reliability, and baloney. *Educational and Psychological Measurement,* 1950, *10,* 94–96.

Gardner, E. F. Comments on selected scaling techniques with a description of a new type of scale. *Journal of Clinical Psychology*, 1950, *6*, 38–43.

Ghiselli, E. E. *Theory of Psychological Measurement.* New York: McGraw-Hill, 1964, 408 pp.

Gulliksen, H. O. *Theory of Mental Tests.* New York: Wiley, 1950, 486 pp.

Loevinger, Jane. The attenuation paradox in test theory. *Psychological Bulletin,* 1954, *51,* 493–504.

Lord, F. M. The relation of test score to the trait underlying the test. *Educational and Psychological Measurement,* 1953a, *13,* 517–549.

Lord, F. M. On the statistical treatment of football numbers. *American Psychologist,* 1953b, *8,* 750–751.

Lord, F. M. Some perspectives on "the attenuation paradox in test theory." *Psychological Bulletin,* 1955, *52,* 506–510.

Lord, F. M. A strong true-score theory, with applications. *Psychometrika,* 1965, *30,* 239–270.

Lumsden, J. The construction of unidimensional tests. *Psychological Bulletin,* 1961, *58,* 122–131.

Stevens, S. S. Measurement and man. *Science,* 1958, *127,* 383–389.

Sutcliffe, J. P. Measurement and permissible statistics. *Australian Journal of Psychology,* 1958, *10,* 257–268.

Thurstone, L. L. The unit of measurement in educational scales. *Journal of Educational Psychology,* 1927, *18,* 505–524.

Thurstone, L. L. The absolute zero in intelligence measurement. *Psychological Review*, 1928, *35*, 175–197.

Unit Two:

NORMS

INTRODUCTION

8. Gardner, Eric F., *Normative Standard Scores*
9. Ebel, Robert L., *Content Standard Test Scores*

A unit on norms is an important part of every course in educational measurement. Norms provide a frame of reference for the interpretation of individual raw scores. The authors of the following two articles discuss two possible frames of reference: (1) The performance of a well-defined group of examinees (a norm group), and (2) the content of the test itself. It should be emphasized that these are complementary rather than competing frames of reference. Gardner emphasizes the importance of norms, but would certainly not suggest that knowledge of the content of the test adds nothing to the meaningfulness of the scores. Ebel readily admits that normative meaning is necessary but that content meaning in test scores is an important supplement that deserves more attention. As he states: "It is unfortunate, I think, that some specialists in measuring educational achievement have seemed to imply that knowing how many of his peers a student can excel is more important than knowing what he can do to excel them." While Ebel centers his discussion around the content of achievement tests, knowledge of the content of other types of tests would also aid in their interpretation.

Angoff (1962) presents a very provocative point of view that differs from those presented by Gardner and Ebel. He suggests that the scale of numbers should be chosen arbitrarily and then forgotten. The meaning of the scores should come directly from the *user* himself.

8. Normative Standard Scores

ERIC F. GARDNER

A single isolated test score is of little or no value. For a score to have meaning and be of social or scientific utility, some sort of frame of reference is needed. A number of different frames of reference have been proposed and have been found to have value.

One possible frame of reference is the content of the test itself. Among derived scores one of the earliest was the per cent of a defined

Gardner, E. F. Normative standard scores. *Educational and Psychological Measurement*, 1962, *22*, 7–14. Reprinted with the permission of the publisher and author.

sample of tasks which an individual has completed satisfactorily. The deficiencies inherent in these kinds of scores have been discussed so many times in the literature no attempt will be made here to go into detail again. A few of the issues are the lack of comparability of per cent scores on the same test for different people, the lack of comparability from test to test, and the lack of algebraic utility. The following comments illustrate these points. John and Jane might each have scores of 60 per cent on the same test but have answered correctly very different items. A score of 80 per cent on a hard test is obviously not comparable to a score of 80 per cent on an easy test. For algebraic utility, equal units throughout the scale are desirable. It is not reasonable to assume that the difference between scores of 60 per cent and 70 per cent represents the same difference in ability as that between 90 per cent and 100 per cent. Such scores ignore differences between items of the test in representativeness, difficulty and importance. Also it is obvious that the meaning of such scores is entirely dependent upon the particular sample of items included.

The content provided by the items of a test yields scores which may be directly related to standards set by the examiner who prepared the test. He may regard a score as good or poor on the basis of his judgments of the difficulties of the items and the expected performance of those taking the examination. Such judgments are difficult to make and frequently are not related to the realities of the situation. For example, when teachers or examining boards discover that very large proportions of those examined have fallen below the standard they originally built into the examination, they generally revise their judgments about the test and re-evaluate the test results. Thus the content or "absolute" frame of reference is supplemented by a relative frame of reference based upon knowledge of the performance of the group of examinees.

The inadequacy of the content frame of reference led to a consideration of additional approaches. One of the most commonly used frames of reference is the performance of some well-defined group of examinees. The College Board score scale, with a mean of 500 and a standard deviation of 100 for a group of examinees on which it was established some years ago, is one type of normative standard score. The I.Q. and grade scores are different types of basically normative standard scores.

This type of score provides a meaningful report of the examinee's performance in relation to those of members of a defined reference group. For example, it may be more useful to know how an examinee's performance on a particular test compares with those of his peers, than to know how it compares with the standards of the examiners. For many purposes, such as selection, placement and prediction, it is useful to know the location of a given score with respect to a particular frequency distribution of scores. For example, a grade score of 6.5 incorporates in it the information that the subject has obtained a score that is the same as the average of the normative group of sixth-graders who have been half a year in school. An I.Q. of 100 indicates that on the particular intelligence test the subject performed at the same level as the average of the normative group. A standard score of 600 indicates performance which is one standard deviation above the mean of the normative group.

In most cases the test user is concerned about frames of reference based on both content and group performance. He is interested in having knowledge about the specific responses of the individual to the items of the test and also knowledge about the performance of the individual relative to that of other individuals.

SOME DESIRABLE PROPERTIES OF ITEMS

If we ignore practical considerations and concern ourselves with characteristics of items that would aid in scaling and test interpretation, there are a number of desirable properties that can be mentioned. Some of these are difficult or impossible to obtain; while others, if obtained, would almost certainly prevent our achieving more important characteristics. Considering each specific issue in isolation and simultaneously assuming that all other necessary requirements for a good test are met, we could argue the following properties would be desirable:

1. *The test consists of items which constitute a representative sample of the domain tested.* It should be a sample of behaviors that represent the objectives which have previously been defined.
2. *The items in the test form a Guttman Scale.* This property implies that the items selected can be ranked in the same order of difficulty for each individual. Once the items have been so ranked, any examinee will answer correctly all those items of less difficulty and incorrectly all those of greater difficulty. Thus a score of 17 means that the person answered correctly the first seventeen items and incorrectly all others. Such an arrangement of items permits an unambiguous interpretation of the score 17 in that all people who score 17 have answered correctly the same items.
3. *The items in the test can be arranged along a continuum of the variable under consideration in such a way that the raw scores constitute an interval scale.* The items included in such a test would have the property of representing equal differences in ability between adjacent items. For example, the difference in ability represented by scores of 53 and 54 would be the same as that represented by scores of 85 and 86.

4. *The items are of such nature that a zero score on the test represents zero amount of the ability being tested.* If the condition specified in property 3 is now added, the scale becomes a ratio scale which is amenable to all four arithmetic operations.
5. *The items provide a scale unit which is meaningful.* There are advantages in having the size of unit related to the standard error of measurement in such a way that a user has some idea as to the likelihood of a difference being entirely due to error.

A test possessing the properties just enumerated (that is, consisting of items which (1) adequately represent the domain to be tested and (2) can be ranked in order of difficulty, and starting with an absolute zero will provide successively equal increments of knowledge) provides a raw score scale with very desirable characteristics. Unfortunately these properties, although desirable, are difficult to achieve and in many practical situations the achievement of one results in less success in achieving another. For example, I would argue that property 1 is paramount for any achievement test. That is—a good achievement test should itself define the objectives measured. These objectives are set up by those agents of society who are responsible for decisions concerning educational objectives, and the test constructor must attempt to incorporate that definition in the building of the examination. This point of view implies that the method of scaling an educational achievement test should not be permitted to determine the content of the test or to alter the definition of objectives implied in the test. It is most probable that an attempt to select items so that the raw score scale produced has properties 2 and 3 (an interval Guttman Scale) would eliminate from the test sample important concepts and skills.

SAMPLING FROM POPULATIONS OF ITEMS AND EXAMINEES

This discussion so far has suggested that the interpretation of achievement test scores requires one to consider two very different types of frames of reference, each associated with a particular sampling problem.

The first problem is concerned with an acceptable sample of items. For a test score to be meaningful the particular variable under consideration must be defined, and the user must have knowledge about the adequacy of the items to sample this domain. Hence, specific knowledge of the field and of the items included in the test is necessary for the adequate interpretation of a raw score.

The second problem is concerned with a sample of examinees. Information about such things as item or test difficulty, functioning of decoys, norms and predictive effectiveness are dependent upon empirical data. To be meaningful these indices must be derived from an acceptable sample of people obtained from a well-defined population. A difficulty index for a reading item obtained from a typical fourth grade obviously does not have the same meaning as one obtained from a typical sixth grade. A person scoring at the eighty-fourth percentile, or obtaining a T-score of 60 in an arithmetic test where the score is calculated from a typical seventh grade sample, is not performing at the same level as one whose standing at the eighty-fourth percentile on the same test is calculated from a below-average seventh grade. Likewise a pupil with a vocabulary grade score of 6.2 obtained from a representative sample of fifth graders, in say, Mississippi, is certainly not comparable to a pupil making a score of 6.2 based on a national representative sample. By the same token, one would hardly expect a set of decoys for an arithmetic multiple-choice item to function in the same fashion in both a fifth and ninth grade. The importance of the particular reference population which is used cannot be overemphasized.

CURRENT PRACTICE

In the construction of an achievement test, the issue of the sampling of the items is considered under the concept of validity—usually content validity. Appropriate objectives are defined, tables of specifications are established, and trial items are constructed to sample the variable described.

Data are then obtained to give information about the statistical characteristics of the items. In the light of this additional information, the test is assembled in such a way that the items will sample both content defined by the objectives and the ability of the examinees for which it is designed.

Attempts are then made by scaling procedures to approximate some of the other desirable properties which the test does not acquire solely through the relationship of the items to each other. Current methods of scaling educational achievement tests are based upon the statistical properties of the test, or of the individual items constituting the test with reference to a particular population of examinees. That is, such scales are derived from normative data.

Raw scores on some educational achievement tests are meaningful in themselves in terms of content of the test. For example, a score of 30 on a test built of 50 basic addition combinations gives some information about the particular student without regard for the performance of any other person. However, groups of such items arranged with reference to such a meaning do not constitute scales. You cannot compare 30 out of these 50 basic addition facts with 30 out of a different set, or six out of 15 rules of grammar, or with a possible number of vocabulary items in Russian. Some frame of reference is needed so that performance from person to person and group to group can be compared. The scaling job still remains to be done.

Any added meanings of scaled scores is due entirely to the contribution of the normative data, and that meaning applies, strictly speaking, only to the particular reference population involved in the scaling process. This statement holds whether the scale is based solely upon item statistics or upon some operations on the total score. Normative standard scores are dependent upon the sample of subjects selected (Gardner, 1953, pp. 13-21).

Let us consider the role of the population in several common scaling procedures. A familiar frame of reference is provided by the performance of individuals in a single well-defined group on a particular test at a particular time. Two commonly used scales have been derived within such a frame of reference. The simplest are ordinal scales, such as percentile scores, in which the scale number describes relative position in the group. The second type are interval scales where an effort has been made to obtain algebraic utility by definition. The T-scores of McCall represent an interval scale where equal units have been defined as equal distances along the abscissa of a postulated normal population frequency distribution. A variation is the College Entrance Examination Board scores with a mean of 500 and standard deviation of 100 for the parent normally distributed population.

A second type of frame of reference is provided by the test performance of individuals belonging to well-defined subgroups where the subgroups have a specific relationship to each other within the composite group.

Within this frame of reference both ordinal and interval scales have been derived. Initially the basic problem is to obtain ordinally related subgroups such as grades 1 to 9 or age groups from a specific population for the scaling operation. Age scores and grade scores provide ordinal scales which have had wide utility in the elementary grades. Attempts have been made to obtain the merits of an algebraically manipulatable scale by utilizing ordinal relationship of subgroups but introducing restrictions in terms of the shape of frequency distributions. Efforts to obtain interval scales within such frames of reference have been made by Flanagan (1939) in the development of Scaled Scores of the Cooperative Tests and by Gardner (1950) in the development of K-Scores.

Test scores are used by administrators, teachers and research workers to make comparisons in terms of rank, level of development, growth and trait differences among both individuals and groups. Hence many types of scales and norms have been developed depending upon the intended use. Each is consistent within itself but the properties of the scales are not completely consistent from one type of scale to another. For example, a grade scale is not appropriate for measuring growth in a function unless one is willing to accept the assumption that growth is linearly related to grade. The scaling of the Binet items involves the assumption of a linear relationship between Mental Age and Chronological Age. As valuable and useful as the Binet Scale has been for the purpose for which it was designed, it has obvious limitations when we try to infer the "true" nature of intellectual growth.

It should be emphasized that the adoption of any one of the scales available does not exclude the use of any of the others. In fact, most situations require the test user to utilize more than one type of scale or norm for an adequate interpretation of test results.

CONCLUSION

Normative standard scores are measures obtained from scales having certain specific properties, and they incorporate in the numerical values certain information about the normative group used. They are obtained by statistically manipulating the raw score responses of a defined group of people on a defined sample of content. It is desirable to facilitate the interpretation of test scores by giving them as much direct meaning as possible. As Flanagan (1950) has said ". . . if much information is built into the score itself, continual use makes its interpretation more and more direct and immediate. It is also of great assistance if such fundamental built-in meanings can be as constant from one test to the next as possible." However, the amount of meaning that can be built into any single reference scale will constitute only a very small part of the total amount of meaning to be desired by all of the test users from those results. It is almost always necessary to supplement the knowledge inherent in the scores with other normative data. Norms based on a variety of different groups have considerable merit. Different types of norms such as grade scores, percentile scores and various types of standard scores all have their place. The case for all normative standard scores stands or falls on their ability to provide additional and more useful information than can be obtained from the raw scores from which they were derived.

REFERENCES

Flanagan, John C. "Scaled Scores." The Cooperative Test Service of the American Council on Education, 1939.

Flanagan, John C. "Units, Scores and Norms." In *Educational Measurement* (E. F. Lindquist, Editor). Washington, D.C.: American Council on Education, 1950.

Gardner, Eric F. "Comments on Selected Scaling Techniques with a Description of a New Type of Scale." *Journal of Clinical Psychology,* VI (1950), 38–42.

Gardner, Eric F. "The Importance of Reference Groups in Scaling Procedure." *Proceedings of the 1952 Invitational Conference on Testing Problems.* Princeton, N.J.: Educational Testing Service, 1953.

9. Content Standard Test Scores

ROBERT L. EBEL

By the term *content standard test score* in this discussion we will mean a number that indicates the per cent of a systematic sample from a defined domain of tasks which an individual has performed successfully. For example, if a school child is asked to add each of the 100 possible pairs of single digit numbers, the number of sums he gives correctly, which in this special case is numerically equal to the per cent correct, is his content standard score.

If a college student is asked to match the appropriate definition with a sample of words selected systematically from a specified dictionary, the per cent of correct matchings he achieves is his content standard score on this test.

The word *content* in the term we are defining signifies that the score is based directly on the tasks which make up or provide the content of the test. This is in contrast to normative standard scores, which are based on the relative performances of those who have taken the test.

The word *standard* in this term signifies two rather different things. The first, and less crucial, is that the scores are reported on a common scale in which each performance is scored as a per cent of the maximum possible performance. In this respect content standard scores are conceptually identical with the familiar but now generally discredited per cent scores applied to subjectively evaluated essay tests, and to the once popular but equally questionable per cent marks on course achievement. Normative standard scores are also standard in the sense that they are based on a common scale, although of course the common scale is not a per cent scale but one in which the mean, standard deviation, and sometimes the shape of the distribution, are specified.

Ebel, R. L. Content standard test scores. *Educational and Psychological Measurement,* 1962, *22,* 15–25. Reprinted with the permission of the publisher and author.

The second and more crucial significance of *standard* in content test score is that the processes by which the scores are obtained—the test construction, administration and scoring—are explicit and objective enough so that independent investigators would obtain substantially the same scores for the same persons. Normative standard scores are seldom "standard" in this second sense. It is also important to note that a per cent score on a subjectively chosen collection of tasks would not be a content standard test score, as we use the term. Unless the score is based on a systematic sample from a defined domain of tasks, it cannot provide a very sound basis for inferences as to the examinees' performance on similar collections of tasks.

Content standard test scores are obviously related closely to raw scores, which many test specialists appear to hold in low esteem. Referring to Johnny's score of 15 on his spelling test, Thorndike and Hagen (1955) say, "Actually as it stands it has no meaning at all and is completely uninterpretable." Noll (1957) says much the same thing, ". . . A single score on a given test is merely a number and has no meaning in and of itself." Stanley and Ross (1954) also dismiss raw scores with only a little clemency, "But a raw or point score by itself means very little."

Statements like these are commonly used to introduce, and to justify, discussions of derived scores and standard scores in many measurement textbooks. In a strict literal sense such statements are very nearly true. But in a practical sense they may be misleading. Raw scores are seldom obtained or reported in a contextual void. It is true, as Travers (1955) says, that "A raw score suffers from the defect of being uninterpretable unless additional data are provided." But a standard score suffers from exactly the same defect. No test score, raw or standard, has much meaning as an abstract number. Additional data for interpretation must always be provided, either by the test producer or by the test user from his own knowledge and experience. The numbers which report standard scores are no more intrinsically meaningful, and no more self-interpreting, than raw scores.

To know that a student answered correctly 72 per cent of the items in a test is meaningful only to the extent of one's knowledge of the test items. To know that a student answered more questions correctly than 67 per cent of a group of students is likewise meaningful only to the extent of one's knowledge of the group of students. It is no more reasonable to assume that a test score can be interpreted adequately in the absence of knowledge of the test itself than to assume that it can be interpreted adequately in the absence of normative data. Both are essential.

The fact remains that normative standard scores are currently far more popular than content standard scores. The history of educational measurement suggests that the popularity of normative standard scores was greatly encouraged by the apparent instability of raw content scores on objective tests. When subjectively scored essay tests were used, the scorer could correct for errors in estimating the probable difficulty of the questions, easing up in his scoring of questions which turn out to be too difficult and becoming more particular in scoring the questions which seem too easy. But with objective test questions the die was cast when the question was written. To have insisted on a minimum passing score of 70 per cent correct responses to objective test questions, or any other predetermined per cent, was obviously unreasonable in the face of evidence such as that reported by Monroe (1918) on the unreliability of teacher's estimates of the difficulty of essentially objective mathematics test items. It was also recognized quite early in the development of objective tests that a test on which the mean score was 85 per cent would probably be far less efficient in differentiating levels of achievement than a test on which the mean score was nearer 50 per cent.

Hence, with the introduction and widespread use of objective tests, content standard scores expressed as per cents of correct response lost favor. Travers (1955) speaks of "the famous but discredited system of converting raw scores into percentages . . ." and characterizes it as ". . . another attempt on the part of the teacher to convert a relatively meaningless score into one which has some commonly accepted meaning." The alternative was to transform the unstable raw score into a standard score related to the actual performances of students in some norm group. This alternative has become extremely popular. Several methods of transformation, and a wide variety of normative standard score scales, have been developed. At present the use of normative standard scores as the basis for the interpretation of standard test scores is almost universal in the United States.

Unfortunately, something important tends to get lost when raw scores are transformed into normative standard scores. What gets lost is a meaningful relation between the score on the test and the character of the performance it is supposed to measure. It is not very useful to know that Johnny is superior to 84 per cent of his peers unless we know what it is that he can do better than they, and just how well he can do it! The very first sentence in John Flanagan's chapter (1950), "Units, Scores and Norms," in *Educational Measurement* makes this point. "Test scores are meaningful and valuable to the extent that they can be interpreted in terms of capacities, abilities and accomplishments of educational significance." Later in the chapter this comment is added: "The raw score is a very fundamental piece of information, and should not be relinquished in favor of some other type of score without good reason." Rulon, and others, have also stressed this point. It is unfortunate, I think, that some specialists in measuring educational achievement have seemed to imply that knowing how many of his peers a student can excel is more important than knowing what he can do to excel them. Note that we are not here objecting to invidious comparisons nor supporting the allegation of psycho-social harm in competition. Our point is that when comparative scores are not clearly related to specific achievements they tend to have rather limited meaning and educational value.

To be meaningful any test scores must be related to test content *as well as* to the scores of other examinees. Most widely used standard test scores can be interpreted in terms of test content only in the most general way. If raw scores are reported, and if a copy of the test is available, the meaning of a score in terms of "capacities, abilities, and accomplishments" can be determined. But raw scores often are not reported and copies of the test are not often available. I am persuaded that the usefulness of educational measurements is seriously limited by the prevailing neglect of content-meaningful test scores. In the remainder of this paper I would like to suggest two ways in which I believe test scores having content-meaning can be secured.

The first involves the use of "scale books" of selected items. Figure 1 displays a selection of ten items representing the content of the Mathematics Section of the 1959 Preliminary Scholastic Aptitude Test, Form HPT2.

As a first step in selecting these ten, all 50 items in the test were classified by inspection and judgment in the content categories shown in Table 1. The items are identified by their numbers in Form HPT2.

TABLE 1. Classification of PSAT Mathematics Items

Category	Item Numbers
1. Calculations with fractions	66, 73, 80, 91
2. Verbal problems	67, 69, 77, 85, 87, 89
3. Percentage and statistics	68, 71, 98, 104
4. Problems in algebra	70, 72, 75, 78, 84, 95, 100
5. Algebraic formulation	74, 86, 97, 102, 110, 111
6. Directions and analytic geometry	76, 79, 105, 106, 109
7. Problems in fractions	81, 83, 93, 107, 113
8. Areas and volumes	82, 90, 94
9. Triangles	88, 92, 96, 99, 112
10. Circles	101, 103, 108, 114, 115

Next a measure of the discriminating power of each item was obtained by subtracting the proportion of correct response in a low scoring group (100 students whose scaled score on the Mathematics test was below

FIGURE 1. Ten Items Representing PSAT Mathematics Test, Form HPT2[1]

74. If there are P girls and R boys in a class, what is the ratio of the number of girls to the total number of boys and girls in the class?

A. $\frac{P-R}{P+R}$ B. $\frac{P}{P+R}$ C. $\frac{P}{R}$ D. $\frac{R}{P}$
E. $\frac{P+R}{P}$

77. A certain test of 100 problems is scored by subtracting from 100 one point for each problem not answered and 2 points for each problem answered incorrectly. If a pupil does not answer $\frac{1}{5}$ of the problems, what is the greatest number of problems he can have wrong and still get a score of 20 on this test?

A. 20 B. 30 C. 35 D. 40 E. 60

80. $\frac{6}{7} + \frac{4}{(?)} = \frac{52}{56}$

A. 7 B. 8 C. 9 D. 28 E. 56

82. A square carpet with an area of 169 square feet must have 2 feet cut off one of its edges in order to be a perfect fit for a rectangular bedroom floor. What is the area in square feet of the bedroom floor?

A. 117 B. 121 C. 143 D. 165
E. 167

84. If $r = 5.5(t - 60) + 110$, for what value of t does $r = 0$?

A. −9.2 B. 0 C. 30.9 D. 40
E. 60

88. A square and an equilateral triangle have equal perimeters. What is the length of a side of the triangle if the area of the square is 9 ?

A. 3 B. 4 C. 6 D. 9 E. 12

93. If a boy earns $28 and spends $\frac{3}{4}$ as much as he saves, how much does he save?

A. $4.90 B. $7 C. $14 D. $16
E. $21

104. Par on a certain 18-hole golf course is 75. If a golfer wants his score to equal par and has a score of 42 on the first 9 holes of this course, how much <u>less</u> must he average per hole on the last 9 holes than he averaged per hole on the first 9 holes?

A. $\frac{1}{2}$ B. 1 C. 2 D. $3\frac{2}{3}$ E. $4\frac{1}{2}$

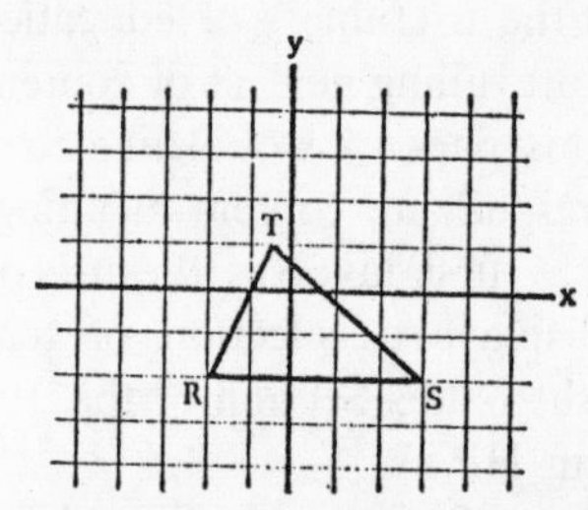

105. In the figure above, each unit along the x-axis represents $\frac{1}{3}$ foot and each unit along the y-axis represents $\frac{1}{2}$ foot. What is the area (in square feet) of $\triangle$ RST ?

A. $\frac{5}{4}$ B. $\frac{3}{2}$ C. $\frac{5}{3}$ D. 2 E. $\frac{5}{2}$

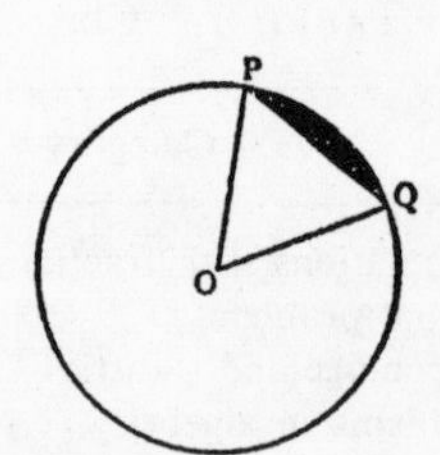

108. In the figure above, POQ is an equilateral triangle with each side equal to 12 inches. What is the perimeter (in inches) of the blackened portion?

A. $12 + 4\pi$ B. $12 + 6\pi$ C. $12 + 12\pi$
D. $12 + 24\pi$ E. $12 + 36\pi$

[1] The answer key for the Ten Items Representing PSAT Mathematics Test, Form HPT2:

Item	74	77	80	82	84	88	93	104	105	108
Key	B	B	E	C	D	B	D	B	A	A

300[2]) from the corresponding proportion in a group whose scaled scores were above 700. The item in each category which showed the highest discriminating power was included in the representative set. We then scored the ten selected items on six sets of 100 answer sheets which had standard scores near 750, 650, 550, 450, 350, and 250, respectively. The results are shown in Table 2.

TABLE 2. Frequency Distributions of Scores by Standard Score Level on the Ten Representative Items

Score on	Standard Score Level					
10 Items	750	650	550	450	350	250
10	40	13	1			
9	41	30				
8	16	33	9			
7	3	15	28			
6		8	29	5	1	
5		1	19	15	1	
4			13	24	4	
3			1	28	15	
2				20	30	1
1				8	32	27
0					17	72

On the basis of this table it is possible to say that in these samples of answer sheets the most frequent number of correct answers to the ten representative items was 9 for those whose scaled scores were near 750, 8 for those whose scaled scores were near 650, and so on. Smoothing and interpolating lead to the estimates shown in Table 3.

It is our belief that this set of items, together with Tables 2 and 3, will contribute to a more informative answer to the question, "What does a score of 600 on Scholastic Aptitude Test mathematics mean?" than has been available previously. It seems reasonable to believe that equally useful interpretive data could be obtained for verbal scores on the Preliminary Scholastic Aptitude Test, and for other tests as well.

The second, and possibly more basic way to secure test scores which have content-meaning is to build the meaning into the test, and hence into the test score, by systematic, explicitly specified processes of test construction.

Specialists in educational measurement generally recognize that most objective tests rest on highly subjective foundations. The abilities, values, and idiosyncrasies of the test constructor have played a major part in determining the contents of most tests. Test specifications sometimes

[2] These scaled scores have a mean of approximately 500 and a standard deviation of approximately 100.

TABLE 3. Most Probable Scores on Sample Items for Examinees Receiving Various Scaled Scores on the Entire Test

Scaled Score	Score on Sample Items
800	10
750	9
700	8 or 9
650	8
600	7
550	6
500	4 or 5
450	3
400	2 or 3
350	2
300	1
250	0

exist only in the mind of the test constructor, or in a few brief written guidelines. When written they often have more to say about the form of the test than about its content. Seldom are the test specifications sufficiently explicit and so comprehensive that competent test constructors, working independently, could be expected to produce forms on which *raw* scores are essentially equivalent. The processes of test construction often appear to have more in common with artistic creation than with scientific measurement!

In this respect, educational tests are distinctly different from most physical, chemical, or biological tests and measurements. In those more scientific fields, carefully specified measurement operations are designed to yield highly consistent results, almost regardless of the operator. The quantitative sophistication of many specialists in educational measurement is displayed, not in the precision and elegance of their procedures for obtaining initial measurements, but rather in the statistical transformations, elaborations, and analyses they are prepared to perform on almost any raw data given them. The term "raw" may be particularly appropriate when applied to the original data yielded by many educational tests. What we often overlook is the limited power of statistical transformations to refine these raw data and make them more precisely meaningful. If more systematic and standardized processes of test production could be developed and used, our educational measurements should become not only more consistently reproducible, but what is perhaps even more important, they should become more meaningful.

Bridgman and others have argued that the meaning of a quantitative concept may be well defined by specifying the operations used to measure the quantity involved. Granting this, it follows logically that tests of educational traits should yield more meaningful scores if the operations by which they were produced could be stated more explicitly. A test produced by objectively defined processes may be less efficient, or lack some kinds of excellence which a creatively artistic test constructor might achieve, but the increase in objective meaningfulness and reproducibility could more than offset the cost.

At this point it may be desirable to illustrate what is meant by an objectively defined process of test construction, and to demonstrate that a useful test of at least one educational achievement can be constructed by such a process. It seemed to make sense to begin with something simple—a test of knowledge of word meanings. Parallel forms of the test were produced, one by a test specialist and the other by an intelligent secretary who had no special training in test construction. Both tests were built on the basis of detailed written specifications and directions. The tests were based on a spaced sample of 100 words from a specified dictionary. Explicit instructions were given for choosing a unique but representative sample, and for limiting the sample to words appropriate for the test. For each word the first synonym or defining phrase was copied from the dictionary.

The words were arranged in alphabetical order in a single list. The defining phrases were also placed in alphabetical order and numbered from 1 to 100. The student's task was to match the definitional phrase with the appropriate word. A twenty-item example of such a test is given in Figure 2.

The two forms of the test were administered to 30 graduate students in a course on education evaluation at the University of Southern California in August, 1960. Half of the students took Form A first; the other half took Form B first. Their scores yielded the test analysis data shown in Table 4.

TABLE 4. Analysis Data for Two Forms of an Objective Test of Word Knowledge

	Form A		Form B
I. Student Scores			
Mean	37.3		32.8
Standard Deviation	12.5		14.8
Reliability	.92		.95
Intercorrelation		.86	
II. Item Difficulty			
Mean	11.19		9.84
Variance	79.34		72.02
Standard Error of Diff.		1.24	
t		1.09	

FIGURE 2. Test of Knowledge of Word Meanings[3]

Directions to the Examinee: First read all the words in the List of Words. Then look at the first definitional phrase, identified by the number "1" in the List of Definitions. If you recognize it as the definition of one of the words, write the number "1" on the line to the left of that word. If not, make no marks. In the same way match each of the other definitions, if you can, with the appropriate word, writing its number opposite the word it matches.

List of Words

1. ______ aroint
2. ______ bosh
3. ______ cineole
4. ______ crossing
5. ______ dowry
6. ______ fandango
7. ______ giant
8. ______ horse
9. ______ jaborandi
10. ______ lowery
11. ______ morsel
12. ______ overlay
13. ______ plumb
14. ______ rajah
15. ______ sangaree
16. ______ smew
17. ______ sunken
18. ______ toed
19. ______ uplift
20. ______ whither

List of Definitions

1. A huge mythical manlike or monstrous being of more than mortal but less than Godlike power and endowment.
2. A large solid-hoofed herbivorous mammal domesticated by man since a prehistoric period, used as a beast of burden, a draft animal or for riding.
3. A liquid of camphor-like odor.
4. A lively Spanish dance, or a tune in its rhythm.
5. A point of intersection.
6. A small quantity.
7. A tropical drink of wine, water and sometimes brandy, sweetened and spiced.
8. A weight of lead attached to a line and used by builders, etc. to indicate a vertical direction.
9. Cloudy.
10. Driven obliquely, as a nail.
11. Empty talk.
12. Lying on the bottom of a river or other water.
13. The money, goods, or estate which a woman brings to her husband in marriage.
14. Title of an Indian king, prince or chief, or of a Malay or Javanese ruler.
15. To improve the condition of, especially mentally or emotionally.
16. To superimpose or cover.
17. A merganser (Mergus albellus) of northern Europe and Asia, white crested in the male.
18. Begone.
19. The dried leaflets of a shrub of the rue family.
20. To what place.

[3] The answer key for the sample Test of Knowledge of Word Meanings:

1.	18	6.	4	11.	6	16.	17
2.	11	7.	1	12.	16	17.	12
3.	3	8.	2	13.	8	18.	10
4.	5	9.	19	14.	14	19.	15
5.	13	10.	9	15.	7	20.	20

The difference between Forms A and B in statistics of both student scores and item difficulty values may seem large for tests which purport to be equivalent. But the differences turn out to be well within expected limits of sampling error in terms of the wide range of difficulty in the domain of tasks from which the samples were drawn. The magnitude of these sampling fluctuations, however, suggests that tests of far more than one hundred items would be required to yield reasonably equivalent scores from alternate forms.

These tests constitute *one* operational definition of the proportion of words in a certain dictionary for which a person "knows" the meaning, and hence of the size of his vocabulary in a certain sense. No doubt better operational definitions, and more acceptable estimates of vocabulary size, are possible. But whatever their limitations, the raw scores on these tests are *not* meaningless. On the contrary, they are objectively meaningful.

Systematic test construction, based on explicitly prescribed operations, will not be so simple in other areas of educational achievement, but there is no apparent reason why it should be impossibly difficult or unrewarding. While a systematically constructed test is not likely to be as efficient as one constructed by an expert, or one built with the help of item tryout data, this problem might be circumvented also. It is quite conceivable that systematically constructed tests could become the *criteria* against which more efficient operational tests are calibrated.

In this presentation our purpose has been to emphasize the need for and to demonstrate the possibility of test scores which report what the examinee can do. Content-meaning in test scores supplements but does not replace normative meaning. Both kinds are essential, in our view. The more simply, directly, and clearly they can be presented, the more useful and educationally fruitful our tests are likely to be.

REFERENCES

Flanagan, John C. "Units, Scores and Norms." In *Educational Measurement* (E. F. Lindquist, Editor). Washington, D.C.: American Council on Education, 1950.

Monroe, Walter Scott. *Measuring the Results of Teaching*. Boston: Houghton Mifflin Company, 1918.

Noll, Victor H. *Introduction to Educational Measurement*. Boston: Houghton Mifflin Company, 1957.

Stanley, Julian C. and Ross, C. C. *Measurement in Today's Schools*. New York: Prentice Hall, 1954.

Thorndike, Robert L. and Hagen, Elizabeth. *Measurement and Evaluation in Psychology and Education*. New York: John Wiley and Sons, Inc., 1955.

Travers, Robert M. W. *Educational Measurement*. New York: The Macmillan Company, 1955.

10. Estimating Norms by Item Sampling[1]

FREDERIC M. LORD

The previous two articles both indicate the need for norms. Quite often, what is desired is something called a national norm. The practical problems inherent in the estimation of national norms are great if not overwhelming. In the following paper, Lord suggests a simplified approach to establishing norms, using an item-sampling technique. This method should help alleviate one of the major problems—that of school noncooperation. But while item sampling shows promise, the three limitations Lord points out should not be overlooked.

There has been continued research in the area following publication of this article. Plumlee (1964) investigated the value of using the item sampling approach in developing test norms for the industrial personnel situation—where the number of subjects was small. Her conclusions were much the same as Lord's—that this technique is quite adequate for power tests. Cook and Stufflebeam (1965) extended Lord's research and corrected the procedural step of item sampling with replacement which Lord mentions as being less efficient and a poorer procedure than sampling without replacement. Their results also support Lord's conclusions.

An earlier article by Lord (1959) also deals with the problems of obtaining a national norms sample. In this article he points out that the number of schools sampled is more directly related to the size of the sampling errors than to the number of students in the sample. He also points out that one obtains a biased estimate of the population mean through simple cluster sampling (i.e., including all students in each school selected in the sample) and suggests the alternative of doing two-stage sampling (i.e., drawing a random sample of schools and then drawing a random sample of students within each school selected). This article is highly recommended for those interested in methods of sampling to obtain unbiased estimates of the norms population.

Truly representative national norms are seldom obtained for any published test. The most serious obstacle is the fact that not every school is willing, at the request of some test publisher, to suspend its accustomed activities and require its students to spend a class period or more taking tests. As a result, published "national" norms usually

---

Lord, F. M. Estimating norms by item sampling. *Educational and Psychological Measurement*, 1962, *22*, 259–267. Reprinted with the permission of the publisher and author.

[1] This work was supported by contract Nonr-2752(00) between the Office of Naval Research and Educational Testing Service. Reproduction in whole or in part for any purpose of the United States Government is permitted.

do not represent the nation's schools, but, at best, only those willing at a particular time to cooperate with a particular test publisher.

The problem of getting each school's cooperation would be less serious if only a few moments of each student's time were required, rather than an entire class period. This raises the question of whether the performance of a large group on a long test can be estimated by administering only a few items to each student.

If such methods of estimating group performance were possible, they would be helpful not only for norming a single test, but even more for norming a number of tests simultaneously. They might also be helpful in any research study of group performance where the testing time or the scoring costs would otherwise be prohibitive.

In such cases, it will not always be a question of substituting a doubtful estimate obtained by item-sampling for a wholly satisfactory determination of the scores desired. When the administration of an entire test to an entire population of examinees is impossible, the question is whether estimates obtained by item sampling are better or worse than estimates obtainable by other methods, such as sampling of schools or of examinees.

The present study is concerned with just such a comparison of estimates. The effectiveness of item-sampling for estimating a group's mean score was investigated in an earlier study (Johnson & Lord, 1958). Now the attempt is made to estimate the entire frequency distribution of scores, rather than just the group mean.[2]

The plan of the study is described in section 1. The rationale for estimating the norms distribution by item-sampling is outlined in section 2. The results obtained are given in section 3, which is followed by a brief discussion.

1. PLAN OF STUDY

Suppose we have a 70-item test and a norms population of 1,000 individuals. We need an estimate of the score distribution for the entire norms population. Unfortunately, either available testing time or available scoring facilities are so limited that we can administer the 70-item test to only 100 examinees. Is it possible that we can obtain a better estimate of the norms distribution by testing each of the 1,000 individuals in the norms population with just 7 items than we can by giving the actual 70-item test to a random sample of 100 individuals?

In the present study, an answer to this question was sought from the vocabulary-test answer sheets of a nationwide sample of 1,000 college seniors. The recorded responses for the first 70 items only were used.

---

[2] The writer is indebted to Robert L. Ebel for suggesting the present study and pointing out its importance.

Since everyone finished these items in the testing time available, the problem of "not-reached" items does not enter the picture.

The "population norms" distribution to be estimated is taken to be the distribution of the test scores of all 1,000 examinees on the 70-item test. Each score referred to here is simply the number of right answers marked by the examinee, as are all other test scores involved in the present study.

The population was subdivided at random into 10 nonoverlapping groups of 100 examinees each. The frequency distribution of the 70-item test score for each group is here considered as a conventional "examinee-sample" estimate of the population norms distribution.

An index of the accuracy of each of the 10 examinee-sample estimates was obtained by computing the following measure of discrepancy:

$$D = \frac{1}{10} \sum \frac{(\hat{\phi}_1 - \phi)^2}{\phi}, \tag{1}$$

where ϕ is the frequency in the norms distribution and $\hat{\phi}_1$ is 10 times the frequency in the 100-examinee sample. For computing D, adjacent test scores were grouped into score intervals where necessary in order that each ϕ should be at least 10. The summation in (1) is over the 48 score intervals thus obtained.

The discrepancy measure D is obviously related to chi-square. Since it cannot be used to make a significance test, however, it will be better here to think of it simply as a measure of the "distance" or discrepancy between two frequency distributions. (There is clearly no need for a significance test here since it is known in advance that each group really is a random sample drawn from the norms population.)

A single "item-sample" estimate of the norms distribution was next obtained, as described in the following section. Another value of D was obtained by substituting the item-sample estimate of ϕ for $\hat{\phi}_1$ in equation (1). The relative merits of the examinee-sample and the item-sample estimates are judged from the various values of D.

2. THE ITEM-SAMPLE ESTIMATE

Ten samples of 7 items each were drawn with replacement, independently, and at random from the 70 items involved in the present study. Each sample of items was treated as a 7-item test. The ten 7-item tests were assigned at random, one to each of the 10 groups of 100 examinees. The answer sheet of each examinee in each group was then scored on the appropriate 7-item test.

(In retrospect, the foregoing item-sampling procedure is seen to have been unnecessarily inefficient. Items were sampled with replacement after each sampling for the reason that such sampling is effectively the same as sampling from an infinite pool of items, and the available formulas in Lord (1960) for utilizing the resulting data are discussed in terms of sampling from an infinite pool. It would have been better to sample without replacement, thus dividing the 70 items at random into 10 nonoverlapping 7-item tests. Hooke's (1956) basic derivations show that the same formulas would be valid for such sampling, without replacement. This would obviously be preferable since, in the actual sampling with replacement, 18 of the 70 items were drawn more than once and 25 were never drawn at all.)

The following statistics were computed for each group from the data on the 7-item scores:

$$g_{26} = \frac{1}{100} \sum_{a=1}^{100} x_a = \bar{x}, \tag{2}$$

$$g_{25} = \sum_{i=1}^{7} \pi_i^2, \tag{3}$$

$$g_{24} = \frac{1}{100} \sum_{a=1}^{100} x_a^2, \tag{4}$$

$$g_{23} = g_{26}^2, \tag{5}$$

where x_a is the 7-item score of examinee a and π_i is the proportion of examinees in the group answering item i correctly.

As shown by Lord (1960, Table 2), corresponding statistics for a randomly parallel 70-item test can be estimated from these values for each group by the formulas

$$\hat{g}_{26} = 10 g_{26}, \tag{6}$$

$$\hat{g}_{24} = 115 g_{24} - 105 g_{26}, \tag{7}$$

$$\hat{g}_{23} = 115 g_{23} - 105 g_{25}. \tag{8}$$

The mean and variance of the 70-item test are then estimated for each group by

$$\hat{m} = \hat{g}_{26}, \tag{9}$$

$$\hat{v} = \frac{100}{99} (\hat{g}_{24} - \hat{g}_{23}). \tag{10}$$

The values obtained for each of the 10 groups from (9) and (10), respectively, were averaged together to obtain, finally, one estimate of the mean and one estimate of the variance of the 70-item test scores in the 1000-case norms population. These two "item-sampling" estimates will be denoted by $\hat{M}$ and $\hat{V}$.

These estimates should be good ones since only a bare minimum of assumptions were made in obtaining them. The main purpose, however, is to obtain an estimate of the entire norms distribution, not merely of its mean and variance. An effective procedure would probably be to use the available formulas in Lord (1960) to estimate higher-order moments of the norms distribution, and then to estimate the shape of this distribution by fitting a Pearson Type I curve, say, to the estimated moments.

The use of higher-order moments was avoided, however, as too laborious computationally. Instead, the relatively simple method was adopted of fitting a negative hypergeometric distribution [to be denoted by $H(x)$] to the three parameters $\hat{M}$, $\hat{V}$, and n (= 70), the number of items. (This distribution has some theoretical basis and, more important, has been found (Keats & Lord, in press) to provide a reasonably good fit for quite a variety of test-score distributions when the test score is the number of right answers.) The fitted distribution is, for present purposes, the item-sample estimate of the norms distribution.

In practical norming work, the 7-item tests would have been administered by themselves, not as part of a longer test. Any practical application of the item-sampling method thus involves the further assumption that the examinees' performance on the items is not too greatly affected by the context in which they are administered. Statistical theory can hardly be expected to dispense with the need for this assumption. Presumably the assumption will be tolerable in some practical situations but not in others; it must therefore be justified empirically for the actual practical situation in which the theory is to be applied.

3. RESULTS

Table 1 shows comparative statistics for (a) the 10 examinee-sample estimates, arranged in order according to their value of D, (b) the item-sample estimate of the norms distribution, (c) the norms population. It is seen that the item-sample estimate of the mean is closer to the norms-population mean than are 7 of the 10 examinee-sample estimates. The item-sample estimate of the variance is closer to the norms-population variance than 5 of the 10 examinee-sample estimates.

The negative hypergeometric distribution with a mean and variance equal to the item-sample estimates is much closer to the norms-population distribution than are any of the 70-item test-score distributions obtained by sampling examinees—the discrepancy index for the former is $D = 5.7$, whereas those for the latter range from 33.0 to 49.3, as shown in the antepenultimate column of Table 1. This is hardly a fair comparison, however, since most of the discrepancies counted against the examinee-sample distributions are due to local irregularities, arising from sampling fluctuations. These could be eliminated by replacing the jagged actual distributions by smooth, fitted distributions.

TABLE 1. Comparison of Estimates of Norms Distribution

Data	Number of items per examinee	Number (N) of examinees	Mean	Variance*	D for raw distribution	D for fitted $H(x)$	D' for fitted $H(x)$
Examinee-Sample							
Group 5	70	100	42.9	214.5	49.3	10.6	10.0
9	70	100	44.3	199.1	44.4	6.6	5.5
0	70	100	46.5	188.0	41.0	7.7	3.8
6	70	100	44.1	212.6	39.2	8.4	6.6
2	70	100	48.1	194.1	38.1	19.2	5.3
1	70	100	46.3	174.8	37.4	5.9	4.2
7	70	100	45.1	150.5	36.7	7.6	7.6
4	70	100	46.1	155.0	34.4	6.3	6.1
8	70	100	45.8	153.7	33.8	6.5	6.4
3	70	100	46.3	170.5	33.0	5.72	4.5
Item-Sample	7	1000	46.1	162.1	—	5.67	5.1
Norms Population	70	1000	45.5	181.7	—	—	—

$^*\sum_{1}^{N}(x-\bar{x})^2/(N-1)$.

A fairer comparison is provided in the next-to-last column of the table. Here each examinee-sample distribution has been replaced by a negative hypergeometric with the same mean and variance, and a D has been computed between this $H(x)$ and the actual norms distribution. This comparison still shows the item-sample estimate to be closer to the norms population than any of the $H(x)$ in any of the 10 groups of 100 examinees.

A closer study of the terms summed to obtain D showed them all to be reasonably small, except, in several groups, the term contributed by test scores of 67 and above. This indicates that $H(x)$ does not adequately represent certain groups at the very top of the score distribution. The discrepancy index D', shown in the last column of the table, was obtained by omitting from D the unduly large term for scores $\geqq 67$, so as to provide a still fairer comparison. This shows that when discrepancies near the test ceiling are excluded, the item-sample estimate is superior to the examinee-sample estimate obtained from 7 out of the 10 samples.

Each of the values in the last two columns of Table 1 represents discrepancies between an estimated norms distribution, in the form of an $H(x)$, and the actual, unsmoothed norms. The question of course arises: How well can the actual norms distribution be approximated by *any* $H(x)$? To answer this question, an $H(x)$ was fitted to the actual norms distribution. The resulting index of discrepancy is $D = 5.4$ or $D' = 2.4$. The value of D corresponds roughly to a chi-square of 54.4

with 45 degrees of freedom, which would be at about the 15 per cent significance level. Examination of Figure 1 and a breakdown of the chi-square into portions with single degrees of freedom shows that $H(x)$ provides a reasonably good fit to the actual norms distribution, except, perhaps, at the very top.

FIGURE 1. Norms Group Frequency Distribution and Various Estimates of It

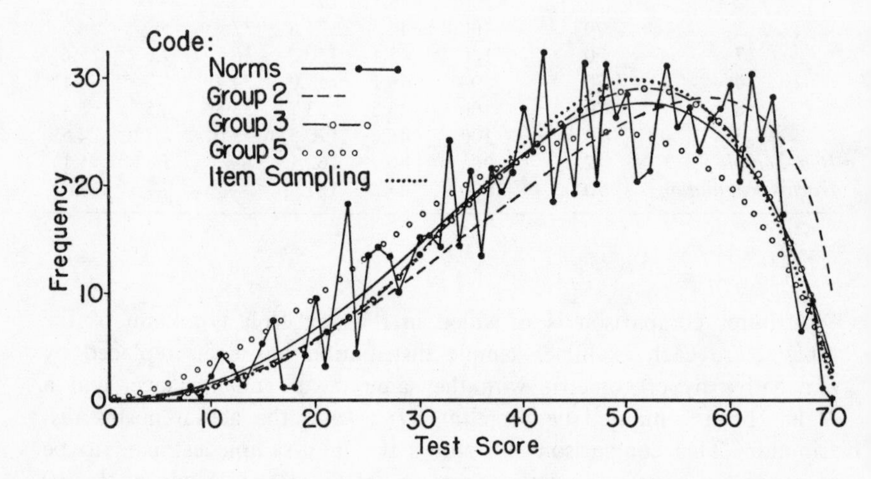

4. DISCUSSION

The results of this study suggest that, if a choice must be made, it may be better in some cases to estimate norms by sampling items rather than by sampling examinees. Because of the labor involved, only one item-sample estimate was made in the present study; hence there is much need to test out this tentative conclusion on other sets of data.

On the other hand, there is good reason to hope for still better results than those obtained here, since in another study the items should be sampled without replacement, so that all items are represented in the samples rather than only two-thirds of them as happened here. Further improvement could be obtained by drawing more item-samples so that each item would appear in several different short tests.

The following limitations and comments on the method should be noted:

1. The item-sample method assumes that performance on an item does not depend on the context in which it occurs. This is a se-

rious assumption that must be evaluated carefully in each new practical situation.

2. In particular, the foregoing assumption means that the method cannot be satisfactory for speeded tests.
3. Granted the assumption made in 1 above, the item-sample method gives an unbiased estimate of the norms mean and variance. As described here, the success of the method then depends on the possibility of estimating the entire norms distribution from this estimated mean and variance. Experience (backed up by a little theory) indicates that the negative hypergeometric distribution is frequently adequate for this purpose for tests that are scored number right. There is as yet no experience with tests scored by other methods.

Higher moments of the norms distribution could be estimated effectively if desired; however, this would be computationally laborious and expensive.

An obvious question asks for the optimum number of items and of examinees to use for a particular norming job. Further experience will be needed before answering this question. To do so will require evaluating the various possibilities of trading items for people in a wide variety of situations.

REFERENCES

Hooke, Robert. "Symmetric Functions of a Two-Way Array." *Annals of Mathematical Statistics,* XXVII (1956), 55–79.

Johnson, M. Clemans and Lord, Frederic M. "An Empirical Study of the Stability of a Group Mean in Relation to the Distribution of Test Items Among Pupils." *Educational and Psychological Measurement,* XVIII (1958), 325–329.

Keats, John A. and Lord, Frederic M. "A Theoretical Derivation of the Distribution of Mental Test Scores." *Psychometrika,* in press.

Kendall, Maurice G. and Stuart, Alan. *Distribution Theory.* (Volume I of *The Advanced Theory of Statistics.*) New York: Hafner, 1958.

Lord, Frederic M. "Use of True-Score Theory To Predict Moments of Univariate and Bivariate Observed Score Distributions." *Psychometrika,* XXV (1960), 325–342.

INTRODUCTION

11. Lindquist, E. F., *Equating Scores on Non-Parallel Tests*
12. Angoff, William H., *Technical Problems of Obtaining Equivalent Scores on Tests*
13. Lennon, Roger T., *Equating Non-Parallel Tests*

Thus far in this unit we have presented two articles indicating why norms are necessary and one article suggesting a method of estimating population norms. Another problem in norming is that of the equating of non-parallel test scores, discussed in the following three articles. The articles are papers originally read at the 1964 Annual Meeting of the National Council on Measurement in Education.

One goal of equating is to eliminate, for example, the necessity of a high school student taking the College Entrance Examination Board Scholastic Aptitude Test (CEEB-SAT), the American College Test (ACT) test battery, the College Qualification Tests (CQT), the Cooperative School and College Ability Tests (SCAT), and the Minnesota Scholastic Aptitude Test (MSAT) just because the various colleges to which a student applies demand scores on different tests prior to admission. One of these tests could be taken and the score on it converted into equivalent scores on the other tests; the colleges could then make their decisions on the basis of the converted scores. Both Lindquist and Angoff discuss the problems of obtaining and interpreting such "equated" scores. (Note the last paragraph in Lindquist's article.)

Lennon addresses himself to a different problem. The equating suggested in his article is not for the purpose of using one score in place of another, but rather to equate the scores so that they can be interpreted as if they were derived from the same norm group, thus making the comparison of the scores meaningful. His equating of scores is more what Lindquist would call establishing comparable scales. While the *techniques* are similar, interpretation is somewhat different in the two situations.

11. Equating Scores on Non-Parallel Tests[1]

E. F. LINDQUIST

I have chosen to organize my discussion of the problem of equating non-parallel tests around a specific example, and to emphasize some of the practical, rather than theoretical, aspects of the problem. It seems to me that the theory involved is already in reasonably good shape so far as practical needs are concerned, and that the major need now is for more effective education of test users. Through this example, I hope not only to make a bit more evident some of the dimensions and complexities of the general educational problem involved, but also to make some direct contribution to a better understanding of the particular problem used in the illustration.

The example is provided by the College Entrance Examination Board and the American College Testing Program, and by the widespread demand from college people for ways of rendering "comparable" the scores reported from the Scholastic Aptitude Test and the ACT test battery. Many colleges are now enrolling students some of whom have taken one of these tests and some the other. Many of these colleges would like to be able to use the scores from these two test batteries interchangeably, particularly for purposes of selective admission. What they think they need is a dependable and "approved" conversion table for translating ACT total scores to SAT totals, or vice versa, so that comparable "cut off" points may be established for the two tests. There seems to be some feeling, also, that the two programs have been somewhat remiss in not having cooperated to provide an "officially approved" conversion table of this type.

I am not in a position here to speak officially for either of these two testing organizations. I believe it is safe to say, however, that both agencies have been somewhat reluctant to cooperate in an equating study of the kind suggested. One reason for this reluctance is the great impracticability of producing a satisfactory conversion table of this type. Even though it could be done, the cost would probably far exceed the value of the results obtained. Another reason, perhaps, is that neither agency is willing, either for political or for technical and theoretical

Lindquist, E. F. Equating scores on non-parallel tests. *Journal of Educational Measurement*, 1964, *1*, 5–9. Reprinted with the permission of the publisher and author.

[1] Paper read at the Annual Meeting of the National Council on Measurement in Education, in Chicago, Illinois, February 1964, as part of a symposium, The Equating of Non-Parallel Test Scores.

reasons, to suggest or admit that the results from the two batteries really are interchangeable for any purpose. In my own opinion, the latter reason, political considerations aside, is the compelling one. If the two agencies were jointly to provide an approved conversion table, no matter what precautions were taken to guard against misuses and misinterpretations, the total effect would probably be increased misuses of the test results, or a more widespread failure to use the test results in the best way possible.

I shall try to substantiate this opinion later, but first let me review what some of the test users have been doing to try to supply such conversion tables for themselves. The usual procedure has been to collect ACT and SAT scores for students who have taken both tests, for whatever reason, and to consider as "equivalent" total (obtained) scores on the two batteries that have the same percentile rank for the particular "happenstance" group of students selected. The groups used have in all cases been composed of students who have *happened* to have taken both tests, rather than students who were selected to be representative of any defined population and then required to take both tests. In every sample used, also, many of the students undoubtedly took one of the tests weeks or even months before they took the other, so that a significant growth increment "favored" one of the two tests. In no instance is it known how the time intervals between the taking of the two tests are distributed for the whole sample, or to what extent these differences operated systematically to depress the scores on one of the two tests. It is practically certain, however, that there were substantial differences of this kind in most of the comparisons. I think that it is safe, therefore, to say that the tables established have been uniformly undependable and unsatisfactory.

Before proceeding further with this illustration, it might be well to consider briefly the extent to which these two test batteries are, in fact, non-parallel. Unfortunately, we do not have on hand any very conclusive empirical evidence concerning this question, and I shall have to rely primarily on inferences drawn from an examination of the test batteries themselves. The most obvious difference is that one of these batteries is curriculum oriented, and is organized into four subtests corresponding to the four major curriculum areas: mathematics, English, social studies, and natural sciences. The other battery is presumably factor oriented, yielding two scores labeled Mathematical and Verbal. Aside from this major difference in organization, there are a number of fairly marked differences in the character and content of individual items. The ACT battery contains an entire subtest completely devoted to specific writing skills. The SAT contains no such items. In the ACT battery, an attempt is made to measure as directly as possible the student's ability to do the same kinds of highly complex and relatively concrete reasoning that he will later be called upon to do in the college learning situation. In general, the SAT items are more homogeneous or purer in the factorial sense, and are to a larger extent concerned with abstract reasoning. In the ACT battery, an effort is made to secure separate measures of the kinds of complex reasoning characteristic of the social studies and the natural sciences—emphasizing in one case rigorous, precise, quantitative and objective reasoning and, in the other case, reasoning leading to value judgments as often as to strictly logical conclusions, reasoning concerned with matters of opinion as much as with matters of fact, and the ability to evaluate opinionated and slanted writing as well as to interpret writing intended only to inform. In the SAT battery, no effort is made to separate materials along these lines.

I am not at all concerned at this time with the possible relative merits of these two batteries with reference to any specific purpose. I do wish to emphasize, however, that there is strong reason to believe that the total scores on these two tests do measure quite different things. This would be a safe statement to make if only because of the difference in organization and scaling of the two batteries. It would be true even though the two tests were comprised of identical items. In both batteries, the part scores are scaled so as to yield equally variable distributions of scaled scores for a given reference population. The reported total score in each case is a simple average or unweighted composite of the part scores. In the SAT, accordingly, the mathematics or quantitative items are given the same weight in the total score as the remainder of the items, while in the ACT battery the math items are given only 1/3 as much weight as the remaining items. Certainly no one would question that there are very marked differences in what is measured by the math or quantitative items and the remaining, predominantly verbal, items in either of the two batteries. Accordingly, even though there were no other differences, that is, even though the two batteries were comprised of identical items, the total scores on these two tests would still measure quite different things, in that the SAT total would place considerably heavier emphasis upon mathematical or quantitative abilities than the ACT total. As I have already suggested, there are probably many other differences in what is measured by the battery totals, but this one difference is all that I need to refer to to make the points that I wish to make.

For this one reason alone, it is of course quite important that the sample used to establish any so-called equivalence table be representative of the population for which it is to be used. A table established for students that do relatively well in mathematics would, for this reason, probably differ considerably from one for students who do relatively poorly in mathematics. For the same reason, a table established for men would probably differ noticeably from one for women, or one for engineering students from one for teachers-college students, etc.

No matter how representative the sampling, however, the table will of course not make the scores interchangeable for the population sampled. For any population, it will presumably be to the advantage of students of relatively high mathematics ability to report SAT scores, and for students of relatively low math ability or relatively high English ability to report ACT scores. Students in the lowest 10% of the SAT distribution will probably compare quite unfavorably in mathematics with students in the lowest 10% of the ACT distribution. Girls will, in general, do better to report ACT scores, boys to report SAT scores, etc. There are undoubtedly other differences, also, but these are the most obvious.

The statements just made are true, of course, primarily because simple averages or *unweighted* composites of the part scores were used. These statements would not be true if, in the composites used, the part scores were optimally weighted for the particular population involved. These statements *should* not be true of any important use of these tests, since in any important use involving composites the part scores should be optimally and differentially weighted rather than arbitrarily and equally weighted.

Colleges that are using the ACT or SAT scores for purposes of selective admission presumably do so because they wish to make as certain as possible that the students who are admitted are those most likely to succeed, as determined by the colleges' own criterion of academic success or failure. Otherwise stated, a major purpose is to minimize the failure rate among the students admitted. The ability to succeed or to make satisfactory grades depends very much more on ability in mathematics in some colleges or in some curricula than in others. Accordingly, the mathematics or quantitative scores should be much more heavily weighted for purposes of admission and guidance in some colleges or in some curricula than in others. Again, this is only a part of the whole story, but it is sufficient for present purposes.

There surely should be no need, however, with an audience of this kind, to argue for the use of best weighted composites in situations in which the weights vary so widely from college to college as they do with these two test batteries. In the ACT program as you may know, a special effort has been made to encourage good practice in this respect by determining for each college population separately the best weighting of the various predictor variables used, and by computing and reporting this best weighted composite for each ACT test student seeking admission to that college. For 136 colleges for which these weights were computed in 1961, the median correlation with the grade point average criterion was .48 for the unweighted total on the ACT battery and .68

for the weighted composite of all available predictor variables. I am sure that a somewhat similar situation exists with reference to the SAT scores. There can be very little question, then, that the unweighted battery total should never be used alone for college admissions purposes. It is easy to see, also, why there *should* be considerable reluctance to supply "official" conversion tables which would only encourage even more widespread use than at present of unweighted totals for this purpose.

If an equating is to be done in this situation, therefore, the measures that should be equated are the measures that *should* be used. In other words, the measures, if any, that should be equated are the best weighted composites of all contributing predictor variables—one composite containing ACT part scores together with other variables, the other composite including SAT part scores. Since the weights would differ markedly from college to college, furthermore, this equating should be done separately for each college.

Having said this, it is hardly necessary to add that any such equating is utterly impracticable even for a single college. Consider how impracticable it would be to equate the unweighted totals for a single sample representative of a single general population. To do the job properly, one would have to select a representative and fairly large sample from this population and would have to arrange for each student in the sample to take both complete batteries under controlled conditions at approximately the same time, preferably counterbalancing the order of taking the two batteries. Ideally, to permit equating on the basis of estimated distributions of true scores, one should require each student to take each of the batteries two times so as to permit computing equivalent forms reliabilities for the total scores. To do anything like this separately for each of the hundreds of colleges involved is just too fantastic for any serious consideration.

There is a good deal more to be learned from this example, but time will not permit any further discussion of it. In conclusion, I would like to summarize briefly what I have said in terms of one or two broad generalizations supported by this and many other similar concrete examples.

In my opinion, the most important generalization is that the problem of equating scores on simple one-part tests is essentially of rather trivial importance. The scores that are by far the most widely used and those that we most wish to equate are scores on multi-test batteries which, like the ACT and SAT batteries, seem to be serving the same general purpose. I refer, of course, to general intelligence tests, general achievement tests, and general aptitude tests. In nearly all of these instances, we are or should be as much or more interested in the subtest scores as in the total scores. In nearly all instances, while the batteries do seem to serve the same general purpose, they are quite differently organized, and only rarely are the subtest scores in one battery anywhere near parallel to any corresponding subtest scores in the other battery. In general, therefore, the difference in organization alone prevents any interchangeable use of the two batteries through equivalence tables established for the tests.

My second broad generalization is simply a restatement of a foregone conclusion. It is that the expression "equating non-parallel tests" is a contradiction in itself. We can, in a certain sense, establish "comparable scales" for such tests, but we cannot *equate* the scores to one another. That is, we cannot use non-parallel tests interchangeably.

12. Technical Problems of Obtaining Equivalent Scores on Tests[1]

WILLIAM H. ANGOFF

One suggested solution to the recent complaint of excessive testing in the schools calls for the preparation of equivalency tables which would allow the conversion of scores obtained on the test of one publisher to the score scale of another publisher. These conversions would presumably make it possible for a student to take only one test, instead of many, and then to submit to each college admissions officer or scholarship agency a converted score reported in terms of the score scale that is considered acceptable by that agency.

Although this solution to the problem of excessive testing (if such a problem indeed exists) has obvious attractions, it also has some objectionable features which may be summarized by saying that the tests of different publishers will not always be parallel forms (in the sense of measuring the same psychological function) and that in such instances it is not possible to provide a unique conversion that will be appropriate for all groups who are likely to take the tests or for all purposes for which the tests are likely to be given, a condition which may ordinarily

Angoff, W. H. Technical problems of obtaining equivalent scores on tests. *Journal of Educational Measurement*, 1964, *1*, 11–13. Reprinted with the permission of the publisher and author.

[1] Paper read at the Annual Meeting of the National Council on Measurement in Education, in Chicago, Illinois, February 1964, as part of a symposium, The Equating of Non-Parallel Test Scores.

be expected to occur when the tests are parallel in function. In such instances, in which it is appropriate to think of conversion as a translation from one set of units to another (as from inches to centimeters, for example) we cannot expect precisely the same line to result in one equating experiment after another but we *can* postulate a single *true* line and expect random variation in successive equating experiments to occur about this line. These variations will result from factors such as the unreliability of the tests themselves, the method of equating used in the particular instance, and the size of the samples used for equating. In contrast to this, the problem of converting scores across tests of different function—a problem in which the issues may be clarified by the use of the term "comparable scores"—differs from equivalent scores for parallel forms in the respect that it is not possible to postulate a single conversion line appropriate to all situations. Here, it is expected that, *in addition* to the kinds of variation that are characteristic of parallel forms, lines relating nonparallel tests will differ and predictably so, depending upon: 1) the particular definition of comparability employed, that is to say, the sense in which the scores are defined to be comparable; 2) the ability characteristics of the group that is used to establish the line of comparability; and 3) the nature of the selection to which each group has been subjected.

In addition, there are problems of interpretation to consider in the conversion of non-parallel tests. For example, there is the erroneous assumption in the minds of many test users that converted scores should behave in all respects like the scores on the test whose scale they have adopted, even to the extent of possessing their reliability and validity. It is interesting to note that this assumption gives an unfair advantage to the poorer, less reliable, and valid test just as it gives an unfair advantage to the test for which the standards of security and test administration are less rigidly guarded.

Other kinds of misinterpretation also result when regression methods are used to establish the conversion line. Unlike other kinds of conversion, regression methods are not symmetrical with respect to the two tests and will necessarily yield scores that have reduced standard deviations—scores that should not be merged with original, unregressed scores. Yet it is for the very purpose of pooling such data that conversion tables are ordinarily called for. Furthermore, regression methods permit students to adopt unfair strategy in competition with other students. For example, good students would be well advised to adopt the strategy of taking the test for which scores are predicted, rather than to allow their scores to be predicted and thereby to suffer a loss due to downward regression. Poor students, on the other hand, would be well advised to take the test which would be directly subjected to regression effects, since in this process they stand to gain points that they could not otherwise earn on their own merit. Finally, it is interesting to note that this effect applies with greater force, the lower the correlation that exists between the tests.

The foregoing enumeration of limitations in the use of comparable scores is not intended as a wholesale condemnation of their use. There *are* situations in which such conversions are useful if it is borne in mind that their usefulness is a function of 1) the similarity of the tests for which comparable scores are to be developed; 2) the appropriateness of the group for whom the table is to be used, in relation to the group on whom the table is based; and 3) the amount of error that can be safely tolerated for the particular use under consideration.

Sometimes, when the use for which a table of comparable scores is required may not be questioned, we are free to choose the kind of group to use in forming such a table. Three such groups are: 1) the national norms group; 2) a set of differentiated norms groups; and 3) the local norms group. A fourth method—of basing the table on a group of people for whom data happen to be convenient and available—is simply to go through the motions of comparability without considering its meaning. Such a table has a highly restricted use, at best.

Of the various kinds of comparability, the one based on differentiated norms groups is the most highly defensible. This procedure would yield a number of conversion tables, each based on and appropriate for a different norms group. The user would then be forced to choose the appropriate table with care, keeping in mind the group and the purpose for which it is to be used.

The local norms approach is similar to the one involving differentiated norms, but is restricted to a single normative group rather than many. Here, the important cautions are 1) that the group has not been directly selected on either score; 2) that there are sufficient cases to ensure reliable conversions; and 3) that the conversions are applied only in the school where they were developed or in schools known to be similar to it.

The national norms approach will result in errors to the extent that the definition of the national norms population differs from one test to another. Even when the definition of the population is the same, differences in methods of sampling will result in errors of bias in the equivalency tables. Finally, even if the national norms groups are quite similar, this approach also requires either that the tests be closely parallel or that the equivalences are applied only to groups closely similar to the national norms groups. Unlike the differentiated norms approach, the national norms approach fails to reveal the extent to which equivalency tables would differ from one group to another. Its sole merit seems to be that it is relatively easy to use, since national norms are available for many tests.

Clearly, the different uses of these tables require different levels of precision. When they are used interchangeably for admissions purposes, only the highest degree of precision should be allowed. On the other hand, when they are used for placement purposes and for estimating *group* performance, high levels of precision are not so crucial. In general, the problem of comparable scores is similar to other problems in which it is impossible to make categorical evaluations that hold fast in all situations. There are many conditions that permit the free use of tables of comparable scores. To demand that these conditions all hold in every situation is unnecessary and also unnecessarily restrictive. However, if in any instance too few of them are fulfilled, then we may find the appropriateness of the tables to be too seriously circumscribed for use in any situation whose characteristics are not clearly understood in complete detail.

13. Equating Non-Parallel Tests[1]

ROGER T. LENNON

The topic to which I shall address myself is the development of a set of scores, having one particular type of comparability, for a series of achievement tests covering a variety of secondary school subjects. These tests, constituting a series known as the *Evaluation and Adjustment Series* of secondary school tests, are designed for the most part as end-of-course examinations, although several of them, particularly in the language arts field, cover the work of all four years of secondary school. Results of such tests serve the obvious purpose of providing an assessment of attainment of the goals of instruction in the respective courses, but, in addition, scores for an individual student on two or more of the tests are indicative of intra-individual strengths or weaknesses and thus potentially of guidance value in much the same manner as scores on an aptitude battery or scores on an interest inventory. A first condition for the realization of this potential guidance value, how-

---

Lennon, R. T. Equating non-parallel tests. *Journal of Educational Measurement*, 1964, *1*, 15–18. Reprinted with the permission of the publisher and author.

[1] Paper read at the Annual Meeting of the National Council on Measurement in Education, in Chicago, Illinois, February 1964, as part of a symposium, The Equating of Non-Parallel Test Scores.

ever, is that results on the several tests be convertible to some common language, or in some manner rendered comparable to one another.

The chief difficulty in achieving such comparability resides, of course, in the fact that the several tests are not, and in the nature of things cannot, be administered to a common or single standardization group; and the standardization groups that are appropriate for the several tests differ systematically from one another in significant respects, the most important of these, in all likelihood, being their respective scholastic aptitude or general mental ability. There is, first, a general selectivity occurring as students progress through secondary school, resulting in increases in the general level of mental ability as one moves from grade 9 to grade 10 to grade 11 to grade 12. And there is more specific selection, self- or school-induced, with respect to particular courses: for example, students enrolled in physics constitute a more select group than those enrolled in World History; students in second-year algebra are of greater scholastic aptitude than students enrolled in general science or general mathematics; etc.

The consequence of this selectivity is that percentile ranks or other interpreted scores derived solely from the respective standardization groups for the various tests cannot be considered comparable to one another, even if one were willing to disregard such differences as might arise from the fact that the several tests are not necessarily standardized at the same time, or in the same school systems. There exists, therefore, a need to develop a system of interpreted scores for all of the tests that will surmount the variations in ability among the standardizing groups.

The problem under discussion, like most matters having to do with score comparability, is not a new one, nor have efforts to deal with it been lacking. Both the Scaled Scores developed for the original editions of Cooperative Achievement Tests in the late 1930's, and the standard score system developed for the first editions of the *Evaluation and Adjustment Series* tests in 1950 and 1951 represented efforts to cope with the issue. The system whereby scores on the achievement tests of the College Entrance Examination program are translated to a common scale is another such effort. And the scheme outlined in this paper has borrowed from all of these. It is, I think, correct to report that the rationale underlying these several systems, and the resulting properties of the types of "comparable" scores they generate are less well understood than they might be, even by persons making wide use of the tests involved; simplicity, it appears, is much to be sought in any set of derived scores for which the test maker aspires to popular understanding and acceptance.

The approach on which we are presently looking with favor as we work upon new editions of some fifteen of the tests in the *Evaluation and Adjustment Series* may be considered in essence an attempt to achieve comparability through an anchor test approach.[2] We envision the development, for the several tests in the series of a uniform system of interpreted scores, such that a given score on any one of the tests will always denote the same relative performance in a hypothetical population having a specified mean and standard deviation on an anchor test, the anchor test being a measure of mental ability or scholastic aptitude, on the assumption that this is the most important differentiating feature among the various standardization populations.

The procedure contemplated may be described as follows:

1. The *Otis Quick Scoring Mental Ability Test—Gamma Test* was selected as an appropriate anchor measure. It is a general mental ability test known to correlate consistently from .55 to .75 with earlier editions of the tests in the series.
2. It was decided to use as the hypothetical common reference population a group having an average IQ on Otis of 107, and standard deviation of 12, these values being chosen as best available estimates for an unselected ninth-grade population on this test.
3. In the standardization program for each of the tests in the series, the anchor test is to be administered, along with the achievement test in question to a group supposedly representative of the students who will regularly be taking the test. The correlation between IQ and achievement test scores will be found, and corrected if necessary for restriction in range to yield an estimated value in a population having the same variability as the hypothetical reference group (i.e., s.d. of 12).
4. On the basis of the correlation of achievement test scores and Otis IQ's, and the corollary regression data, a hypothetical distribution of achievement test scores will be created for a population having an Otis average IQ of 107, and standard deviation of 12.
5. Raw scores in the distribution for the hypothetical reference population will be converted, via an area transformation, to a uniform standard score system, having a mean of 50 and a standard deviation of 15.
6. In the case of tests intended for use at several grade levels, the procedure outlined above will be repeated at each grade, so that separate conversions of raw to standard scores will be developed for the successive grades.

What results from the procedure just described is a translation of, let us say, the raw score corresponding to the 75th percentile of the stan-

[2] I should like to acknowledge the work of Drs. Walter Durost and Victor Noll, editorial coordinators for the series, and of Drs. Harold Bligh and Norman Maberly of Test Department staff, in developing the scheme here reported on.

dardization group's distribution to a standard score value that will fluctuate from test to test but will always presumably represent the same level of performance for the hypothetical uniform reference group. Translation of the test scores to percentile ranks and stanines based on performance of the standardization group is, of course, provided; but there has now been created a way of expressing scores on the various achievement measures in terms of what they denote for a common or uniform basic reference population. We have sought, in other words, to achieve a state of affairs similar to that which prevails in the case of elementary achievement or other batteries, where all sub-tests are standardized on the same population.

Some features of the method outlined are worth noting:

1. First, it may be seen that the correlations among the various achievement measures do not enter into or affect the establishment of this kind of comparability among them. "Comparability" in the sense in which it is used here may be imputed to the scores of two or more tests which may correlate not at all or but very slightly with one another, as well as to scores of tests which are substantially correlated. However, the appropriateness or usefulness of making such comparisons among tests will in many cases depend on the magnitude of such correlations and on the demonstrated guidance or predictive significance of interest differences. There is a comedian whose routine includes a question to his audience. "Do you think I'm too handsome for my height?" What is funny about that, supposedly, is the implied comparison of two qualities where there is no logical basis for positing a relationship. Equally incongruous comparisons can also be made with test scores.
2. Secondly, there is a measure of artificiality in the procedure. The distribution that is created to depict the performance of a hypothetical unselected group on a physics test, for example, is somewhat unrealistic: if such an unselected group really pursued a physics course, the nature of the course, and hence of the achievement as measured at its conclusion, would undoubtedly be different from the hypothetical one. We recognize this limitation, and trust that such error as it introduces is tolerable.

You may be disposed to wonder why a more direct equating of tests in the series to one another is not the more satisfactory way of dealing with the problem. The question of comparing results of a student on two or more of the tests only becomes relevant for those students who take the tests in question. Unless the numbers taking various pairs or other combinations is appreciable, the matter of comparability is of little importance; and if the number taking combinations is appreciable then, indeed, it should be possible to establish direct equivalences. The answer is a practical one: the several tests are not standardized simultaneously, nor are the courses which they cover taken simultaneously by students; moreover, the number of combinations for which it would be necessary to study equivalences directly according to this plan would be prohibitively large; and finally, the samples entering into the determination of the various sets of comparable scores would be of varying qualities, and we know that "comparability" is always relative to the group from which it is derived. For these reasons the anchor test approach seems much preferable. The goodness of the anchor-test approach can, however, be judged by individual studies of the direct equivalence between various pairs or among combinations of tests, and we will be making such checks.

UNIT TWO: NORMS
ADDITIONAL READINGS

Angoff, W. H. Scales and nonmeaningful origins and units of measurement. *Educational and Psychological Measurement,* 1962, *22,* 27–34.

Cattell, R. B. Psychological measurement: Ipsative, normative and interactive. *Psychological Review,* 1944, *51,* 292–303.

Cook, D. L., and Stufflebeam, D. L. Estimating test norms from variable size item and examinee samples. Mimeograph, 1965.

Lord, F. M. Test norms and sampling theory. *Journal of Experimental Education,* 1959, *27,* 247–263.

Plumlee, Lynnette B. Estimating means and standard deviations from partial data—an empirical check on Lord's item sampling technique. *Educational and Psychological Measurement,* 1964, *24,* 623–630.

Schrader, W. B. Norms. *Encyclopedia of Educational Research,* 3rd edition. New York: Macmillan, 1960, 922–926.

Seashore, H. G., and Ricks, J. H., Jr. Norms must be relevant. *Test Service Bulletin,* 1950, *39,* 2–3.

Unit Three:

RELIABILITY

INTRODUCTION

14. Kuder, G. Frederic, and Richardson, Marion W., *The Theory of the Estimation of Test Reliability*
15. Rulon, Phillip J., *A Simplified Procedure for Determining the Reliability of a Test by Split-Halves*
16. Hoyt, Cyril J., *Test Reliability Estimated by Analysis of Variance*

Many articles have been written on the meaning of reliability, how it should be determined, and the relationship between method and meaning. Three distinctive methods of estimating reliability are the Kuder-Richardson, the Rulon, and the Hoyt methods. The first three articles in this unit contain the original derivations of the formulas these methods use.

The Rulon method requires the splitting of the test into two halves. The estimate of the error variance is the variance of the difference scores of the two halves. The Kuder-Richardson and Hoyt methods do *not* require a division of the test. The Kuder-Richardson method uses the sum of the variances of the individual items for an estimate of the error variance. Hoyt's method, which gives the same results as the K-R 20, obtains the error variance from an analysis of variance design.

Other articles, not included in this book, which relate very closely to these three are listed in the suggested readings.

14. The Theory of the Estimation of Test Reliability

G. FREDERIC KUDER
MARION W. RICHARDSON

The theoretically best estimate of the reliability coefficient is stated in terms of a precise definition of the equivalence of two forms of a test. Various approximations to this theoretical formula are derived, with reference to several degrees of completeness of information about the test and to special assumptions. The familiar Spearman-Brown Formula is shown to be a special case of the general formulation of the problem of reliability. Reliability coefficients computed in various ways are presented for comparative purposes.

The reliability coefficient is of interest because it gives, by the simple assumption that a test score has two components, viz., true score and variable error, an (indirect) estimate of the random error variance present in an obtained test score variance. No matter how computed, the reliability coefficient is only an *estimate* of the percentage of the total variance that may be described as true variance, i.e., not due to error.

The usual methods of estimating test reliability are too well known to justify description here. These methods differ in such a fashion that no close estimate can be made of the results of one method, knowing the estimate obtained by another method. It is always desirable, even necessary, for the investigator to state how he made his estimate of the reliability coefficient.* The retest coefficient on the same form gives, in general, estimates that are too high, because of material remembered on the second application of the test. This memory factor cannot be eliminated by increasing the length of time between the two applications, because of variable growth in the function tested within the population of individuals. These difficulties are so serious that the method is rarely used.

Although the authors have made no actual count, it seems safe to say that most test technicians use the split-half method of estimating

---

Kuder, G. F., and Richardson, M. W. The theory of the estimation of test reliability. *Psychometrika*, 1937, *2*, 151–160. Reprinted with the permission of the publisher and author.

* The critical reader will reflect that, in addition, the investigator must report the range, or better, the variance of the group tested. The present study is not concerned with that matter.

reliability. This method involves an arbitrary division of the test into two parts, and the computation of the correlation-coefficient of the two sets of scores thus derived. The correlation coefficient thus obtained is taken as an estimate of the reliability of either half, and the Spearman-Brown formula for double length is then used to estimate the reliability coefficient of the whole test. The split-half method is commonly supposed to give estimates that are too high; this is an uncertain generalization unless one has some definitely defensible standard. A more pertinent observation about the split-half coefficient is that *it is not a unique value*. There are $\frac{n!}{2(\frac{n}{2}!)^2}$ different ways of dividing a test of n items into two halves. Each one of these ways of splitting the test gives its own estimate of the reliability coefficient.* True enough, not all these ways of splitting are equally defensible on *a priori* grounds. It remains true, however, that there are large fluctuations in the value of the reliability coefficient as obtained from different ways of constituting the two halves.†

The supposedly best method of estimating the reliability coefficient is to find the correlation between two *equivalent* forms, given at the same time. The crux of the matter here is *equivalence*. Actually the difficulties discussed in connection with the split-half coefficient still apply, in perhaps smaller degree. Again, there is no unique value of the reliability coefficient. In the quest for equivalence, the shift of items from one form to the other will affect the magnitude of the coefficient. In this situation, there are $\frac{(2n!)}{2(n!)^2}$ different coefficients, again not equally defensible.

In view of the limitations briefly described in the foregoing, the authors present certain deductions from test theory which lead to unique values of the reliability coefficient.‡ The least exact approximation we

---

*With certain assumptions as to the distribution of inter-item correlations it would be possible to estimate, theoretically, the expected distribution of reliability coefficients thus to be computed. The most representative value (perhaps the mean) could then be taken as the best estimate and the problem thus solved. It is likely, however, that the solution would be enormously complicated by the possibility that the matrix of inter-item coefficients would have a rank greater than one. See Mosier, Charles I., "A Note on Item Analysis and the Criterion of Internal Consistency," *Psychometrika*, 1936, **1**, pp. 275–282.

† Brownell, Wm. A., "On the Accuracy with which Reliability May be Measured by Correlating Test Halves," *J. Exper. Educ.*, 1933, 1, pp. 204–215.

‡ It should be mentioned that the main outlines of the simple argument in this article were derived independently by the two authors. In a chance conversation it developed that the two had reached similar conclusions by methods similar in principle.

shall describe involves assumptions no more unreasonable than those basic to the Spearman-Brown formula. Any one of the formulas will give a unique estimate of the coefficient in all situations to which it is applicable. In certain cases, the commonly calculated parameters of the test score distribution will afford, in two minutes of time, a fairly good estimate of the reliability coefficient.

We shall consider a test variable t made up of n unit-weighted items applied to a population of N individuals. In the general case, we shall allow for the possibility of the inter-item coefficients varying between their possible limits, and also for varying proportions of correct answers; items need not be equally difficult or equally correlated with other items. This enables us to state the formally complete and theoretically most exact method of estimating the reliability of test t.

CASE I.

The data required are the number of items in the test, the difficulties of the items, the inter-item correlations, and the standard deviation of the total test. In one of the possible solutions suggested it is assumed that the matrix of inter-item correlations has a rank of one.

The correlation between two forms of a test is given by

$$r(a+b+\ldots+n)\,(A+B+\ldots+N) = \qquad (1)$$

$$\frac{r_{aA}\,\sigma_a\,\sigma_A + r_{aB}\,\sigma_a\,\sigma_B + \cdots + r_{n(N-1)}\,\sigma_n\,\sigma_{N-1} + r_{nN}\,\sigma_n\,\sigma_N}{\begin{array}{l}[\sigma_a{}^2 + \sigma_b{}^2 + \cdots + \sigma_n{}^2 + 2(r_{ab}\,\sigma_a\,\sigma_b + r_{ac}\,\sigma_a\,\sigma_c + \cdots + r_{n(n-1)}\,\sigma_n\,\sigma_{n-1})]^{\frac{1}{2}} \times \\ {[\sigma_A{}^2 + \sigma_B{}^2 + \cdots \sigma_N{}^2 + 2(r_{AB}\,\sigma_A\,\sigma_B + r_{AC}\,\sigma_A\,\sigma_C + \cdots + r_{N(N-1)}\,\sigma_N\,\sigma_{N-1})]^{\frac{1}{2}}}\end{array}},$$

in which $a, b, \ldots n$ are items of the test, and $A, B, \ldots N$ are corresponding items in a second hypothetical test. Equivalence is now defined as interchangeability of items a and A, b and B, etc.; the members of each pair have the same difficulty and are correlated to the extent of their respective reliabilities. The inter-item correlations of one test are the same as those in the other. These relationships constitute the operational definition of *equivalence* which is to be used.*

By this definition of equivalence, the two expressions in the denominator of equation (1) are identical. It may then be seen that the numerator and denominator are the sums of the entries in square tables which are the same except for the entries in the principal diagonals. The entries in the principal diagonal of the numerator are the reliabilities of the items multiplied by their variance, while the entries in the diagonal

---

* It should be noted that this definition of equivalence is more rigid than the one usually stated.

of the denominator are merely the variances of the items. The formula for test reliability then becomes:

$$r_{tt} = \frac{r_{aa}\,\sigma_a^2 + r_{bb}\,\sigma_b^2 + \cdots + r_{nn}\,\sigma_n^2 + 2(r_{ab}\,\sigma_a\,\sigma_b + r_{ac}\,\sigma_a\,\sigma_c + \cdots + r_{n(n-1)}\,\sigma_n\,\sigma_{n-1})}{\sigma_a^2 + \sigma_b^2 + \cdots + \sigma_n^2 + 2(r_{ab}\,\sigma_a\,\sigma_b + r_{ac}\,\sigma_a\,\sigma_c + \cdots + r_{n(n-1)}\,\sigma_n\,\sigma_{n-1})}. \tag{2}$$

The denominator of equation (2) is simply the expression for the variance of the sum of the items *a* to *n*, when each item is given a score of one. We can therefore substitute σ_t^2, the obtained variance of test scores, directly in the denominator, and also in the numerator by use of a suitable correction.

In order to write the numerator term, we must adjust the variance for the fact that the entries in the diagonals of the numerator and denominator tables are different. We therefore subtract from the obtained variance the sum of the variances of the items $(\sum_1^n pq)$ and substitute the sum of the products of the variance and reliability of each item $(\sum_1^n r_{ii}pq)$. The variance of any item *i* is p_iq_i.

The formula then becomes

$$r_{tt} = \frac{\sigma_t^2 - \sum_1^n pq + \sum_1^n r_{ii}pq}{\sigma_t^2}, \tag{3}$$

where σ_t^2 is the obtained test variance, $\sum_1^n pq$ is the sum of the item variances, and $\sum_1^n r_{ii}pq$ is the sum of the products of item reliabilities and their variances.

Equation (3), while basic, is not adapted to calculations, because the r_{ii}'s are not operationally determinable except by use of certain assumptions. However, certain approximations are possible. If the inter-item correlations are available, two methods of estimating the *n* different values of r_{ii} suggest themselves. One is to use the average correlation of item *i* with the *n*—1 other items of the test as an estimate of the reliability of item *i*. This method, or other methods, of estimating the reliability of an item may be thought to be crude; however, it will be noted by reference to the square tables previously suggested that the r_{ii}'s comprise for a 100-item test only one per cent of the total number of entries whose values enter into the determination of the reliability coefficient of the whole test. Reasonable guesses as to the values of r_{ii} would probably not affect the final result very much, unless the tests were very short.

Another method is to estimate the unknown r_{ii} as the average computed from all the second-order minors of the matrix of inter-item correlations in which r_{ii} is the single unknown. By this method,

$$r_{ii} = \frac{\Sigma \dfrac{r_{ij}\, r_{ik}}{r_{jk}}}{\frac{1}{2}\,(n-1)\,(n-2)}, \tag{4}$$

where i, j, and k are all different, and where the Σ means the sum of the separate determinations of r_{ii} from the $\frac{1}{2}\,(n-1)\,(n-2)$ minors. This method assumes that the matrix is of rank one, or that the test measures one function. This method would be justified only where n is fairly small.

CASE II.

The data required are the numbers of items in the test, the difficulties of the items, the item-test correlations, and the standard deviation of the test. It is assumed that the matrix of inter-item correlations has a rank of one.

A more usable approximation is adapted to those situations in which an item analysis giving values of item-test correlations has been made. If we care to assume that item and test measure the same thing (which, of course, we do when we put the item into the test), we may write

$$\frac{r_{it}}{\sqrt{r_{ii}\, r_{tt}}} = 1, \tag{5}$$

where r_{it} is the correlation between the item and the test, r_{ii} and r_{tt} are the reliabilities of item and test respectively.

Then

$$r_{ii} = \frac{r_{it}^2}{r_{tt}}\,. \tag{6}$$

Substituting $\dfrac{r_{it}^2}{r_{tt}}$ for r_{ii} in equation (3), we have

$$r_{tt} = \frac{\sigma_t^2 - \sum_1^n pq + \dfrac{\sum_1^n r_{it}^2 pq}{r_{tt}}}{\sigma_t^2}\,. \tag{7}$$

Solving for r_{tt}:

$$r_{tt} = \frac{\sigma_t^2 - \Sigma pq}{2\sigma_t^2} \pm \sqrt{\frac{\Sigma r_{it}^2 pq}{\sigma_t^2} + \left(\frac{\sigma_t^2 - \Sigma pq}{2\sigma_t^2}\right)^2}\,. \tag{8}$$

In practice, only the positive value of the radical in the right member of the equation is admissible. Equation (8) gives an estimate of the reliability coefficient in those situations in which the techniques of item analysis have been applied. In each case, Σ denotes summation over the n items.

CASE III.

The data required are the number of items in the test, the difficulties of the items, and the standard deviation of the test. It is assumed that the matrix of inter-item correlations has a rank of one and that all intercorrelations are equal.

In other situations, we may be willing to assume that the items are equally intercorrelated, but allow their difficulties to vary over a wide range. We shall proceed, therefore, to investigate this case. By assuming r_{ij} to be constant and equal to $\bar{r}_{ii}$ in equation (2) we have

$$r_{tt} = \frac{\bar{r}_{ii} \left(\sum_{i=1}^{n} \sqrt{p_i q_i} \right)^2}{\sigma_t^2}, \tag{9}$$

in which $\sqrt{p_i q_i}$ is the standard deviation of item i. Equation (9) gives an estimate of the reliability coefficient. An approximation to equation (9) is given by

$$r_{tt} = \frac{\bar{r}_{it} \Sigma \sqrt{pq}}{\sigma_t} \tag{10}$$

by assuming $\bar{r}_{ii} = \dfrac{\bar{r}_{it}^2}{r_{tt}}$, where $\bar{r}_{it}$ is the average item-test coefficient.

Since the test t is the sum of its items $a, b, \cdots n$, the variance of test scores is given by

$$\sigma_t^2 = \sigma_a^2 + \sigma_b^2 \cdots + \sigma_n^2 + 2 (r_{ab}\,\sigma_a\,\sigma_b + r_{ac}\,\sigma_a\,\sigma_c + \cdots + r_{(n-1)n}\,\sigma_{n-1}\,\sigma_n, \tag{11}$$

in which $a, b, \cdots n$ are items of the test.

If all intercorrelations are assumed equal ($\bar{r}_{ii}$), and $\sqrt{p_i q_i}$ is used as the σ for an item,

$$\sigma_t^2 = (\Sigma \sqrt{pq})^2 \bar{r}_{ii} - \Sigma pq \bar{r}_{ii} + \Sigma pq, \tag{12}$$

in which

$$\Sigma \sqrt{pq} = \text{sum of the } \sqrt{pq\text{'s}} \text{ for items } a \text{ to } n,$$

and

$$\bar{r}_{ii} = \frac{\sigma_t^2 - \Sigma pq}{(\Sigma \sqrt{pq})^2 - \Sigma pq}. \tag{13}$$

Substituting for $\bar{r}_{ii}$ in formula (9)

$$r_{tt} = \frac{\sigma_t^2 - \Sigma pq}{(\Sigma \sqrt{pq})^2 - \Sigma pq} \cdot \frac{(\Sigma \sqrt{pq})^2}{\sigma_t^2}. \tag{14}$$

Again, all summations are over the items.

This formula is recommended for use when there is reason to believe that the inter-item correlations are approximately equal.

We shall digress slightly to illustrate the degree of approximation involved in the various steps. Let us suppose that, with reference to equation (9), we are in addition willing to assume equal standard deviations of items. With such an assumption, we have

$$r_{tt} = \frac{r_{ii} n^2 \overline{pq}}{\sigma_t^2} \qquad (15)$$

in which $\overline{pq}$ is the average item variance.

But

$$\sigma_t^2 = n\overline{pq}\,[1 + (n - 1)\, r_{ii}], \text{ from } (12) \qquad (16)$$

by similar assumptions. Substituting (16) in (15), we have

$$r_{tt} = \frac{n\bar{r}_{ii}}{1 + (n - 1)\,\bar{r}_{ii}}. \qquad (17)$$

Equation (17) is, of course, the familiar Spearman-Brown formula, which is predicated upon test length as the only variable affecting reliability, given a constant value of the reliability of the element.

It is now convenient to introduce another variant of equation (3), with assumptions similar to those involved in the Spearman-Brown formula.

From equation (12),

$$r_{ii} = \frac{\sigma_t^2 - n\overline{pq}}{(n - 1)\, n\overline{pq}}, \qquad (18)$$

since $\Sigma pq = n\overline{pq}$.

Substituting this value of r_{ii} in equation (15) we have

$$r_{tt} = \frac{\sigma_t^2 - n\overline{pq}}{(n - 1)\, n\overline{pq}} \cdot \frac{n^2\overline{pq}}{\sigma_t^2}, \qquad (19)$$

which simplifies to

$$r_{tt} = \frac{n}{n - 1} \cdot \frac{\sigma_t^2 - n\overline{pq}}{\sigma_t^2}. \qquad (20)$$

Equation (20) gives an estimate of the reliability of a test, knowing the number of items, the standard deviation, and the *average* variance of the items. This would not seem to be ordinarily a useful formula since it requires essentially the same basic data as formula (14), but involves one more approximation. Empirical evidence presented at the end of this paper, however, shows that reliabilities obtained by formula (20) do not for the tests used, vary more than .001 from those obtained from formula (14). Since formula (20) eliminates the necessity for computing $\sqrt{pq}$ for each item, it accomplishes a material saving in labor. It serves, too, as a basis for the formula recommended for use in Case IV.

CASE IV.

The data required are the number of items in the test and the standard deviation and mean of the total scores. It is assumed in this case that the matrix of inter-item correlations has a rank of one, that these correlations are equal, and that all items have the same difficulty.

Solution of formula (20) becomes greatly simplified if we make the rigid assumption that all items have the same difficulty. As the formula now stands it is necessary to obtain the average variance. The average variance ($\overline{pq}$) is equal to the product of average p and average q, ($\bar{p}\,\bar{q}$), if the items all have the same difficulty. In this case,

$$r_{tt} = \frac{n}{n-1} \cdot \frac{\sigma_t^2 - n\,\bar{p}\,\bar{q}}{\sigma_t^2}. \qquad (21)$$

The average value of p may be easily obtained from the formula

$$\bar{p} = \frac{\Sigma X_t}{nN} = \frac{M_t}{n}, \qquad (22)$$

when ΣX_t is the sum of the scores of N subjects on a test of n items, and M_t is the mean of the test scores.

The difference between equations (20) and (21) should be noted. Equation (20) calls for the average of the item variances ($\overline{pq}$); equation (21) calls for the average of the item difficulties ($\bar{p}$) and this value subtracted from 1.00, ($\bar{q}$). When all items have the same difficulty, $\overline{pq}$ is equal to $\bar{p}\,\bar{q}$, but if there is variation in difficulty among the items, $\bar{p}\,\bar{q}$ becomes larger than $\overline{pq}$, and this discrepancy increases as the variation increases. This means that the estimate of reliability obtained by formula (21) is equal to or less than that obtained by formula (20). If Equation (22) is used to get an estimate of $\bar{p}$, the reliability coefficient can be quickly estimated from the mean, standard deviation, and the number of items. This formula may be regarded as a sort of foot-rule method of estimating test reliability without the necessity of splitting halves, rescoring twice, and calculating a correlation coefficient. According to theory and to the applications already made, the formula may be expected to give an underestimate of the reliability coefficient in situations not favorable for its application. If Equation (21) should give a higher value than the split-half, one would suspect the latter of being abnormally low because of some unfavorable way of splitting. The split-half Spearman-Brown coefficient cannot be regarded as the standard from which to judge other estimates. The split-half method involving use of the Spearman-Brown formula may produce estimates of reliability which are either too high or too low. Reliabilities obtained from the formulas presented here are never overestimates. When the assumptions are rigidly fulfilled, the figures obtained are the exact values of test reliability as herein defined; if the assumptions are not met, the figures obtained are underestimates.

It may be useful to suggest an interpretation of Equation (21) which has some bearing on the general problem of reliability. For r_{tt} to be positive, σ_t^2 must exceed $n\bar{p}\,\bar{q}$. Now $n\bar{p}\,\bar{q}$ is the variance of n equally difficult items when they are uncorrelated, by the familiar binomial theory.* Hence r_{tt} is positive for any average inter-item correlation that is positive. But negative reliability is inadmissible; hence only to the extent to which test items are positively intercorrelated will a test have reliability. It is implicit in all formulations of the reliability problem that *reliability is the characteristic of a test possessed by virtue of the positive intercorrelations of the items composing it.*

Table I presents a comparison of reliability coefficients computed by equation (21) with a split half coefficient for various tests. The time of computation was approximately two minutes for each test, applying Equation (21).

TABLE I

Test No.	Nature	Range of values of p	$\bar{p}$	n	σ_t	Reliability Coefficient: By equation (21)	Reliability Coefficient: Split-half, Spearman-Brown
1	College Achievement	.05-.22	.156	50	6.56	.864	.880
2	"	.23-.40	.318	50	9.24	.891	.906
3	"	.41-.59	.522	50	10.96	.914	.923
4	"	.60-.77	.672	50	8.69	.872	.896
5	"	.78-.95	.852	50	6.57	.871	.888

Table II presents results from several formulas. As in Table I, three decimal figures are retained, merely to illustrate the differences obtained by the various formulas.

The foregoing results are not intended to confirm the theory developed, but they may serve to illustrate the degree of divergences of results that may be expected in actual application. In comparing these estimates, it should be noted that all the tests are short; longer tests may be expected to give less variable estimates. Several algebraic variants are not here presented; they may be easily derived when their use is indi-

* Dunlap, J. W. and Kurtz, A. K., *Handbook of Statistical Nomographs, Tables and Formulas*, World Book Company, New York. Formula No. 46.

TABLE II

Test No.	Nature	Mean Score	n	σ_t	Reliability Coefficient, as estimated by Case II Equation (8)	Case III Equation (14)	Case III Equation (20)	Case IV Equation (21)
6	multiple choice vocabulary	24.39	65	7.62	.823	.808	.808	.733
7	do	24.13	65	7.92	.839	.826	.825	.758
8	general information	....	25	....	.729	.716	.716	.714

cated. The choice of formula to be used in any actual situation will depend upon the amount of information about the components of the test, and upon the degree of accuracy desired. It is the belief of the authors that in many cases the quick estimate afforded by Formula (21) may be good enough for all practical purposes; if the items vary greatly in difficulty, Formula (20) appears to be adequate in any case.

15. A Simplified Procedure for Determining the Reliability of a Test by Split-Halves

PHILLIP J. RULON

A common procedure in estimating the reliability of a test is to divide it into comparable halves, score the halves separately, compute the correlation between the resulting pairs of scores, and apply the Spearman-Brown formula to the correlation coefficient to estimate what correlation would be found between two complete comparable forms of the test. To obtain a still more useful (for many purposes) index of the dependability of the test, the standard error of the score from the test is then estimated by multiplying the standard deviation of the

---

Rulon, P. J. A simplified procedure for determining the reliability of a test by split-halves. *Harvard Educational Review*, 1939, 9, 99–103. Reprinted with the permission of the publisher and author.

distribution of scores by the square root of the complement of the estimated reliability coefficient.

This procedure may be represented symbolically as follows:

Let N be the number of persons tested.

Let X_a be the score of any person on one of the comparable halves of the test, and let X_b be his score on the other half of the test, so that $X_w = X_a + X_b$ is his score on the whole test.

Let $M_a = \frac{\Sigma X_a}{N}$ and $M_b = \frac{\Sigma X_b}{N}$.

Let $x_a = X_a - M_a$ and $x_b = X_b - M_b$.

Then X_a and X_b are determined for each person and r_{ab} computed from them. This result is entered in the Spearman-Brown formula,

$$r_w = \frac{2r_{ab}}{1 + r_{ab}}, \qquad [1]$$

where r_w is the estimated reliability coefficient for the whole test.

Next X_w is obtained for each of the N persons and σ_w is computed as the standard deviation of these scores.[1]

Finally r_w and σ_w are used in the formula,

$$\sigma_e = \sigma_w \sqrt{1 - r_w}, \qquad [2]$$

to estimate the standard error of the score from the whole test.

Some time ago the writer noticed that this whole process can be short-cut by simply computing the standard deviation of the differences $(X_a - X_b)$ between the scores on the *halves* of the test and taking it directly as the estimated standard error (σ_e) of the score from the *whole test*.[2] This simplification has proved extremely useful on a number of occasions and has recently been adopted by the Cooperative Test Service in deriving published standard errors. It is therefore appropriate to set forth the validity of the technique.

Remembering that $X_w = X_a + X_b$, we see from the usual formula for the variance of a sum that

$$\sigma^2_w = \sigma^2_a + \sigma^2_b + 2r_{ab}\sigma_a\sigma_b.$$

If the halves of the test are comparable, σ^2_a must equal σ^2_b and

$$\sigma^2_w = 2\sigma^2_a\ (1 + r_{ab}), \qquad [3]$$

and after squaring equation [2] we can rewrite it:

$$\sigma^2_e = 2\sigma^2_a\ (1 + r_{ab})\ (1 - r_w). \qquad [4]$$

---

[1] Professor T. L. Kelley reminds me that even when the Spearman-Brown technique is employed, σ^2_w is often computed from Formula [3] or the one preceding it.

[2] Otis has observed a similar useful relationship between scores from different forms of a test. See Arthur S. Otis, *Statistical Method in Educational Measurement* (Yonkers, N.Y.: World Book Company, 1925, p. 250).

For r_w in this expression we now substitute the right-hand member of equation [1] and get

$$\sigma^2_e = 2\sigma^2_a \ (1 + r_{ab}) \ (1 - \frac{2r_{ab}}{1 + r_{ab}}) \ ,$$

which reduces to

$$\sigma^2_e = 2\sigma^2_a \ (1 - r_{ab}) \ . \qquad [5]$$

The right-hand member of this can be obtained directly by computing the variance of the N differences between half-scores from the test. From the usual formula for the variance of a difference, we see that, where $d = X_a - X_b$,

$$\sigma^2_d = \sigma^2_a + \sigma^2_b - 2r_{ab} \, \sigma_a \sigma_b \ ,$$

and again setting $\sigma^2_a = \sigma^2_b$, we have

$$\sigma^2_d = 2\sigma^2_a \ (1 - r_{ab}) \ . \qquad [6]$$

From [5] and [6] we see that $\sigma^2_e = \sigma^2_d$, so $\sigma_e = \sigma_d$.

It may be noticed that in arriving at Equations [3] and [6], we assumed the test halves to be comparable. This may appear at first glance to be a limitation of the technique, since in any particular application we might not succeed in arranging exactly comparable halves, in which case σ^2_a would not equal σ^2_b. In fact, this contingency may arise, but wherever it does, it points up a limitation in the Spearman-Brown technique itself, so that the simplified procedure is not singularly subject to this criticism.[3] Indeed, when the two procedures give different results, the avoidance of assumptions would lead to adopting the simpler of the two, since the derivation of the Spearman-Brown formula involves several assumptions while that of the simpler process actually involves only two, both highly conventional: that the difference between the two true scores for the two half-tests is constant for all individuals studied, and that the errors of measurement in the two half-scores are chance errors, and hence uncorrelated.[4]

---

[3] Dr. John Flanagan points out that actually the Spearman-Brown formula as ordinarily used in this situation is unnecessarily inexact: that instead of Formula [1] above, a more nearly exact form would be

$$r_w = \frac{4\sigma_a\sigma_b r_{ab}}{\sigma^2_a + \sigma^2_b + 2\sigma_a\sigma_b r_{ab}} = \frac{4\sigma_a\sigma_b r_{ab}}{\sigma^2_w} ,$$

and when this form is used for Formula [1] as outlined at the beginning of this treatment, the result will always agree with that of the proposed simplified procedure. He points out also that even if one is primarily interested in the reliability coefficient, time would be saved in computation by utilizing the relationship

$$r_w = l - \frac{\sigma^2_d}{\sigma^2_w} ,$$

in which $d = X_a - X_b$, as already defined.

[4] It has been suggested that it is necessary also to assume that the two halves are equally reliable, so that σ^2_{ea}, the variance of errors in the scores from one half of the test, shall equal σ^2_{eb}, the variance of the errors for the other half. I believe the treatment which follows shows this assumption to be unnecessary.

Let X_{ta} be the true score of any individual on one half of the test and X_{tb} his true score on the other half. Let e_a be the error of measurement involved in the obtained score on one half and e_b the error in the score on the other half, so that

$$\left.\begin{aligned} X_{ta} + e_a &= X_a \\ X_{tb} + e_b &= X_b \end{aligned}\right\} \qquad [7]$$

where X_a and X_b are, as previously defined, the obtained scores from the two halves.

By subtraction, since $X_{ta} = X_{tb} + c$, c constant,

$$c + e_a - e_b = X_a - X_b\,,$$

and since the constant, c, on the left-hand side does not affect the variance, $\sigma^2{}_{de} = \sigma^2{}_{dx}$ where $de = e_a - e_b$ and $dx = X_a - X_b$.

But $X_{ta} + X_{tb} = X_{tw} =$ the true score on the whole test.

Also $X_a + X_b = X_w =$ the obtained score on the whole test. From this and Equation [7] we see that

$$\begin{aligned} X_w &= X_a + X_b \\ &= X_{ta} + X_{tb} + e_a + e_b \\ &= X_{tw} + e_a + e_b\,. \end{aligned}$$

Hence $e_w = X_w - X_{tw} = e_a + e_b$.

Now if the errors e_a and e_b are uncorrelated, then

$$\sigma^2{}_{se} = \sigma^2{}_{de}$$

where de has already been defined and $se = e_a + e_b$.

Hence $\sigma^2{}_e = \sigma^2{}_{de}$, where the w has been dropped from the subscript in the left-hand member. That is, the variance of the errors in X_w is equal to the variance of the differences between e_a and e_b. And since we have already observed the equality of $\sigma^2{}_{de} = \sigma^2{}_{dx}$, we now see that the variance of the errors in X_w is equal to the variance of the differences between half-scores.

There remains only the assumption that the variance of errors ($\sigma^2{}_e$) here dealt with—where there are N of the e_w's for N individuals—is a good estimate of the variance to be expected among a series of errors arising from measuring the same individual a number of times. It should be pointed out that this assumption is implicit in the use of Formula [2], that it appears to be an entirely reasonable assumption when the range (or variance $\sigma^2{}_{tw}$) of the true scores is not large,[5] and

[5] Professor Kelley points out that the range of true scores is a function of the unit of measurement and that "the range is not large" is an ambiguous expression. Of course this is true. In practice, one estimates the standard error of the score at various score levels, and the more different levels studied, the narrower the range of obtained scores included in each determination. For examples of this practice, see T. L. Kelley, G. M. Ruch, and L. M. Terman, *New Standard Achievement Test, Guide for Interpreting (Revised)* (Yonkers, N.Y.: World Book Company, 1929, pp. 8–9).

that it is nearly always possible to arrange for this in any application by restricting the range of obtained scores (X_w) studied.

Further, it should be noted that the technique prompts the derivation of an *unbiased* estimate of the standard error of the score by the use of the relationship

$$\sigma^2_u = \frac{N}{N-1}\sigma^2_e ,$$

where σ^2_u is the estimated variance of the universe from which the sample of size N was drawn for the calculation of σ^2_e.

16. Test Reliability Estimated by Analysis of Variance

CYRIL J. HOYT

A formula for estimating the reliability of a test, based on the analysis of variance theory, is developed and illustrated. The data needed for the required computation are the number of correct responses to each item and the score for each subject. The results obtained from this formula are identical with those from one of the special cases of the Kuder-Richardson formulation. The relationships of the new procedure to other approaches to the problem are indicated.

This paper is composed of two parts, the first of which describes the procedures followed in computing the estimated reliability of a test by analysis of variance while the second part contains the mathematical derivation of the formulas.

I

The coefficient of reliability of a test gives the percentage of the obtained variance in the distribution of test scores that may be regarded as true variance, that is, as variance not due to the unreliability of the measuring instrument. Out of Rulon's* work on a short method of estimating the reliability coefficient by means of "split-halves" comes the relationship

$$r_n = 1 - \frac{\sigma_d^2}{\sigma_t^2}$$

Hoyt, C. J. Test reliability estimated by analysis of variance, *Psychometrika,* 1941, *6,* 153–160. Reprinted with the permission of the publisher and author.

* Rulon, Phillip J. A simplified procedure for determining the reliability of a test by split-halves. *Harvard Educational Review,* 1939, 9, 99–103.

where σ_d^2 is the variance of the distribution of differences obtained by subtracting a student's score on the odd items of a test from that on the even items, or vice versa, and σ_t^2 is the variance of the distribution of the students' scores on the test. From this information, it is apparent that σ_d^2 is used as a measure of the discrepancy between the obtained variance and the true variance, σ_∞^2. If the odd-even split of the test happens to be an unlucky one, σ_d^2 as thus computed may be an underestimate or an overestimate of the discrepancy between the obtained variance and the true variance. It was this difficulty that led the writer to seek a better estimate of this discrepancy. Table I shows the results of a hypothetical test where each item is scored either one or zero.

TABLE I

Student	Items 1	2	3	n	Scores
1					t_1
2					t_2
3					t_3
.					.
.					.
.					.
k					t_k
Totals	p_1	p_2	p_3	p_n	$\sum_{i=1}^{n} p_i = \sum_{i=1}^{k} t_i$

The sum of squares "among students" is

$$\frac{1}{n} \sum_{i=1}^{k} t^2{}_i - \frac{(\sum_{i=1}^{k} t_i)^2}{nk}. \tag{1}$$

The sum of squares "among items" is

$$\frac{1}{k} \sum_{i=1}^{n} p^2{}_i - \frac{(\sum t_i)^2}{nk}. \tag{2}$$

The total sum of squares is

$$\frac{(\sum_{i=1}^{k} t_i)\ (nk - \sum_{i=1}^{k} t_i)}{nk}, \tag{3}$$

or simply the number of correct responses times the number of incorrect responses divided by the total number of responses, nk. This last result can be verified as follows.

Let n_1 equal the number of correct responses and n_2 equal the number of incorrect responses. Then the mean is $\frac{n_1(1) + n_2(0)}{n_1 + n_2}$ or $\frac{n_1}{n_1 + n_2}$.

The sum of the squares of the deviations from the mean is

$$n_1\left(1 - \frac{n_1}{n_1 + n_2}\right)^2 + n_2\left(\frac{n_1}{n_1 + n_2} - 0\right)^2 = \frac{n_1\, n_2^2 + n_1^2\, n_2}{(n_1 + n_2)^2} \text{ or } \frac{n_1\, n_2}{n_1 + n_2}.$$

In terms of the notation of the analysis of variance problem above, this sum is clearly (3).

By subtracting the "among students" and the "among items" sums of squares from the total sum of squares, we have left the residual sum of squares which is used as the basis of estimating the discrepancy between the obtained variance and the true variance. This estimate of the discrepancy is a better one than that obtained by dividing the test into odd and even halves because in the latter case the particular split of the test, which is only one of many possible ways of splitting a test, may be an unlucky division and may result in either an overestimate or an underestimate of the coefficient of reliability. Furthermore, it has been shown, as the reader will see in Part II, that the particular estimate of the discrepancy between the obtained and the "true" scores is the best linear estimate where "best" is considered in the light of the least squares' criterion. Hence, it is clear that this method of estimating the reliability of a test gives a better estimate than any method based upon an arbitrary division of the test into halves or into any other fractional parts. From a practical point of view, the labor involved in computation is not excessive although probably not much less than is required for the computation by split-halves. The data needed to compute the reliability are the number of correct responses to each item and the score for each subject. The use of the item counter on the International Scoring Machine makes it possible to obtain these item counts immediately.

The method of obtaining the coefficient of reliability will be illustrated by a specific example. A test of 250 items was administered to 33 students in a class in botany in the College of Pharmacy of the University of Minnesota.

TABLE II. Analysis of Variance of Test of 250 Items in Botany, Administered to 33 Students

Source of Variation	d.f.	Sum of Squares	Variance
Total	8249	2002.42533	.24275
Among Items	249	593.81927	2.38482
Among Individuals	32	82.82933	2.58842
Remainder	7968	1325.77673	.16639

The coefficient of reliability of the test may be expressed

$$r_{tt} = \frac{2.58842 - .16639}{2.58842} = .936.$$

The standard error of measurement is $\sqrt{1325.77673/32}$ or 6.44. That measure of reliability which Jackson* has called the sensitivity, γ, can be obtained immediately as,

$$\gamma^2 = \frac{2.42203}{.16639} = 14.556 \text{ and } \gamma = 3.82\,.$$

γ is interpreted on the normal probability scale as follows. If $\gamma = 2.57$ for example, using the obtained scores as estimates of a certain capacity of the individual, we would expect to make an error as great as or greater than one standard deviation (of the true scores) only once in a hundred times.

It may be interesting to some who are familiar with the work of Kuder and Richardson† that the foregoing method of estimating the coefficient of reliability gives precisely the same result as formula (20) of their paper. This fact can be easily verified algebraically.

If two or more equivalent forms of the test are administered to the same group of students it is easy to extend this procedure so that it is possible to separate out another source of variation, the "between forms" variance which might be considered to be due to practice effect.

More extended examination of the "among items" variance would make it possible to decide on heterogeneity of the respective difficulties of the items while a more extended examination of the "among students" variance would make it possible to answer certain pertinent questions regarding the individual differences among students.

II

The method used in developing the formulas for estimating the reliability of a test by means of analysis of variance as described in Part I is essentially the method suggested by Johnson and Neyman‡ and later used by Jackson§. This particular approach does not give new or different results for the problems of tests of significance but does possess considerable advantage in attacking problems of estimation.

---

* Jackson, Robert W. Reliability of mental tests. *British Journal of Psychology*, 1939, **29**, 267–87.

† Kuder, G. F. and Richardson, M. W. The theory of the estimation of test reliability. *Psychometrika,* 1937, **2**, 151–60.

‡ Johnson, Palmer O. and Neyman J. Tests of certain linear hypotheses and their application to some educational problems. *Statistical Research Memoirs,* 1936, **1**, 57–93.

§ Jackson, *op. cit.*

The problem of chief concern here is clearly a problem of estimation, since only rarely would the reliability of a test be so low that its difference from zero would be a major issue, although this could be tested by the use of the variance ratio $|(n-1)S_2 - S_0|/S_0$. (See equations (9) and (17) for definitions of these quantities).

Assume that the score, X_{is}, of the s-th student on the i-th item of the test may be represented as the sum of four independent factors or components (i.e., the vector X_{is} is resolved into four mutually perpendicular components). These four components may be described as follows:

(1) a component common to all individuals and to all items;
(2) a component associated with the item;
(3) a component associated with the individual;
(4) an error component that is independent of (1), (2), and (3) but includes a multitude of small variations produced by a multitude of causes which, though each by itself is relatively unimportant and unpredictable, taken together may be thought of as being distributed normally with variance σ^2, the precise value of which is unknown.

This may be expressed in mathematical form by assuming that

$$X_{is} = A + t_i + p_s + y_{is},$$

where $i = 1, 2, \cdots, n$ and $s = 1, 2, \cdots, k$, represents the score of the s-th individual on the i-th item of the test. Here A is the component common to all individuals irrespective of the particular item under consideration; it will be shown to be a constant for all students and all items. In the foregoing expression for X_{is}, t_i is the component associated with the item and p_s is the component associated with the student. (It will be seen later that $(A + t_i)$ is the quantity often called the difficulty of the item.) If a student were an "average student" his "true score" on the i-th item would be $(A + t_i)$; however, if he were above "average" his "true score" would be higher than $(A + t_i)$, such as $(A + t_i + p_s)$. (If he were below "average" p_s would be negative.)

We must further assume that the error component, y_{is}, of the i-th item is normally distributed with the same variance, σ^2, as is the error component of every other item, and that y_{is} is independent of y_{js} where $i \neq j$.

Then, since

$$y_{is} = (X_{is} - A - t_i - p_s) \tag{1}$$

is distributed normally with standard deviation, σ,

$$\sum_{i=1}^{n} \sum_{s=1}^{k} y^2_{is} = \sum_{i=1}^{n} \sum_{s=1}^{k} (X_{is} - A - t_i - p_s)^2$$

is distributed as χ^2.

Hence

$$\chi^2 = \sum_{i=1}^{n} \sum_{s=1}^{k} (X_{is} - A - t_i - p_s)^2 \tag{2}$$

The reliability coefficient of a test is the ratio of the variance of the "true scores" to the variance of the obtained scores, or in other words, gives the percentage of the obtained variance that may be spoken of as "true" variance or not due to the unreliability of the test. If we let $\sigma^2{}_t$ represent the variance of the obtained scores and $\sigma_d{}^2$ the discrepancy between the variance of the obtained scores and the variance of the "true" scores, the reliability coefficient is given by the ratio: $r_{tt} = (\sigma^2{}_t - \sigma^2{}_d)/\sigma^2{}_t$. The variance of the error term, y_{is}, or $\sigma^2{}_d$, is the expression of which we wish to obtain the best estimate. According to Markoff's theorem,* the best linear estimate of y_{is} can be obtained, in the situation where the σ's of the independent observations are all equal, by minimizing the sum of squares (2) with respect to A, t_i, and p_s as independent variables and substituting these values, A°, $t_i{}^\circ$, and $p_s{}^\circ$, in (1) to give y_{is}', the best linear estimate of the discrepancy between the obtained score and the "true" score.

A first necessary condition for minimizing (2) is that the partial derivatives with respect to A, t_i and p_s must vanish.

$$\frac{\partial \chi^2}{\partial A} = -\ 2 \sum_{i=1}^{n} \sum_{s=1}^{k} (X_{is} - A - t_i - p_s)\ ; \tag{3}$$

$$\frac{\partial \chi^2}{\partial t_i} = -\ 2 \sum_{s=1}^{k} (X_{is} - A - t_i - p_s) \quad \text{for each } i = 1, 2, \cdots, n\ ; \tag{4}$$

$$\frac{\partial \chi^2}{\partial p_s} = -\ 2 \sum_{i=1}^{n} (X_{is} - A - t_i - p_s) \quad \text{for each } s = 1, 2, \cdots, k\ . \tag{5}$$

Setting each of these partial derivatives equal to zero and solving simultaneously gives the values for A, t_i, and p_s which minimize χ^2. These values of A, t_i, and p_s which render χ^2 a minimum will be designated by A^0, $t_i{}^0$, and $p_s{}^0$.

$$A^0 = \frac{1}{nk} \sum_{i=1}^{n} \sum_{s=1}^{k} X_{is} - \frac{1}{n} \sum_{i=1}^{n} t_i{}^0 - \frac{1}{k} \sum_{s=1}^{k} p_s{}^0\ ; \tag{6}$$

$$t_i{}^0 = \frac{1}{k} \sum_{s=1}^{k} (X_{is} - p_s{}^0) - A^0 \quad (i = 1, 2, \cdots, n)\ ; \tag{7}$$

$$p_s{}^0 = \frac{1}{n} \sum_{i=1}^{n} (X_{is} - t_i{}^0) - A^0 \quad (s = 1, 2, \cdots, k) \tag{8}$$

---

* Neyman, J. The Markoff method and Markoff theorem on least squares. *Journal of the Royal Statistical Society*, 1934, **97**, 593–594.

Substituting these values of A^0, t_i^0, and p_s^0 in (2) gives the minimum value of χ^2 which is designated by S_0.

$$S_0 = \sum_{i=1}^{n} \sum_{s=1}^{k} (X_{is} - A^0 - t_i^0 - p_s^0)^2$$

$$= \sum_{i=1}^{n} \sum_{s=1}^{k} (X_{is} - \bar{x}_{i.} - \bar{x}_{.s} + \bar{x})^2 , \quad (9)$$

where

$$\bar{x}_{i.} = \frac{1}{k} \sum_{s=1}^{k} X_{is} \; ; \bar{x}_{.s} = \frac{1}{n} \sum_{i=1}^{n} X_{is} \; ; \; \bar{x} = \frac{1}{nk} \sum_{i=1}^{n} \sum_{s=1}^{k} X_{is} \, . \quad (10)$$

Substituting these values of A^0, t_i^0, and p_s^0 in (1) gives the best linear estimate of y_{is} (i.e., the error component of the response of the s-th student to the i-th item).

Thus

$$y'_{is} = X_{is} - \bar{x}_{i.} - \bar{x}_{.s} + \bar{x} \, , \quad (11)$$

Since $\sum_{i=1}^{n} \sum_{s=1}^{k} y'_{is} = 0$, $S_0 = \sum_{i=1}^{n} \sum_{s=1}^{k} (y'_{is} - \bar{y})^2$, so that S_0 is f times the variance of the y'_{is}, the error component, where f is the number of degrees of freedom or the number of independent variates necessary to express the sum, S_0. It is clear that $f = (n-1)\ (k-1)$ if we consider the nk X_{is}'s arranged in n rows and k columns, so there are $(n-1)$ independent variates in each of the $(k-1)$ columns. Hence the best estimate of the variance of the error component is

$$\frac{S_0}{(n-1)\ (k-1)} . \quad (12)$$

In order to determine the best estimate of σ^2_s, the variance of the component p_s associated with the student, assume p_s to be normally distributed with variance σ^2_s. Since p_s is independent of y_{is},

$\sum_{i=1}^{n} \sum_{s=1}^{k} (y_{is} + p_s)^2$ is distributed as χ^2.

Then

$$\chi^2 = \sum_{i=1}^{n} \sum_{s=1}^{k} (X_{is} - A - t_i)^2; \quad (13)$$

$$\frac{\partial \chi^2}{\partial A} = -2 \sum_{i=1}^{n} \sum_{s=1}^{k} (X_{is} - A - t_i) \; ; \quad (14)$$

$$\frac{\partial \chi^2}{\partial t_i} = -2 \sum_{s=1}^{k} (X_{is} - A - t_i) \quad (i = 1, 2, \cdots, n.) \quad (15)$$

Setting each of these partial derivatives equal to zero and solving simultaneously gives the values of A' and t'_i which, when substituted in (13), will give $\sum_{i=1}^{n} \sum_{s=1}^{k} (y_{is} + p_s)^2$ its minimum value which is designated here as S_1.

Then

$$S_1 = \sum_{i=1}^{n} \sum_{s=1}^{k} (X_{is} - \bar{x}_{i.})^2. \tag{16}$$

This sum of squares gives the basis for estimating the variance σ_s^2, since $(S_1 - S_0)$ is the "among students" sum of squares.

Let

$$S_2 = S_1 - S_0 . \tag{17}$$

Then $\frac{S_2}{k-1}$ is the obtained variance "among students." The obtained variance "among students" is not the best estimate of the true variance in case the hypothesis of homogeneity of the sample has been refuted as will usually be the case in test item responses. Instead, according to the work of Irwin,* the best estimate of the variance "among students" is obtained by subtracting the estimate of the error variance $\frac{S_0}{(n-1)(k-1)}$ from the obtained variance "among students."

Thus

$$\frac{S_2}{k-1} - \frac{S_0}{(n-1)(k-1)} \tag{18}$$

is the best estimate of the true variance of the students' responses. Hence the percentage of the obtained variance that is not associated with unreliability of the test is

$$r_{tt} = \frac{\dfrac{S_2}{(k-1)} - \dfrac{S_0}{(k-1)(n-1)}}{\dfrac{S_2}{k-1}} \tag{19}$$

or

$$\frac{(n-1)\,S_2 - S_0}{(n-1)\,S_2}. \tag{20}$$

Formula (19) is the one used for the computation of estimated test reliability in Part I.

---

* Irwin, J. O. Mathematical theorems involved in analysis of variance. *Journal of the Royal Statistical Society,* 1931, **94**, 284–300.

17. Estimation of the Reliability of Ratings

ROBERT L. EBEL*

Hoyt's article has shown how reliability estimates can be obtained from analysis of variance computations. This article illustrates the application of this approach to ratings. While there is no difference in the concept of reliability as applied to ratings or to test scores, there ordinarily is a difference in the data on which the computations must be based. Ratings lend themselves especially well to analysis of variance computations.

In this article, Ebel undertakes to explain the rationale of the formula used, to illustrate its application, and to explain why it gives results that do not agree completely with those from other procedures intended to serve the same purpose. He discusses briefly the conditions under which certain sources of variation in the ratings may or may not be included appropriately in the error variance. He also shows how the analysis of variance data provides for estimates of the precision of the reliability coefficients.

A procedure for estimating the reliability of sets of ratings, test scores, or other measures is described and illustrated. This procedure, based upon analysis of variance, may be applied both in the special case where a complete set of ratings from each of k sources is available for each of n subjects, and in the general case where k_1, k_2, ..., k_n ratings are available for each of the n subjects. It may be used to obtain either a unique estimate or a confidence interval for the reliability of either the component ratings or their averages. The relations of this procedure to others intended to serve the same purpose are considered algebraically and illustrated numerically.

THE PROBLEM

The process of estimating test reliability by correlating two sets of scores is well known. The two sets of scores are usually obtained from two equivalent forms, split halves, or two administrations of the test. But when one is dealing with measures other than test scores, such as performance ratings, it frequently happens that more than two parallel sets are available. For example, in one study which concerned us recently, nineteen English instructors graded each of five themes. We desired a measure of their agreement with each other, both before they

Ebel, R. L. Estimation of the reliability of ratings. *Psychometrika,* 1951, *16*, 407–424. Reprinted with the permission of the publisher and author.

* The writer wishes to acknowledge the helpful comments and suggestions of Professors E. E. Cureton, Harold Gulliksen, and E. F. Lindquist.

had received special training in theme rating and again after that training. A complete table of ratings was available in this study, since each instructor rated each of the themes.

In other similar studies, however, the available sets of ratings are sometimes incomplete. An example of this is provided by a study in which eight physics professors rated the research potentialities of twenty-two graduate students. We wished to measure the agreement among the raters in order to establish the reliability of the average ratings as a criterion for validating a selection test. Each professor was asked to rate only those students whose work he knew well. Hence the table of ratings in this study was incomplete.

Problems similar to those just mentioned arise frequently in educational and psychological research. Several formulas have been proposed to deal with them, but there has been no general agreement on a best method. Peters and Van Voorhis (8) present a formula for average intercorrelation (No. 118) which is appropriate in certain situations. While this formula is derived on the basis of a complete table of ratings, further derivation leads to another formula (No. 119) which may be used where ratings are incomplete. Clark (1) has reported a study in which such a formula was applied to data which did not provide a complete table of ratings.

Fisher's work on intraclass correlation (3) has led to a formula based upon the analysis of variance. This formula is presented in convenient form by Snedecor (9). It is applicable to either complete or incomplete sets of ratings. Horst (5) developed a generalized formula for the reliability of measures which is also applicable to either complete or incomplete sets of ratings. Horst's formula yields the reliability of *average* ratings. However, the Spearman-Brown transformation may be used to obtain the reliability of individual ratings.

At this point a question is likely to arise. Is it better to estimate the reliability of individual ratings or the reliability of average ratings? If decisions are based upon average ratings, it of course follows that the reliability with which one should be concerned is the reliability of those averages. However, if the raters ordinarily work individually, and if multiple scores for the same theme or student are only available in experimental situations, then the reliability of individual ratings is the appropriate measure. Since the reliability of average ratings is determined completely by the reliability of the component ratings, and by the number of components, it is always possible to determine the reliability of individual ratings, or of averages, no matter which value a formula gives initially. Formulas using both approaches will be presented in the following section.

A somewhat different approach to the problem of rater agreement has been suggested by Gulliksen (4). This approach, based on the Wilks-

Votaw tests for compound symmetry, does not yield a quantitative estimate of the *degree of agreement* between ratings, but provides instead a statistical criterion upon which to base a categorical statement that the raters do or do not agree. If the distributions of scores from different sources are similar enough so that one can not reject at the five per cent level of confidence the hypothesis that the sets of ratings are random samples from the same population, Gulliksen recommends that the sources of ratings be regarded as parallel (or in agreement). If this hypothesis can be rejected at the one per cent level of confidence, he recommends that the sources be regarded as not parallel. Gulliksen's suggestion has another application in the study of rater agreement. If one has *a priori* reason to believe that different "schools of thought" may exist among the raters, it is possible to use the Wilks-Votaw tests to check this hypothesis. One should not, however, test the hypothesis on the same set of data that suggested it.

THE INTRACLASS CORRELATION FORMULA

When the formulas of Peters, Snedecor, and Horst for estimating the reliability of ratings were applied to the same sets of data, they yielded some inconsistent coefficients. An analysis of the sources of these inconsistencies has led to the conclusion that the formula for intraclass correlation is the most convenient and generally useful. The derivation of this formula is outlined here, since it has not been widely used in studies of educational and psychological ratings, and since few textbooks on measurement contain any discussion of it.

Suppose we have a sample of k estimates of a trait in each of a sample of n persons. Each estimate may be considered to consist of a true component and an error. The true component is constant in all k estimates for any one person, but varies from person to person. Let A represent the variance of these true components in the population of persons from which we have sampled.

The error component varies from estimate to estimate for the same person, but this variance is assumed to be substantially the same in all sets of ratings for the various persons. Let B represent the variance of these errors in the population of estimates. The total observed variance of the estimates is thus $A + B$.

The reliability of the estimates is defined as that portion of the observed variance which is true variance, or

$$r = \frac{A}{A+B}. \tag{1}$$

Suppose we have analyzed the variance of the foregoing sample of estimates to obtain a mean square for error (M) and a mean square for persons ($M_{\bar{x}}$). The mean square for error is a direct estimate of B, the variance of the population of errors of estimate, or

$$M = B. \tag{2}$$

The mean square for persons, however, is not a direct estimate of A. Rather, it represents k times the variance of the means of the estimates for each of the n persons. The variance of these n means is not attributable to A alone, but also includes an error component attributable to B. Each mean consists of a true component, drawn from a population with variance A, and an error component, which is the mean of k errors drawn from a population with variance B. Hence the variance of the means is $A + B/k$. The mean square for persons is k times the variance of the means. Hence

$$M_{\bar{x}} = kA + B. \tag{3}$$

Solving equations (2) and (3) for A and B, and substituting these values in formula (1), we obtain the formula given by Snedecor,

$$r_1 = \frac{M_{\bar{x}} - M}{M_{\bar{x}} + (k-1)M}. \tag{4}$$

This is the formula for the reliability of individual ratings. Cureton (2) suggests the following parallel derivation of a formula for the reliability of average ratings.

For the average scores, the variance ratio analogous to (1) is

$$r_k = \frac{A}{A + \bar{B}}, \tag{a}$$

where $\bar{B}$ is the error variance of the person means. The estimate of A is still given by (3) and (2); i.e.,

$$A = \frac{M_{\bar{x}} - M}{k}, \tag{b}$$

and the estimate of $\bar{B}$ is given by the usual formula for the error variance of a mean,

$$\bar{B} = \frac{M}{k}. \tag{c}$$

Substituting from (b) and (c) in (a), we obtain at once,

$$r_k = \frac{M_{\bar{x}} - M}{M_{\bar{x}}}. \tag{d}$$

It is worth noting that formula (d) may also be derived by applying the Spearman-Brown formula to formula (4) given above.

ILLUSTRATIONS

Snedecor's formula is applied to a simple problem involving a complete table of ratings in Table 1. Those not familiar with analysis of variance may refer to Table 4 for the formulas used. In this analysis, three components, attributable to pupils, raters, and error, may be separated. Thus it is possible, if desired, to remove the "between-raters" variance from the error term. This overcomes the chief objection of Peters and Van Voorhis to intraclass correlation coefficients, which is that such coefficients are seriously distorted by differences between raters in general level of rating. In Table 1, the "between-raters" variance is zero, so retention or removal gives the same result.

Whether or not it is desirable to remove "between-raters" variance in estimating the reliability of ratings depends upon the way in which the ratings are ultimately used in grading, classification, or selection. In any case where differences from rater to rater in general level of rating do not lead to corresponding differences in the ultimate grades, classifications, or selections, the "between-raters" variance should be removed

TABLE 1. Analysis of Ratings for Problem 1—Complete Sets

	Rater 1	Rater 2	Sum	Sum^2
Pupil 1	3	1	4	16
Pupil 2	1	3	4	16
Pupil 3	5	4	9	81
Pupil 4	4	5	9	81
Sum	13	13	26	194
Sum^2	169	169	338	

Sum of squared ratings		=	102
Product of sum and mean	$26 \times \frac{26}{8}$	=	84.5
Sum of squares			
For raters	$\frac{338}{4} - 84.5$	=	0.0
For pupils	$\frac{194}{2} - 84.5$	=	12.5
For total	$102 - 84.5$	=	17.5
For error	$17.5 - 12.5 - 0.0$	=	5.0
Mean square			
For pupils	$12.5 \div 3$	=	4.1667
For error	$5.0 \div 3$	=	1.6667
Reliability of ratings	$\frac{4.1667 - 1.6667}{4.1667 + (2-1)\ 1.6667}$	=	.4286
Reliability of average ratings	$\frac{4.1667 - 1.6667}{4.1667}$	=	.6000

from the error term. Specifically, the "between-raters" variance *should be removed* where the final ratings on which decisions are based consist of averages of complete sets of ratings from all observers, or ratings which have been equated from rater to rater such as ranks, Z-scores, etc. Likewise, if comparisons are never made practically, but only experimentally, between ratings of pupils by different raters, the "between-raters" variance should be removed. But if decisions are made in practice by comparing single "raw" scores assigned to different pupils by different raters, or by comparing averages which come from different groups of raters, then the "between-raters" variance should be included as part of the error terms.

Table 2 illustrates application of this formula to a simple problem in which the table of ratings is incomplete and the sources of ratings are not identified. In this case only two components of the variance, attributable to pupils and error, are separated. Thus any difference in general level of ratings between the various raters is automatically included in the error term.

The application of this reliability formula in Table 2 presents a special problem. The formula requires a value of k, the number of ratings of each person. But in Table 2 this number is not the same for each person. Snedecor (9, p. 234) suggests the following formula for an average k:

$$k_0 = \frac{1}{n-1}\left[\sum k - \frac{\sum k^2}{\sum k}\right]. \qquad (5)$$

TABLE 2. Analysis of Ratings for Problem 5—Incomplete Sets

	Ratings	k	Sum
Pupil 1	8 6 4 4 3	5	25
Pupil 2	6 9 9 4 9 6 5 10 8	9	66
Pupil 3	4 9 10	3	23
	Sums	17	114
Sum of squared ratings			858
Sum of products (pupil sum times pupil mean)			785.3333
Product of sum and mean			764.4706
Sum of squares			
For total	858 — 764.4706	=	93.5294
For pupils	785.3333 — 764.4706	=	20.8627
For error	93.5294 — 20.8627	=	72.6667
Mean square			
For pupils	20.8627 ÷ 2	=	10.4314
For error	72.6667 ÷ 14	=	5.1905
Average value of k			5.1176
Reliability	$\frac{10.4314 - 5.1905}{10.4314 + (4.1176)\,(5.1905)}$	=	.1648

The average k thus obtained is approximately the harmonic mean of the k's for each pupil.

ESTIMATES OF PRECISION

When the reliability of ratings is estimated on the basis of a sample of products or raters or both, a description of the precision of the reliability estimate obtained is useful in judging the adequacy of the sample or the confidence which can be placed in the obtained estimate. The intraclass formula lends itself readily to such a description. The method used here was suggested by Jackson and Ferguson's description of confidence intervals for their sensitivity coefficient (6).

The first step in obtaining this estimate is to express the variance between products, and the error variance as a single ratio, here designated by F_s. In equation form

$$F_s = \frac{M_{\bar{x}}}{M}. \tag{6}$$

Using this ratio it is possible to transform the intraclass formula as follows:

$$r = \frac{F_s - 1}{(F_s - 1) + k}. \tag{7}$$

Now if the sample values of $M_{\bar{x}}$ and M are considered as having been drawn from separate populations, it is obvious that the ratio (F_p) for the populations might be either greater or less than the ratio observed in the sample. How much greater or less one should believe it to be, at any selected level of confidence, can be read from a Table for F, given the degrees of freedom for the sample values of $M_{\bar{x}}$ and M. To obtain an estimate for the upper limit of the variance ratio between two populations, one must multiply the variance ratio observed in the samples (F_s) by the maximum ratio expected if the populations had been equal in variance. This value (F_t) may be read in the table, given the number of degrees of freedom in the samples, and the level of confidence desired. In entering the table for F it is important to remember that at the upper limit $M_{\bar{x}}$ is the larger variance, so that the degrees of freedom for $M_{\bar{x}}$ should be located on the marginal headings for the larger variance. Similarly, to obtain the lower limit of (F_p) one must multiply the sample value by the reciprocal of the value given in the table. Remember that at the lower limit, M is the larger variance, so that in this case the degrees of freedom for M should be located on the marginal headings for the larger variance. Substituting these two limiting values for the population variance ratio in formula 6 yields upper and lower limits of the confidence interval for the estimate of reliability obtained from a particular sample.

The application of this procedure to several sample problems is illustrated in Table 3. The data for problems 1 and 3 are taken from Table 5, and the data for problem 5 are taken from Table 2. Because of the smallness of the samples involved, the confidence limits for these reliability coefficients are very wide indeed. Reliability estimates based upon such small samples are little better than blind guesses.

TABLE 3. Confidence Limits (5%) for Reliability Coefficients From Sample Data

Problem	1	3	5
Unique Estimate	.4286	.3429	.1648
k	2.	2.	5.1176
F_s	2.500	2.0435	2.0096
F_t (upper 5% limit)	9.28	9.28	3.74
(lower 5% limit)	9.28	9.28	19.42
F_p (upper 5% limit)	23.125	18.964	7.5159
(lower 5% limit)	.2694	.2202	.1035
r (upper 5% limit)	.92	.90	.56
(lower 5% limit)	−.58	−.64	−.21

RELATIONSHIPS AMONG THE FORMULAS

The fact that various formulas have been presented for estimating the reliability of ratings, and that these formulas do not always yield consistent results when applied to the same set of data was mentioned in the first section of this paper. It is therefore appropriate to consider the relationships among them first analytically and then, by way of illustration, empirically. Consider first the relation between the Pearson product-moment formula and the formula for average intercorrelation given by Peters and Van Voorhis. As usually presented these formulas are

(1) Product moment:

$$r = \frac{\Sigma xy}{N \sigma_x \sigma_y}. \qquad (8)$$

(2) Average intercorrelation:

$$r = \frac{(\sigma_s^2/\sigma_i^2) - a}{a^2 - a}. \qquad (9)$$

We note that the quantity $\frac{\Sigma xy}{N}$ is the covariance of the scores for each *product* from two *observers*. The symbol ζ will be used to represent this covariance.

It is easy to show (8, p. 196) that the variance of the sums of scores from k observers is

$$\sigma_s^2 = k\sigma_i^2 + (k^2 - k)\zeta_{ij} \,. \tag{10}$$

If this value is substituted for σ_s^2 in formula (9) the result is

$$r = \frac{\zeta_{ij}}{\sigma_i^2} \,. \tag{11}$$

Since the product-moment formula may be written

$$r = \frac{\zeta}{\sqrt{\sigma_x^2 \, \sigma_y^2}} \,, \tag{12}$$

it is clear that when $k = 2$, (the only case in which the product-moment formula is applicable) and when the table of ratings is complete (which must be true for either formula to apply) the numerators are identical. But since σ_i^2, which represents the variance of scores from either observer, is estimated by taking the *arithmetic mean* of the variances of scores from each observer, σ_i^2 will not equal the geometric mean of these variances, $\sqrt{\sigma_x^2 \, \sigma_y^2}$ except in the special case where $\sigma_x^2 = \sigma_y^2$. Hence, differences in coefficients obtained from these two formulas are attributable to the difference in methods of calculating the average variance within observers.

It is interesting to note in passing that ζ provides a direct estimate of A, the variance of the population of true scores. Recalling the definitions of A and B given earlier in this paper, one may see that

$$\sigma_s^2 = k^2 A + k B \tag{13}$$

and

$$\sigma_i^2 = A + B \,. \tag{14}$$

Substituting these in (9) and simplifying leads to the expression

$$A = \zeta \,. \tag{15}$$

Consider next the relation between the formulas for average intercorrelation (9) and intraclass correlation (4). The notation used in this and the following comparison is presented in Table 4. Since

$$\sigma_s^2 = \frac{\Sigma P^2}{n} - \left(\frac{T}{n}\right)^2$$

or

$$n \, \sigma_s^2 = \Sigma P^2 - \frac{T^2}{n} \,,$$

and since

$$S_p = \frac{\Sigma P^2}{k} - \frac{T^2}{nk}$$

or

$$k \, S_p = \Sigma P^2 - \frac{T^2}{n} \,,$$

TABLE 4. Notation for Analysis of Ratings
(Complete Arrays)

A. Data

n products	k observers					Sums
	0_1	0_2	0_3 . . .	0_j . . .	0_k	
P_1	x_{11}	x_{12}	x_{13} . . .	x_{1j} . . .	x_{1k}	P_1
P_2	x_{21}	x_{22}	x_{23} . . .	x_{2j} . . .	x_{2k}	P_2
P_3	x_{31}	x_{32}	x_{33} . . .	x_{3j} . . .	x_{3k}	P_3
.	.	.	.	.	.	.
.	.	.	.	.	.	.
.	.	.	.	.	.	.
.	.	.	.	.	.	.
P_i	x_{i1}	x_{i2}	x_{i3} . . .	x_{ij} . . .	x_{ik}	P_i
.	.	.	.	.	.	.
.	.	.	.	.	.	.
.	.	.	.	.	.	.
.	.	.	.	.	.	.
P_n	x_{n1}	x_{n2}	x_{n3} . . .	x_{nj} . . .	x_{nk}	P_n
Sums	0_1	0_2	0_3 . . .	0_j . . .	0_k	T

B. Analysis of Variance

Source	Degrees of Freedom	Sums of Squares	Mean Square
Products	$n-1$	$S_p = \frac{\Sigma P^2}{k} - \frac{T^2}{nk}$	$M_p = \frac{S_p}{n-1}$
Observers	$k-1$	$S_o = \frac{\Sigma 0^2}{n} - \frac{T^2}{nk}$	$M_o = \frac{S_o}{k-1}$
Error	$(n-1)(k-1)$	$S_e = S_t - S_p - S_o$	$M_e = \frac{S_e}{(n-1)(k-1)}$
Total	$nk-1$	$S_t = \Sigma x^2 - \frac{T^2}{nk}$	

it follows that

$$\sigma_s{}^2 = \frac{k\,S_p}{n}. \tag{16}$$

Further, since

$$\sigma_i^2 = \frac{\Sigma\,\Sigma\,x^2}{nk} - \frac{\Sigma\,0^2}{n^2k}$$

or

$$n\,k\,\sigma_i^2 = \Sigma\,\Sigma\,x^2 - \frac{\Sigma\,0^2}{n},$$

and since

$$S_e + S_p = S_t - S_o = \Sigma \Sigma x^2 - \frac{\Sigma 0^2}{n},$$

then

$$\sigma_i^2 = \frac{S_e + S_p}{nk}. \tag{17}$$

Substituting the foregoing values of σ_s^2 and σ_i^2 in formula (9) gives, upon simplification,

$$r = \frac{S_p - \frac{S_e}{k-1}}{S_p + S_e}. \tag{18}$$

But

$$S_p = (n-1)M_p$$

and

$$S_e = (n-1)\ (k-1)M_e\,.$$

Substituting these values in formula (18) and simplifying gives

$$r = \frac{M_p - M_e}{M_p + (k-1)M_e} = \frac{M_{\bar{x}} - M}{M_{\bar{x}} + (k-1)\ M}.$$

In terms of these derivations, the average intercorrelation appears identical with the intraclass correlation formula. This will be true, however, only if the "between-raters" variance is not included as part of the error variance in either formula, or if it *is* included in both. As was previously pointed out, some situations require inclusion of the "between-raters" variance and others do not. The user of the intraclass formula finds it convenient to choose either procedure. The user of the average intercorrelation formula may also exercise an option in this matter. He may include the "between-raters" variance by calculating the average "within-raters" variance (σ_i^2) about the general mean for all raters. Or, he may exclude it by calculating that variance about the mean for each rater separately, as was indicated in the foregoing derivation.

It is also worth noting that the formulas give identical coefficients in spite of the fact that the average intercorrelation formula uses sample statistics whereas the intraclass formula uses estimates of population parameters. Since the reliability coefficient is basically a ratio of true and observed variances, application of the sample correction to both variances of the ratio does not change its value.

Consider finally the relation between the intraclass correlation formula and generalized formula for the reliability of averages. The latter, as given by Horst, is

$$r_{\text{av}} = 1 - \frac{\frac{\Sigma \frac{\sigma_i^2}{n_i - 1}}{N}}{\sigma_M^2}. \tag{19}$$

In the case where a complete table of ratings is available so that $n_1 = n_2 = n_3 = \cdots\cdots = n_i = k$, the formula may be written (substituting n for Horst's N)

$$r_{\text{av}} = 1 - \frac{\sum \sigma_i^2}{n(k-1)\sigma_M^2}. \tag{20}$$

The formula relating the reliability of an average of k equally weighted scores to the reliability of the scores themselves is

$$r_{\text{av}} = \frac{kr}{1 + (k-1)r}. \tag{21}$$

If the right hand members of equations (20) and (21) are equated and the equation solved for r, we obtain

$$r = \frac{\sigma_M^2 - \dfrac{\sum \sigma_i^2}{n(k-1)}}{\sigma_M^2 + \dfrac{\sum \sigma_i^2}{n}}. \tag{22}$$

Now since

$$\sigma_M^2 = \frac{\sum \left(\dfrac{P}{k}\right)^2}{n} - \left(\frac{T}{nk}\right)^2$$

or

$$nk^2\, \sigma_M^2 = \sum P^2 - \frac{T^2}{n},$$

and since, as was shown previously,

$$k\, S_p = \sum P^2 - \frac{T^2}{n},$$

then

$$n\, k^2\, \sigma_M^2 = k\, S_p$$

or

$$\sigma_M^2 = \frac{1}{n\,k} S_p.$$

Since, further,

$$\sum \sigma_i^2 = \frac{\sum\sum x^2}{k} - \sum \left(\frac{P}{k}\right)^2$$

or

$$k \sum \sigma_i^2 = \sum\sum x^2 - \sum \frac{P^2}{k},$$

and since

$$S_0 + S_e = S_t - S_p = \sum\sum x^2 - \frac{\sum P^2}{k},$$

then

$$k \sum \sigma_i^2 = S_0 + S_e$$

or

$$\sum \sigma_i^2 = \frac{S_0 + S_e}{k}.$$

Substituting the above values for $\sigma_M{}^2$ and $\sum \sigma_i{}^2$ in formula (22), we find

$$r = \frac{S_p - \dfrac{(S_0 + S_e)}{k-1}}{S_p + (S_0 + S_e)}. \tag{23}$$

Comparing this formula with formula (18) we observe that the sole difference is that the "error term" of formula (23) includes the "between-raters" sum of squares, whereas the formula (18) does not.

Hence, whenever there is a difference between the means of the ratings from various raters, the generalized reliability formula will give a lower value for the reliability of the ratings than is given by the intraclass formula as here calculated. The circumstances of each problem determine whether the "between-raters" variance should be included as part of the error term. As pointed out previously, the user of the intraclass formula may easily include or exclude "between-raters" variance as part of the error term. The user of the generalized reliability formula can not conveniently exclude "between-raters" variance even where it appears desirable to do so. In particular, the generalized reliability formula should not be used in estimating reliability of averages to which each rater has contributed by rating each product. Attention was called earlier to the fact that "between-raters" variance does not belong in the error term in this situation.

In this connection it should be mentioned that "between-raters" variance is always removed in the process of calculating the product-moment formula. Hence, as Gulliksen has pointed out in a private communication, the product-moment formula should not be used in cases where the "between-raters" variance is properly part of the error.

Both the intraclass formula and the generalized reliability formula are applicable to situations where the table of ratings is incomplete, that is, where k varies from product to product. But here again a computational difference appears which results in different reliability coefficients. With the intraclass formula the mean square for error based on two component analysis is

$$Me = \frac{1}{N-n}\left[\ \sum\sum x^2 - \frac{\sum P^2}{k}\right], \tag{24}$$

so that each score contributes equally to the estimate of error variance. With the generalized reliability formula, however, the error variance for each product is figured separately and the separate error variances are then averaged, as indicated by the numerator of the fraction in formula (19). A "within-product" variance based on many scores is given the same weight as one based on few scores. Thus, a score in a small group is weighted more heavily than one in a large group.

A similar difference is observed in calculation of the variance of the means for products. In analysis of variance each product mean is weighted in proportion to the number of scores on which it is based. But in the generalized reliability formula each product mean is given equal weight. Since unweighted averages are seldom the same as weighted averages from the same data, the reliability estimates obtained when in the two formulas are applied to incomplete tables of scores are usually different.

Table 5 presents four sample problems, the data of which illustrate various combinations of equal or unequal means and variances. Below the data are given the reliability coefficients obtained by applying each of the four formulas which have just been discussed. The values obtained confirm the analytical findings.

TABLE 5. Rater Reliability by Various Formulas for Problems Illustrating Various Conditions

Problem	1	2	3	4
Condition				
Means	Equal	Unequal	Equal	Unequal
Variances	Equal	Equal	Unequal	Unequal
Scores (Test 1 and Test 2)				
Pupil 1	3 1	3 3	6.25 2	3 2
Pupil 2	1 3	1 5	4.25 6	1 6
Pupil 3	5 4	5 6	8.25 8	5 8
Pupil 4	4 5	4 7	7.25 10	4 10
Reliability				
Product-Moment	.4286	.4286	.4286	.4286
Intraclass	.4286	.4286	.3429	.3429
Average Intercorrelation	.4286	.4286	.3429	.3429
Generalized Reliability	.4286	−.0196	.3429	−.0944

In Problem 1, with equal means and variances, all four formulas yield identical coefficients of reliability. In Problem 2, where only the means of the two sets of scores differ, the generalized reliability formula gives a much lower coefficient than the other three. This is due to the previously noted fact that systematic differences between the sets of scores are included as part of the error term in the generalized reliability formula, whereas these differences are removed in the other three formulas.

In Problem 3, where only the variances of the two sets of scores differ, all three of the special formulas yield coefficients which disagree with that from the product-moment formula, but which agree perfectly with each other. This is due to the fact that the product-moment formula uses a geometric mean of the variances of the scores from each observer, whereas all of the other formulas are based upon arithmetic means of these variances. In Problem 4, both the means and the variances of the two sets of scores differ, with the result that the intraclass coefficient and the average intercorrelation coefficient are somewhat lower, and the generalized reliability coefficient is very much lower, than the product-moment coefficient.

If the generalized reliability formula is applied to the data of Table 2 it yields a reliability coefficient of —.0582 compared with .1648 given by the intraclass formula. Here the discrepancy occurs because the generalized reliability formula uses a simple mean of the error variances within each person, and a simple variance of the person means, whereas the analysis of variance formula uses a weighted mean and a weighted variance.

The formula used by Clark was

$$r = \frac{(a\,\sigma_{av}^2/\sigma_i^2) - 1}{a - 1}. \quad (25)$$

The σ_{av}^2 is the variance of the averages for each product, and the σ_i^2 is, in this case, the total variance of all ratings. When this formula is applied to the data of Table 2 it yields a reliability coefficient of .2060 instead of the .1648 given by the intraclass formula. Here the discrepancy is partly due to the use in Clark's formula of a simple variance of the pupil means, and partly due to the estimation of the variance of the population of ratings from three sets of related ratings, which are treated as if they constituted a single random sample of the population of all ratings. Fisher (3, 225) has called attention to the error introduced by the second of these procedures. These two differences in procedure no doubt cause much more apparent error in the small illustrative sample presented in Table 2 than they did in the more extensive data upon which Clark based his report. However the possibility of such errors when formula (25) is applied to incomplete sets of ratings should be recognized.

CONCLUSIONS

In view of the foregoing findings, there are three reasons for preferring the intraclass formula to the average intercorrelation or generalized reliability formulas. First, the intraclass formula permits the investigator to choose whether to include or exclude "between-raters" variance as part of the error variance, in terms of the circumstances of the particular problem. Second, a convenient means for estimating the precision of the reliability coefficients is available to the user of the intraclass formula. Third, the intraclass formula uses the familiar statistics and routine computational procedures of analysis of variance.

In the case of incomplete sets of ratings, the intraclass formula also has advantages over the generalized reliability formula and the variant of the average intercorrelation formula which Clark used in this situation. First, in determining the variances used in the intraclass formula, each observation is weighted equally, whereas in both the other formulas it is groups of unequal numbers of observations that are weighted equally. Second, Clark's formula involves a biased estimate of the population variance. Third, the advantages of the analysis of variance approach in estimating the precision of the reliability coefficient, and in computation, also apply in the case of unequal sets of ratings.

REFERENCES

1. Clark, Edward L. Reliability of college grades. Unpublished paper presented to American Psychological Association in September, 1950.
2. Cureton, Edward E. Reliability of a set of averages of unequal numbers of scores. Unpublished paper read at the March, 1951, meeting of the Southern Society for Philosophy and Psychology.
3. Fisher, R. A. Statistical methods for research workers. (10th Ed.) Edinburgh: Oliver and Boyd, 1946.
4. Gulliksen, Harold. Theory of mental tests. New York: John Wiley and Sons, 1950.
5. Horst, Paul. A generalized expression for the reliability of measures. *Psychometrika,* 1949, **14**, 21–31.
6. Jackson, R. W. B., and Ferguson, George A. Studies on the reliability of tests. Toronto: Univ. of Toronto Press, 1941.
7. Lindquist, E. F. Statistical analysis in educational research. Boston: Houghton Mifflin Company, 1940.
8. Peters, Charles C., and Van Voorhis, Walter R. Statistical procedures and their mathematical bases. New York: McGraw Hill Book Company, 1940.
9. Snedecor, George W. Statistical methods. (4th Ed.) Ames, Iowa: Iowa State Coll. Press, 1946.

INTRODUCTION

18. Cronbach, Lee J., *Coefficient Alpha and the Internal Structure of Tests*
19. Cureton, Edward E., *The Definition and Estimation of Test Reliability*

The following two articles treat reliability theory extensively. While the authors disagree concerning some aspects, careful study of their respective points of view will be rewarding. Two parts of Cronbach's article deserve particular attention. Guilford (p. 143) is quoted, then criticized: Cronbach disagrees with the second and third lines of the quotation, not with the first line. The issue is whether a test with low internal consistency is necessarily a poor test.* Recall Humphreys' point that one should not always try to maximize test reliability since it is a function of homogeneity as well as item reliability. Coombs (1950) also discusses the relationship between reliability and homogeneity.

In Part IV, 5, Cronbach defends the use of the *phi* coefficient against Loevinger's (1947) criticism. Loevinger (1954) refutes this defense in her article on the attenuation paradox—the one Humphreys was responding to in Unit 1. A study of both of Loevinger's articles, as well as Humphreys', concurrently with Cronbach's would be valuable.

Cureton pays particular attention to the assumptions required in the derivation of various reliability formulas. In Part II he discusses investigation of the stringency of equal reliability and variance assumptions of the Spearman-Brown formula. Results suggest that debate concerning which assumptions the formulas *really* require is of more theoretical than practical importance.

Recent highly theoretical discussions of reliability, such as the article by Cattell in the validity unit (Unit 4), as well as articles by Cronbach *et al.* (1963), LaForge (1965), and Rajaratnam *et al.* (1964) are recommended reading. The articles by Cronbach *et al.* and Rajaratnam *et al.* interpret reliability as the adequacy with which one can generalize to a universe of observations. The LaForge article suggests a multiple-factor analysis approach to reliability rather than the analysis of variance approach.

18. Coefficient Alpha and the Internal Structure of Tests

LEE J. CRONBACH**

A general formula (α) of which a special case is the Kuder-Richardson coefficient of equivalence is shown to be the mean of all split-half coefficients resulting from different splittings of a test. α is therefore an estimate of the correlation between two random sam-

Cronbach, L. J. Coefficient alpha and the internal structure of tests. *Psychometrika,* 1951, *16,* 297–334. Reprinted with the permission of the publisher and author.

* See, for example, the review of Fricke's OAIS test by Crites and Fricke's response to the review, 1965.

** The assistance of Dora Damrin and Willard Warrington is gratefully acknowledged. Miss Damrin took major responsibility for the empirical studies reported. This research was supported by the Bureau of Research and Service, College of Education, University of Illinois.

ples of items from a universe of items like those in the test. α is found to be an appropriate index of equivalence and, except for very short tests, of the first-factor concentration in the test. Tests divisible into distinct subtests should be so divided before using the formula. The index $\bar{r}_{ij}$, derived from α, is shown to be an index of inter-item homogeneity. Comparison is made to the Guttman and Loevinger approaches. Parallel split coefficients are shown to be unnecessary for tests of common types. In designing tests, maximum interpretability of scores is obtained by increasing the first-factor concentration in any separately-scored subtest and avoiding substantial group-factor clusters within a subtest. Scalability is not a requisite.

I. HISTORICAL RESUMÉ

Any research based on measurement must be concerned with the accuracy or dependability or, as we usually call it, reliability of measurement. A reliability coefficient demonstrates whether the test designer was correct in expecting a certain collection of items to yield interpretable statements about individual differences (25).

Even those investigators who regard reliability as a pale shadow of the more vital matter of validity cannot avoid considering the reliability of their measures. No validity coefficient and no factor analysis can be interpreted without some appropriate estimate of the magnitude of the error of measurement. The preferred way to find out how accurate one's measures are is to make two independent measurements and compare them. In practice, psychologists and educators have often not had the opportunity to recapture their subjects for a second test. Clinical tests, or those used for vocational guidance, are generally worked into a crowded schedule, and there is always a desire to give additional tests if any extra time becomes available. Purely scientific investigations fare little better. It is hard enough to schedule twenty tests for a factorial study, let alone scheduling another twenty just to determine reliability.

This difficulty was first circumvented by the invention of the split-half approach, whereby the test is rescored, half the items at a time, to get two estimates. The Spearman-Brown formula is then applied to get a coefficient similar to the correlation between two forms. The split-half Spearman-Brown procedure has been a standard method of test analysis for forty years. Alternative formulas have been developed, some of which have advantages over the original. In the course of our development, we shall review those formulas and show relations between them.

The conventional split-half approach has been repeatedly criticized. One line of criticism has been that split-half coefficients do not give the same information as the correlation between two forms given at different times. This difficulty is purely semantic (9, 14); the two coefficients are measures of different qualities and should not be identified by the same unqualified appellation "reliability." A retest after an interval, using the identical test, indicates how stable scores are and therefore can be called a coefficient of *stability*. The correlation between two forms given virtually at the same time, is a coefficient of *equivalence*, showing how nearly two measures of the same general trait agree. Then the coefficient using comparable forms with an interval between testings is a coefficient of equivalence and stability. This paper will concentrate on coefficients of equivalence.

The split-half approach was criticized, first by Brownell (3), later by Kuder and Richardson (26), because of its lack of uniqueness. Instead of giving a single coefficient for the test, the procedure gives different coefficients depending on which items are grouped when the test is split in two parts. If one split may give a higher coefficient than another, one can have little faith in whatever result is obtained from a single split. This criticism is with equal justice applicable to any equivalent-forms coefficient. Such a coefficient is a property of a pair of tests, not a single test. Where four forms of a test have been prepared and intercorrelated, six values are obtained, and no one of these is *the* unique coefficient for Form A; rather, each is the coefficient showing the equivalence of one form to another specific form.

Kuder and Richardson derive a series of coefficients using data from a single trial, each of them being an approximation to the interform coefficient of equivalence. Of the several formulas, one has been justifiably preferred by test workers. In this paper we shall be especially concerned with this, their formula (20):

$$r_{tt(KR20)} = \frac{n}{n-1}\left(1 - \frac{\sum_i p_i q_i}{\sigma_t^2}\right); \quad (i = 1, 2, \ldots n). \tag{1}$$

Here, i represents an item, p_i the proportion receiving a score of 1, and q_i the proportion receiving a score of zero on the item.

We can write the more general formula

$$\alpha = \frac{n}{n-1}\left(1 - \frac{\sum_i V_i}{V_t}\right). \tag{2}$$

Here V_t is the variance of test scores, and V_i is the variance of item scores after weighting. This formula reduces to (1) when all items are scored 1 or zero. The variants reported by Dressel (10) for certain weighted scorings, such as Rights-minus-Wrongs, are also special cases of (2), but for most data computation directly from (2) is simpler than by Dressel's method. Hoyt's derivation (20) arrives at a formula identical to (2), although he draws attention to its application only to the case where items are scored 1 or 0. Following the pattern of any of the other published derivations of (1) (19, 22), making the same assumptions but imposing no limit on the scoring pattern, will permit one to derive (2).

Since each writer offering a derivation used his own set of assumptions, and in some cases criticized those used by his predecessors, the precise meaning of the formula became obscured. The original derivation unquestionably made much more stringent assumptions than necessary, which made it seem as if the formula could properly be applied only to rare tests which happened to fit these conditions. It has generally been stated that α gives a lower bound to "the true reliability"—whatever that means to that particular writer. In this paper, we take formula (2) as given, and make no assumptions regarding it. Instead, we proceed in the opposite direction, examining the properties of α and thereby arriving at an interpretation.

We introduce the symbol α partly as a convenience. "Kuder-Richardson Formula 20" is an awkward handle for a tool that we expect to become increasingly prominent in the test literature. A second reason for the symbol is that α is one of a set of six analogous coefficients (to be designated β, γ, δ, etc.) which deal with such other concepts as like-mindedness of persons, stability of scores, etc. Since we are concentrating in this paper on equivalence, the first of the six properties, description of the five analogous coefficients is reserved for later publication.

Critical comments on the Kuder-Richardson formula have been primarily directed to the fact that when inequalities are used in deriving a lower bound, there is no way of knowing whether a particular coefficient is a close estimate of the desired measure of equivalence or a gross underestimate. The Kuder-Richardson method is an overall measure of internal consistency, but a test which is not internally homogeneous may nonetheless have a high correlation with a carefully-planned equivalent form. In fact, items within each test may correlate zero, and yet the two tests may correlate perfectly if there is item-to-item correspondence of content.

The essential problem set in this paper is: How shall α be interpreted? α, we find, is the average of all the possible split-half coefficients for a given test. Juxtaposed with further analysis of the variation of split-half coefficients from split to split, and with an examination of the relation of α to item homogeneity, this relation leads to recommendations for estimating coefficients of equivalence and homogeneity.

II. A COMPARISON OF SPLIT-HALF FORMULAS

The problem set by those who have worked out formulas for split-half coefficients is to predict the correlation between two equivalent whole tests, when data on two half-tests are at hand. This requires them to define equivalent tests in mathematical terms.

The first definition is that introduced by Brown (2) and by Spearman (33), namely, that we seek to predict correlation with a test whose halves are c and d, possessing data from a test whose halves are a and b, and that

$$V_a = V_b = V_c = V_d; \quad \text{and}$$
$$r_{ab} = r_{ac} = r_{ad} = r_{bc} = r_{bd} = r_{cd}. \qquad (3)$$

This assumption or definition is far from general. For many splittings $V_a \neq V_b$, and an equivalent form conforming to this definition is impossible.

A more general specification of equivalence credited to Flanagan [see (25)] is that

$$V_{(a+b)} = V_{(c+d)}; \quad \text{and}$$
$$r_{ab}\sigma_a\sigma_b = r_{ad}\sigma_a\sigma_d = r_{bc}\sigma_b\sigma_c = r_{cd}\sigma_c\sigma_d = \cdots. \qquad (4)$$

This assumption leads to various formulas which are collected in the first column of Table 1. All formulas in Column A are mathematically identical and interchangeable.

TABLE 1. Formulas for Split-Half Coefficients

Entering Data*	Formulas Assuming Equal Covariances Between Half-Tests	Formulas Assuming $\sigma_a = \sigma_b$
$r_{ab}\ \sigma_a\ \sigma_b$	1A† $\dfrac{4\sigma_a\sigma_b r_{ab}}{\sigma_a^2 + \sigma_b^2 + 2\sigma_a\sigma_b r_{ab}}$	1B‡ $\dfrac{2r_{ab}}{1 + r_{ab}}$
$\sigma_t\ \sigma_a\ \sigma_b$	2A§ $2\left(1 - \dfrac{\sigma_a^2 + \sigma_b^2}{\sigma_t^2}\right)$	
$\sigma_t\ \sigma_a\ r_{at}$	3A‖ $\dfrac{4(r_{at}\sigma_a\sigma_t - \sigma_a^2)}{\sigma_t^2}$	
$\sigma_t\ \sigma_a$	4A¶ $1 - \dfrac{\sigma_a^2}{\sigma_t^2}$	4B(≡4A) $1 - \dfrac{\sigma_d^2}{\sigma_t^2}$
$\sigma_a\ \sigma_d\ r_{ad}$	5A $\dfrac{4(\sigma_a^2 - \sigma_a\sigma_d r_{ad})}{4\sigma_a^2 + \sigma_d^2 - 4\sigma_a\sigma_d r_{ad}}$	5B $\dfrac{2(2\sigma_a^2 - \sigma_d^2)}{4\sigma_a^2 - \sigma_d^2}$

*In this table, a and b are the half-test scores, $t = a + b$, $d = a - b$.
†After Flanagan (25)
‡Spearman-Brown (2, 33)
§Guttman (19)
‖After Mosier (28)
¶Rulon (31)

When a particular split is such that $\sigma_a = \sigma_b$, the Flanagan requirement reduces to the original Spearman-Brown assumption, and in that case we arrive at the formulas in Column B. Formulas 1B and 5B are not identical, since the assumption enters the formulas in different ways. No short formula is provided opposite 2A or 3A, since these exact formulas are themselves quite simple to compute.

Because of the wide usage of Formula 1B, the Spearman-Brown, it is of interest to determine how much difference it makes which assumption is employed. If we divide 1B by any of the formulas in Column A we obtain the ratio

$$k_1 = \frac{2mr + m^2 + 1}{2m(1 + r)}, \tag{5}$$

in which $m = \sigma_b/\sigma_a$, $\sigma_a < \sigma_b$, and r signifies r_{ab}. The ratio when 5B is divided by any of the formulas in the first column is as follows:

$$k_5 = \frac{(2mr - m^2 + 1)\ (1 + 2mr + m^2)}{2mr(2mr - m^2 + 3)}. \tag{6}$$

When m equals 1, that is, when the two standard deviations are equal, the formula in Column B is identical to that in Column A. As Table 2 shows, there is increasing disagreement between Formula 1B and those in Column A as m departs from unity. The estimate by the Spearman-Brown formula is always slightly larger than the coefficient of equivalence computed by the more tenable definition of comparability.

TABLE 2. Ratio of Spearman-Brown Estimate to More Exact Split-Half Estimate of Coefficient of Equivalence when S.D.'s are Unequal

Ratio of Half-Test S.D.'s (greater/lesser)	Correlation Between Half-Tests					
	.00	.20	.40	.60	.80	1.00
1	1	1	1	1	1	1
1.1	1.005	1.004	1.003	1.003	1.003	1.002
1.2	1.017	1.014	1.012	1.010	1.009	1.008
1.3	1.035	1.029	1.025	1.022	1.020	1.017
1.4	1.057	1.048	1.041	1.036	1.032	1.029
1.5	1.083	1.069	1.060	1.052	1.046	1.042

Formula 5B is not so close an approximation to the results from formulas in Column A. When m is 1.1., for example, the values of k_5 are as follows: for $r = .20$, .62; for $r = .60$, .70; for $r = 1.00$, .999.

It is recommended that the interchangeable formulas 2A and 4A be used in obtaining split-half coefficients. These formulas involve no assumptions contradictory to the data. They are therefore preferable to the Spearman-Brown formula. However, if the ratio of the standard deviations of the half-tests is between .9 and 1.1, the Spearman-Brown formula gives essentially the same result. This finding agrees with Kelley's earlier analysis of much the same question (2, 3).

III. α AS THE MEAN OF SPLIT-HALF COEFFICIENTS

To demonstrate the relation between α and the split-half formulas, we shall need the following notation:

Let n be the number of items.

The test t is divided into two half-tests, a and b. i' will designate any item of half-test a, and i'' will designate any item of half-test b. Each half-test contains n' items, where $n' = n/2$.

V_t, V_a, and V_b are the variances of the total test and the respective half-tests.

C_{ij} is the covariance of two items i and j.

C_a is the total covariance for all items in pairs within half-test a, each pair counted once; C_b is the corresponding "within-test" covariance for b.

C_t is the total covariance of all item pairs within the test.

C_{ab} is the total covariance of all item pairs such that one item is within a and the other is within b; it is the "between halves" covariance.

Then

$$C_{ab} = r_{ab}\sigma_a\sigma_b\,; \tag{7}$$

$$C_t = C_a + C_b + C_{ab}\,; \tag{8}$$

$$V_t = V_a + V_b + 2C_{ab} = \sum_i V_i + 2C_t;\ \text{and} \tag{9}$$

$$V_a = \sum_{i'} V_{i'} + 2C_a \ \text{and}\ V_b = \sum_{i''} V_{i''} + 2C_b. \tag{10}$$

These identities are readily visible in the sketches of Figure 1, which is based on the matrix of item covariances and variances. Each point along the diagonal represents a variance. The sum of all entries in the square is the test variance.

Rewriting split-half formula 2A, we have

$$r_{tt} = 2\left(1 - \frac{V_a + V_b}{V_t}\right) = 2\,\frac{V_t - V_a - V_b}{V_t}. \tag{11}$$

$$r_{tt} = \frac{4C_{ab}}{V_t}. \tag{12}$$

This indicates that whether a particular split gives a high or low coefficient depends on whether the high interitem covariances are placed in the "between halves" covariance or whether the items having high correlations are placed instead within the same half.

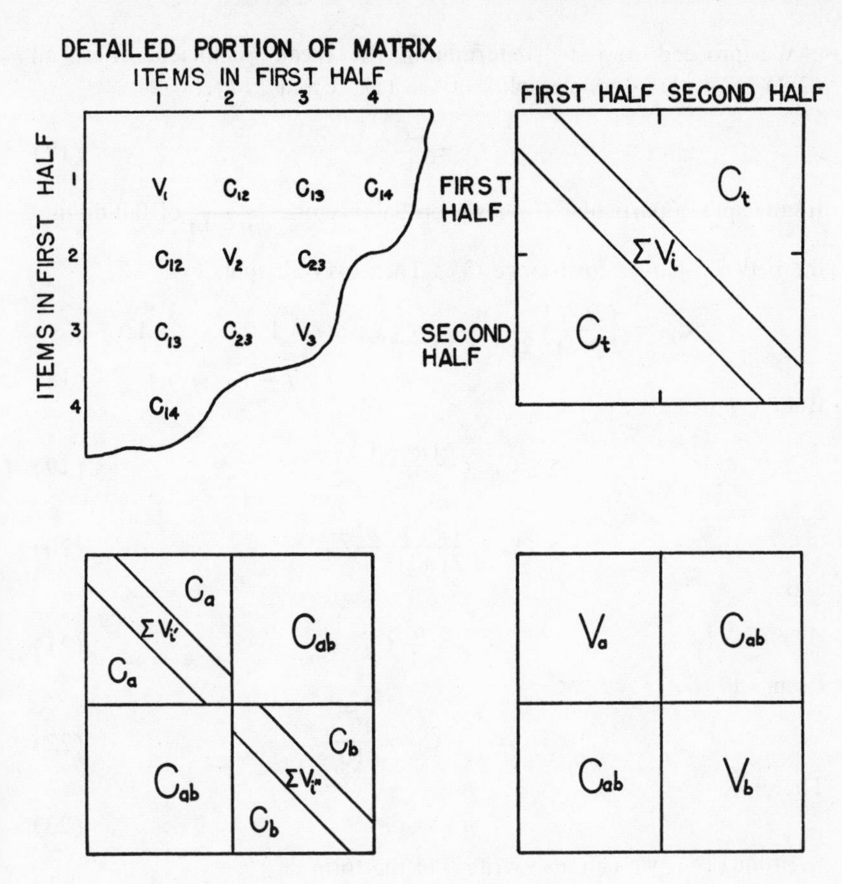

FIGURE 1. Schematic Division of the Matrix of Item Variances and Covariances.

Now we rewrite α:

$$\alpha = \frac{n}{n-1}\left(1 - \frac{\sum_i V_i}{V_t}\right) = \frac{n}{n-1}\left(\frac{V_t - \sum_i V_i}{V_t}\right). \tag{13}$$

$$\alpha = \frac{n}{n-1} \cdot \frac{2C_t}{V_t}. \tag{14}$$

$$\overline{C}_{ij} = \frac{C_t}{n(n-1)/2}. \tag{15}$$

Therefore

$$\alpha = \frac{n^2 \, \overline{C}_{ij}}{V_t}. \tag{16}$$

We proceed now by determining the mean coefficient from all $(2n')!/2(n'!)^2$ possible splits of the test. From (12),

$$\bar{r}_{tt} = \frac{4\,\bar{C}_{ab}}{V_t}. \quad (17)$$

In any split, a particular C_{ij} has a probability of $\frac{n}{2(n-1)}$ of falling into the between-halves covariance C_{ab}. Then over all splits,

$$\Sigma\, C_{ab} = \frac{(2n')!}{2(n'!)^2}\,\frac{n}{2(n-1)}\sum_i\sum_j C_{ij}\,;\ (i = 1, 2, \cdots n{-}1;\ j = i+1, \cdots, n). \quad (18)$$

But

$$\sum_i\sum_j C_{ij} = \frac{n(n-1)}{2}\,\bar{C}_{ij}. \quad (19)$$

$$\Sigma\, C_{ab} = \frac{(2n')!}{2(n'!)^2}\,\frac{n^2}{4}\,\bar{C}_{ij}, \quad (20)$$

and

$$\bar{C}_{ab} = \frac{n^2}{4}\,\bar{C}_{ij} \quad (21)$$

From (17),

$$\bar{r}_{tt} = \frac{4n^2}{4V_t}\,\bar{C}_{ij} = \frac{n^2\bar{C}_{ij}}{V_t}. \quad (22)$$

Therefore

$$\bar{r}_{tt} = \alpha\,. \quad (23)$$

From (14), we can also write α in the form

$$\alpha = \frac{n}{n-1}\,\frac{\sum_i\sum_j C_{ij}}{V_t};\ (i, j = 1, 2, \cdots n;\ i \neq j). \quad (24)$$

This important relation states a clear meaning for α as $n/(n-1)$ times the *ratio of interitem covariance to total variance*. The multiplier $n/(n-1)$ allows for the proportion of variance in any item which is due to the same elements as the covariance.

α As a Special Case of the Split-Half Coefficient

Not only is α a function of all the split-half coefficients for a test; it can also be shown to be a special case of the split-half coefficient.

If we assume that the test is divided into equivalent halves such that $\bar{C}_{i'i''}$ (i.e., C_{ab}/n'^2) equals $\bar{C}_{ij}$, the assumptions for formula 2A still hold. We may designate the split-half coefficient for this splitting as r_{tt_0}.

$$r_{tt} = \frac{4\,C_{ab}}{V_t}. \quad (12)$$

Then

$$r_{tt_0} = \frac{4n'^2 \overline{C}_{i'i''}}{V_t} = \frac{4n'^2 \overline{C}_{ij}}{V_t} = \frac{n^2 \overline{C}_{ij}}{V_t}. \quad (25)$$

From (16),

$$r_{tt_0} = \alpha \quad (26)$$

This amounts to a proof that α is an exact determination of the parallel-form correlation when we can assume that the mean covariance between parallel items equals the mean covariance between unpaired items. This is the least restrictive assumption usable in "proving" the Kuder-Richardson formula.

α As the Equivalence of Random Samples of Items

The foregoing demonstrations show that α measures essentially the same thing as the split-half coefficient. If all the splits for a test were made, the mean of the coefficients obtained would be α. When we make only one split, and make that split at random, we obtain a value somewhere in the distribution of which α is the mean. If split-half coefficients are distributed more or less symmetrically, an obtained split-half coefficient will be higher than α about as often as it is lower than α. This average that is α is based on the very best splits and also on some very poor splits where the items going into the two halves are quite unlike each other.

Suppose we have a universe of items for which the mean covariance is the same as the mean covariance within the given test. Then suppose two tests are made by twice sampling n items at random from this universe without replacement, and administered at the same sitting. Their correlation would be a coefficient of equivalence. The mean of such coefficients would be the same as the computed α. α is therefore an estimate of the correlation expected between two tests drawn at random from a pool of items like the items in this test. Items are not selected at random for psychological tests where any differentiation among the items' contents or difficulties permits a planned selection. Two planned samplings may be expected to have higher correlations than two random samplings, as Kelley pointed out (25). We shall show that this difference is usually small.

IV. AN EXAMINATION OF PREVIOUS INTERPRETATIONS AND CRITICISMS OF α

1. *Is α a Conservative Estimate of Reliability?*

The findings just presented call into question the frequently repeated statement that α is a conservative estimate or an underestimate or a lower bound to "the reliability coefficient." The source of this conception is the original derivation, where Kuder and Richardson set up a definition of two equivalent tests, expressed their correlation algebraically, and proceeded to show by inequalities that α was lower than this correlation. Kuder and Richardson assumed that corresponding items in test and parallel test have the same common content and the same specific content, i.e., that they are as alike as two trials of the same item would be. In other words, they took the zero-interval retest correlation as their standard. Guttman also began his derivation by defining equivalent tests as identical. Coombs (6) offers the somewhat more satisfactory name "coefficient of precision" for this index which reports the absolute minimum error to be found if the same instrument is applied twice independently to the same subject. A coefficient of stability can be obtained by making the two observations with any desired interval between. A rigorous definition of the coefficient of precision, then, is that it is the limit of the coefficient of stability, as the time between testings becomes infinitesimal.

Obviously, any coefficient of equivalence is less than the coefficient of precision, for one is based on a comparison of different items, the other on two trials of the same items. To put it another way: α or any other coefficient of equivalence treats the specific content of an item as error, but the coefficient of precision treats it as part of the thing being measured. It is very doubtful if testers have any practical need for a coefficient of precision. There is no practical testing problem where the items in the test and only these items constitute the trait under examination. We may be unable to compose more items because of our limited skill as testmakers but any group of items in a test of intelligence or knowledge or emotionality is regarded as a sample of items. If there weren't "plenty more where these came from," performance on the test would not represent performance on any more significant variable.

We therefore turn to the question, does α underestimate appropriate coefficients of equivalence? Following Kelley's argument, the way to make equivalent tests is to make them as similar as possible, similar in distribution of item difficulty and in item content. A pair of tests so designed that corresponding items measure the same factors, even if each one also contains some specific variance, will have a higher correlation than a pair of tests drawn at random from the pool of items. A planned split, where items in opposite halves are as similar as the test permits, may logically be expected to have a higher between-halves covariance than within-halves covariance, and in that case, the obtained coefficient would be larger than α. α is the same type of coefficient as the split-half coefficient, and while it may be lower, it may also be higher than the value obtained by actually splitting a particular test at random. Both the random or odd-even split-half coefficient and α will theoretically be lower than the coefficient from parallel forms or parallel splits.

2. *Is α Less Than the Coefficient of Stability?*

Some writers expect α to be lower than the coefficient of stability. Thus Guttman says (34, p. 311):

> For the case of scale scores, then, . . . we have the assurance that if the items are approximately scalable [in which case α will be high], then they necessarily have very substantial test-retest reliability.

Guilford says (16, p. 485):

> There can be very low internal consistency and yet substantial or high retest reliability. It is probably not true, however, that there can be high internal consistency and at the same time low retest reliability, except after very long time intervals. If the two indices of reliability disagree for a test, we can place some confidence in the inference that the test is heterogeneous.

The comment by Guttman is based on sound thinking, provided we reinterpret test-retest coefficient on the basis of the context of the comment to refer to the instantaneous retest (i.e., coefficient of precision) rather than the retest after elapsed time. Guilford's statement is acceptable only if viewed as a summary of his experience. There is no mathematical necessity for his remarks to be true. In the coefficient of stability, variance in total score between trials (within persons) is regarded as a source of error, and variance in specific factors (between items within persons) within trials is regarded as true variance. In the coefficient of equivalence, such as α, this is just reversed: variance in specific factors is treated as error. Variation between trials is non-existent and does not reduce true variance (9). Whether the coefficient of stability is higher or lower than the coefficient of equivalence depends on the relative magnitude of these variances, both of which are likely to be small for long tests of stable variables. Tests are also used for unstable variables such as mood, morale, social interaction, and daily work output, and studies of this sort are becoming increasingly prominent. Suppose one builds a homogeneous scale to obtain students' evaluations of each day's classwork, the students marking the checklist at the end of each class hour. Homogeneous items could be found for this. Yet the scale would have marked instability from day to day, if class activities varied or the topics discussed had different interest value for different students.

The only proper conclusion is that α may be either higher or lower than the coefficient of stability over an interval of time.

3. *Are Coefficients from Parallel Splits Appreciably Higher than Random-Split Coefficients or α?*

The logical presumption is strong that planned splits as proposed by

Kelley (25) and Cronbach (7) would yield coefficients nearer to the equivalent-tests coefficient than random splits do. There is still the empirical question whether this advantage is large enough to be considered seriously. This raises two questions: Is there appreciable variation in coefficients from split to split? If so, does the judgment made in splitting the test into *a priori* equivalent halves raise the coefficient? Brownell (3), Cronbach (8), and Clark (5) have compared coefficients obtained by splitting a test in many ways. There is doubt that the variation among coefficients is ordinarily a serious matter; Clark in particular found that variation from split to split was small compared to variation arising from sampling of subjects.

Empirical evidence. To obtain further data on this question, two analyses were made. One employs responses of 250 ninth-grade boys who took Mechanical Reasoning Test Form A of the Differential Abilities Tests. The second study uses a ten-item morale scale, adapted from the Rundquist-Sletto General Morale Scale by Donald M. Sharpe and administered by him to teachers and school administrators.*

The Mechanical Reasoning Test seems to contain items requiring specific knowledges regarding pulleys, gears, etc. Other items seem to be answerable on the basis of general experience or reasoning. The items seemed to represent sufficiently heterogeneous content that grouping into parallel splits would be possible. We found, however, that items grouped on *a priori* grounds had no higher correlations than items believed to be unlike in content. This finding is confirmed by Air Force psychologists who made a similar attempt to categorize items from a mechanical reasoning test and found that they could not. These items, they note, "are typically complex factorially" (15, p. 309).

Eight items which some students omitted were dropped. An item analysis was made for 50 papers. Using this information, ten parallel splits were made such that items in opposite halves had comparable difficulty. These we call Type I splits. Then eight more splits were made, placing items in opposite halves on the basis of both difficulty and apparent content (Type II splits). Fifteen random splits were made. For all splits, Formula 2A was applied, using the 200 remaining cases. Results appear in Table 3.

There are only 126 possible splits for the morale test, and it is possible to compute all half-test standard deviations directly from the item variances and covariances. Of the 126 splits, six were designated in advance as Type II parallel splits, on the basis of content and an item analysis of a supplementary sample of papers. Results based on 200 cases appear in Table 4.

---

* Thanks are expressed to Dr. A. G. Wesman and the Psychological Corporation, and to Dr. Sharpe, for making available the data for the two studies, respectively.

TABLE 3. Summary of Data from Repeated Splittings of Mechanical Reasoning Test (60 items; $\alpha = .811$)

	All Splits			Splits Where $1.05 > \sigma_b/\sigma_a > .95$		
Type of Split	No. of Coefficients	Range	Mean	No. of Coefficients	Range	Mean
Random	15	.779-.860	.810	8	.795-.860	.817
Parallel Type I	10	.798-.846	.820	6	.798-.846	.822
Parallel Type II	8	.801-.833	.817	4	.809-.826	.818

TABLE 4. Summary of Data from Repeated Splittings of Morale Scale (10 items; $\alpha = .715$)

	All Splits			Splits Where $1.1 > \sigma_b/\sigma_a > .9$		
Type of Split	No. of Coefficients	Range	Mean	No. of Coefficients	Range	Mean
All Splits	126	.609-.797	.715	82	.609-.797	.717
Parallel (Type II)	6	.681-.780	.737	5	.712-.780	.748

The highest and lowest coefficients for the mechanical test differ by only .08, a difference which would be important only when a very precise estimate of reliability is needed. The range for the morale scale is greater (.20), but the probability of obtaining one of the extreme values in sampling is slight. Our findings agree with Clark, that the variation from split to split is less than the variation expected from sample to sample for the same split. The standard error of a Spearman-Brown coefficient based on 200 cases using the same split is .03 when $r_{tt} = .8$, .04 when $r_{tt} = .7$. The former value compares with a standard deviation of .02 for all random-split coefficients of the mechanical test. The standard error of .04 compares with a standard deviation of .035 for the 126 coefficients of the morale test.

This bears on Kelley's comment on proposals to obtain a unique estimate: "A determinate answer would result if the mean for all possible splits were gotten, but, even neglecting the labor involved, this would seem to contravene the judgment of comparability." (25, p. 79). As our tables show, the splittings where half-test standard deviations are unequal, which "contravene the judgment of comparability," have coefficients about like those which have equal standard deviations.

Combining our findings with those of Clark and Cronbach we have studies of seven tests which seem to show that the variation from split to split is too small to be of practical importance. Brownell finds appreciable variation, however, for the four tests he studied. The apparent contradiction is explained by the fact that the former results applied to tests having fairly large coefficients of equivalence (.70 or over). Brownell worked with tests whose coefficients were much lower, and the larger range of r's does not represent any greater variation in z values at this lower level.

In Tables 3 and 4, the values obtained from deliberately equated half-tests differ slightly, but only slightly, from those for random splits. Where α is .715 for the morale scale, the mean of parallel splits is .748—a difference of no practical importance. One parallel split reaches .780, but this split could not have been defended *a priori* as more logical than the other planned splits. In Table 3, we find that neither Type I nor Type II splits averaged more than .01 higher than α. Here, then, is evidence that the sort of judgment a tester might make on typical items, knowing their content and difficulty, does not, contrary to the earlier opinion of Kelley and Cronbach, permit him to make more comparable half-tests than would be obtained by random splitting. The data from Cronbach's earlier study agree with this. This conclusion seems to apply to tests of any length (the morale scale has only ten items). Where items fall into obviously diverse subgroups in either content or difficulty, as, say, in the California Test of Mental Maturity, the tester's judgment could provide a better-than-random split. It is dubious whether he could improve on a random division *within subtests*.

It should be noted that in this empirical study no attempt was made to divide items on the basis of r_{it}, as Gulliksen (18, p. 207-210) has recently suggested. Provided this is done on a large sample of cases other than those used to estimate r_{tt}, Gulliksen's plan might indeed give parallel-split coefficients which are consistently at least a few points higher than α.

The failure of the data to support our expectation led to a further study of the problem. We discovered that even tests which seem to be heterogeneous are often highly saturated with the first factor among the items. This forces us not only to extend the interpretation of α, but also to reexamine certain theories of test design.

Factorial composition of the test variance. To make fully clear the relations involved, our analytic procedure will be spelled out in detail. We postulate that the variance of any item can be divided among $k + 1$ orthogonal factors (k common with other items and one unique). Of these, we shall refer to the first, f_1, as the general factor, even though it is possible that some items would have a zero loading on this factor.*

* This factor may be a so-called primary or reference factor like Verbal, but it is more likely to be a composite of several such elements which contribute to every item.

Then if f_{zi} is the loading of common factor z on item i,

$$1.00 = N^2(f^2{}_{1i} + f^2{}_{2i} + f^2{}_{3i} + \cdots + f^2{}_{Ui}). \tag{27}$$

$$C_{ij} = N^2\, \sigma_i\, \sigma_j (f_{1i}\, f_{1j} + f_{2i}\, f_{2j} + \cdots + f_{ki}\, f_{kj}). \tag{28}$$

$$C_t = \Sigma\Sigma C_{ij} = N^2 \sum_i \sum_j \sigma_i\, \sigma_j\, f_{1i}\, f_{1j} + \cdots + N^2 \sum_i \sum_j \sigma_i\, \sigma_j\, f_{ki}\, f_{kj}\,;$$

$$(i = 1, 2, \cdots n-1; j = i+1, \cdots, n). \tag{29}$$

$$V_t = N^2 \sum_i \sigma^2{}_i\, (f^2{}_{1i} + \cdots f^2{}_{ki} + f^2{}_{Ui}\ ) + 2N^2 \sum_i \sum_j \sigma_i\, \sigma_j\, f_{1i}\, f_{1j}$$

$$+ \cdots + 2N^2 \sum_i \sum_j \sigma_i\, \sigma_j\, f_{ki}\, f_{kj}\,. \tag{30}$$

If n_1 items contain non-zero loadings on factor 1, and n_2 items contain factor 2, etc., then V_t consists of

$n_1{}^2$ terms of the form $N^2\sigma_i\, \sigma_j\, f_{1i}\, f_{1j}$, plus
$n_2{}^2$ terms of the form $N_2\sigma_i\, \sigma_j\, f_{2i}\, f_{2j}$, plus (31)
$n_3{}^2$ terms of the form $N^2\sigma_i\, \sigma_j\, f_{3i}\, f_{3j}$, plus and so on to
n_{k2} terms of the form $N^2\sigma_i\, \sigma_j\, f_{ki}\, f_{kj}$, plus
n terms of the form $N^2\sigma_i{}^2\, f_{U_i}^2$.

We rarely know the values of the factor loadings for an actual test, but we can substitute values representing different kinds of test structure in (30) and observe the proportionate influence of each factor in the total test.

First we shall examine a test made up of a general factor and five group factors, in effect a test which might be arranged into five correlated subtests. $k = 6$. Let $n_1 = n$, so f_1 is truly general, and let $n_2 = n_3 = n_4 = n_5 = n_6 = 1/5\, n$. To keep the illustration simple, we shall assume that all items have equal variances and that any factor has the same loading (f_z) in all items where it appears. Then

$$\frac{1}{N^2\sigma_i{}^2} V_t = n^2\, f_1{}^2 + \frac{n^2}{25} f_2{}^2 + \frac{n^2}{25} f_3{}^2 + \cdots + \frac{n^2}{25} f_6{}^2 + \sum_i f_{U_i}^2\,. \tag{32}$$

It follows that in this particular example, there are n^2 general factor terms, $n^2/5$ group factor terms, and only n unique factor terms. There are, in all, $6n^2/5 + n$ terms in the variance. Let $f^2{}_{zt}$ be the proportion of test variance due to each factor. Then if we assume that all the terms making up the variance are of the same approximate magnitude,

$$f^2{}_{1t} = \frac{5n^2}{6n^2 + 5n} = \frac{5n}{6n+5}\,. \tag{33}$$

$$\lim_{n\to\infty} f^2{}_{it} = \frac{5}{6} = .83\,. \tag{34}$$

$$f^2{}_{2t} = \cdots = f^2{}_{6t} = \frac{n^2/5}{6n^2 + 5n}\,. \tag{35}$$

$$\lim_{n\to\infty} f^2{}_{2t} = .03. \tag{36}$$

$$\Sigma f^2{}_{U_i t} = \frac{5}{6n+5}. \tag{37}$$

$$\lim_{n\to\infty} \sum_i f^2{}_{U_i t} = 0. \tag{38}$$

Note that among the terms making up the variance of any test, the number of terms representing the general factor is n times the number representing item specific and error factors.

We have seen that the general factor cumulates a very large influence in the test. This is made even clearer by Figure 2, where we plot the trend in variance for a particular case of the above test structure. Here we set $k = 6$, $n_1 = n$, $n_2 = n_3 = n_4 = n_5 = n_6 = n/5$. Then we assume that each item has the composition: 9% general factor, 9% from some one group factor, 82% unique. Further, the unique variance is divided by 70/12 between error and specific stable variance. It is seen that even with unreliable items such as these, which intercorrelate only .09 or .18, the general factor quickly becomes the predominant portion of the variance. In the limit, as n becomes indefinitely large,

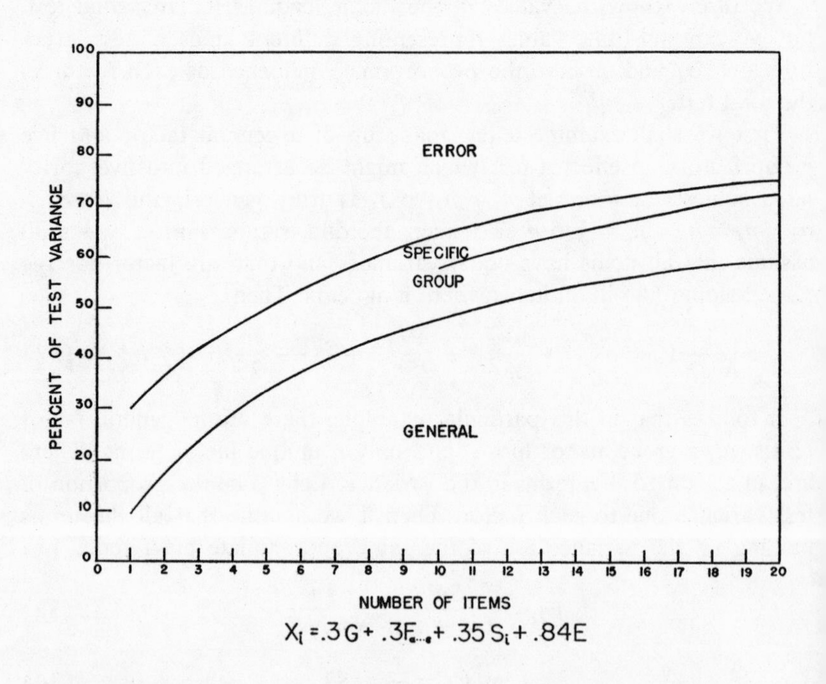

FIGURE 2. Change in Proportion of Test Variance due to General, Group, and Unique Factors among the Items as n Increases.

the general factor is 5/6 of the variance, and each group factor is 1/30 of the total variance.

This relation has such important consequences that we work out two more illustrative substitutions in Table 5. We first consider the test which is very heterogeneous in one sense, in that each group of five items introduces a different group factor. No factor save factor 1 is found in more than 5 items. Here great weight in each item is given to the group factor, yet even so, the general factor quickly cumulates in the covariance terms and outweighs the group factors.

The other illustration involves a case where the general factor is much less important in the items than two group factors, each present in half the items. In this type of test, the general factor takes on some weight through cumulation, but the group factors do not fade into insignificance as before. We can generalize that when the proportion of items containing each common factor remains constant as a test is lengthened (factor loadings being constant also), the ratio of the variances contributed by any two common factors remains constant. That is, in such a test pattern each item accounts for a nearly constant fraction of the non-unique variance.

While our description has discussed number of terms, and has simplified by holding constant both item variances and factor loadings, the same general trends hold if these conditions are not imposed. The mathematical notation required is intricate, and we have not attempted a formal derivation of these general principles:

If the magnitude of item intercorrelations is the same, on the average, in successive groups of items as a test is lengthened,

(a) Specific factors and unreliability of responses on single items, account for a rapidly decreasing proportion of the variance if the added items represent the same factors as the original items. Roughly, the contribution is inversely proportional to test length.

(b) The ratio in which the remaining variance is divided among the general factor and group factors
   (i) is constant if these factors are represented in the added items to the same extent as in the original items;*
   (ii) increases, if the group factors present in the original items have less weight in the added items.

As a test is lengthened, the general factor accounts for a larger and larger proportion of the total variance. In the case where only a few group factors are present no matter how many items are added, these also account for an increasing and perhaps substantial portion of the

* This is the case discussed in the recent paper of Guilford and Michael (17). Our conclusion is identical to theirs.

TABLE 5. Factor Composition of Tests Having Certain Item Characteristics as a Function of Test Length

Pattern	Factors	Per Cent of Variance in Any Item	Number of Items Containing Factor	Percent of Total Test Variance (assuming equal item variances)				
				$n=1$	$n=5$	$n=25$	$n=100$	$n\to\infty$
One general factor, new group factors in each set of 5 items:	f_1	9	n	9	13	44	76	100
$\frac{n}{5}+1 \leqq k \leqq \frac{n+4}{5}+1$	f_2	50	1 to 5	50	74	10	1	0
	.	.	0 to 5			.	.	.
	.	.	"			.	.	.
	.	.	"			.	.	.
	f_k	50 (if present)	"			10	1	0
	$\Sigma f_2 \ldots f_k$			50	74	48	21	0
	f_{v_i}	41	1					
	Σf_{v_i}		n	41	12	8	3	0
				$n=1$	$n=6$	$n=26$	$n=100$	$n\to\infty$
One general factor, two group factors each in half the items	f_1	9	n	9	22	25	26	26
	f_2	50 or 0	$n/2$	50	31	35	36	37
	f_3	0 or 50	$n/2$	0	31	35	36	37
	f_{v_i}	41	1					
	Σf_{v_i}		n	41	17	4	1	0

variance. But when each factor other than the first is present in only a few items, the general factor accounts for the lion's share of the variance as the test reaches normal length. We shall return to the implications of this for test design and for homogeneity theory.

Next, however, we apply this to coefficients of equivalence. We may study the composition of half-tests just as we have studied the total test. And we may also examine the composition of C_{ab}, the between-halves covariance. In Table 6, we consider first the test where there is a general factor and two group factors. If the test is divided into halves such that every item is factorially identical to its opposite number, save for the unique factor in each, the covariance C_{ab} nonetheless depends primarily upon the general-factor terms. Note, for example, the twenty-item test. Two-thirds of the covariance terms are the result of item similarity in the general factor. Suppose that these general factor terms are about equal in size. Then, should the test be split differently, the covariance would be reduced to the extent that more than half the items loaded with (say) factor 2 fall in the same half, but even the most drastic possible departure from the parallel split would reduce the covariance by only one-third of its terms. In the event that the group-factor loadings in the items are larger than the general-factor loadings, the size of the covariance is reduced by more than one-third. It is in this case that the parallel split has special advantage: where a few group factors are present and have loadings in the items larger than the general factor does.

The nature of the split has even less importance for the pattern where each factor is found in but a few items. Suppose, for example, that we are dealing with the 60-item test containing 15 factors in four items each. Then suppose that it is so very "badly" split that items containing 5 of the factors were assigned only to one of the half-tests, and items containing the second 5 factors were assigned to the other half-test. This would knock out 40 terms from the between-halves covariance, but such a shift would reduce the covariance only by 40/960 of its terms. Only in the exceptional conditions where general factor loadings are miniscule or where they vary substantially would different splits of such a test produce marked differences in the covariance.

It follows from this analysis that marked variation in the coefficients obtained when a test is split in several ways can result only when

(a) a few group factors have substantial loadings in a large fraction of the items or

(b) when first-factor loadings in the items tend to be very small or where they vary considerably. Even these conditions are likely to produce substantial variations only when the variance of a test is contributed to by only a few items.

TABLE 6. Composition of the Between-Halves Covariance for Tests of Certain Patterns

Pattern	Common Factors	No. of Items Having Non-Zero Loadings in Factor	No. of Terms Representing Each Factor in Between-Halves Covariance (ΣC_{ij}) When an Ideal Split is Made, for Varying Numbers of Items			
			$n = 2$	$n = 8$	$n = 20$	$n = 60$
One general factor, two group factors each in half the items	1	n	1	16	100	900
	2	$n/2$		4	25	225
	3	$n/2$		4	25	225
Total No. of Terms in C_{ab}			1	24	150	1350
Total No. of Terms in V_t			8	104	620	5460
			$n = 2$	$n = 8$	$n = 20$	$n = 60$
One general factor, new group factors in each set of 5 items:	1	n	1	16	100	900
	2	4	1	4	4	4
	3	4		4	4	4
$\frac{n}{5} + 1 \leq k \leq \frac{n+4}{5} + 1$	$4 \cdots k$	4 each			4 each	4 each
Total No. of Terms in C_{ab}			2	24	120	960
Total No. of Terms in V_t			10	104	500	3900

In the experimental tests studied by Clark, by Cronbach, and in the present study, general-factor loadings were probably greater, on the whole, than group-factor loadings. Moreover, none of the tests seems to have been divisible into large blocks of items each representing one group factor. (Such large "lumps" of group factor content are most often found in tests broken into subtests, viz., the Number Series, Analogies, and other portions of the ACE Psychological Examination.)

This establishes on theoretical grounds the fact that for certain common types of test, there is likely to be negligible variation among split-half coefficients. Therefore α*, the mean coefficient, represents such tests as well as any parallel split.*

This interpretation differs from the Wherry-Gaylord conclusion (38) that "the Kuder-Richardson formula tends to underestimate the true reliability by the ratio $(n-K)/(n-1)$ when the number of factors, K, is greater than one." They arrive at this by highly restrictive assumptions: that all factors are present in an equal number of items, that no item contains more than one factor, that there is no general factor, and that all items measuring a factor have equal variances and covariances. This type of test would never be intended to yield a psychologically interpretable score. For psychological tests where the intention is that all items include the same factor, our development shows that the quoted statement does not apply.

The problem of differential weighting has been studied repeatedly, the clearest mathematical analyses being those of Richardson (30) and Burt (4). This problem is closely related to our own study of test composition. Making different splits of a test is essentially the same as weighting the component items differently. The conditions under which split-half coefficients differ considerably are identical to those where differential weighting of components alters a total score appreciably: few components, lack of general factor or variation in its loadings, large concentrations of variance in group factors. The more formal mathematical studies of weighting lead to the same conclusions as our study of special cases of test construction.

4. *How is* α *Related to the Homogeneity, Internal Consistency, or Saturation of a Test?**

During the last ten years, various writers (12, 19, 27) directed attention to a property they refer to as homogeneity, scalability, internal consistency, or the like. The concept has not been sharply defined, save

* Several of the comments made in the following sections, particularly regarding Loevinger's concepts, were developed during the 1949 APA meetings in a paper by Humphreys (21) and in a symposium on homogeneity and reliability. The thinking has been aided by subsequent discussions with Dr. Loevinger.

in the formulas used to evaluate it. The general notion is clear: In a homogeneous test, the items measure the same things.

If a test has substantial internal consistency, it is psychologically interpretable. Two tests, composed of different items of this type, will ordinarily give essentially the same report. If, on the other hand, a test is composed of groups of items, each measuring a different factor, it is uncertain which factor to invoke to explain the meaning of a single score. *For a test to be interpretable, however, it is not essential that all items be factorially similar.* What is required is that a large proportion of the test variance be attributable to the principal factor running through the test (37).

α estimates the proportion of the test variance due to all common factors among the items. That is, it reports how much the test score depends upon general and group, rather than item specific, factors. If we assume that the mean variance in each item attributable to common factors $(\overline{\sum_z \sigma_i^2 f_{zi}^2})$ equals the mean interitem covariance $\overline{\sum_z (\sigma_i \sigma_j f_{zi} f_{zj})}$,

$$\frac{1}{n} \sum_z \sum_i \sigma_i^2 f_{zi}^2 = \frac{2}{n(n-1)} \sum_i \sum_j C_{ij} = \frac{2}{n(n-1)} C_t . \tag{39}$$

$$\sum_z \sum_i \sigma_i^2 f_{zi}^2 = \frac{2}{n-1} C_t , \tag{40}$$

and the total variance (item variance plus covariance) due to common factors is $2 \frac{n}{n-1} C_t$. Therefore, from (14), α is the proportion of test variance due to common factors. Our assumption does not hold true when the interitem correlation matrix has rank higher than one. Normally, therefore, α underestimates the common-factor variance, but not seriously unless the test contains distinct clusters.

The proportion of the test variance due to the first factor among the items is the essential determiner of the interpretability of the scores. α is an upper bound for this. For those test patterns described in the last section, where the first factor accounts for the preponderance of the common-factor variance, α is a close estimate of first-factor concentration.

α applied to batteries of tests or subtests. Instead of regarding α as an index of *item* consistency, we may apply it to questions of *subtest* consistency. If each subtest is regarded as an "item" composing the test, formula (2) becomes

$$\alpha = \frac{n}{n-1} \left(1 - \frac{\sum V_{\text{subtests}}}{V_{\text{test}}}\right). \tag{41}$$

Here n is the number of subtests. If this formula is applied to a test or battery composed of separate subtests, it yields useful information about the interpretability of the composite. Under the assumption that the variance due to common factors within each subtest is on the average equal to the mean covariance between subtests, α indicates what proportion of the variance of the composite is due to common factors among the subtests. In many instruments the subtests are positively correlated and intended to measure a general factor. If the matrix of intercorrelations is approximately hierarchical, so that group factors among subtests are small in influence, α is a measure of first-factor concentration in the composite.

Sometimes the variance of the test is not immediately known, but correlations between subtests are known. In this case one can compute covariances ($C_{ab} = \sigma_a \sigma_b r_{ab}$), or the variance of the composite (V_t is the sum of the subtest variances and covariances), and apply formula (41). But if subtest variances are not at hand, an inference can be made directly from correlations. If all subtests are assigned weights such that their variances are equal, i.e., they make equal contributions to the total,

$$\alpha = \frac{n}{n-1}\left(\frac{2\sum_i\sum_j r_{ij}}{n + 2\sum_i\sum_j r_{ij}}\right); \ (i = 1, 2, \cdots n-1; j = i+1, \cdots n). \tag{42}$$

Here i and j are subtests, of which there are n. This formula tells what part of the total variance is due to the first factor among the subtests, when the weighted subtest variances are equal.

A few applications will suggest the usefulness of this analysis. The California Test of Mental Maturity, Primary, has two part scores, Language and Non-Language. For a group of 725, according to the test authors, these scores correlate .668. Then, by (42), α, the common-factor concentration, is .80. Turning to the Primary Mental Abilities Tests, we have a set of moderate positive correlations reported when these were given to a group of eighth-graders (35). The question may be asked: How much would a composite score on these tests reflect common elements rather than a hodgepodge of elements each specific to one subtest? The intercorrelations suggest that there is one general factor among the tests. Computing α on the assumption of equal subtest variances, we get .77. The total score is loaded to this extent with a general intellective factor. Our third illustration relates to four Air Force scores related to carefulness. Each score is the count of number *wrong* on a plotting test. The four scores have rather small intercorrelations (15, p. 687), and each score has such low reliability that its use alone as a measure of carefulness is not advisable. The question therefore arises whether the tests are enough intercorrelated that the general factor would cumulate in a preponderant way in their total. The sum of the six intercorrelations is 1.76. Therefore α is .62. I.e., 62% of the variance in the equally weighted composite is due to the common factor among the tests.

From this approach comes a suggestion for obtaining a superior coefficient of equivalence for the "lumpy" test. It was shown that a test containing distinct clusters of items might have a parallel-split coefficient appreciably higher than α. If so, we should divide the test into subtests, each containing what appears to be a homogeneous group of items. α is computed for each subtest separately by (2). Then $\sigma_i^2\alpha$ gives the covariance of each cluster with the opposite cluster in a parallel form, and the covariance between subtests is an estimate of the covariance of similar pairs "between forms." Hence

$$r_{t_1 t_2} = \frac{\sum_i \sum_j \sigma_i \sigma_j r_{ij}}{V_t}; \; (i = 1, 2, \cdots n; \; j = 1, 2, \cdots n), \tag{43}$$

where α_i is entered for r_{ii}, i and j being subtests. To the extent that α_i is higher than the mean correlation between subtests, the parallel-forms coefficient will be higher than α_t computed from (2).

The relationships developed are summarized in Figure 3. α falls somewhere between the proportion of variance due to the first factor and the proportion due to all common factors. The blocks representing "other common factors" and "item specifics" are small, for tests not containing clusters of items with distinctive content.

An index unrelated to test length. Conceptually, it seems as if the "homogeneity" or "internal consistency" of a test should be independent of its length. A gallon of homogenized milk is no more homogeneous than a quart. α increases as the test is lengthened, and so to some extent do the Loevinger-Ferguson homogeneity indices. We propose

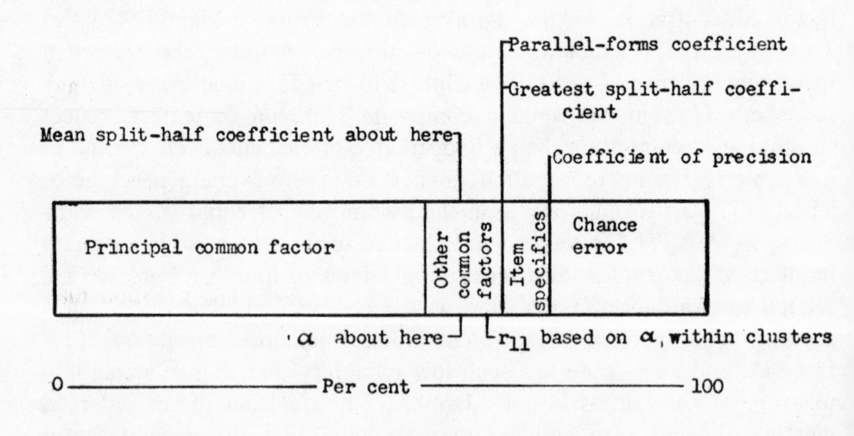

FIGURE 3. Certain Coefficients related to the Composition of the Test Variance.

to obtain an indication of interitem consistency by applying the Spearman-Brown formula to α_t, thereby estimating the mean correlation between items. The formula is entered with the reciprocal of the number of items as the multiple of test length. The formula can be simplified to

$$\bar{r}_{ij\,(\text{est})} = \frac{\alpha}{n + (1 - n)\alpha} \tag{44}$$

or (cf. 24, p. 213 and 30, p. 387),

$$\bar{r}_{ij\,(\text{est})} = \frac{1}{n-1} \cdot \frac{V_t - \Sigma V_i}{\Sigma V_i}. \tag{45}$$

$\bar{r}_{ij\,(\text{est})}$ (r bar) is the correlation required, among items having equal variances and equal covariances, to obtain a test of length n having common-factor concentration α. $r_{ij\,(\text{est})}$ or its special case $\bar{\phi}$ for dichotomously-scored items is recommended as an overall index of internal consistency, if one is needed. It is independent of test length. It is not, in my opinion, important for a test to have a high $\bar{r}$ if α is high. Woodbury's "standard length" (39) is an index of internal consistency which can be derived from $\bar{r}_{ij}$ and has the same advantages and limitations. n_i, the standard length, is the number of items which yields an α of .50 . Then

$$n_i = \frac{1 - \bar{r}_{ij}}{\bar{r}_{ij}}. \tag{46}$$

If $\bar{r}$ is high, α is high. But α may be high even when items have small intercorrelations. If $\bar{r}$ is low, the test may be a smooth mixture of items all having low intercorrelations. In this case, each item would have some loading with the general factor and if the test is long α could be high. Such items are illustrated by very difficult psychophysical discriminations such as a series of near-threshold speech signals to be interpreted; with enough of these items we have a highly satisfactory measuring instrument. In fact, save for random error of performance, it may be unidimensional. A low value of $\bar{r}$ may instead indicate a lumpy test composed of discrete and homogeneous subtests. Guttman (34, p. 176n.) describes a questionnaire of this type. The concept of homogeneity has no particular meaning for a "lumpy" test. It is logically meaningless to inquire whether a set of ten measures of physical size plus ten intercorrelated vocabulary items is more homogeneous than twenty slightly correlated biographical questions. A high $\bar{r}$ is sufficient but not necessary evidence that the test lacks important group factors. When $\bar{r}$ is low, only a study of correlations among items or trial clusters of items shows whether the test can be broken into more homogeneous subtests.

Comparison with the index of reproducibility. Guttman's coefficient of reproducibility has appeared to some reviewers (Loevinger, 28;

Festinger, 13) as an *ad hoc* index with no mathematical rationale. It may therefore be worthwhile to note that this coefficient can be approximated by a mathematical form which makes clear what it measures. The correlation of any two-choice item with a total score on a test may be expressed as a phi coefficient, and this is common in conventional item analysis. Guttman dichotomizes the test scores at a cutting point selected by inspection of the data. We will get similar results if we dichotomize scores at that point which cuts off the same proportion of cases as pass the item under study. (Our ϕ_{it} will be less in some cases than it would be if determined by Guttman's inspection procedure.) Simple substitution in Guttman's definition (34, p. 117) leads to

$$R \doteq \sqrt{1 - 2\sigma_i^2(1 - \phi_{it})}, \tag{47}$$

where the approximation is introduced by the difference in ways of dichotomizing. The actual R obtained by Guttman will be larger than that from (47). For multiple-alternative items, a similar but more complex formula involving the phi coefficient of the alternative with the test is required to approximate Guttman's result. R is independent of test length; if a Guttman scale is divided into equivalent portions, the two halves will have the same R as the original test. In this respect, R is most comparable to our $\bar{r}$. Both ϕ_{it} and $\bar{r}$ are low, so long as items are unreliable or contain substantial specific factors.

5. *Is the Usefulness of α Limited by Properties of the Phi Coefficient Between Items Having Unequal Difficulties?*

The criticism has been made, most vehemently by Loevinger (27), that α is a poor index because, being based on product-moment correlations, it cannot attain unity unless all items have distributions of the same shape. For the pass/fail item, this requires that all p_i be equal. The inference is drawn that since the coefficient cannot reach unity for such items, α and $\bar{r}$ do not properly represent homogeneity.

There are two ways of examining this criticism. The simpler is empirical. The alleged limitation upon the product-moment coefficient has no practical effect upon the coefficient, for items of the sort customarily employed in psychological tests. To demonstrate this, we consider the change in ϕ with changes in item difficulty. To hold constant the relation between the "underlying traits," we fix the tetrachoric correlation. When the tetrachoric coefficient is .30, $p_i = .50$ and p_j ranges from .10 to .90, ϕ_{ij} ranges only from .14 to .19. Figure 4 shows the relation of ϕ_{ij} to p_i and p_j for three levels of correlation: $r_{tet} = .30$, $r_{tet} = .50$, and $r_{tet} = .80$. The correlation among items in psychometric tests is ordinarily below .30. For example, even for a five-grade range of talent, the $\bar{\phi}_{ij}$ for the California Test of Mental Maturity subtests range only

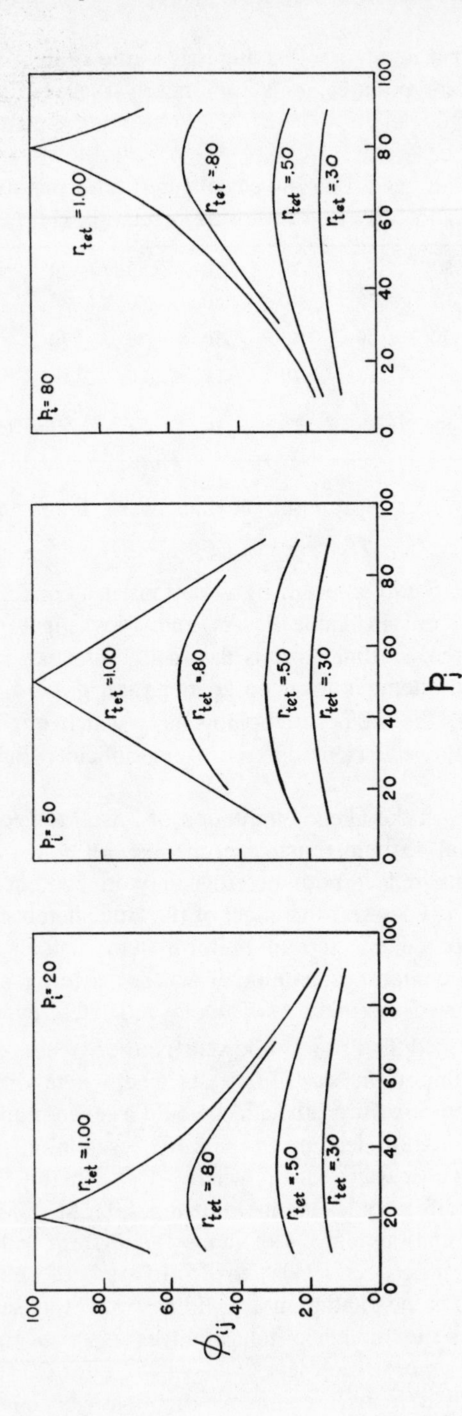

FIGURE 4. Relation of ϕ_{ij} to p_i and p_j for Several Levels of Correlation.

from .13 to .25 . That is, for tests having the degree of item intercorrelation found in present practice, ϕ is very nearly constant over a wide range of item difficulties.

TABLE 7. Variation in Certain Indices of Interitem Consistency with Changes in Item Difficulty (Tetrachoric Correlation Held Constant)

p_i	.50	.50	.50	.50	.50	.50	.50	.50	.50
p_j	$\rightarrow$.00	.10	.20	.40	.50	.60	.80	.90	$\rightarrow$1.00
$r_{ij\,tet}$	.30	.30	.30	.30	.30	.30	.30	.30	.30
ϕ_{ij}	$\rightarrow$.00	.14	.17	.19	.19	.19	.17	.14	$\rightarrow$.00
H_{ij}	$\rightarrow$1.00	.42	.34	.23	.19	.23	.34	.42	$\rightarrow$1.00

Examining Loevinger's proposed coefficient of homogeneity (29),

$$H_{ij} = \phi_{ij}/\phi_{ij(\max)} \;, \tag{48}$$

we find that *it* is markedly affected by variations in item difficulty. One example is worked out in Table 7. As many investigators including Loevinger have noted, Guttman's R is drastically affected by item difficulty. For any single item, R must be greater than p_i or q_j , whichever is greater. Evidently the indices of homogeneity which might replace $\bar{\phi}$ suffer more from the effects of differences in difficulty than does the phi coefficient.

Further evidence on the alleged limitation of α is obtained by preparing four hypothetical 45-item tests. In each case, all $r_{ij(\text{tet})}$ are fixed at .30 . Phi coefficients reflect both heterogeneity in content and heterogeneity in difficulty. To assess the effect of the latter heterogeneity upon $\bar{\phi}$ and α , we compared one test of uniform item difficulty, where all heterogeneity is in content, with another where "heterogeneity due to difficulty" was allowed to enter. As Table 8 indicates, even when extreme ranges of item difficulty are allowed, neither $\bar{\phi}$ nor α is affected in any practically important way. For tests where item difficulties are higher, or correlations are lower, the effect would be even more negligible.

Still another small study leading to the same essential conclusion was made by examining a "perfect scale," where all p_{ij} equal $\phi_{ij(\max)}$. Items were placed at five difficulty levels, the p_i being .50 , .58 , .71 , .80 , and .89 . Then the correlations (phis) of items range from 1.00 (at same level) to .85 (highest between levels) to .36. In a test of only five items, α reaches .86 . This is the maximum α could have, for this set of 5 items and specified p_i . As the number of items increases, α rises toward 1.00 . Thus, for 10 items, two at each level $\alpha_{\max} = .951$; for 20 items, .977 . It follows that even if items are much more homogeneous in content than present tests and much freer from error, the cumulative properties

TABLE 8. Comparison of $\bar{\phi}$ and α for Hypothetical 45-Item Tests With and Without "Heterogeneity Due to Item Difficulty"

Test	Distribution of Difficulties	Range of p_i	$\bar{p}_i$	$\bar{\phi}$	Diff.	α	Diff.
A	Normal	.20 to .80	.50	.181	*.011*	.909	*.005*
A′	Peaked	.50	.50	.192		.914	
B	Normal	.10 to .90	.50	.176	*.016*	.906	*.008*
B′	Peaked	.50	.50	.192		.914	
C	Normal	.50 to .90	.70	.170	*.011*	.902	*.007*
C′	Peaked	.70	.70	.181		.909	
D	Rectangular	.10 to .90	.50	.153	*.039*	.892	*.022*
D′	Peaked	.50	.50	.192		.914	

of covariance terms make the failure of all ϕ's to reach unity of next-to-no importance. α_{max} would be lower if difficulties range over the full scale, but the same principle holds. α is a good measure of common-factor concentration, for tests of reasonable length, in spite of the fact that it falls short of 1.00 if items vary in difficulty.

In the case of the perfect scale, of course, $\bar{\phi}$ does fall well short of unity and for such tests it does not reflect the homogeneity in content. From the five-item case just considered, $\bar{\phi}$ is .54 .

The second way to analyze this criticism is to examine the nature of redundancy (using a term from Shannon's information theory, 32). If two items repeat the same information, they are totally redundant. Thus, if one item divides people 50/50, and the second item does also, the two items always placing exactly the same people together, the second item gives no new information about individual differences. (Cf. Tucker, 36). Suppose, though, that the second item is passed by 60 per cent of the subjects. Even if $r_{ij(\text{tet})} = 1.00$, this second item conveys new information because it discriminates among the fifty people who failed the first item. A five-item test where all items have perfect tetrachoric intercorrelations, and the p_i are .40 , .45 , .50 , .55 , .60 , is perfectly homogeneous (a la Guttman, Loevinger, et al.). So is a ten-item test composed of these items plus five others whose p's are .30 , .35 , .65 , .70 , .75 . The two tests are not equivalent in measuring power, however; the second makes a much greater number of discriminations. Because there is less redundancy, the longer test has a lower $\bar{\phi}$.

From the viewpoint of information theory, we should be equally concerned with heterogeneity in content and heterogeneity in difficulty. We get one bit of information when we place the person as above the mean in (say) pitch discrimination. Now with another item or set of items, we might place him relative to the mean in visual acuity. The two tests together place him in one of four categories. If our second test had been a further measure of pitch, placing the subject above or below the 75th percentile, then the two tests would have placed him in one of four categories. Either set of tests gives the same amount of information. Which information we most want depends on practical considerations.

The phi coefficient reports whether a second item gives new information that the first does not. Then a tetrachoric r must be computed to determine if the new information relates to a new content dimension or to a finer discrimination on the same content dimension. If the phi coefficient between true scores is 1.00, redundancy is complete and there is no new information. Redundancy is desirable when accuracy of a single item is low. To test whether men can hear a 10-cycle difference, the best way is to use a large number of items of just that difficulty. Such items usually also discriminate to some degree at other points on the scale, but cannot give information about ability at the 5-cycle level if a single item is extremely reliable. With very accurate items a pitch test which is not homogeneous will be better for differentiation all along the scale. The "factors" found by Ferguson (11) due to the higher correlation (redundancy) of items with equal difficulty need not be regarded as artifacts (38).* These "difficulty factors" are factors on which the test gives information and on which the tester may well want information. They are not "content factors," but they must be considered in test analysis. For example, if one regards pitch tests in this light, it is seen that a test containing 5-cycle items, 10-cycle items, and 15-cycle items will be slightly influenced by undesired factors, when the criterion requires discrimination only at the 15-cycle level. (Problems of this type occur in validating tests for selecting military personnel using detection apparatus.) One would maximize the loading in the test of the group factor among 15-cycle items, to maximize validity. This factor is of course a mathematical factor, and not a property of the auditory machinery. While the mathematics is not clear, it seems very likely that the group factors found among phi coefficients are interchangeable with Guttman's "components of scale analysis" to which he gives serious psychological interpretation.

From this point of view, the phi coefficient which tells when items do and do not duplicate each other is a better index *just because* it does not reach unity for items of unequal difficulty. Phi and r_{tet} are both useful in test analysis. Brogden (1, pp. 199, 201) makes a similar point, although approaching the problem from another tack.

---

* It is not *necessary,* as Ferguson seems to think, for difficulty factors to emerge if product-moment correlations are used with multi-category variates. On *a priori* grounds, difficulty factors will appear only if the shapes of the distributions of the variates are different. In Ferguson's data it appears likely that the hardest and easiest tests were skewed in opposite directions.

IMPLICATIONS FOR TEST DESIGN

In view of the relations detailed above, we find it unnecessary to create homogeneous scales such as Guttman, Loevinger, and others have urged.

It is true that a test where all items represent the same content factor with no error of measurement is maximally interpretable. Everyone attaining the same score would mark items in the same way. Yet the question we really wish to ask is whether the individual differences in test score are attributable to the first factor within the test. If a large proportion of the score variance relates to this factor, the residue due to specific characteristics of the items little handicaps interpretability. It has been shown that a high first-factor saturation indicated by a high α can be attained by cumulating many items which have low correlations. The standard proposed by Ferguson, Loevinger, and Guttman is unreasonably severe, since it would rule out tests which do have high first-factor concentrations.

These writers seem to wish to infer the person's score on each item from his total score. This appears unimportant, but even if it were important, the interest would attach to predicting his *true* standing on the item, not his fallible obtained score. For the unreliable items used in psychological and educational tests, the aim of Guttman et al. will not be approached in practice. Perhaps sociological data have such greater reliability that prediction of obtained scores is tantamount to predicting true scores.

Increasing interpretability by lengthening a test is not without its disadvantages. Using more and more time to get at the same information employs the principle of redundancy (32). When a message is repeated over and over, it is easier to infer the true message even when there is substantial interference (item unreliability). But the more you repeat messages already transmitted, the less time is allowed for conveying other information. A set of redundant items can carry much less information than a set of independent items. In other words, when we lengthen certain tests or subtests to make their scores more interpretable, we sacrifice the possibility of obtaining separate measures of additional factors in the same time.

From the viewpoint of both interpretability and efficient prediction of criteria, the smallest element on which a score is obtained should be a set of items having a substantial α and not capable of division into discrete item clusters which themselves have high α. Such separately interpretable tests can sometimes be combined into an interpretable composite, as in the case of the PMA tests. Although it is believed that the test designer should seek interitem consistency, and judge the effectiveness of his efforts by the coefficient α, the pure scale should not be viewed as an ideal. It should be remembered that Tucker (36) and Brogden (1) have demonstrated that increases in internal consistency may lead to decreases in the product-moment validity coefficient when the shape of the test-score distribution differs from that of the criterion distribution.

SUMMARY

1. Formulas for split-half coefficients of equivalence are compared, and those of Rulon and Guttman are advocated for practical use rather than the Spearman-Brown formula.

2. α, the general formula of which Kuder-Richardson formula 20 is a special case, is found to have the following important meanings:

(a) α is the mean of all possible split-half coefficients.

(b) α is the value expected when two *random* samples of items from a pool like those in the given test are correlated.

(c) α is a lower bound for the coefficient of precision (the instantaneous accuracy of this test with these particular items). α is also a lower bound for coefficients of equivalence obtained by simultaneous administration of two tests having matched items. But for reasonably long tests not divisible into a few factorially-distinct subtests, α is nearly equal to "parallel-split" and "parallel-forms" coefficients of equivalence.*

(d) α estimates, and is a lower bound to, the proportion of test variance attributable to common factors among the items. That is, it is an index of common-factor concentration. This index serves purposes claimed for indices of homogeneity. α may be applied by a modified technique to determine the common-factor concentration among a battery of subtests.

(e) α is an upper bound to the concentration in the test of the first factor among the items. For reasonably long tests not divisible into a few factorially-distinct subtests, α is very little greater than the exact proportion of variance due to the first factor.

3. Parallel-splits yield coefficients little larger than random splits, unless tests contain large blocks of items representing group factors.

* W. G. Madow suggests that the amount of disagreement between two random or two planned samples of items from a larger population of items could be anticipated from sampling theory. The person's score on a test is a sample mean, intended to estimate the population mean or "true score" over all items. The variance of such a mean from one sample to another decreases rapidly as the sample is enlarged by lengthening the test, whether samples are drawn at random or are drawn after stratifying the universe as to difficulty and content. The conditions under which the random splits correlate about as highly as parallel splits are those in which stratified sampling has comparatively little advantage. Madow's comment has implications also for the preparation of comparable forms of tests and for developing objective methods of selecting a sample of items to represent a larger set of items so that the variance of the difference between the score based on the sample and the score based on the universe of items is as small as possible.

For such tests, α computed for separate blocks and combined by a special formula gives a satisfactory estimate of first-factor concentration.

4. Interpretability of a test score is enhanced if the score has a high first-factor concentration. A high α is therefore to be desired, but a test need not approach a perfect scale to be interpretable. Items with quite low intercorrelations can yield an interpretable scale.

5. A coefficient $\overline{r}_{ij}$ (or $\overline{\phi}_{ij}$) is derived which is the intercorrelation required, among items with equal intercorrelations and variances, to reproduce a test of n items having common-factor concentration α. $\overline{\phi}$, as a measure of item interdependence, draws attention to heterogeneity in both difficulty and content factors. Heterogeneity in test difficulty merits the attention of the test designer, since the validity of the test may be increased by capitalizing on "difficulty factors" present in the criterion.

6. To obtain subtest scores for interpretation or to be weighted in an empirical composite, the ideal set of items is one having a substantial α and not further divisible into a few discrete smaller blocks of items.

REFERENCES

1. Brogden, H. E. Variation in test validity with variation in the distribution of item difficulties, number of items, and degree of their intercorrelation. *Psychometrika,* 1946, **11,** 197–214.
2. Brown, W. Some experimental results in the correlation of mental abilities. *Brit. J. Psychol.,* 1910, **3,** 296–322.
3. Brownell, W. A. On the accuracy with which reliability may be measured by correlating test halves. *J. exper. Educ.,* 1933, **1,** 204–215.
4. Burt, C. The influence of differential weighting. *Brit. J. Psychol., Stat. Sect.,* 1950, **3,** 105–128.
5. Clark, E. L. Methods of splitting vs. samples as sources of instability in test-reliability coefficients. *Harvard educ. Rev.,* 1949, **19,** 178–182.
6. Coombs, C. H. The concepts of reliability and homogeneity. *Educ. psychol. Meas.,* 150, **10,** 43–56.
7. Cronbach, L. J. On estimates of test reliability. *J. educ. Psychol.,* 1943, **34,** 485–494.
8. Cronbach, L. J. A case study of the split-half reliability coefficient. *J. educ. Psychol.,* 1946, **37,** 473–480.
9. Cronbach, L. J. Test "reliability": its meaning and determination. *Psychometrika,* 1947, **12,** 1–16.
10. Dressel, P. L. Some remarks on the Kuder-Richardson reliability coefficient. *Psychometrika,* 1940, **5,** 305–310.
11. Ferguson, G. The factorial interpretation of test difficulty. *Psychometrika,* 1941, **6,** 323–329.
12. Ferguson, G. The reliability of mental tests. London: Univ. of London Press, 1941.
13. Festinger, L. The treatment of qualitative data by "scale analysis." *Psychol. Bull.,* 1947, **44,** 149–161.

14. Goodenough, F. L. A critical note on the use of the term "reliability" in mental measurement. *J. educ. Psychol.,* 1936, **27,** 173–178.
15. Guilford J. P., ed. Printed classification tests. Report No. 5, Army Air Forces Aviation Psychology Program. Washington: U. S. Govt. Print. Off., 1947.
16. Guilford, J. P. Fundamental statistics in psychology and education. Second ed. New York: McGraw-Hill, 1950.
17. Guilford, J. P., and Michael, W. B. Changes in common-factor loadings as tests are altered homogeneously in length. *Psychometrika,* 1950, **15,** 237–249.
18. Gulliksen, H. Theory of mental tests. New York: Wiley, 1950.
19. Guttman, L. A basis for analyzing test-retest reliability. *Psychometrika,* 1945, **10,** 255–282.
20. Hoyt, C. Test reliability estimated by analysis of variance. *Psychometrika,* 1941, **6,** 153–160.
21. Humphreys, L. G. Test homogeneity and its measurement. *Amer. Psychologist,* 1949, **4,** 245.
22. Jackson, R. W., and Ferguson, G. A. Studies on the reliability of tests. Bull. No. 12, Dept. of Educ. Res., University of Toronto, 1941.
23. Kelley, T. L. Note on the reliability of a test: a reply to Dr. Crum's criticism. *J. educ. Psychol.,* 1924, **15,** 193–204.
24. Kelley, T. L. Statistical method. New York: Macmillan, 1924.
25. Kelley, T. L. The reliability coefficient. *Psychometrika,* 1942, **7,** 75–83.
26. Kuder, G. F., and Richardson, M. W. The theory of the estimation of test reliability. *Psychometrika,* 1937, **2,** 151–160.
27. Loevinger, J. A systematic approach to the construction and evaluation of tests of ability. *Psychol. Monogr.,* 1947, **61,** No. 4.
28. Loevinger, J. The technic of homogeneous tests compared with some aspects of "scale analysis" and factor analysis. *Psychol. Bull.,* 1948, **45,** 507–529.
29. Mosier, C. I. A short cut in the estimation of split-halves coefficients. *Educ. psychol. Meas.,* 1941, **1,** 407–408.
30. Richardson, M. Combination of measures, pp. 379–401 in Horst, P. (Ed.) The prediction of personal adjustment. New York: Social Science Res. Council, 1941.
31. Rulon, P. J. A simplified procedure for determining the reliability of a test by split-halves. *Harvard educ. Rev.,* 1939, **9,** 99–103.
32. Shannon, C. E. The mathematical theory of communication. Urbana: Univ. of Ill. Press, 1949.
33. Spearman, C. Correlation calculated with faulty data. *Brit. J. Psychol.,* 1910, **3,** 271–295.
34. Stouffer, S. A., et al. Measurement and prediction. Princeton: Princeton Univ. Press, 1950.
35. Thurstone, L. L., and Thurstone, T. G. Factorial studies of intelligence, p. 37. Chicago: Univ. of Chicago Press, 1941.
36. Tucker, L. R. Maximum validity of a test with equivalent items. *Psychometrika,* 1946, **11,** 1–13.
37. Vernon, P. E. An application of factorial analysis to the study of test items. *Brit. J. Psychol., Stat. Sec.,* 1950, **3,** 1–15.

38. Wherry, R. J., and Gaylord, R. H. The concept of test and item reliability in relation to factor pattern. *Psychometrika,* 1943, **8,** 247–264.
39. Woodbury, M. A. On the standard length of a test. Res. Bull. 50–53, Educ. Test Service, 1950.

19. The Definition and Estimation of Test Reliability

EDWARD E. CURETON

It has been common practice to define the reliability coefficient as the correlation between equivalent forms of a test—either two actual forms or one actual form and one hypothetical form to which it is rationally equivalent. Equivalence then becomes a matter for further definition and for empirical judgment, and different authors have given conflicting definitions and conflicting criteria to guide empirical judgment. Under several of these definitions, however, it can be shown that the reliability coefficient is the variance ratio of true scores to total scores on each of the equivalent forms. The present writer prefers to reverse this procedure, defining the reliability coefficient of any one form of a test as the variance ratio of true scores to total scores. This shifts the ground of a difficulty indicated by Kelley [6], that under the correlation definition we cannot discuss directly the reliability of one form of a test. Under the proposed definition such discussion is entirely possible so long as it remains formal, and we see that the second form is needed only when we come to the *estimation* of the reliability of the first form. Moreover, by employing this approach we can avoid certain pitfalls inherent in the rational-equivalence model, which have led in some cases to the use of more restrictive assumptions than are actually necessary, and in others to the use of assumptions which are actually more restrictive than they appear to be. Finally, this approach seems to provide clearer guides to empirical judgments about equivalence.

Previous attempts to define error of measurement without defining true score, or to define true score without defining error of measurement, appear inherently unsatisfactory to the writer. The definition of a true

Cureton, E. E. The definition and estimation of test reliability. *Educational and Psychological Measurement,* 1958, *18,* 715–738. Reprinted with the permission of the publisher and author.

score as the mean score on an infinite number of forms is rejected specifically, along with all definitions which imply even an infinite item universe. In all questions of item sampling we limit ourselves deliberately to a finite population which can be identified in practice with the pool of items which a test author actually uses in constructing several forms of a test. The definitions of error of measurement and true score turn out to be opposite faces of the same coin, and the assumptions underlying reliability formulas provide explicit rules for the allocation of items to forms.

Most existing treatments of reliability fail to maintain consistently the distinction between the population (of individuals) and the sample. This leads to logical absurdities such as the assumption that errors of measurement are statistically independent of one another and of true scores *in the sample*. In the present treatment these assumptions are applied only to the population. Formulas are derived for the population, and the question of point estimation from the sample is then discussed for each such formula. From the unsatisfactory nature of most of these discussions it will be apparent that consideration of interval estimation would be fruitless. There are no unbiased estimators for any of the basic formulas of reliability; in particular, the writer is unable to find an unbiased estimator for the product-moment correlation coefficient.* For a few of the basic formulas there are maximum likelihood estimators, and for the rest we must simply use "parallel estimators": formulas in which we merely replace the population standard deviations, variances, covariances, and/or correlation coefficients by their sample values.

When we have two or more forms of a test, they can be alike in at least four distinct respects: a) measuring the same function or combination of functions (factorially alike), b) equally reliable, c) equally variable, and d) equally difficult (having equal means). Each of the basic formulas is derived on the basis of the minimum necessary number of these varieties of alikeness.

This treatment is limited to the classical linear model, assuming linear regression of true scores on raw scores, and omitting all discussion of variation in reliability with score level. The special problems of recognition-type items are also ignored, in particular the fact that we do not yet know how to scale them for difficulty even on the assumption that the underlying ability is normally distributed in the scaling sample. All of these problems are important, and further progress in reliability theory will come mainly through their solution. It appears, however, that a more rigorous consideration of the classical

* After this manuscript was submitted for publication, the formula appeared: Olkim, I., and Pratt, J. W. "Unbiased Estimation of Certain Correlation Coefficients." *Annals of Mathematical Statistics,* XXIX (1958), 201–211.

problems will provide a better foundation for work on these more advanced and complex problems.

1. THE RELIABILITY COEFFICIENT

We start with the *linear model:* the assumption that the total score on any test is the *sum* of the true score and the error score, and that the true score and the error score are statistically independent of each other in the population of examinees for whom the test is to be considered suitable. If a second test measures the same function as the first, and the errors of measurement of the two tests are statistically independent of *each other* as well as of the true scores, they are *parallel* (but not necessarily equivalent) forms of the same test. Let the total scores be x_a and x_b, the common true score x, and the error scores e_a and e_b, all taken as deviations from their respective *population* means. Since we have not assumed that the two forms are equally reliable or equally variable, or that their units of measurement are equal, we require weighting constants, c_a and c_b, for x in x_a and x_b. The error scores e_a and e_b may be assumed without loss of generality to be measured in the same units as x. We then have,

$$x_a = c_a(x + e_a), \qquad (1)$$

$$x_b = c_b(x + e_b). \qquad (2)$$

Let σ with one subscript denote a standard deviation, σ^2 with one subscript a variance, ρ with two subscripts a correlation, and σ with two subscripts a covariance ($\sigma_{ab} = \rho_{ab}\sigma_a\sigma_b$). Then, remembering that x, e_a, and e_b are statistically independent,

$$\sigma_{ab} = c_a c_b \sigma_x^2, \qquad (3)$$

$$\rho_{ab} = \frac{\sigma_{ab}}{\sigma_a\ \sigma_b} = \frac{c_a c_b \sigma_x^2}{\sigma_a\ \sigma_b}. \qquad (4)$$

The operational meaning of the assumption of statistical independence is that if we judge two tests to be parallel forms of the same test, we agree to define everything causing correlation between them as true score, and everything causing unique variability in each of them as error of measurement.

If R_a and R_b are reliability coefficients of the two forms, then by the variance-ratio definition of reliability,

$$R_a = c_a^2\ \sigma_x^2/\sigma_a^2, \qquad (5)$$

$$R_b = c_b^2\ \sigma_x^2/\sigma_b^2. \qquad (6)$$

From (4), (5), and (6), it follows immediately that

$$\sqrt{R_a\ R_b} = \rho_{ab}; \qquad (7)$$

i.e., the correlation between any two parallel forms of the same test is the geometric mean of their reliability coefficients. If in addition the two forms are *equally reliable,*

$$R_a = R_b = \rho_{ab}. \tag{8}$$

This is the further condition for equivalence; i.e., two parallel forms of the same test are *equivalent* if they are equally reliable, and the correlation between two equivalent forms is the reliability coefficient of each of them. Note that so far we have *not* found it necessary to assume that $\sigma_a = \sigma_b$. Two forms can be equally reliable but unequally variable if one has a larger number of less discriminating items and the other a smaller number of more discriminating items, or if their scoring formulas are different, or if their scales differ arbitrarily.

For forms which are merely equivalent, the maximum-likelihood estimate of ρ_{ab} (and hence of R_a and R_b) is r_{ab}, the product-moment correlation coefficient [5].

2. THE SPEARMAN-BROWN FORMULA

From (1), (2), and the variance-ratio definition of reliability,

$$R_{a+b} = \frac{(c_a + c_b)^2 \sigma_x^2}{\sigma^2_{a+b}} = \frac{(c_a^2 + c_b^2 + 2c_a c_b)\sigma_x^2}{\sigma_a^2 + \sigma_b^2 + 2\sigma_{ab}}. \tag{9}$$

If we assume that $c_a = c_b = c$, and then make in the numerator of (9) the substitution indicated in (3); namely, $c^2 \sigma_x^2 = \sigma_{ab}$,

$$R_{a+b} = \frac{4\sigma_{ab}}{\sigma_a^2 + \sigma_b^2 + 2\sigma_{ab}}. \tag{10}$$

This formula is credited to Flanagan by Kelley [6], and is quoted by Cronbach [1] and Thorndike [8] as being independent of the assumption of equal variances. The original derivation was based on the correlation definition of reliability and a rational-equivalence model. Assume two hypothetical forms, x_f and x_g, equivalent to x_a and x_b in the sense defined by the following two assumptions:

$$\sigma_{ab} = \sigma_{af} = \sigma_{ag} = \sigma_{bf} = \sigma_{bg} = \sigma_{fg}, \tag{11}$$

$$\sigma_{a+b} = \sigma_{f+g}. \tag{12}$$

The reliability coefficient of $(x_a + x_b)$ is then taken as

$$\rho_{(a+b)(f+g)} = \frac{\sigma_{af} + \sigma_{ag} + \sigma_{bf} + \sigma_{bg}}{\sigma_{a+b}\, \sigma_{f+g}} = R_{a+b}. \tag{13}$$

From (11) and (12) we can substitute σ_{ab} for each term of the numerator and σ_{a+b} for each factor of the denominator. Then

$$R_{a+b} = \frac{4\sigma_{ab}}{\sigma_a^2 + \sigma_b^2 + 2\sigma_{ab}},$$

which is identical with (10).

If, however, we set up for the hypothetical forms, x_f and x_g, equations analogous to (1) and (2),

$$x_f = c_f(x + e_f),$$
$$x_g = c_g(x + e_g),$$

there will be five more equations analogous to (3), two of which are

$$\sigma_{af} = c_a\, c_f\, \sigma_x^2,$$
$$\sigma_{bf} = c_b\, c_f\, \sigma_x^2.$$

From the assumption of (11), $\sigma_{af} = \sigma_{bf}$, and hence from the two equations above, $c_a = c_b$; i.e., the assumption (11) implies the assumption preceding (10). We shall next investigate the significance of this assumption. Substituting c^2 for c_a^2 and c_b^2 in (5) and (6),

$$R_a = c^2\, \sigma_x^2/\sigma_a^2,\ c^2\, \sigma_x^2 = R_a\, \sigma_a^2,$$
$$R_b = c^2\sigma^2{}_x/\sigma^2{}_b,\ c^2\sigma^2{}_x = R_b\sigma^2{}_b\,,$$
$$R_a\sigma_a^2 = R_b\sigma_b^2; \tag{14}$$

i.e., the reliability coefficients of the two forms are *inversely* proportional to their variances. This restriction is at best improbable in practice. If two forms measure in the same units and are unequally reliable, the more reliable form will have the greater variability. To prove this statement we must first define equality of units of measurement.

Flanagan argues cogently that any two forms have equal units of measurement if and only if the same raw deviation score on each form predicts the same true deviation score [3]: the regression coefficient of true scores on raw scores must be the same for both forms; i.e.,

$$\rho_{xa}\sigma_x/\sigma_a = \rho_{xb}\sigma_x/\sigma_b\ ;$$
$$\rho_{xa}/\sigma_a = \rho_{xb}/\sigma_b\ .$$

Now from (1) and (5),

$$\rho_{xa} = \frac{E[xc_a(x+e_a)]}{\sigma_x\sigma_a} = \frac{c_a\sigma_x^2}{\sigma_x\sigma_a} = \frac{c_a\sigma_x}{\sigma_a} = \sqrt{R_a},$$

and $\rho_{xb} = \sqrt{R_b}$. Substituting in the previous formula and squaring both sides,

$$R_a/\sigma_a^2 = R_b/\sigma_b^2; \tag{15}$$

i.e., if the units of measurement of two forms of a test are equal, their reliabilities are *directly* proportional to their variances.

Equations (14) and (15) can be true simultaneously only if $R_a = R_b$ *and* $\sigma_a = \sigma_b$. And if the units of measurement of x_a and x_b are not equal, their sum, whose reliability is our present subject of discussion, is meaningless. Letting $\sigma_a = \sigma_b$ in (10), and dividing numerator and denominator by $2\,\sigma_a\,\sigma_b$ $(= 2\,\sigma_a^2 = 2\sigma_b^2)$, we obtain at once

$$R_{a+b} = 2\,\rho_{ab}/(1 + \rho_{ab}), \tag{16}$$

which is the usual form of the Spearman-Brown formula. The restrictions on (10) are *not* less stringent than those on (16): both require the assumption of equivalence *and* the assumption of equal variances.

If we start directly from (9), and substitute in the numerator from (3), (5), and (6), we obtain

$$R_{a+b} = \frac{R_a\sigma_a^2 + R_b\sigma_b^2 + 2\sigma_{ab}}{\sigma_a^2 + \sigma_b^2 + 2\sigma_{ab}}.$$

Assuming equivalence in order to evaluate R_a and R_b,

$$R_{a+b} = \frac{\rho_{ab}\,(\sigma_a^2 + \sigma_b^2 + 2\sigma_a\sigma_b)}{\sigma_a^2 + \sigma_b^2 + 2\rho_{ab}\sigma_a\sigma_b}.$$

The assumption of equal units of measurement, (15), now requires that $\rho_{ab}/\sigma_a^2 = \rho_{ab}/\sigma_b^2$, or $\sigma_a^2 = \sigma_b^2 = \sigma^2$, and

$$R_{a+b} = \frac{4\sigma^2\,\rho_{ab}}{2\sigma^2\,(1+\rho_{ab})} = \frac{2\,\rho_{ab}}{1+\rho_{ab}},$$

which is identical with (16). *If two forms are equivalent and measure in the same units, they are equally variable.* In this case it is clear from (5) and (6) that $c_a = c_b$. Hence, *if and only if we assume both equivalence and equal units of measurement at the outset, the weighting factors, c_a and c_b, may be omitted from the original factor patterns.*

We shall next investigate the stringency of the assumptions of equal reliability and equal variance with some numerical examples. If we start with the formula following (16) and divide numerator and denominator by $\sigma_a\sigma_b$ we obtain

$$R_{a+b} = \frac{R_a(\sigma_a/\sigma_b) + R_b(\sigma_b/\sigma_a) + 2\,\rho_{ab}}{\sigma_a/\sigma_b + \sigma_b/\sigma_a + 2\rho_{ab}}.$$

Let $R_a = R_b = \rho_{ab} = .6$, and let $\sigma_a = \sigma_b$. Then $R_{a+b} = .750$, which is identical with the value given by (16).

Now let $\sigma_a = 2\sigma_b$. Then from the formula above, $R_{a+b} = .730$, and the same result is obtained if $\sigma_b = 2\,\sigma_a$. If the two forms are equivalent, the requirement of equal standard deviations is apparently not very stringent.

Next let $\sigma_a = \sigma_b$, but let $R_a = .4$, $R_b = .9$, and from (7), $\rho_{ab} = .6$ as before. Then $R_{a+b} = .781$. If the standard deviations are equal, the requirement of equal reliabilities is not very stringent either.

Next let $R_a = .4$, $R_b = .9$, $\rho_{ab} = .6$, and $\sigma_a = 2\sigma_b$. Then $R_{a+b} = .662$. If $R_a = .4$, $R_b = .9$, $\rho_{ab} = .6$, and $\sigma_b = 2\sigma_a$, $R_{a+b} = .865$. When both assumptions are violated as badly as in these examples, (16) gives a rather poor estimate, and there is little to choose as between $\sigma_a = 2\sigma_b$ and $\sigma_b = 2\sigma_a$.

In practice, the assumption that $\sigma_a = \sigma_b$ can be checked by the sample data, but the assumption that $R_a = R_b$ can not. If a statistical test does not reject the hypothesis that $\sigma_a = \sigma_b$ (or $\sigma_a^2 = \sigma_b^2$) at the 5 per cent level, say, with N large enough for the useful study of reliabilities, equation (16) should be adequate in all cases in which the reliabilities of the two forms are assumed equal merely because they have the same number of items, with allocation of items to forms (on the basis of indices of discrimination) no worse than random.

When there is only one variance in the population, the maximum-likelihood estimate of ρ_{ab} is no longer the product-moment correlation [5], but is

$$r'_{ab} = \frac{2\Sigma x_a x_b}{\Sigma x_a^2 + \Sigma x_b^2} = \frac{2s_{ab}}{s_a^2 + s_b^2}; \tag{17}$$

the denominator is the arithmetic mean of the sample sums of squares of deviations or the sample variances, rather than their geometric mean. The maximum-likelihood estimate of (16) itself has not been derived, so far as the writer is aware; and the best we can do is to take $2\, r'_{ab}/(1 + r'_{ab})$ as the sample estimate.

If the original units of measurement of two equivalent forms are unequal, they can be equalized by any convenient linear transformation, such as the use of some arbitrary standard score system, for purposes of summing.

Horst [4] gives the formula for the reliability of the sum of scores on two forms of unequal length which have the same units of measurement and are equally reliable *per unit length.* It is

$$R_{a+b} = \frac{\rho_{ab}\sqrt{[\rho_{ab}^2 + 4pq(1 - \rho_{ab}^2)]} - \rho_{ab}^2}{2pq(1 - \rho_{ab}^2)}, \tag{18}$$

where p and q are the relative lengths of x_a and x_b $(p + q = 1)$. If we set $p = .7$ and $q = .3$, so that one form is 2.333 times as long as the other, and let $\rho_{ab} = .7$, we find from (18) that $R_{a+b} = .844$. If we now substitute $\rho_{ab} = .7$, directly in (16), we obtain $R_{a+b} = .824$. If the units of measurement of the two forms are equal, the requirement of equal reliability for the validity of the Spearman-Brown formula is shown again to be fairly weak.

The more general Spearman-Brown formula for the reliability of a test n times as long as *one* of the original forms is

$$R_n = \frac{n\rho_{ab}}{1 + (n - 1)\rho_{ab}}. \tag{19}$$

Here the two original forms must be of equal length and equal reliability and must measure in the same units. If we have two forms of unequal length, measuring in the same units and presumably equally reliable per unit length, and the longer form is not more than say 1.5 times as long as the shorter form, the formula,

$$R_{n'} = \frac{2n'\rho_{ab}}{1 + (2n' - 1)\rho_{ab}} \tag{20}$$

should give a fairly valid estimate of the reliability of a parallel form n' times as long as forms a and b combined. For greater accuracy, we can of course compute R_{a+b} by (18) and then $R_{n'}$ by (19), using R_{a+b} as the ρ_{ab} of (19).

3. COMPLEX TRUE SCORES AND ERRORS

The preceding derivations have used a single symbol, x, to represent the true score, and a single symbol, e_i, to represent the error measurement of each form. Hence we have not yet ruled out the possibility that the true scores and/or the errors of measurement of each form must represent unitary traits. The factor analysis literature indicates quite clearly that the true scores on most tests do *not* represent unitary traits, and we know also that errors of measurement result from sampling in several distinct (but not necessarily independent) universes: the universe of possible test items, the universe of reactions of an individual to the same test item at different times, etc.

We shall investigate the case of two distinct general factors and two distinct errors of measurement for each form; the generalization to more than two factors and more than two errors per form will be fairly obvious. In place of (1) and (2), we write

$$x_a = c_a(w_{a^1}x_1 + w_{b^2}x_2 + e_{a^1} + e_{a^2}), \tag{21}$$

$$x_b = c_b(w_{b^1}x_1 + w_{a^2}x_2 + e_{b^1} + e_{b^2}), \tag{22}$$

where x_1 and x_2 are true scores for two different abilities, the w's are the weights of x_1 and x_2 in x_a and x_b, and the e's are errors of measurement. This is still a linear model: x_a and x_b are weighted linear combinations of x_1, x_2, and the e's. Then in place of (5) and (6), we have

$$R_a = c_a{}^2(w_{a^1}{}^2\sigma_2{}^2 + w_{a^2}{}^2\sigma_2{}^2 + 2w_{a^1}w_{a^2}\sigma_{12})/\sigma_a{}^2, \tag{23}$$

$$R_b = c_b{}^2(w_{b^1}{}^2\sigma_2{}^2 + w_{b^2}{}^2\sigma_2{}^2 + 2w_{b^1}w_{b^2}\sigma_{12})/\sigma_b{}^2. \tag{24}$$

Here R_a and R_b are again the true-score variance of each form divided by its total variance. Note that we have *not* assumed that x_1 and x_2 are uncorrelated.

We now add the assumptions for parallel forms: that e_{a^1} and e_{a^2} are uncorrelated with e_{b^1} and e_{b^2}, and that all e's are uncorrelated with x_1 and x_2. We do *not* assume that e_{a^1} is uncorrelated with e_{a^2} or that e_{b^1} is uncorrelated with e_{b^2}. We assume merely that all sources of covariation of x_a and x_b are to be attributed to their common true scores, and that all sources of unique variance in each form are to be attributed to errors of measurement. As noted previously, this assumption is actually a definition of parallel forms. With these assumptions,

$$\rho_{ab} = c_a c_b\,(w_{a^1}w_{b^1}\sigma_2{}^2 + w_{a^2}w_{b^2}\sigma_2{}^2 + w_{a^1}w_{b^2}\sigma_{12} + w_{a^2}w_{b^1}\sigma_{12})/\sigma_a\sigma_b. \tag{25}$$

The basic assumptions used in writing (25) are necessary conditions for parallel forms, but they are no longer sufficient. If all causes of common variance (with their weights) are to be taken as true-score variance in each form, it is necessary that the terms in parentheses in (23), (24), and (25) all be equal. Comparing these terms, it is evident that this can occur only if $w_{a^1} = w_{b^1} = w_1$, say, and $w_{a^2} = w_{b^2} = w_2$. The total true score, x, must be the same *combination* of x^1 and x^2 in each form; i.e., the two forms must have the same common-factor structure with the same *relative* factor loadings. If the two forms are *equivalent,* so that $c_a/\sigma_a = c_b/\sigma_b$, they must have the same common-factor structure and the same actual factor loadings. Note that this requirement applies only to the total forms. It is *not* required that the factorial structure of each form be duplicated in every item; i.e., that each form be factorially homogenous.

4. COEFFICIENT ALPHA (KUDER-RICHARDSON FORMULA 20)

Ferguson [2] and Cronbach [1] have presented derivations of the Kuder-Richardson Formula 20 [7]—termed "Coefficient Alpha" by Cronbach—using fewer assumptions than were used by Kuder and Richardson. Consider a variance-covariance matrix for k items, partitioned into two equal subsets of $k/2$ representing two half-tests, x_a and x_b. There will be $k/2$ variances of the type σ_a^2, and $k/2$ of the type σ_b^2. There will be $(k/2)\ (k/2-1)/2$ or $k(k-2)/8$ covariances of the type $\sigma_{aa'}$, and $k(k-2)/8$ of the type $\sigma_{bb'}$. There will also be $(k/2)^2$ or $k^2/4$ covariances of the type σ_{ab}. We denote by Σ' a sum of $k/2$ variances, by Σ'' a sum of $k(k-2)/8$ covariances, by Σ^* a sum of $k^2/4$ covariances, by Σ a sum of k variances, and by Σ^{**} a sum of $k(k-1)/2$ covariances. In this notation, the general formula for the correlation between the sum of $k/2$ items and the sum of $k/2$ other items is

$$\rho_{ab} = \frac{\Sigma^*\sigma_{ab}}{\sqrt{(\Sigma'\sigma_a^2 + 2\Sigma''\sigma_{ad'})(\Sigma'\sigma_b^2 + 2\Sigma''\sigma_{bb'})}}. \tag{26}$$

Assume now that there is at least one possible division of the k items into the two half-tests, x_a and x_b, such that these two half-tests are equally reliable and equally variable, and that (26) represents the correlation between two such half-tests. If they are equally variable, the two factors of the denominator must be equal, or

$$k\overline{\sigma_a^2}/2 + 2k(k-2)\overline{\sigma_{aa'}}/8 = k\overline{\sigma_b^2}/2 + 2k(k-2)\overline{\sigma_{bb'}}/8.$$

Now if $\overline{\sigma_a^2} > \overline{\sigma_b^2}$, say, it follows that $\overline{\sigma_{aa'}} < \overline{\sigma_{bb'}}$. In this case the $\rho_{aa'}$ will in general have smaller numerators and larger denominators than the $\rho_{bb'}$, contrary to the assumption of equal reliability of the two half-tests.

Hence

$$\Sigma'\sigma_a{}^2 = \Sigma'\sigma_b{}^2 = \Sigma\sigma_i{}^2/2, \qquad (27)$$

$$\overline{\sigma_{aa'}} = \overline{\sigma_{bb'}} = \overline{\sigma_{ii'}},$$

and (26) becomes

$$\rho_{ab} = \frac{k^2\overline{\sigma_{ab}}}{2\Sigma\sigma_i{}^2 + k(k-2)\overline{\sigma_{ii'}}}$$

Applying the Spearman-Brown formula, (16),

$$R_{a+b} = \frac{2k^2\overline{\sigma_{ab}}}{2\Sigma\sigma_i{}^2 + k(k-2)\overline{\sigma_{ii'}} + k^2\overline{\sigma_{ab}}}$$

It is evident that this formula cannot be used unless we know the particular division into half-tests which distinguishes $\overline{\sigma_{ab}}$ from $\overline{\sigma_{ii'}}$. We therefore assume further that

$$\overline{\sigma_{ab}} = \overline{\sigma_{ii'}} = \overline{\sigma_{ij}} \qquad (28)$$

i.e., that the mean within-half-test item covariances are not only equal to each other but are equal also to the mean between-half-test item covariance. With this added assumption,

$$\text{R}_{a+b} = \frac{k^2\overline{\sigma_{ij}}}{\Sigma\sigma_i{}^2 + k(k-1)\overline{\sigma_{ij}}}. \qquad (29)$$

Ferguson's derivation [2] used both (27) and (28) explicitly; Cronbach's [1] used only (28) explicitly, but used a form of the Spearman-Brown formula algebraically equivalent to (10), in which the assumption of (27) is not explicit until we consider the requirement that the two half-tests must have equal units of measurement.

$$\overline{\sigma_{ij}} = \frac{\Sigma^{**}\sigma_{ij}}{k(k-1)/2} = \frac{2\Sigma^{**}\sigma_{ij}}{k(k-1)}$$

and substituting this value in (29),

$$R_{a+b} = \frac{2k}{k-1} \cdot \frac{\Sigma^{**}\sigma_{ij}}{\Sigma\sigma_i{}^2 + 2\Sigma^{**}\sigma_{ij}}. \qquad (30)$$

The variance of the total scores is

$$\sigma_t{}^2 = \Sigma\sigma_i{}^2 + 2\Sigma^{**}\sigma_{ij}, \qquad (31)$$

and hence

$$\Sigma^{**}\sigma_{ij} = (\sigma_t{}^2 - \Sigma\sigma_i{}^2)/2. \qquad (32)$$

Substituting from (31) in the denominator of (30) and from (32) in the numerator,

$$R_{a+b} = \frac{k}{k-1}\left(1 - \frac{\Sigma\sigma_i{}^2}{\sigma_t{}^2}\right), \qquad (33)$$

which is Coefficient Alpha or Kuder-Richardson Formula 20.

If all items are scored + 1 when answered correctly and 0 when answered incorrectly, $\sigma_i{}^2 = \text{p}_i\text{q}_i$, and the unbiased estimate of p_iq_i is

$N_i(N-N_i)/N(N-1)$, where N is the number in the sample and N_i is the number giving the correct answer to the i-th item. The unbiased estimate of σ_t^2 is $s_t^2 = [NSX^2 - (SX)^2]/N(N-1)$, where S indicates summation over the N individuals in the sample. A convenient raw-score computing formula equivalent to (33) is therefore

$$\tilde{R}_{a+b} = \frac{k}{k-1}\left(1 - \frac{N\Sigma N_i - \Sigma N_i^2}{NSX^2 - (SX)^2}\right). \tag{34}$$

This is *not* an unbiased estimate of R_{a+b}; the writer has not seen either an unbiased estimate or a maximum-likelihood estimate.

In the previous discussion, the assumption that $\overline{\sigma_{ab}} = \overline{\sigma_{ii'}}$ was introduced because it was necessary in order to arrive at a formula which did not require explicit differentiation between the items of one half-test and those of the other. Let us now examine the consequences of this assumption, with particular regard to the factorial structures of the items. We set up the following hypothetical factor pattern for a test consisting of just four items:

$$a = cx_1 + fx_2 + e_a, \tag{35}$$

$$a' = c'x_1 + gx_3 + e_{a'}, \tag{36}$$

$$b = cx_1 + fx_2 + e_b, \tag{37}$$

$$b' = c'x_1 + gx_3 + e_{b'}. \tag{38}$$

In this factor pattern, x_1 is a true-score variable common to all items with weight c in items a and b and weight c' in items a' and b', x_2 is common to a and b with weight f in both, x_3 is common to a' and b' with weight g in both, and the e's are errors of measurement unique to each item. We omit the general constants, c_a and c_b, since we are assuming at the outset that the two half-tests, $x_a = a + a'$ and $x_b = b + b'$, are equally reliable and equally variable. We assume as usual that e_a and $e_{a'}$ are uncorrelated with e_b and $e_{b'}$, and that all e's are uncorrelated with all x's; but we do *not* assume that the x's are uncorrelated with one another or that e_a is uncorrelated with $e_{a'}$ or e_b with $e_{b'}$. From these factor patterns, the factor patterns for the two half-tests are

$$a + a' = (c + c')x_1 + fx_2 + gx_3 + e_a + e_{a'} \tag{39}$$

$$b + b' = (c + c')x_1 + fx_2 + gx_3 + e_b + e_{b'}. \tag{40}$$

The two half-tests have the same common factors with the same weights; and if they are equally reliable and equally variable, it follows from the argument of Section 3 that $R_{a+a'} = R_{b+b'} = \rho_{(a+a')(b+b')}$.

Let us now examine the covariances of the a's and b's of (35), (36), (37), and (38).

$$\sigma_{aa'} = \sigma_{bb'} = cc'\sigma_1^2 + c'f\sigma_{12} + cg\sigma_{13} + fg\sigma_{23}, \tag{41}$$

$$\sigma_{ab'} = \sigma_{a'b} = cc'\sigma_1^2 + c'f\sigma_{12} + cg\sigma_{13} + fg\sigma_{23}, \tag{42}$$

$$\sigma_{ab} \;= c^2\sigma_1^2 + f^2\sigma_2^2 + 2cf\sigma_{12}, \tag{43}$$

$$\sigma_{a'b'} = c'^2\sigma_1^2 + g^2\sigma_3^2 + 2c'g\sigma_{13}. \tag{44}$$

From these equations it is clear that σ_{ab} can be equal to $\sigma_{ii'}$ only if

$$(c^2 + c'^2)\sigma_1^2 + f^2\sigma_2^2 + g^2\sigma_3^2 + 2cf\sigma_{12} + 2c'g\sigma_{13}$$
$$= 2cc\,\sigma_1^2 + 2c\,f\sigma_{12} + 2cg\sigma_{13} + 2fg\sigma_{23}.$$

If we assume that $c = c'$ and $f = g$: i.e. that the relative weights of x_1 and x_2 in a and b are the same as the relative weights of x_1 and x_3 in a' and b' this reduces to

$$\sigma_2^2 + \sigma_3^2 = 2\sigma_{23}.$$

This equality can hold only if $\sigma_2^2 = \sigma_3^2$ and $\rho_{23} = 1$. If $\sigma_2^2 \neq \sigma_3^2$, ρ_{23} will exceed unity. But if the weights are equal, the variances are equal, and the correlation is unity, the two variables, x_2 and x_3 are not distinct.

We conclude, therefore, that the assumption that $\overline{\sigma_{ab}} = \overline{\sigma_{ii'}}$ carries the implied restriction that *every item of the test must measure the same true function or combination of true functions.* Under this restriction we are back at once to almost the original Kuder-Richardson assumption: the rank of the matrix of inter-item correlations must be unity, apart from possible "difficulty factors" generated by the use of ϕ-coefficients. Coefficient Alpha—the Kuder-Richardson Formula 20—applies only to factorially homogeneous tests. If we use the split-half technique, on the other hand, it is only required that the two half-tests have the same factorial structure.

5. CONSTRUCTION OF EQUIVALENT FORMS

The requirements for equivalence are that two forms have the same common factors *with the same weights,* and if the units of measurement are equal the total error variances must be equal also. This means in effect that each pair of subsets of items having the same factorial structure must be equally reliable, and the reliability implied here is the *within-subset* reliability. In preparing a test battery, the items of each factorially homogeneous subtest should be item-analyzed against the total score on the experimental edition of *that subtest* to obtain the indices of discrimination needed for allocation of items to forms, and the allocation should be made in such a manner as to yield almost-identical distributions of item-discrimination indices for each subtest. In preparing a non-homogeneous test (an achievement test, e.g., where the forms must be balanced with respect to content), the same considerations apply; and we can reasonably assume that the items covering each *topic* represent a subtest. When a test outline contains both major topics and subtopics, the choice as to which represents a subtest is ordinarily a matter of judgment—guided by the principles that the within-topic content homogeneity of the items should be sufficient to justify the assumption of factorial homogeneity, and that there must be enough items on each topic to permit balancing of the distributions of indices of discrimination. A better but much more time-consuming method would be to allocate items to subgroups on the basis of Wherry-Gaylord procedure [9] rather than on the basis of judged content similarity.

If item-analysis against an external criterion or against a double criterion (both external and internal) is used to select items in such a manner as to maximize the validity of the final test for the specific external criterion, allocation of items to forms must still be based on the subset internal-consistency data alone, if ρ_{ab} is to be a reliability coefficient.

It is not uncommon for test constructors to pick pairs of items which appear to be exceptionally similar in content, and to allocate one to one form and one to the other. In effect this practice is equivalent to taking each item of one form as a separate homogeneous subtest. This procedure can never be justified where a major objective is construction of *equivalent* forms, because of the impossible requirement that every individual pair of items so allocated must have equal indices of discrimination. If two items are judged to be too much alike to be included in the same form, they are certainly too much alike to be included in two equivalent or even parallel forms. The very judgment "too much alike," is in fact a judgment that the two items will generate correlated errors of measurement. Correlated errors of measurement (doublets and narrow group factors) among the items of one form are quite all right; but correlated errors of measurement between items, one in one form and one in another, violate the definition of parallel forms and give rise to inter-form correlations which exceed the reliabilities of the forms. Hence whenever two or more items appear to be exceptionally similar in content, they should all be allocated to the *same* form. This requirement is *at least* as important as the requirement of balanced subset reliabilities. With these procedures the true score is defined as the general factor plus every group factor common to all items of any subtest or topic in which it has a significant loading. Group factors narrower than this, including item doublets, are taken as representing correlated errors of measurement. Allocation by most-similar pairs, on the other hand, implies that *all* causes of inter-item correlation are to be included in the true score. If considerations of proposed use justify this definition (e.g., if the second form is to be used mainly to examine students who missed the session at which the first form was given), it must be recognized that the correlation between the forms will not be a reliability coefficient.

There are some types of tests—paragraph reading, table and diagram interpretation, and the like—in which several test items measure comprehension of, or ability to interpret the message given by, a larger content or problem unit. All test items associated with any one such unit must be assumed to have correlated errors of measurement. Hence the unit and all associated test items must be allocated to one form. In computing Kuder-Richardson Formula 20 for such a test, as well as for tests or subtests containing pairs or sets of items which are unusually similar, the "item" must be the unit and all its associated test items, or the pair or set of unusually similar items. We can actually compute σ_i^2 for the test items of each unit or pair or set, and then substitute in (33). The requirement of factorial homogeneity then applies only to the "items" as defined above, rather than to all the separate test items. In allocating "items" to forms, the average inter-"item" correlations of a subtest should be the same within each of the two forms, and the same as the average inter-"item" correlation between "items" one from one form and one from the other.

All of these "musts," of course, apply only to the construction of forms which are intended to be equivalent. Some lack of equivalence may well be tolerated in practice in order to gain other ends. Thus no mention has been made above of balancing the item difficulties, because equivalence does not require such balance. If, on the other hand, items are so allocated to forms as to balance very closely the total joint distributions of item difficulties and item discriminations, with some loss thereby in the topic-by-topic discrimination balance, the result will be two forms yielding the same distribution of raw scores, and one table of norms will serve for both forms. This consideration may be practically more important than that of constructing two forms, the correlation between which will be precisely a reliability coefficient.

6. VARIETIES OF UNRELIABILITY

For an objective test there are just two measurable types of unreliability: that associated with sampling in the universe of possible items, and that associated with sampling in the universe of possible reactions of the same individuals to the same items on different occasions. For a subjective test—any test which requires evaluation of the responses by a judge in order to yield a score—there are two more: that associated with sampling in the population of possible judges, and that associated with sampling in the universe of evaluations of the same papers by the same judge on different occasions. Sampling in a defined population of examinees does not affect the reliability of the test in that population; it affects only the accuracy with which test reliability can be estimated. And sampling in the universe of specific populations for which the test might be suitable is a problem concerning which there is as yet no useful theory. At present *all* discussions of reliability are relevant only to one defined population of potential examinees.

Considering first the case of an objective test, we note that errors of measurement which result from sampling in the universe of occasions can be eliminated experimentally: we can sample on one occasion only. If the test has more than one form, the two or several forms must be administered *simultaneously*. This is, in effect, what we are doing when we compute a reliability coefficient by Kuder-Richardson Formula 20 or by the split-half method and the Spearman-Brown formula. When we use the later method, all of the considerations of the previous section apply to the allocation of items to half-tests, along with one further consideration: the items of the two half-tests must be so interwoven into the total test as to preserve simultaneity of administration. The usual procedure is to let one form consist of the odd-numbered items and the other the even-numbered items. Even this procedure leaves something to be desired: the whole "even" form is administered one item later than the whole "odd" form. A better arrangement—but quite possibly a hair-split in this case—is to arrange the items as follows (for a 12-item test):

Form a:	1			4	5			8	9			12
Form b:		2	3			6	7			10	11	

This pattern will work only for a test having a number of items which is a multiple of four.

Errors associated with the universe of occasions occur second by second and minute by minute, as well as day by day and week by week. They include differential (different from examinee to examinee) fatigue effects, differential progressive changes in motivation, working procedures, attitudes toward the test, and the like, and in particular, differential variations in working speed. Since these last variations are the same for the two half-tests they will introduce occasion-associated errors of measurement with correlation almost unity if the whole test has a time limit. Whenever a test is timed, the two forms must be administered with experimentally independent time limits; and this precludes their administration simultaneously. Hence every examinee must have ample time to attempt every item if reliability based on sampling in the item-universe only is to be computed by Kuder-Richardson Formula 20 or by the split-half technique and the Spearman-Brown formula without serious overestimation. These formulas cannot properly be used with any test which has a time limit—even a "generous" time limit—let alone with any actual speed test.

We shall term a coefficient computed by Kuder-Richardson Formula 20 or by the split-half technique and the Spearman-Brown formula a "coefficient of internal consistency," and refer to the "internal consistency" of a test when we mean its relative freedom from errors associated with sampling in the item universe. This usage agrees generally with the term "criterion of internal consistency" in item analysis, where the criterion is the total score on the experimental test or some subgroup of its items. The term "coefficient of equivalence" is less satisfactory. The term "equivalence" has a definite meaning when applied to two forms of a test; and when they are absolutely equivalent the coefficient is not unity, but merely an experimentally unbiased estimate of the corresponding parameter of the item universe defined by the two forms; i.e., the universe of all items from which further forms equivalent to the given two must be constructed.

The coefficient of internal consistency of a test yields a gross overestimate of its practical reliability. Errors associated with time are real and substantial, and their variances are different for different kinds of test materials. For the test constructor, however, internal consistency is of major interest, since it is the only aspect of reliability which can be improved by using better items in an objective test.

There are several varieties of errors of measurement which result from sampling in the universe of occurrences. Relative to a given set of test items, each examinee will have at any time a large number of interrelated items of information and misinformation, working skills, and mental abilities. Some are relevant, some are partially relevant, and some are irrelevant but are believed by him to be more or less relevant to the tasks set by the test. We will term the sum total of these his *true ability* at the given time. Logically, the true score of an examinee should be his true ability, measured in the units of the given form of the test.

But over and above the elements of his true ability, each examinee will have at any time a greater or less than average (for him) *mobilization level.* This includes his reactions to session differences in the examiner's statements and procedures and in the working conditions, and random and cyclic variations in emotional control, general fatigue, motivation, attitudes toward the test, anxiety, working procedures including working speed, ability to concentrate, resistance to distraction, and access to his memory. Even if the *probability* that he will mark the right answer to a given item is the same on two occasions, and is neither 0 nor 1, he may mark it right on one occasion and wrong on another. We shall term the aggregate effect of all these factors upon test-score differences from session to session the *stability* of the test. Actually, of course, it is the average stability of the defined population of examinees in preforming the tasks set by the test.

Variations in true ability with time will result from mental growth, mental deterioration, learning, and forgetting. We must distinguish between forgetting, which is a one-way process affecting true ability, and access to memory, which is a fluctuating process affecting mobilization level. Ideally, test reliability should be determined from experimentally independent test sessions so close together that the true abilities of the examinees do not change during the interval. In practice, no interval is short enough. Some elements of the differential practice effect of the first form upon the second represent real learning and (through proactive inhibition) real forgetting. From this standpoint, the longer the interval between sessions, the better.

To obtain an unbiased measure of stability or reliability, the mobilization levels of the examinees at the second session should be uncorrelated with their mobilization levels at the first session. But since variations in some elements of mobilization level are cyclic, this would require an interval between sessions at least half as long as the mean value of the longest cycle. Since differential *seasonal* variation in at least some elements of mobilization level is a tenable hypothesis, and since emotional cycles may also in some cases last for periods of several months or even years, the indicated interval is much too long to satisfy the requirement of minimum change in the true abilities. For experimentally independent administration of two forms of a test, no interval is short enough for both forms to measure the same true abilities; and no practical interval is long enough to justify the assumption of uncorrelated mobilizational-level errors.

If the time interval is too short, correlated mobilization-level errors will appear as spurious elements of true score in the interform correlation, leading to overestimation of the test reliability. This overestimation will decrease with increasing interval. If the interval is greater than zero, changes in the true abilities will appear as spurious elements of instability, leading to underestimation of the test reliability. This underestimation will increase with the interval. For any given test and population then, there should be an optimum interval: the interval across which the overestimation due to correlated mobilization-level errors is just balanced by the underestimation due to differential changes in the true abilities. The true score would then represent the mean true ability over the optimum interval, and the time-associated errors of measurement would be equal to the instability.

The writer, so far, is unable to quantify this theory, or to suggest any experimental design for determining the optimum interval. In the absence of any such theory or information, the following very rough guess is offered: give the first form near the beginning of one week and the second near the end of the following week, one form in the morning and one in the afternoon. This will at least partially control the effects of any diurnal and weekly cycles in mobilization level; and this interval, including one week-end, should be sufficient to reduce within reasonable limits the differential practice effects of the first form upon the second. The mean practice effect has, of course, no effect upon the estimation of reliability.

Whenever a test performance must be evaluated by a judge or reader to yield a score, there is a judge or reader error. Relative freedom from such errors is commonly termed the *objectivity* of the test. In general it is not useful to try to separate the elements of subjectivity associated with different judges from those associated with evaluations by the same judge at different times. No judge can read the same set of papers on a second occasion without perseverative (correlated) errors of judgment occurring, and no two judges can be "synchronized" so that each of them reads the papers while he is at the same relative position as the other on all cyclical functions affecting errors of judgment. If two judges evaluate the same papers or performances independently, the correlation between their marks is a coefficient of objectivity. Possibly one should read the papers in the morning and one in the afternoon, one near the beginning of a week and one near the end, but no further experimental control appears necessary. This last statement, of course, does not apply to the many types of control designed to *reduce* errors of judgment, but only to those designed to permit experimentally unbiased *estimation* of objectivity.

It is the writer's conviction that no useful information is provided by the correlation between scores on the same form administered to the same group at two different times. It is not a coefficient of stability, because the mobilization-level error is cancelled in part by perseveration effects, quite probably including for some items actual recall on the second occasion of the answer given on the first occasion. The correlation is therefore higher than the actual stability of the test, and there is no way of estimating how much higher.

There is, moreover, a better method for estimating the stability of a test. One form is given at the beginning of the optimum interval, and a parallel form at the end. The internal consistency of each form is then determined by Kuder-Richardson Formula 20 or by the split-half technique and the Spearman-Brown formula. The coefficient of stability is then formally equivalent to the correction for attenuation: it is the inter-form correlation divided by the geometric mean internal consistency. The two forms do not have to be either equally reliable or equally variable. The proof is as follows: Let

$$\begin{aligned}
x_a &= c_a(x + e_a + s), \\
x_b &= c_b(x + e_b + s), \\
R_a &= c_a^2(\sigma_x^2 + \sigma_s^2)/\sigma_a^2, \\
R_b &= c_b^2(\sigma_x^2 + \sigma_s^2)/\sigma_b^2,
\end{aligned}$$

where e_a and e_b are the errors of internal consistency, s is the stability error, and R_a and R_b are the coefficients of internal consistency. Then

$$\rho_{ab} = c_a c_b \sigma_x^2 / \sigma_a \sigma_b,$$

$$\frac{\rho_{ab}}{\sqrt{(R_a R_b)}} = \frac{c_a c_b \sigma_x^2 / \sigma_a \sigma_b}{c_a c_b (\sigma_x^2 + \sigma_s^2) / \sigma_a \sigma_b} = \frac{\sigma_x^2}{\sigma_x^2 + \sigma_s^2}. \qquad (45)$$

By the variance-ratio definition, $\sigma_x^2/(\sigma_x^2 + \sigma_s^2)$ is the coefficient of stability, provided the interval is optimum. For shorter intervals it is an overestimate; for longer intervals it is an underestimate. We have not assumed that $R_a = R_b$ nor that $\sigma_a = \sigma_b$. However, R_a and R_b must each meet all the conditions mentioned in previous sections as requirements for their interpretation as coefficients of internal consistency. The stability error is assumed to be uncorrelated with the errors of internal consistency, and the estimate of this error does not depend on the internal consistencies of the forms. The higher their internal consistencies, however, the more accurate will be the estimate given by (45), for given N. The only available estimate is again a simple substitution estimate: replacing ρ_{ab} by r_{ab}, and R_a and R_b by Kuder-Richardson Formula 20 or by the sample half-test correlations $r'_{aa'}$ and $r'_{bb'}$, raised by the Spearman-Brown formula.

The term "reliability" should be reserved for cases in which *all* elements of unreliability have a chance to operate. The reliability of an objective test is estimated by the correlation between equivalent forms administered at times separated by the experimenter's best estimate of the optimum interval. The reliability of an essay examination or any other subjective test requires two equivalent forms also. The forms are administered at times separated by the best estimate of the optimum interval. Each reader must read all answers to a given question if he reads any of them, and there must be zero overlap among the readers of the Form *a* answers and the readers of the Form *b* answers. When all these conditions are met, and then only, the correlation between the Form *a* grades and the Form *b* grades may be considered an estimate of the *reliability* of the subjective test.

REFERENCES

1. Cronbach, L. J. "Coefficient Alpha and the Internal Structure of Tests." *Psychometrika,* XVI (1951), 297–334.
2. Ferguson, G. A. "A Note on the Kuder-Richardson Formula." *Educational and Psychological Measurement*, XI (1951), 612–615.
3. Flanagan, J. C. "Units, Scores, and Norms." In E. F. Lindquist (Editor), *Educational Measurement*. American Council on Education, 1951. Chapter 17.
4. Horst, Paul. "Estimating Total Test Reliability from Parts of Unequal Length." *Educational and Psychological Measurement*, XI (1951), 368–371.

5. Jackson, R. W. B. and Ferguson, G. A. Studies on the Reliability of Tests. Bulletin No. 12, Department of Educational Research, University of Toronto, 1941. (Appendix A)
6. Kelley, T. L. "The Reliability Coefficient." *Psychometrika,* VII (1942), 75–83.
7. Kuder, G. Frederic and Richardson, M. W. "The Theory of the Estimation of Test Reliability." *Psychometrika,* II (1937), 151–160.
8. Thorndike, R. L. "Reliability." In E. F. Lindquist (Editor), *Educational Measurement.* American Council on Education, 1951. Chapter 15.
9. Wherry, R. M. and Gaylord, R. H. "The Concept of Test and Item Reliability in Relation to Factor Patterns." *Psychometrika,* VIII (1943), 247–264.

20. Correcting the Kuder-Richardson Reliability for Dispersion of Item Difficulties

PAUL HORST

Horst, in the following article, agrees with Loevinger (1947) that the Kuder-Richardson reliability formulas are estimates of item homogeneity as well as of test reliability. (Before reading this article the student may wish to reread the views of Humphreys and Cronbach.) Loevinger's attempt to derive a formula that takes into account the deficiency (in her opinion) of the *phi* coefficient is examined by Horst; he concludes she stopped short of her goal. He suggests an additional step that yields a more realistic estimate of reliability than the K-R 20 if items are of unequal difficulty. His statement, in the second to the last paragraph, "We still have to remember that the basic assumption in all these formulas is that all items measure the same function . . . " is worth noting. We may, theoretically, get low internal consistency reliabilities and still obtain high retest reliability.

The relationship between item difficulty and reliability is also examined in the article by Cronbach and Warrington in Unit 5. Other references pertaining to this relationship are mentioned in the introduction to that paper.

Loevinger (**5**) has insisted, quite rightly, that the Kuder-Richardson (**4**) reliability formulas are actually estimates of item homogeneity as

Horst, P. Correcting the Kuder-Richardson reliability for dispersion of item difficulties. *Psychological Bulletin,* 1953, *50,* 371–374. Reprinted with the permission of the publisher and author.

well as of test reliability. She proceeds, then, to point out that K-R 20[1] has unity as an upper limit only when the items in the test are all of equal difficulty, and regards as a serious defect of formula K-R 20 the fact that its upper limit is a function of the dispersion of item difficulties. She argues that a test of perfectly homogeneous items is justified only if there is a range of difficulty in the items. Otherwise, a single item will give the same discrimination as any number of equally difficult perfectly homogeneous items. Therefore, she contends, what is needed is a coefficient of homogeneity which has unity as its maximum value, irrespective of the dispersion of item difficulties. Accordingly, she develops a formula which has this property. It is given in somewhat different notation by

$$H_t = \frac{\sigma_t^2 - \Sigma pq}{\sigma_m^2 - \Sigma pq} \tag{1}$$

where H_t is the coefficient of homogeneity of the test; σ_t^2 the test variance; σ_m^2 is the maximum variance possible for a test which has the same distribution of item difficulties as the test under consideration; Σpq is the sum of the item variances in the test. It is clear, therefore, that as σ_t^2 approaches σ_m^2, H_t approaches unity. It has been shown by Carroll (1) in somewhat different notation that the maximum possible value of the variance of a work limit test, with score being number of items correct, is given by

$$\sigma_m^2 = 2\Sigma i p_i - M_t(1 + M_t) \tag{2}$$

where M_t is the test mean and $\Sigma i p_i$ means that the p's are ranked in descending order of magnitude, each p is multiplied by its rank order, and the sum of the products is taken.

Suppose now we attempt to relate equation (1) to one of the more familiar reliability functions. Kuder and Richardson have shown (4) that the reliability of a test is given by

$$r_{tt} = \frac{\sigma_t^2 - \Sigma pq + \Sigma r_{ii} pq}{\sigma_t^2} \tag{3}$$

where r_{tt} is the reliability of the test; σ_t^2 is the variance of the test; p is the difficulty of an item; $q = 1 - p$; r_{ii} is the reliability of item i.

The problem in using (3) is to get plausible estimates of the item reliabilities. Kuder and Richardson in deriving their well-known formula 20 assumed, in effect, that all item reliabilities are equal. Although they proceeded somewhat differently, we may, from this assumption, rewrite (3) as

$$r_{tt} = \frac{\sigma_t^2 - (1 - r_{ii})\Sigma pq}{\sigma_t^2}. \tag{4}$$

[1] This formula is

$$r_{tt} = \frac{n}{n-1}\left(\frac{\sigma_t^2 - \Sigma pq}{\sigma_t^2}\right)$$

If now we let r_{ii} be the ratio of the average item covariance to the average item variance, we have shown elsewhere (2) that

$$r_{ii} = \frac{\sigma_t^2 - \Sigma pq}{(n-1)\Sigma pq}. \tag{5}$$

Except for a slight difference in notation, equation (5) gives the same estimate of item reliability which Kuder and Richardson derived by somewhat different methods in their formula 18. Substituting (5) in (4), we get

$$r_{tt} = \frac{\sigma_t^2 - \left[1 - \left(\frac{\sigma_t^2 - \Sigma pq}{(n-1)\Sigma pq}\right)\right]\Sigma pq}{\sigma_t^2} \tag{6}$$

which reduces to

$$r_{tt} = \frac{n}{n-1}\left(\frac{\sigma_t^2 - \Sigma pq}{\sigma_t^2}\right). \tag{7}$$

Equation (7) is, of course, the well-known Kuder-Richardson Formula 20 for estimating test reliability.

Let us now examine equation (5) in the light of Loevinger's criticism. For a set of items of specified difficulties, r_{ii} will be a maximum only when σ_t^2, or the variance, is as large as possible. This maximum value, σ_t^2, is given by equation (2). First we shall write (5) in the form

$$r_{ii} = \frac{\sigma_t^2 - \Sigma pq}{n\Sigma pq - \Sigma pq}. \tag{8}$$

We shall prove that (8) cannot be unity unless all of the items are of equal difficulty. It is well known that the variance of a test can be expressed as a function of the item variances and the interitem correlations, if the score is number correct and the test is not speeded. This function is

$$\sigma^2 = \left|\begin{array}{llll} s_1^2 & + s_1s_2r_{12} + & \cdots & + s_1s_nr_{1n} \\ + s_1s_2r_{12} + & s_2^2 + & \cdots & + s_2s_nr_{2n} \\ \cdots & \cdots & \cdots & \cdots \\ + s_ns_nr_{1n} & + s_2s_nr_{2n} + & \cdots & + s_n^2 \end{array}\right| \tag{9}$$

where $S_i = \sqrt{p_iq_i}$ and the r_{ij} are phi coefficients. If we prove that

$$\sigma_t^2 < n\Sigma pq \tag{10}$$

for items of unequal difficulty, we shall have proved that r_{ii} is less than unity, since the last terms of both numerator and denominator of (8) are equal. Since $S_i = \sqrt{p_iq_i}$ we must prove that

$$\sigma_t^2 < n\Sigma s_i^2. \tag{11}$$

It can readily be shown that a phi coefficient must be less than unity unless both items are equally difficult. In no case can they exceed unity.

If we prove that, even though all r's in (9) are unity, the inequality in (11) must still hold for unequal S's, then we will also have proved it for the case of some r's less than unity. Assuming all r's in (9) unity, we write

$$\sigma_t^2 = (\Sigma s)^2. \tag{12}$$

Substituting (12) in (11),

$$(\Sigma s)^2 < n\Sigma s^2. \tag{13}$$

We indicate the variance of the s's by σ_s^2 and, from the standard formula, write

$$\sigma_s^2 = \frac{\Sigma s^2}{n} - \left(\frac{\Sigma s}{n}\right)^2$$

or

$$(\Sigma s)^2 = n\Sigma s^2 - n^2\sigma_s^2. \tag{14}$$

Substituting (14) in (13),

$$n\Sigma s^2 - n^2 - n^2\sigma_s^2 < n\Sigma s^2 \tag{15}$$

or

$$n^2\sigma_s^2 < 0. \tag{16}$$

Obviously, (16) holds unless the variance of the item sigmas is zero. But the variance of the item sigmas cannot be zero unless all the item difficulties are equal, or unless some of them are equal to a constant p and all the others are equal to a constant $1 - p$. But in the latter case not all of the phi coefficients could be unity. So the only case in which σ_i^2 could be as large as $n\,\Sigma pq$ is when the item variances are all equal and the phi coefficients are all unity, and this can be true only when all items are of equal difficulty.

Loevinger (**6**) and Johnson (**3**) have proposed that, in order to make a phi coefficient independent of the disparity of its item difficulties, we should divide it by the maximum phi which is possible for the two obtained difficulties. Generalizing from this rationale, we shall apply the procedure to r_{ii} in (5).

$$r_m = \frac{\sigma_m^2 - \Sigma pq}{(n-1)\Sigma pq} \tag{17}$$

where σ_m^2 is the maximum variance of a test with specified item difficulties. We then let ρ_{ii} be the adjusted value of r_{ii} and write

$$\rho_{ii} = \frac{r_{ii}}{r_m} \tag{18}$$

or substituting (5) and (17) in (18),

$$\rho_{ii} = \frac{\sigma_t^2 - \Sigma pq}{\sigma_m^2 - \Sigma pq}. \tag{19}$$

But we see that equation (19) is precisely equation (1), or Loevinger's coefficient of homogeneity. This is the coefficient which she preferred to K-R 20. However, this preference does not seem entirely appropriate. As we have seen, it gives an estimate of average item intercorrelation corrected for dispersion of item difficulties. Loevinger's proposal lacks one essential step. To get a more realistic estimate of test reliability, we should substitute her formula for the estimate of average item reliability in equation (4). Substituting equation (19) in (4) we get

$$r_{tt} = \frac{\sigma_t^2 - \left(1 - \dfrac{\sigma_t^2 - \Sigma pq}{\sigma_m^2 - \Sigma pq}\right) \Sigma pq}{\sigma_t^2} \qquad (20)$$

which reduces to

$$r_{tt} = \left(\frac{\sigma_t^2 - \Sigma pq}{\sigma_m^2 - \Sigma pq}\right) \frac{\sigma_m^2}{\sigma_t^2}. \qquad (21)$$

Equation (21) would seem to provide a more realistic estimate of the reliability coefficient than K-R 20. It yields a higher estimate if the items are of unequal difficulty and will have unity as an upper limit irrespective of the dispersion of item difficulties. Because of the factor σ_m^2/σ_t^2, it yields a higher value than Loevinger's homogeneity coefficient given by (1).

The chief disadvantage of using (21) rather than K-R 20 is, of course, the added time required to compute σ_m^2 as given by (2). However, the major part of the labor involved in using K-R 20 is getting the item counts for the *pq* values. Once the *p*'s are obtained, it is not a great deal more work to get Σip required in equation (2) to get σ_m^2.

If we have a wide distribution of item difficulties, the difference between K-R 20 and our equation (21) may actually be quite large. Suppose, for example, we have for seven items in ascending order of difficulty, the following values: .80, .70, .60, .50, .40, .30, and .20. Suppose the variance of the test is 5.25. We have, then, the following values:

$$n = 7$$

$$M_t = \Sigma p = 3.50$$

$$\sigma_t^2 = 5.25$$

$$\Sigma pq = 1.470$$

$$\Sigma ip = 11.20$$

For the K-R 20 value we have

$$r_{tt} = \frac{7}{6}\left(\frac{5.25 - 1.47}{5.25}\right) = .84 .$$

For the adjusted value given by our equation (21) we must first compute the maximum variance given by equation (2). This is

$$\sigma_m^2 = 2 \times 11.20 - (3.50)\ (4.50) = 6.65.$$

Substituting the required values in (21), we have

$$r_{tt} = \left(\frac{5.25 - 1.47}{6.65 - 1.47}\right) \frac{6.65}{5.25} = .92\,.$$

In this particular case, therefore, with a rectangular distribution of item difficulties ranging from .80 down to .20, our estimate of reliability is almost 10 per cent higher than that given by K-R 20. It should be emphasized that, even with the correction we suggest, we are compensating only for the attenuation introduced by the dispersion of item difficulties. We still have to remember that the basic assumption in all these formulas is that all items measure the same function, and that the failure of maximum item intercorrelation is due only to the unreliability of the items. Thus, even our formula (21) should be regarded as only a lower bound to the Kuder-Richardson type of reliability even though this lower bound may be somewhat higher than that given by K-R 20.

It should be emphasized that the type of reliability which we refer to is consistency of behavior within a very limited time interval, that is, the time interval during which the items in the test are being responded to. This is, of course, also the type of reliability implied by the Kuder-Richardson formulas. However, it should also be observed that this "short term" reliability is comparable to the correlation between two tests taken within a short time interval, e.g., at the same sitting or on the same day.

REFERENCES

1. Carroll, J. B. The effect of difficulty and chance success on correlation between items or between tests. *Psychometrika,* 1945, **10,** 1–19.
2. Horst, P. Relationships between several Kuder-Richardson reliability formulas. *J. educ. psychol. Measmt,* in press.
3. Johnson, H. M. Maximal selectivity, correctivity and correlation obtainable in 2 × 2 contingency-tables. *Amer. J. Psychol.,* 1945, **58,** 65–68.
4. Kuder, G. F., & Richardson, M. W. The theory of the estimation of test reliability. *Psychometrika,* 1937, **2,** 151–160.

5. Loevinger, Jane. A systematic approach to the construction and evaluation of test of ability. *Psychol. Monogr.,* 1947, **61,** No. 4 (Whole No. 285).
6. Loevinger, Jane. The technique of homogeneous tests. *Psychol. Bull.,* 1948, **45,** 507–529.

21. Do Tests of the Same Length Have the Same Standard Error of Measurement?

FREDERIC M. LORD

Test reliability coefficients are often used as indicators of the precision of test scores. Most users recognize, however, that a reliability coefficient depends not only on characteristics of the test but also on those of the individuals tested. The spread of ability among the examinees, as well as the number of items in the test, the discriminating power of the items, and other factors determine the size of the reliability coefficient.

In these circumstances a measure of score precision that does not depend on group variability looks attractive. Such a measure is the standard error of measurement. But it turns out to be rather difficult to interpret. For, paradoxically enough, good tests tend to have larger standard errors of measurement, when expressed in raw score units, than do poor tests. One thing that helps to make them good, *i.e.,* the number of items they include, also gives them more opportunities to err and thus contributes to larger standard errors of measurement.

There is worse to come. It also turns out, as Lord demonstrates in this article, that the standard error of measurement of a particular test for a given examinee is only a function of the number of items in the test, and of the examinee's true score. It does not depend on item quality, as reflected by item discrimination indices. Nor does it depend on test quality. Two similar tests, one of which sharply differentiates two examinees of differing ability and the other of which does not differentiate them at all, may have identical standard errors of measurement for a particular examinee.

Recognizing that this conclusion is likely to seem strange, even unreasonable, to some readers, Dr. Lord establishes it with care and then discusses

Lord, F. M. Do tests of the same length have the same standard error of measurement? *Educational and Psychological Measurement,* 1957, *17,* 510–521. Reprinted with the permission of the publisher and author.

a number of questions that it will suggest to the critical reader. His logical reasoning will repay careful reading.

From one very useful point of view, granted certain reasonable restrictions, tests of the same length do have the same standard errors of measurement, which can thus be computed even before the test items have been written. Such standard errors are now in use with certain nationally distributed tests (2). Several puzzling questions regarding these standard errors are discussed here and answers given.

Necessary definitions and restrictions are the following:

1. By test "length" is meant the number of items in the test.

2. The test items are scored 0 or 1; the examinee's score is the sum of his item scores.

3. The examinee's response to an item depends only on the item itself. (In particular, it does not depend on the serial position of the item in the test. This excludes speeded tests from present consideration.)

4. The "standard error of measurement" is defined as the standard deviation of the scores that an individual examinee would be expected to obtain on a very large number of "parallel" test forms, assuming that the individual remains unchanged during the testing and unaffected by practice, fatigue, and so forth. (The precise interpretation to be given to the words "expected" and "parallel" will appear in the course of the discussion. It should be noted that the standard error of measurement is defined with respect to a given examinee, and that two individuals taking the same test will not in general have the same standard error of measurement.)

The formula (5, equation 2; 6, equation 10) for the standard error of measurement of examinee a is the same as the familiar binomial formula commonly used, for example, to represent the sampling error of the number of white balls in a sample drawn at random from an urn containing a large number of white and black balls:

$$\text{S.E.}(t_a) = \sqrt{\frac{1}{n}\,\tau_a(n-\tau_a)} \qquad (1)$$

$$= \sqrt{n\zeta_a(1-\zeta_a)},$$

where t_a is the actual score of examinee a, n is the number of items in the test, τ_a is the "true score" of examinee a, and $\zeta_a = \tau_a/n$ is the "true" proportion-correct score of examinee a.

Equation (1) states that the standard error of measurement for examinee a depends only on the true score of examinee a (which can be estimated from his actual score) and on the number of items in the test. The implications of this formula in its present context are sufficiently novel to suggest to the thoughtful reader a number of questions that seem to cast doubt on its correctness or usefulness.

The Derivation of Equation (1)

Before discussing these questions, it may be well to review the derivation of equation (1).

In the timeworn example, the statistician has an urn that contains a large number of balls some of which are white, the rest being black. Samples, each containing n balls, are drawn at random from the urn, and the number of white balls in each sample is counted. Formulas may be written for various statistical properties of this number, such as its mean, standard deviation, and frequency distribution over a large number of samples.

Paralleling the urn containing a large number of balls, we may imagine a pool containing a large number of test items. If all the items in the pool could be administered to the examinee without practice effect, fatigue effect, and so forth, the ones that he would get right may be thought of as corresponding to the white balls, the ones that he would get wrong as corresponding to the black balls. Each parallel form of the test is thought of as a random sample of items from the pool. The number of "white" (correctly answered) items in each sample is the examinee's score on that form of the test. The standard deviation of this number, found by the usual binomial formula, is the examinee's standard error of measurement, as given by equation (1).

It is obvious that in order to use equation (1), it will ordinarily be necessary to replace the examinee's true score in the equation by his observed score. The resulting formula for the standard error of measurement is

$$\text{S.E.}(t_a) \doteq \sqrt{\frac{1}{n-1}\, t_a(n - t_a)}, \tag{2}$$

$n - 1$ being used in the denominator rather than n in order that the sample estimate of the standard error of measurement shall be unbiased.

An important relation exists between the standard error of (2) and the test reliability, which is defined by the equation

$$r_{tt} = 1 - \frac{\text{S.E.}^2(t)}{s_t^2}, \tag{3}$$

where s_t is the standard deviation of the scores of the examinees tested and $\text{S.E.}^2(t)$ is some sort of average of their standard errors of measurement. It has been shown (6) that if the standard error of equation (2) is squared, averaged over all examinees, and the average substituted for $\text{S.E.}^2(t)$ in (3), the resulting reliability coefficient is mathematically equal to the Kuder-Richardson formula-21 reliability coefficient. This result provides a new basis for the use of that coefficient, whose derivation previously rested on some rather drastic assumptions regarding the test items (4).

Question 1

Equation (1) *depends on the examinee's true score, which is not only unknown but is actually unknowable because of practice effect, etc. How can a statement based on operationally undefinable quantities be put to practical use?*

For considerably more than a century the subtleties of statistical inference have created controversy and confusion, even among leading mathematicians. Rather than attempt a philosophical discussion here, it should be sufficient to point out that the statistician deals habitually and effectively with unknown and unknowable quantities and characteristics that are assumed to characterize populations that are actually nonexistent. The fact that the balls in the statistician's urn may be so numerous as to make it out of the question to count the number of white and the number of black balls accurately does not prevent the statistician from obtaining useful practical estimates from samples drawn from the urn.

Another analogy may be of help. Consider a coin-tossing experiment, in which the coin may be biased. The statistician will assert that equation (1), with suitable redefinition of the symbols, represents the standard error of the number of "heads" to be expected in a set of n tosses. It may be argued that the true value of ζ is unknown for this particular coin and indeed could never be found exactly, since the coin would doubtless begin to wear out appreciably after a few million tosses. The fact is, however, that the true bias of the coin, as represented by ζ, can be estimated with a known degree of accuracy from information obtained on a small number of tosses. From a practical point of view, such estimates are frequently completely satisfactory substitutes for the unknown, unknowable, and operationally undefinable true value.

Question 2

In practice equation (1) *is used by substituting the examinee's observed score for his true score. Is this legitimate? In particular, suppose the examinee's observed score is* 0; *according to the formula his standard error of measurement is also* 0. *How can this be correct?*

Whereas (1) is a rigorously accurate equation, the dot above the equal sign in (2) indicates that the equation is only approximately true, since the examinee's true score has been replaced by his observed score. The utility of (2) obviously depends on the extent to which the observed score provides a good estimate of the true score. If the number of items in the test is very small ($n = 2$ or 3, say), then the examinee's observed score does not supply a very accurate estimate of his true score and little can be inferred about the magnitude of the standard error of measurement.

In large-sample theory, it is, of course, common practice to substitute observed values for "true" values. In most situations, the error introduced by this approximation tends to decrease inversely as $\sqrt{n}$, so that the error can be made arbitrarily small if n is made sufficiently large. The exact effect of the substitution of observed values for true values can perhaps be made clearer with the aid of a numerical example and the use of confidence limits.

Suppose that a given examinee has obtained a score of 80 on a 100-item test. Using the normal-curve approximation that 95 per cent of obtained scores will lie within 1.96 standard deviations from the true score, the 95 per cent confidence limits are found to be 71.1 and 86.7. If $\tau_a = 71.1$, the standard error of an obtained score is found from equation (1) to be 4.5; if $\tau_a = 86.7$, then the standard error is 3.4. (The confidence limits were chosen so that the obtained score of 80 is precisely $1.96 \times 4.5 = 8.9$ score points above 71.1 and $1.96 \times 3.4 = 6.7$ points below 86.7.) Thus the 95 per cent confidence belt for the standard error of measurement for examinee *a* is from 3.4 to 4.5. If the statistician follows this same procedure for a large number of examinees and asserts that the true standard error of measurement of each examinee lies somewhere within his confidence belt, the statistician's assertions will, in the long run, be correct for 95 per cent of the examinees.

If an examinee obtains a perfect (or a zero) score his standard error of measurement as estimated by (2) is zero. In large-sample theory, this result is a reasonably good approximation—if n is sufficiently large, the standard error of measurement for such an examinee will actually be close to zero. A clear understanding of the degree of the approximation involved in any actual case can again be obtained by the use of confidence intervals.

If an examinee obtains a score of 100 on a 100-item test the 95-per cent confidence interval within which his true score may be expected to lie extends from $\tau_a = 100$ to $\tau_a = 96.378$. (The lower limit for the confidence interval is found, without using the normal-curve approximation, by solving for ζ_a the equation $\zeta_a^{100} = .025$, ζ_a^{100} being the probability that 100 items drawn at random will all be items that are answered correctly by the examinee whose true score is ζ_a.) When $\tau = 96.378$, the standard error of measurement is 1.87. Thus the confidence interval for the standard error of measurement for the examinee whose obtained score is 100 ranges from 0 to 1.87. Although this is a larger range of uncertainty than one might wish, it still enables us to assert with confidence that the standard error of measurement for this examinee is less than 1.87, and certainly less than the standard error of measurement of the examinee whose obtained score is 80.

Question 3

An examinee who obtains a high score on the first form of a test is likely also to obtain a high score on other subsequent forms of the test. Does this not mean that the successive independent and random sampling required for the application of the usual binomial formulas does not exist, since successive samples appear to be dependent on each other?

If we consider the scores of two examinees on each of a number of parallel tests, there will be a correlation between the scores of examinee *a* and the scores of examinee *b,* arising from the fact that both examinees will tend to obtain poor scores on those tests that happen to be a little more difficult than the others, and both will tend to obtain higher scores on tests that happen to be rather easy. This type of correlation is not relevant in a discussion of the standard error of measurement of an individual, however, since in discussing the standard error, it is logically necessary to restrict attention to one individual at a time. For a given individual, having a given true score, the scores that he attains on successive parallel forms of the test are all independent of each other.

A related point may be noted here. If a pair of different tests are administered to a single examinee and then this testing is repeated on many successive occasions, each time using a randomly parallel form of each test, theoretically (assuming no practice effect, etc.) there will be no correlation between his successive scores on one test and the corresponding scores on the other. Hence the squared standard error of measurement for the score difference between the two tests will equal the sum of the squared standard errors of measurement for the two separate tests and will not depend on any coefficient of correlation between them.

Question 4

According to formula (1), *the standard errors of measurement of a test do not depend on any of the statistical properties of the items from which the test is constructed. Thus the formula indicates, does it not, that the standard errors of measurement cannot be improved by any attempt to build or to select "good" test items?*

It is a striking fact that *the standard errors of measurement, as here defined, do not depend in any way on the content, form, or statistical characteristics of the items in the test, provided the items are scored* 0 *or* 1. It is still important, however, for the test constructor to use valid, discriminating items. The effectiveness of the test as a measuring instrument depends not on the standard errors of measurement alone, but on the relation of the standard errors of measurement to the standard deviation of the obtained scores of the examinees tested. In fact, the reliability coefficient of the test is defined as a simple function of the ratio of these standard deviations, as seen from equation (3).

The standard deviation of the test scores is a function of the item difficulties and inter-item correlations; an increase in the item inter-correlations (or the item-test correlations) will ordinarily increase the standard deviation of the test scores and will thus increase the reliability of the test. Hence, the use of effective test items remains essential for any good test.

Question 5

The logic underlying equation (1) *requires that "parallel" forms of the test shall be constructed by selecting items at random from a pool of items. Such forms are not parallel in the strictest sense (3, ch. 14), since sampling fluctuations will cause them to differ somewhat in average item difficulty, in average item discriminating power, and even in factorial composition. Furthermore, actual tests are rarely constructed in this way. If more than one form is to be built, some attempt is usually made to match the items on the two forms on item type, item difficulty, subject matter, and so forth. How, therefore, is it possible to apply formula* (1) *in ordinary testing situations?*

First of all, it may be noted that the Kuder-Richardson formula-20 reliability coefficient is likewise based on assumptions about the "rational equivalence" of parallel test forms that are far from being met in practice, yet this fact does not destroy the utility of this coefficient. The derivation of the coefficient assumes that parallel test forms have the same average item difficulty and the same average inter-item covariance. Actual "parallel" forms rarely if ever satisfy this definition, yet the practical value of this reliability coefficient is beyond challenge.

In actual practice, the items in parallel test forms generally are matched to some extent in one way or another. This "matching" is commonly done with somewhat less than complete scientific precaution. To insure the desired result, the available items should be stratified according to one or more important characteristics (content, form, difficulty, et cetera) and then the items within each stratum allocated to the test forms *at random*.

If the phrase "at random" is interpreted, as is frequently done, as describing any process whose bias is not immediately obvious, then it is likely that the "parallel" test forms produced will differ from each other more than if no "matching" had occurred. If the matching is carefully done, however, the resulting parallel forms will resemble each other more than they would if the items in each form had been selected at random from a common pool. Thus when the parallel forms of a test are carefully matched, the standard error of measurement defined by such matched forms must be less for each examinee than that given by equation (1). Equation (1) thus gives a definition of the standard error of measurement that is conservative in comparison to that appropriate for carefully matched test forms.

The degree to which equation (1) overestimates the standard error of measurement in the case of any actual test can be determined by comparing the Kuder-Richardson formula-21 reliability coefficient for the test with the matched-forms reliability of the test. The appropriateness of this comparison derives from the fact (6) that the formula-21 reliability coefficient is identically equal to the coefficient defined by (3) when the standard errors of measurement as defined by (2) are squared and averaged over all examinees and the resulting value substituted for $S.E.^2(t)$ in (3). Since the formula-21 reliability coefficient is usually found to be only a moderate underestimate of the matched-forms reliability coefficient, it follows that the standard error of measurement defined by (1) or (2) is usually only a moderate overestimate of the standard error of measurement defined by matched test forms.

Cronbach (**1**, pp. 309–312) quotes a number of empirical studies tending to the conclusion that, unless the items are exceptionally heterogeneous, ". . . the sort of judgment a tester might make on typical items, knowing their content and difficulty, does not, contrary to the earlier opinion of Kelley and Cronbach, permit him to make more comparable half-tests than would be obtained by random splitting." This conclusion relates to the splitting of a test into parallel half-tests; it would thus apply *a fortiori* to the selection of two parallel tests from a very large pool of test items.

Question 6

It seems intuitively evident that the standard error of measurement at or near the "chance score" level is larger than at higher levels where less guessing occurs. On a test composed of 100 *five-choice items, for example, the "chance score" is* 20, *since an examinee would be expected to obtain a score of* 20 *if he simply marks all items at random. Scores near this level are subject to sizable fluctuations due to lucky or unlucky guessing that are additional to the other errors of measurement afflicting all test scores. Yet according to equation* (1) *the standard error of measurement on a 100-item test, for example, is the same for an examinee with a score of* 80 *as it is for an examinee with a score of* 20*; furthermore, this standard error of measurement remains the same irrespective of whether the test is a free-response test on which guessing cannot occur, a test composed of five-choice items permitting some* *guessing, or a true-false test on which much guessing may be expected. How can this be?*

In a hypothetical test-retest situation in aptitude or achievement testing, it is clear, granted certain reasonable assumptions, that the score of a high-scoring examinee will in general tend to fluctuate less between two administrations of the same test than will the score of a low-scoring examinee. The reason is that the high-scoring examinee knows the answer to most of the questions and will therefore not change his response to them, whereas the low-scoring examinee will respond more or less at random to most of the questions, thus introducing a large random fluctuation from one testing to the next.

A totally different conclusion is reached if the hypothetical retesting is to be done with a randomly parallel form of the test rather than by readministering the original form. As will be shown below, *if two examinees have the same true score (proportion of correct answers for all items in the pool, including correct answers obtained by guessing), the standard error of measurement (the standard deviation of the scores obtained by the examinee on successive randomly parallel forms) will be the same even though one examinee guesses whenever he does not know the correct answer to an item and the other examinee omits any item for which he is not sure of the correct answer.*

Suppose that examinee *a* knows the correct answer to ζ_a of the items in the (infinitely) large pool of items, and that he gives no response to any item for which he does not know the correct answer. The standard error of measurement for examinee *a* is given by equation (1).

Suppose that the proportion of items in the pool that would be answered correctly by examinee *b* is $\zeta_b = \zeta_a$. However, the proportion of items in the pool to which examinee *b* *knows* the correct answer is only π_b; on all other items, examinee *b* responds by guessing. Let κ_b denote his chance of success when guessing, i.e., let κ_b be the ratio of correct guesses to total guesses for the items in the pool. (Note that his guessing is *not* assumed to be at random, nor is his chance of success assumed to be the same for different items.) Thus in the pool,

$$\zeta_b = \pi_b + (1 - \pi_b)\kappa_b. \tag{4}$$

If a given test contains *n* items selected at random from the pool, the probability that examinee *b* will *know* the correct answer to x_b of these is given by the usual binomial formula:

$$\text{Prob}(x) = \binom{n}{x} \pi^x (1 - \pi)^{n-x}, \tag{5}$$

the subscript *b* having been dropped for convenience. The standard deviation of *x* in successive random samples is given by the usual binomial formula:

$$\text{S.E.}(x) = \sqrt{n\pi(1 - \pi)}. \tag{6}$$

There will be $n-x$ items to which the examinee does not know the answer, and to which he will therefore respond by guessing. Let y be the number of items in the test, out of $n-x$, that examinee b answers correctly *by guessing*. Obviously, the frequency distribution of y is *not* independent of the value of x. For given x, y has a binomial distribution, with a mean given by the usual binomial formula:

$$M(y \mid x) = (n-x)\kappa. \tag{7}$$

The standard deviation of y for a given value of x is, by the familiar binomial formula,

$$\text{S.E.}(y \mid x) = \sqrt{(n-x)\kappa(1-\kappa)}. \tag{8}$$

The test score that the examinee actually obtains is equal to the number of items that he knows plus the number that he guesses correctly, i.e., $t = x + y$. The average value of t for fixed x is found with the help of equation (7) to be

$$\begin{aligned} M(t \mid x) &= x + (n-x)\kappa \\ &= (1-\kappa)x + n\kappa. \end{aligned} \tag{9}$$

The desired standard error of t can be obtained from the following general formula, similar to a familiar identity in analysis of variance:

$$\text{S.E.}^2(t) = \epsilon\,[\text{S.E.}^2(y \mid x)] + \text{S.E.}^2[M(t \mid x)], \tag{10}$$

where the first term on the right denotes the average value over all samples of the square of the quantity in (8), and the second term on the right is the squared standard deviation over all samples of the quantity (9). (The symbol ϵ denotes the operation of averaging over all samples of test items; it thus has the same mathematical properties as the symbol Σ and may be manipulated accordingly.)

From (8),

$$\begin{aligned} \epsilon[\text{S.E.}^2(y \mid x)] &= \epsilon(n-x)\kappa(1-\kappa) \\ &= \kappa(1-\kappa)\epsilon(n-x) \\ &= \kappa(1-\kappa)(n-n_\pi), \end{aligned} \tag{11}$$

since n and κ are constants for all samples, and since $\epsilon(x)$, the average value of x over all samples, is n_π.

The standard error of $M(t \mid x)$ is readily found from equations (9) and (6) to be

$$\begin{aligned} \text{S.E.}[M(t \mid x)] &= (1-\kappa)\text{S.E.}(x) \\ &= (1-\kappa)\sqrt{n\pi(1-\pi)}. \end{aligned} \tag{12}$$

From (10), (11), and (12), finally

$$\begin{aligned} \text{S.E.}(t) &= \sqrt{\kappa(1-\kappa)n(1-\pi) + (1-\kappa)^2 n\pi(1-\pi)} \\ &= \sqrt{(1-\kappa)(1-\pi)n(\kappa+\pi-\kappa\pi)} \\ &= \sqrt{n\zeta(1-\zeta)}, \end{aligned} \tag{13}$$

where ζ is the same as ζ_b in equation (4).

Since ζ_b is the same as ζ_a, and since (13) is the same as (1), it follows that the standard error of measurement for the examinee who guessed at the items he did not know is the same as the standard error of measurement for the examinee who omitted the items that he did not know, provided always that both examinees have the same true score.

REFERENCES

1. Cronbach, L. J. "Coefficient Alpha and the Internal Structure of Tests." *Psychometrika,* XVI (1951), 297–334.
2. Educational Testing Service. *Cooperative School and College Ability Tests.* Princeton, New Jersey: Educational Testing Service, 1955.
3. Gulliksen, H. *Theory of Mental Tests.* New York: John Wiley and Sons, 1950.
4. Kuder, G. F. and Richardson, M. W. "The Theory of Estimation of Test Reliability." *Psychometrika,* II (1937), 151–160.
5. Lord, Frederic M. "Sampling Fluctuations Resulting from the Sampling of Test Items." *Psychometrika,* XX (1955), 1–22.
6. Lord, Frederic M. "Estimating Test Reliability." *Educational and Psychological Measurement*, XV (1955), 325–336.

UNIT THREE: RELIABILITY

ADDITIONAL READINGS

Bingham, W. V. Reliability, validity and dependability. *Journal of Applied Psychology,* 1932, *16,* 116–22.

Burt, C. Testing reliability estimated by analysis of variance. *British Journal of Statistical Psychology*, 1955, *8*, 103–118.

Cattell, R. B. Validity and reliability: A proposed more basic set of concepts. *Journal of Educational Psychology*, 1964, *55*, 1–22.

Coombs, C. H. The concepts of reliability and homogeneity. *Educational and Psychological Measurement*, 1950, *10*, 43–56.

Cronbach, L. J. Test "reliability": Its meaning and determination. *Psychometrika*, 1947, *12*, 1–16.

Cronbach, L. J., and Gleser, Goldine C. Interpretation of reliability and validity coefficients: Remarks on a paper by Lord. *Journal of Educational Psychology*, 1959, *50*, 230–237.

Cronbach, L. J., Rajaratnam, Nageswari, and Gleser, Goldine C. Theory of generalizability: A liberalization of reliability theory. *British Journal of Statistical Psychology*, 1963, *16*, 137–163.

Dressel, P. L. Some remarks on the Kuder-Richardson reliability coefficient. *Psychometrika*, 1940, *5*, 305–310.

Gaito, J. Relative and absolute consistency in reliability and validity procedures. *Journal of General Psychology*, 1964, *70*, 139–141.

Horst, P. A generalized expression for the reliability of measures. *Psychometrika.* 1949, *14*, 21–32.

Hoyt, C. J., and Stunkard, C. L. Estimation of test reliability for unrestricted item scoring methods. *Educational and Psychological Measurement,* 1952, *12,* 756–758.

LaForge, R. Components of reliability. *Psychometrika*, 1965, *30*, 187–195.

Loevinger, J. A systematic approach to the construction and evaluation of tests of ability. *Psychological Monograph*, 1947, *61*, No. 4.

Loevinger, J. The attenuation paradox in test theory. *Psychological Bulletin*, 1954, *51,* 493–504.

Lord, F. M. The relation of the reliability of multiple-choice tests to the distribution of item difficulties. *Psychometrika*, 1952, *17*, 181–194.

Lord, F. M. Sampling error due to choice of split in split-half reliability coefficients. *Journal of Experimental Education*, 1956, *24*, 245–249.

Lord, F. M. The utilization of unreliable difference scores. *Journal of Educational Psychology*, 1958, *49*, 150–152.

Lord, F. M. Tests of the same length do have the same standard error of measurement. *Educational and Psychological Measurement*, 1959, *19*, 233–239.

Lorr, M. Relations between the intraclass correlations and the Kuder-Richardson reliability formulas. *Journal of Clinical Psychology*, 1960, *16*, 447–450.

Patterson, C. H. A note on the standard error of measurement *Journal of Educational Psychology*, 1955, *46*, 239–242.

Rajaratnam, Nageswari, Cronbach, L. J., and Gleser, Goldine C. Generalizability of stratified-parallel tests. *Psychometrika,* 1964, *29,* 39–56.

Remmers, H. H., and Whisler, L. D. Test reliability as a function of method of computation. *Journal of Educational Psychology*, 1938, *29*, 81–92.

Reprint of reviews of the *Opinion, Attitude, and Interest Survey* (OAIS) by Dr. John O. Crites and Dr. Harold D. Webster, and Reprint of two open letters to Dr. Crites by Dr. Benno G. Fricke, 1965, 14 pp.

Richardson, M. W., and Kuder, G. F. The calculation of test reliability coefficients based on the method of rational equivalence. *Journal of Educational Psychology*, 1939, *30*, 681–687.

Saupe, J. L. Some useful estimates of the Kuder-Richardson formula number 20 reliability coefficient. *Educational and Psychological Measurement*, 1961, *21,* 63–71.

Unit Four:

VALIDITY

22. A Critical Examination of the Concepts of Face Validity[1]

CHARLES I. MOSIER

Validity is commonly regarded as the essential quality of any psychological test. What validity means, precisely, and how it should be determined have been subjects of some dispute. A great many of the articles that have been written on the subject of validity have been devoted either to correcting errors which the author believes others have made in defining and assessing validity or to the proposal of some new conception of validity. The articles included in this section illustrate that generalization.

The first of these is an article on *face validity*. Dr. Mosier, whose untimely death deprived quantitative psychology of a keen mind and a persuasive voice, does not think much of face validity. He points out that the term can mean quite diverse things, and the defense of a test on the basis of any of these meanings may be open to question. Mosier would have been pleased to observe, twenty years after his article was published, that the term *face validity* has lost much of its former popularity. But he would be distressed to discover that some of the errors of understanding and interpretation he pointed out are still being made by present-day test users.

Face validity is a term that is bandied about in the field of test construction until it seems about to become a part of accepted terminology. The frequency of its use and the emotional reaction which it arouses—ranging almost from contempt to highest approbation—make it desirable to examine its meaning more closely. When a single term variously conveys high praise or strong condemnation, one suspects either ambiguity of meaning or contradictory postulates among those using the term. The tendency has been, I believe, to assume unaccepted premises rather than ambiguity, and beautiful friendships have been jeopardized when a chance remark about face validity has classed the speaker among the infidels.

An examination of the ways in which the term "face validity" has been used indicates three frequent meanings. These are sufficiently similar as to be confused, yet so different in their implications that to understand one meaning where another was intended leads to a wholly

---

Mosier, C. I. A critical examination of the concepts of face validity. *Educational and Psychological Measurement,* 1947, 7, 191–205. Reprinted with the permission of the publisher.

[1] Opinions expressed in this paper are those of the author and do not necessarily reflect the policies of the War Department.

erroneous interpretation. This paper will analyze the various meanings which have been attributed to the term and it will then recommend that the term (and one of its meanings as well) be banished to outer darkness.

The three meanings which have been attributed to the term may be characterized as: (1) validity by *assumption,* (2) validity by *definition,* and (3) the *appearance* as well as the reality of validity. A fourth concept, validity by hypothesis, is closely related to the first two and deserves consideration in connection with them, although this concept has not generally been termed "face validity."

Validity by assumption: As used in this way, the term "face validity" carries the clear meaning that a test is assumed to be valid for the prediction of an external criterion if the items which compose it "appear on their face" to bear a common-sense relationship to the objective of the test. The assumption of validity in this case is asserted to be so strong that statistical evidence of validity is unnecessary; indeed, statistical evidence showing a lack of validity may be set aside by the strength of the assumption.

Validity by definition: For some tests, the objective is defined solely in terms of the population of questions from which the sample comprising the test was drawn, e.g., when the ability to handle the one hundred number facts of addition is tested by a sampling of those number facts. In these cases, the test is considered to be valid if the sample of items appears to the subject-matter expert to represent adequately the total universe of appropriate questions. The objective of the test is so defined that the index of reliability (the square root of the reliability coefficient) is, by definition, the measure of validity. This is so, not because of a definition of validity, but because of the way the objective of the test is defined. This situation is the one for which the term "face validity" was apparently coined.

Appearance of validity: In this usage, the term "face validity" implies that a test which is to be used in a practical situation should, in addition to having pragmatic or statistical validity, appear practical, pertinent and related to the purpose of the test as well; i.e., it should not only *be* valid but it should *also appear* valid. This usage of the term assumes that "face validity" is not validity in any usual sense of the word but merely an additional attribute of the test which is highly desirable in certain situations.

Validity by hypothesis: This concept, not generally associated with the term "face validity," is nevertheless sufficiently related to validity by assumption and validity by definition as to call for analysis at this point. The term "validity by hypothesis" is used to characterize the following situation. Often, before the validity of a test can be empirically verified for a particular group by demonstration of its relationship to a satisfactory criterion, the test must be used to meet an immediate practical need. In such instances, the use of the test involves the hypothesis that it has a useful degree of validity. This hypothesis is based upon the designed similarity of the particular test to other tests already demonstrated to have known validity for the purpose in question. The validity of the test is not assumed in the sense that no further proof is required; neither is the objective of the test defined in such a way that the reliability of the test is evidence of its validity for the defined purpose. Rather the hypothesis is stated that, because of the sum total of previous knowledge relating to methods of predicting this particular criterion it is reasonable to suppose that a test of this sort will prove to be valid by the conventional statistical tests. This reasonable presumption, however, is subject to empirical verification by fact. Pending the opportunity for such verification, the presumption may be sufficiently strong as to justify the use of the test. Similarly, the physician studies the symptoms and the general condition of the patient and then, on the basis of his knowledge of the past effects of remedies upon similar symptoms in similar patients, prescribes treatment. He does this even though this combination of remedies has not occurred before in his experience and certainly not with this patient (who may have an unsuspected allergy which will defeat the purpose of the remedy).

With these four possible meanings of the term before us, it becomes profitable to examine each one in more detail.

Validity by Assumption

This conception of "face validity" is illustrated by the following quotations from a widely circulated testing handbook:

> Generally speaking, the validity of the test is best determined by using common sense in discovering that the test measures component abilities which exist both in the test situation and on the job. This common-sense approach to the problem of validity can be strengthened greatly by basing the estimate of the component of the job on a systematic observation of job analysis.

The term "face validity" is thus used to imply that the appearance of a relationship between the test and the external criterion is sufficient evidence of pragmatic validity. This use is a pernicious fallacy. This illegitimate usage has cast sufficient opprobrium on the term as to justify completely the recommendation that it be purged from the test technicians' vocabulary, even for its legitimate usage. The concept is the more dangerous because it is glib and comforting to those whose lack of time, resources, or competence prevent them from demonstrating validity (or invalidity) by any other method. Moreover, it is readily acceptable to the ordinary users of tests and its acceptance in these quarters lends the concept strength. This notion is also gratifying to the ego of the unwary test constructor. It implies that his knowledge and skill in the area of test construction are so great that he can unerringly design a test with the desired degree of effectiveness in predicting job success or in evaluating defined personality characteristics, and that he can do this so accurately that any further empirical verification is unnecessary. So strong is this ego complex that if statistical verification is sought and found lacking, the data represent something to be explained away by appeal to sampling errors or other convenient rationalization, rather than by scientific evidence which must be admitted into full consideration.

The concept of validity by assumption gains strength from the legitimate use of the term "face validity" to mean validity by definition. The superficial similarity, however, between the two concepts should not deceive us into accepting either the truth of the one or the necessary falsity of the other.

Any experienced test constructor can cite numerous instances of tests which appear so closely related to the external criterion that a high validity coefficient seems inevitable. The following example is to be considered merely one illustration which most readers can reproduce almost without limit from their own experience.

Two test construction agencies, each having a fairly large and competent staff, began work about the same time on an objective test to measure the clerical skills involved in alphabetical filing. Up to a certain point the two agencies worked independently, each devising its own test. Agency A, after an analysis of the job, constructed a test of which the following item is representative:

> "Below are five names, in random order. If the names were placed in strict alphabetical order, which name would be *third:* (1) John Meeder; (2) James Medway; (3) Thomas Madow; (4) Catherine Meagan; (5) Eleanor Meehan."

The second agency designed a test of skill in alphabetical filing in which the task was as follows:

> "In the following items you have one name which is underlined and four other names in alphabetical order. If you were to put the underlined name into the alphabetical series, indicate by the appropriate letter where it would go:
>
> Robert Carstens
> A.________________
> Richard Carreton
> B.________________
> Roland Casstar
> C.________________
> Jack Corson
> D.________________
> Edward Cranston
> E.________________

There was a general agreement that each of these tests was face-valid and that each consisted of work-samples representative of the filing of alphabetical material. It was also agreed that if one were going to use two different tests to measure filing ability, it would be difficult to get two tests more closely similar than these and still have different tests. Had the concept of validity by assumption prevailed, there is little question that each test would have been considered highly valid.

An actual tryout, however, revealed quite different results from those expected. The correlation of the two tests in a sample of 43 clerical workers was .01, although the Kuder-Richardson reliabilities of the two tests were .81 and .89, respectively. We have here two tests which, on the basis of face validity by assumption, would be equally valid but which correlate substantially zero with one another. If one is valid, the other is not likely to be. What happens when the two tests are studied, not for their correlation with each other, but for their correlation with what seems to be a reasonable criterion, namely supervisors' ratings of speed and accuracy in filing? For 72 employed workers where accuracy of filing materials was an important part of the job, the correlation between the first of the two tests described and the supervisors' rating was .09.[2] For the second test the correlation with the supervisors' ratings of accuracy in alphabetizing was .00. (That these results cannot be attributed to the unreliability of the supervisors' ratings is indicated by correlation coefficients of .40 and above between the same ratings and scores on other tests.) These two examples, therefore, as well as those which the reader's experience will readily bring to bear, are sufficient to demonstrate the fallacy involved in the statement that a test can be assumed to be valid without further verification if only it "measures component abilities which are judged by common sense to exist both in it and in the job."

Validity by Definition

The foregoing discussion has assumed an outside criterion measurable apart from the test itself. The discussion which follows is applicable rather to the situation, very frequent in educational measurement, in which the only available measure of the criterion (that which the test is intended to measure) is, because of the nature of the criterion, directly and intimately related to the test questions themselves. If the objective is the measurement of the pupils' skill in forming the elementary number combinations of addition, a test consisting of the one hundred possible combinations is presumably valid by definition. In this case the index of reliability can be taken as the validity coefficient. Even in this simple situation, the actual validity is limited by the reliability of the particular test, by the form in which the problems are presented, e.g.,

[2] The test did, however, show substantial correlation with other clerical skills and hence was useful in a general clerical battery, though not for its "face-valid" objective.

in words, in columns or in equations (e.g., four plus two equals ———;
$\begin{array}{r} 4 \\ \underline{+\ 2} \end{array}$; 4 + 2 = ——), the arrangement of the items and by the conditions of administration. As soon, however, as the test is reduced from the totality of all situations which constitute the objective of measurement to a sample of those situations, the question recurs as to the extent to which the universe can be predicted from the sample. Moreover, it must be remembered that the relationship between test items and criterion behavior requires careful scrutiny. It is quite possible to design a test which apparently depends on the ability to perform the indicated additions, but is at the same time so dependent on verbal facility in understanding the directions, on speed of reaction, and on coding skills needed to record the answers, that the similarity between test situation and criterion situation is more apparent than real.

A further point which must be remembered in interpreting validity by definition is that it is frequently possible to establish several definitions of the criterion behavior, each obviously valid and yet each bearing far less than perfect relationship to the other. In the investigation of spelling ability, one obviously valid criterion of ability to spell might be the number of words correctly spelled from dictation. Should the words be dictated singly or in sentences, in a Brooklyn, Mobile, or Chicago accent? Another criterion which might be used, however, is a count of the number of words misspelled in compositions written by the pupils. Either of these criteria is, upon its face, a valid reflection of spelling ability. Nevertheless, empirical investigation is unlikely to show a perfect correlation between dictation and correct spelling in compositions, even after correction for attenuation. Which universe should be sampled to provide a face-valid test of spelling?

Finally, in the validation of a test by definition, it must be remembered that *the direction of the argument flows from the test to the definition of the criterion* rather than from the conceptually defined criterion to the test as a valid measure. The only proper statement which can be made about a test in terms of face validity by definition is that this test is a valid measure of that and only that universe of individual behavior patterns for which these items constitute a representative sample. If one is prepared to infer such a universe and consider *that* universe rather than one defined in any other way, such a concept of validity may be useful. The necessity for inferring the conceptual nature of the universe from an examination of the sample still exists as a judgmental process and as one which is peculiarly subject to error.

If we return to the example of the two alphabetizing tests given in the section above we see how readily one may be misled into generalizing beyond the nature of the facts given. It is not difficult to draw the conclusion, from an inspection of the items, that these two tests were representative of the same universe and that therefore either test is a valid measure of the same set of skills. The fallacy of the conclusion, however, is attested by the absence of correlation between the two tests as cited above.

In educational achievement tests it is possible to outline the concepts to be covered in a particular course of study. These concepts may be sampled so systematically and so comprehensively that we are prepared to say the test questions constitute an adequate representation of all of the questions which might be asked on this course, in the light of its content and stated objectives. Even so, the questions may be so formulated that the crucial skills for achieving a high score on the examination are quite different from a knowledge of course content and the achievement of the stated objectives. We are correct in saying that the test is a valid measure of "whatever it measures reliably." We may be far from correct in inferring that the hypostatized "whatever" is what it appears to be on the face of the test. Nevertheless if we rely on validity by definition, we face the obligation of defining that "whatever" in some meaningful terms without running into the pitfall of *assuming* that the "whatever" is synonymous with the test constructor's objective in preparing the test.

As we examine critically the distinction between validity by assumption and validity by definition, we are led to see how tenuous is the dividing line between the scientifically defensible use, "validity by definition," and the totally unscientific and indefensible use, "validity by assumption."

Moreover, we do not escape the dilemma by refusing to recognize anything except external criteria. The validity of the external criterion is just as much open to question as is the validity of the test which is being checked against it. Consider the situation in which a test purporting to measure clerical aptitude is "validated" by correlating test scores with salary (where salary is presumed to reflect the level of duties and responsibilities assigned). A high correlation between test score and salary level might well be taken, however, not as validation of the test but as validation of the agency's promotional system and an indication of the effectiveness with which the placement office had sought out and recommended for promotion the employees with the highest level of knowledge and skill. As Toops has pointed out, the criterion is a complex and elusive concept.[3] This paper is not the place for a systematic analysis of the nature of the criterion. It suffices to point out here that it is frequently possible to define in verbal, as distinct from operational, terms a criterion which is a socially significant independent measure of the behavior to be predicted by the test; such a definition is not in

[3] Toops, H. A. "The Criterion." Educational and Psychological Measurement, IV (1944), 271–297.

itself a sufficient guarantee that the criterion used to validate the test is itself valid.

The Appearance of Validity

In many situations it is highly desirable that the testing instrument should have a high degree of "consumer acceptance." These situations are most commonly found in, but by no means limited to, the field of employment testing. If a test is to be used effectively in achieving its objectives, it is essential that it actually be selected for use and that the results of the test be acceptable to those responsible for action on the basis of these results. In the area of public employment testing, e.g., civil service examining, the test must be acceptable not only to those using the test but to those taking the test as well. To a large extent this is also true in educational situations, particularly in the field of counseling. Up to a certain point the acceptability of the test can be carried by weight of authority. The board of examiners, the test technicians, or the counseling experts assert on the basis of their technical knowledge that the test is good, and their assertion is accepted without question. In other situations, however, this assertion of authority is not sufficient to carry conviction. Moreover, the technical evidence on which such authoritative statements should be based is often neither comprehensible nor completely convincing to those who must be convinced.

In Civil Service situations, the candidate whose score is less than he expected is inclined to attribute his low score, not to his own deficiencies but to the impractical nature of the test in relation to the job for which he is being examined. His dissatisfaction with the test results and his feeling of injustice may, of course, have real merit. We have not yet reached the era of public personnel examining where all tests are technically sound. Whether or not there is merit in his claim, the legislature, the courts, and public opinion, the court of last appeal, are more readily impressed by superficial appearances than by correlation coefficients. It becomes highly important, therefore, that a test to be used in such a situation not only *be* valid in the pragmatic sense of affording reasonably accurate predictions of job competence, but *have the appearance of validity* as well.

This appearance of validity as an added attribute is important in terms of the acceptance of the test, not only by the persons being examined, but also by those operating officials who are charged with the responsibility for taking action based upon the test results. If sound tests are given and accurately reported, but the supervisor, interviewer, or counselor has no confidence in them, the results will not be used effectively.

In passing it should be noted that the concern of the Civil Service or merit system agency with the consumer acceptance of the test should not be merely a negative one of avoiding appeals or legislative pressures. In a democratic society the quality of public service is dependent to a large extent upon the public's opinion of the quality of public servants. If the examination by which public servants are selected (whether it be an objective test or an examination of the candidates' voting records) is such that competent persons in a particular occupation are convinced that they have no opportunity to demonstrate their competence, they will not file for the examination or apply for the position. Since even the best Civil Service system can do no more than to select the best qualified persons of those who apply for positions, it is essential that every possible step be taken to insure that the most competent ones make application. They certainly will not do so if they believe that their examination will be impractical, theoretical, and deny them an opportunity to demonstrate their real ability. Moreover, in the face of such an attitude, statistical evidence on the validity of the test is likely to prove convincing only after an educational campaign extending to several generations of test-takers.

The foregoing discussion does not imply that predictive value is to be sacrificed to superficial appearances. Neither does it imply that a statistically valid test may be used only if it also has the appearance of practicality. It does imply, however, that the appearance of practicality is an objective sufficiently desirable in its own right that it may often be sought as an additional end consistent with the principal objective—predictive value.

The use of the term "face validity" to denote the appearance of a relationship to job performance as an attribute in addition to rather than instead of a statistical relationship, is frequently and unjustifiably confused with the notion of "face validity" by assumption. There is, however, a much clearer distinction between these two usages than between validity by assumption and validity by definition.

Validity by Hypothesis

This fourth view of validity has not, to the writer's knowledge, been explicitly termed face validity, although it contains certain elements of confusion with validity by assumption. In the construction of any test it is necessary to formulate certain hypotheses as to the most valid type and content to achieve a particular purpose. These hypotheses are held with a greater or less degree of confidence depending upon (a) the amount and the convincingness of available data showing that test items X have proved valid in situation Y, (b) the similarity of test item X to the proposed test items X′, and (c) the degree of similarity between situation Y and situation Y′ in which the test is to be used. If the new test is very similar to one previously shown to be valid and if the new situation is very similar to that in which the test was valid, then we may proceed with a high degree of confidence that the proposed test will be valid in the situation in which it is to be used. This confidence, of course, never approaches certainty, and a verification of the hypothesis is always necessary.

Even though the questions and the methods of administration are identical for the two tests (if we may speak of two sets of identical questions as two sets), the measuring instrument will not be identical in its effect if its application has shifted from one group of subjects to another or from one testing situation to another. When a test has been adequately standardized on one population and found to be highly valid for the prediction of a particular skill in that population, the use of the same test for another population involves merely a hypothesis, rather than the certainty, of its validity as a measure of the same skill in the new situation. Even though we may have a high degree of confidence that the hypothesis will be confirmed, it is nevertheless a hypothesis. As we construct alternate forms of a test and apply them to new situations to predict the same set of skills, our degree of confidence becomes substantially less. The confidence level is also reduced when we use the same test to predict a somewhat different set of skills. For example, a test may be used to predict competence in clerical office work of a certain type in one agency when the test has been validated against proficiency in office work of a similar type but in another agency. In all these cases we are dealing with varying amounts of confidence in the validity of a test in a particular situation. The degree of confidence which justifies the use of an examining instrument in advance of its validation in the specific situation is a question of administrative judgment which is not wholly answerable by statistical techniques.

The foregoing discussion makes it clear that a validation study does not completely validate the test for use with another group of subjects but that it merely increases our confidence that the test when applied to a group of "similar" subjects will prove similarly valid. Any selection of an existing test to serve a particular purpose (or construction of a new test to serve that purpose) therefore involves validity by hypothesis to a certain extent. The only situation in which we can escape the conclusion that our knowledge of the validity of a test is a hypothesis is the extremely limited one in which the test is validated on the identical subjects for which it is to be used administratively. Since validation of the test involves obtaining criterion measures (which are presumably superior to the test itself and would be used if it were not for the greater time and cost of securing them), the absurdity of using a test which has been prevalidated in this sense becomes immediately apparent. This does not lead, of course, to the absurd conclusion that a test may never be used; rather, it makes clear that when a test is used, its use is based upon a hypothesis in which we have more or less confidence depending upon the amount of research which has preceded its formulation. Our confidence in the test also depends upon the similarity between the research situation and the service-testing situation. Needless to say, this conclusion applies with equal force to all personnel evaluation and prediction devices.

It will be noted that validity by hypothesis departs from the concept of "face validity" in the preceding usages of the term. The first three usages discussed involve a superficial, common-sense similarity between test content and test objective. For example, in validity by assumption the similarity between test and job, without regard to statistical evidence of validity, is taken as sufficient. In validity by hypothesis, the similarity to a test for which there is statistical evidence of validity is tentatively accepted, without regard to its resemblance to the criterion. In validity by hypothesis, no such superficial similarity is assumed. On the basis of extensive previous research, one might legitimately propose that the ability to identify pictured hands as right hands or left hands would be a valid test for the prediction of the ability to read blueprints, although the superficial resemblance between the two tasks is slight. Nevertheless, certain controversies which have been raised about face validity and the presumed necessity for prevalidating any test before it is used[4] make the discussion of validity by hypothesis appropriate in connection with the other uses of face validity.

Moreover, in validity by assumption, hypothesis, or definition, we are dealing with varying points on a continuum of degrees of certainty. In "assumption" we have, within the scientific frame of reference, no confidence whatever; in "hypothesis" we have varying degrees of confidence depending on the amount, quality and pertinence of the evidence from previous experience; in "definition," our confidence usually is greatest, but—and this must always be remembered—that confidence applies only to the trait or traits actually represented by the test items in relation to the sample and *not* to traits defined in any other way.

Summary and Conclusions

1. This paper has attempted an analysis of the various meanings of the term "face validity." These meanings, although superficially similar, lead to widely different conclusions.

2. The results of the analysis may be summarized as follows. Face validity is variously used to mean that:

---

[4] Strangely enough, many of those who insist upon the prevalidation of each written test continue to urge reliance upon other types of selection techniques which numerous research studies have almost unanimously shown to be without predictive value.

a) The test bears a common-sense relationship to the measurement objective and therefore no statistical verification is necessary (*assumption*).
b) The test sets such a task that the universe of possible tasks (of which the test is a representative sample) is the only practicable criterion and the test is therefore a valid measure of the universe defined in terms of the sample. This implies merely that the test is a valid measure of whatever trait is measured reliably by the test (*definition*).
c) In the interests of the acceptability of the test to those most intimately concerned with its use, it is highly desirable that a test possess not only statistical validity, but also, as an added attribute, the appearance of practicality (*appearance*).
d) In the construction or selection of a particular test to be used for a particular objective with a particular group of subjects, recourse is always had to previous knowledge of the effectiveness of the same or similar tests applied to the same or similar subjects for the prediction of the same or similar attributes. On the basis of this previous research, the hypothesis is proposed that this test will be valid for the particular objective. The hypothesis is one which carries varying degrees of confidence: in some cases enough to justify the use of the test immediately, pending further investigation; in other cases so little confidence that such further investigation seems unprofitable. Even after there has been further investigation, however, we are left with a degree of confidence which is somewhat less than certainty, unless we are dealing with the same test, the same population and the same objectives (*hypothesis*).

3. Since the term "face validity" has become overlaid with a high degree of emotional content and since its referents are not only highly ambiguous but lead to widely divergent conclusions, it is recommended that the term be abandoned. Anyone intending to use the term should, instead, describe fully the *concept* which he originally intended to denote by "face validity." Even though writers may not always follow this recommendation, it is hoped that the foregoing analysis will prevent readers from drawing the improper conclusions that have frequently resulted from the indiscriminate uses made of the term in recent years.

23. Must All Tests Be Valid?

ROBERT L. EBEL

The author of this article questions not just one kind of validity but the very concept itself. He notes the diversity of views about validity and the difficulty of determining how much of it a test may have. Others have attributed these problems to lack of sufficient concern, lack of appropriate effort, or lack of skill on the part of the test builders. This article suggests that the problems may arise from overgeneralization of the validity concept and from attempts to apply criterion-based validation procedures to tests for which no valid criterion can be found or developed.

The author of this article contends that test scores, above all, ought to be meaningful and maintains that this meaning must be rooted ultimately in the operations of measurement by means of which the scores are obtained. To some test specialists these propositions seem almost self-evident—but not to all. For examples, see the *American Psychologist*, Volume 17 (1962), pages 205–207 and 507–508.

Validity has long been one of the major deities in the pantheon of the psychometrician. It is universally praised, but the good works done in its name are remarkably few. Test validation, in fact, is widely regarded as the least satisfactory aspect of test development. For this the blame is usually placed on the lack of good criterion measures. To assuage their guilt feelings about inadequate test validation, test constructors from time to time urge their colleagues to go to work on the criterion problem.

It is the purpose of this paper to develop an alternative explanation of the problem, and to propose an alternative solution. The basic difficulty in validating many tests arises, we believe, not from inadequate criteria but from logical and operational limitations of the concept of validity itself. We are persuaded that faster progress will be made toward better educational and psychological tests if validity is given a much more specific and restricted definition than is usually the case, and if it is no longer regarded as the supremely important quality of every mental test.

DIFFICULTIES WITH VALIDITY

Definitions of Validity

There are at least four indications that all is not well with the concept of validity as applied to mental tests. The first is that test spe-

Ebel, R. L. Must all tests be valid? *American Psychologist,* 1961, *16*, 640–647. Reprinted with the permission of the publisher and author.

cialists tend to differ in their definitions of the concept. Gulliksen (1950b) has said: "the validity of a test is the correlation of the test with some criterion" (p. 88). Cureton (1951) writes: "The validity of a test is an estimate of the correlation between the raw test scores and the 'true' (that is perfectly reliable) criterion scores" (p. 625). Lindquist (1942) suggests: "The validity of a test may be defined as the accuracy with which it measures that which it is intended to measure, or as the degree to which it approaches infallibility in measuring what it purports to measure" (p. 213). Edgerton (1949) says: "By 'validity' we refer to the extent to which the measuring device is useful for a given purpose" (p. 52). Cronbach (1960b) explains: "The more fully and confidently a test can be interpreted, the greater its validity" (p. 1551).

No exact scientist would accept such diverse statements as operationally useful definitions of the same quantitative concept. While there is obviously some conceptual similarity there also are important divergencies. The first specifies correlation with a criterion. The second requires estimation of a corrected correlation coefficient. The third avoids statistical terms, stressing accuracy in relation to the user's intent. The fourth makes validity mean utility. The fifth relates it to interpretability of test scores.

It would be difficult to state in words a core of meaning common to all the various definitions of test validity, of which the foregoing is only a sample. Such a conceptual definition, even if it could be formulated satisfactorily, would probably be too abstract to contribute significantly to more effective test validation. What the test developer needs is an operational definition.

Further, the generality of some of these definitions suggests that in the minds of their authors test validity is almost synonymous with test value. But if validity does mean value, then reliability, convenience in use, adequacy of norms, and even the availability of alternate forms become aspects of validity, and we are left without a term for what Gulliksen and Cureton mean by validity. Using the same term for a variety of concepts leads to serious semantic confusions and to procedural pitfalls as well.

Types of Validity

A closely related indication of difficulty with the concept of validity is seen in the diverse forms it must assume to fit different situations. The APA (1954) and the AERA (1955) Technical Recommendations mention four types of validity: content, predictive, concurrent, and construct. Two of these, content and construct, have little in common with the other two, or with each other. Anastasi (1954) discusses face validity, and factorial validity in addition to content validity, and various types of empirical validity. Gulliksen (1950a) has discussed intrinsic validity, and Mosier (1947) analyzed face validity into validity by assumption, validity by definition, the appearance of validity, and validity by hypothesis.

Again it may be said truly that these types of validity have some common conceptual elements, but the differences are striking. To encompass all the diverse varieties of validity requires an extremely loose and general definition of the basic idea of validity. It is easy to agree with Guilford (1956) that "The question of validity has many facets and it requires clear thinking not to be confused by them." Perhaps one could go farther and suggest that even clear thinking in the frame of reference of the present conceptual structure of validity may not lead to common understanding of a single concept, nor to effective operational use of it. Perhaps what we really need is not clearer thinking about validity, but rather a more concrete and realistic conception of the complex of qualities which make a test good.

Evidence of Validity

A third indication that all is not well with validity is found in this strange paradox. While almost every test specialist agrees that validity is the most important quality of a mental test, almost all of them lament the general inadequacy of test validation. Nearly 30 years ago, in the early years of objective testing, Ruch (1933) made this comment:

> There are in use today at least one thousand different educational and mental tests. Convincing critical and statistical data on the validity, reliability, and norms of these measures are available in probably less than 10 per cent of the cases.

One might reasonably expect that the situation would have improved in the intervening years, but this seems not to have happened. In a spaced sample of reviews of 20 tests in the *Fifth Mental Measurements Yearbook* (Buros, 1959) only one was found in which the reviewer judged the evidence of validity to be adequate. Ten tests were criticized for lack of evidence of validity. Nine reviewers made no comment about the validation of the tests they reviewed. This in itself is surprising, if validity is indeed the most important quality of any mental test.

Some years ago, W. J. Cameron in one of his *Ford Sunday Evening Hour* commentaries observed that when someone tries to do a job the wrong way, nature often teaches him his error by refusing to let the job be done. Our failure to demonstrate consistently that our tests possess the quality we value above all others may mean that we have used the wrong approach in trying to gain evidence of it.

Is Validity Essential

A fourth suggestion that something may be wrong with the mental tester's concept of validity is that corresponding problems of validation seem to be almost nonexistent in the realm of physical measurements. Norman Campbell (1957), P. W. Bridgman (1927), and others have written extensively on the measurement of physical properties, but one searches in vain through their writings for a discussion of the validity of physical measurements. They show much concern for operational definitions of quantitative concepts, for limitations on the measurability of certain properties, and for accuracy of measurement. But the question of the *validity* of a measuring procedure seems to arise only incidentally and indirectly. For some properties, such as the hardness of solids or the viscosity of fluids, different methods of measurement yield inconsistent results. But modern physical scientists seem never to ask which of the methods of measurement is the more valid. One is moved to wonder why this difference between mental and physical measurement. Is it possible that we have fallen into a trap of our own devising when we find it so difficult to validate our mental tests? Have we, in Berkeley's words, "first raised a dust and then complained that we cannot see?"

Refinements in the measurement of distance—by the interferometer—or in the measurement of time—by the atom clock—are not justified on the basis of superior validity, that is, as closer approximations to the measurement of true distance or true time. They are regarded rather as improvements because they permit reproducible measurement to smaller fractions of existing units of measurement, which is to say that they are justified on the basis of superior reliability.

When a shortcut substitute for some more elaborate standard method of measurement is proposed, the question of the validity of the substitute method does arise with logical legitimacy. In such a situation the concept of validity is simple, and the meaning of the term is clear. We will argue for retaining this concept of validity and of restricting the term to this concept. But to ask about the validity of the basic method of measurement, which provides the operational definition of the thing being measured, would seem to most physical scientists as it does to us to be asking a meaningless question.

WHY THE DIFFICULTIES

Scientific Adequacy

These observations suggest that the concept of validity itself may be weak scientifically. Most of the definitions of validity can be shown to be derived from the basic notion that validity is the degree to which a test measures what it is supposed to measure. But how does one know what a test is supposed to measure? On a superficial level, perhaps, it may be suggested by the test title—academic aptitude, mathematics achievement, or social studies background, for example—but these suggestions are by no means definitive.

Does the criterion tell us what the test is supposed to measure? It might if criteria were given to us. Usually they are not. They have to be *devised,* often after the test itself was constructed. Toops (1944) has said:

> Possibly as much time should be spent in devising the criterion as in constructing and perfecting the test. This important part of a research seldom receives half the time or attention it requires or deserves. If the criterion is slighted the time spent on the tests is, by so much, largely wasted.

The ease with which test developers can be induced to accept as criterion measures quantitative data having the slightest appearance of relevance to the trait being measured is one of the scandals of psychometry. To borrow a figure of speech from Thorndike (1922), they will use the loudness of the thunder as a criterion for their measurements of the voltage of the lightning. Even in those rare cases where criterion measures have been painstakingly devised, the validity of the test is not determined unless the validity of the criterion has been established. This requires a criterion for the other criterion, and so on ad infinitum. We can pursue such an infinite regress until we are weary without finding a self-sufficient foundation for a claim that the test is valid. It is an unhappy fact that the general conceptual definition of validity provides no firm basis for operational definitions of validity.

Philosophic Adequacy

The concept of validity is also weak philosophically. It reflects a belief in the existence of quantifiable human characteristics, such as intelligence or skill in arithmetic, independent of any operations used to measure it. Philosophers call this point of view realism but most of them now agree that it is not very realistic. One of Einstein's major contributions was to point out that the concept of time is scientifically meaningless until the clocks used to measure it have been described. As Henry F. Kaiser (1960) said in his review of a measurement book recently:

> Chapter 2 repeatedly exhibits the philosophically naïve faith that there "exists" an "actual" or "true" scale for a particular phenomenon; the author seems to assume a degree of absolute truth inherent in nature which went out of style in the nineteenth century.

This naive faith in the pre-existence of a quantity to be measured is basic to the general conception of validity.

You may recall the story of the three baseball umpires who were discussing their modes of operation and defending their integrity as umpires. "I call 'em as I see 'em," said the first. The second replied, "I call 'em as they are." The third said, "What I call 'em makes 'em what they are." In philosophical terms, the first was an empiricist; the second, a realist; and the third, a positivist. I should like to see test developers be less individualistic in their positivism than baseball umpires are at times, but I think they should be positivists rather than realists. Neither a strike in baseball nor scholastic aptitude in testing is a useful concept until it has been defined in operational terms.

Many of those concerned with mental measurements, however, persist in being philosophical realists. They tend to endow abstractions with a real existence. They think of a real trait which "underlies" a test score, and which is meaningfully there even though their best efforts to measure it will never be more than approximations. They think of intelligence as really existing independent of any operational definition such as those provided by the Binet, the Kuhlman Anderson, or the Wechsler. They seek to use tests to discover what critical thinking or creativity really are instead of using the tests to define what they mean when they use such terms. They have not yet learned that realistic philosophy is productive mainly of verbal discourse, and that it must be shunned if mental measurement is to advance.

So long as what a test is supposed to measure is conceived to be an ideal quantity, unmeasurable directly and hence undefinable operationally, it is small wonder that we have trouble validating our tests. Only if we are willing to accept some actual test, or other actual method of obtaining criterion measures, as a basic (if somewhat arbitrary) operational definition of the thing we wish to measure, and only if we have some other test or measurement procedure that we wish to check against this standard, do we find the concept of test validity useful. Further, if the test we propose to use provides in itself the best available operational definition, the concept of validity does not apply. A basic definition needs to be clearly meaningful, but it does not need to be, and indeed it cannot be validated.

One of the by-products of the realistic philosophy is mistrust of appearances and a reverence for the concealed reality. What a test or test item really measures, we warn ourselves, may be quite different from what it appears to measure. But how a person can possibly determine what it really measures without observing something that it appears to measure is never clearly explained. Those who analyze batteries of tests to determine the "underlying" factors trust appearances of what a test is measuring very little, but even they fall back on appearances when they must name the factors discovered or provide verbal descriptions of them.

The source of our concern over the deceitfulness of appearances is probably that what a test appears to measure sometimes seems to be different to different observers or when viewed in a different light. If we resolve not to trust any appearances at all the problem vanishes, but so does our confidence in the test (and probably our sanity as well). A better course of action is to seek to understand why the appearances were not consistent, and to find an interpretation which makes them consistent.

Mistrust of appearances, in turn, leads one to seek completely empirical and deductive procedures of test validation. But completely empirical validation is seldom possible. Strictly speaking it is impossible in principle. We cannot escape judgment regarding the choice of a criterion, nor can we escape appearances (i.e., observations) in getting criterion data. To avoid an infinite regress of criterion validations one must stop somewhere and accept or proclaim an arbitrary definition of the thing to be measured. Unfortunately this is seldom done. What happens more often is that we accept highly questionable criteria, obtain discouragingly low correlations, and finally give the whole thing up as a bad job.

Overgeneralization of Validity

A third possible explanation for difficulty with validity is that the concept is too broad. If it is made synonymous with value, or utility, or meaning, if it is made to apply to all mental tests including those used to describe persons or control educational processes as well as those used to predict future achievement, it must obviously have many different meanings. Now the trouble with using the same term to mean a variety of different things is that the meanings tend to get tangled up with each other. When the word is used in one particular sense, connotations appropriate to its use in other senses tend to hover about it and suggest irrelevant procedures.

In the case of the term validity, we tend always to expect evidence in the form of a validity coefficient even though such coefficients are completely appropriate only to tests used as convenient operational substitutes for more tedious, if somewhat more precise, standard measurement procedures. But when tests are used to describe educational achievement, or to assist in the control of the educational process, validity coefficients usually are quite irrelevant. The fact that they are not naturally relevant in these situations may account for some of the difficulty we encounter in trying to obtain data from which to calculate them. The obvious natural criteria we need simply do not exist in the real world, and must be conjured up from the realm of abstract ideals. Perhaps this is why evidence for the validity of educational tests is so often inadequate and unsatisfactory. Perhaps the notion of correlating test scores with criterion scores to obtain a basic index of test quality has been overgeneralized. Perhaps we have often sought to use it in situations where it does not logically apply.

It may even be that some of us, unconsciously perhaps, are glad to honor with our words a procedure of test validation which has limited applicability in practice. By so doing we exhibit our good intentions. If the procedure will not work in the absence of a good criterion, and if a good criterion is unavailable, we are excused from further effort to demonstrate test quality. We also have, in the well recognized shortcomings of available criteria, a convenient scapegoat for the lack of good evidence of test quality. It may often be convenient to sweep the problem of test validation under the rug of inadequate or unavailable criteria, especially when we promise ourselves and others to work to get better criteria when we can find the time.

WHAT IS A CRITERION

At this point it may be appropriate to ask what, after all, is the difference between test scores and criterion measures? Is the difference one of substance or only one of function? In the case of predictive validity the distinction is fairly clear. Test scores come first. Criterion measures are obtained later. In the case of concurrent validity the distinction gets blurred. One distinction suggested by frequent practice, is that criterion measures should be ratings based on direct observations of behavior under presumably natural conditions. This would serve to distinguish them from test scores, which are almost always based on assessments of output under carefully controlled and hence somewhat artificial conditions. But ratings based on direct observations of behavior have serious and well known psychometric shortcomings. This limits their value as criteria.

Indeed the limitation may be more serious than is commonly realized. Though it has often been done, it makes little sense to judge the accuracy with which a test does the job it is supposed to do by checking the scores it yields against those obtained from a less accurate measuring procedure. If a new method of measurement involves a better (and hence different) definition of the trait to be measured, it obviously makes no sense to judge its quality on the basis of degree of agreement with inferior measures. If the new method does not involve a better definition, but only more precise observations, it does make sense to require that the new agree with the old so far as their respective reliabilities will permit, but in this case it is hard to see the old, inferior measure as a standard or criterion for judging the quality of the new. If the criterion is used as a standard for judging the accuracy of the scores from the test, it should always exemplify a measurement procedure clearly superior to (i.e., more relevant and precise than) that embodied in the test.

In theory this could provide a useful distinction between test scores and criterion measures. In practice it seldom does. What usually happens is that the test developer pours all the skill, all the energy, and all the time he has into the process of making an outstanding test. He has none left over to spend on obtaining measurements "clearly superior" to those his test will yield, and under the circumstances would have no stomach for the task anyway. Small wonder that many good tests go unvalidated or poorly validated by conventional psychometric standards.

Predictive Validity

Predictive validity has long been recognized as one of the standard types, if not the standard type of validity. Cronbach (1960a, pp. 17–18), Mosier (1951, pp. 767–768), and others have developed the idea that the purpose of all measurement is prediction. There is a special sense in which this is true, though the surveyor or the analytic chemist might be surprised to find himself in the same occupational class as the weather forecaster. Perhaps the statement "All measurement is for prediction" belongs in the same category as the statement "All education is guidance" or even "All flesh is grass." There is a degree of truth in such statements, but if they are taken too literally they can be seriously misleading. If the predictive function of measurement is regarded as the sole function, it leads to the highly questionable conclusion that the best way to judge the quality of a measurement of something is to determine how accurately it predicts something else.

Why should the quality of a Test X as a measure of Trait X be judged by how well it predicts Trait Y when Y is a function not only of X but also of Z, W, and possibly a host of other factors? Is it reasonable to judge the quality of a barometer solely, or even mainly, by the accuracy of the weather forecasts which are made with its help? Or to consider the matter in another way, is it reasonable to suppose that Test X should by itself be a good measure of Trait Y, when Test X consists of verbal analogies, arithmetic problems, etc., while Trait Y is ultimately measured by grades assigned by a variety of teachers in courses from Art to Zoology?

Scores on Test X may indeed be related to measures of Trait Y, and the size of the correlation may indicate, in part, how useful Test X is for a particular task of selection. But loose logic is involved if that correlation is used as a measure of the validity of Test X as a measure of Trait X. An academic aptitude test does not purport to *measure* academic success. It should not claim to do more than part of the job of *predicting* academic success.

Specificity of Validity

Validity, test theorists agree, is specific—specific to a given group of individuals tested, to the treatment given them, and to a given purpose for testing (or to a given criterion). Anyone who uses a published test is almost certain to give it to a different group than the one on which it was validated. For any user's group the test may be more or less valid than it was for the test author's tryout group. Quite possibly the user may even have a somewhat different purpose for testing than the test author had in mind. His criterion may be different. Again this means that the test may be more or less valid than the author reported. Under these conditions, how can a test author possibly publish fully adequate data on validity? The best he can do is to report validity under certain clearly specified and carefully restricted conditions of use. For the majority of possible uses of a test, validation becomes inevitably a responsibility of the test user. There is thus an element of unfairness in the common complaint that test publishers fail to provide adequate data on validity.

ALTERNATIVES

Meaningfulness and Validity

Whether or not you are prepared to agree that validity has serious shortcomings as the primary basis for judging test quality, you may now be interested in what alternatives might be proposed to replace it. What basis for judging test quality would be better than validity? Cronbach's definition cited earlier, may provide a clue. He said: "The more fully and confidently a test can be interpreted, the greater its validity." The interpretability of a test score depends on its meaningfulness. We would suggest that meaningfulness replace validity in the usual lists of major desirable characteristics of a measuring instrument. Before this suggestion is laughed out of hearing, consider what it implies.

One, but only one, of the kinds of information that help to make test scores meaningful is the relation of those scores to other measures of the same persons. When tests are used to predict, or when they are used as convenient substitutes for more exact but more laborious measurement procedures, validity coefficients expressing the relation between test scores and criterion measures may be the most essential basis for meaning. Hence we are not proposing that either the term or the concept of validity be abolished but only that they be restricted to situations in which independent criterion measures are feasible and necessary.

Relationships of test scores to other measures can also add meaning to the test scores even when the other measures do not constitute legitimate criteria. When a test is used in a battery, knowledge of intercorrelations among the scores adds to the meaningfulness of the scores from each test. Such intercorrelations show how much the various tests measure in common, and how much independent information they provide. Campbell and Fiske (1959) have suggested a special technique for using this kind of information. From a "multitrait-multimethod matrix" of intercorrelations they secure data on which to base "convergent and discriminant" test validation. Construct validation also depends on relations between measures of various kinds, but thus far it has been of more direct interest and value to the psychological theorist than to the psychometrist.

Unless a measure is related to other measures it is scientifically and operationally sterile. The validity fallacy arises from the assumption that the relation of the measure to one single other measure (the criterion) is all important. The concept of construct validity has helped to break down this unfortunate stereotype.

Operational Definitions. What of the other kinds of information that help make test scores meaningful? Most important of all, scientifically, is a description of the operations used to obtain the scores. Operational definitions have always been basic to the meaning of measurements of length, mass, time, and other physical quantities. Such operational definitions should be basic to mental measurements as well. They would be, I am persuaded, had we not been misled by an overgeneralized concept of predictive validity.

Operational definitions of some kinds of test scores, such as speed scores in typewriting, ability scores in spelling, or vocabulary knowledge scores, are not particularly difficult to formulate. For other test scores, the problems seem more formidable. We must acknowledge that the excellence of many current tests has resulted more from the skilled intuitions of the test constructor than from preconceived excellence of design, recorded in truly controlling test specifications. But there is no apparent reason why an adequate operational definition of the score from any test should be impossible. Such a definition obviously must cover the critical procedures in test construction, in test administration, and in scoring. The development, use, and publication of such operational definitions would, I am persuaded, not only make the test scores more meaningful, but would lead us rapidly to the production of better tests.

Reliability and Norms. There are two other types of information which contribute substantially to the meaningfulness of test scores. These have to do with the reliability of the scores and with the norms of performance for representative groups of examinees. A completely unreliable score is completely meaningless. A perfectly reliable test score is almost certainly meaningful, though it may not be particularly significant or useful.

The importance of norms in making test scores meaningful requires no defense here. In the case of most educational tests they are highly useful. In a few special cases they may be unimportant or even irrelevant.

Importance and Convenience

The stress we have placed on meaningfulness of test scores, subordinating validity, reliability, and norms to it, does not mean that it can be regarded as the sole basis for judging the quality of a mental test. There are two other very important elements. One is the importance (usefulness as a basis for effective or satisfying behavior) of the knowledge or abilities required by the test. The other is the convenience of the test in use. The many factors which contribute to the convenience of a test have been well outlined by numerous authors.

A measurement can be completely meaningful and still be completely useless. For example, the number of hairs on a person's head is an operationally definable measurement. It can be related to other measurements of a person such as his age or his IQ. We could estimate its reliability and get norms for it. But it would remain, so far as I know, an almost useless measurement, one of little or no importance. Quite properly I think, critics of current educational tests are as much concerned with the importance of what the test is measuring as they are with the meaningfulness of the scores or with the convenience of the test in use.

CONCLUSIONS

It may be helpful now to summarize in outline form the characteristics which we regard as determining the quality of a mental test or measurement procedure. They are:

1. The importance of the inferences that can be made from the test scores
2. The meaningfulness of the test scores, based on
    a. An operational definition of the measurement procedure
    b. A knowledge of the relationships of the scores to other measures, from
        i. Validity coefficients, predictive and concurrent
        ii. Other correlation coefficients or measures of relationship
    c. A good estimate of the reliability of the scores
    d. Appropriate norms of examinee performance
3. The convenience of the test in use

Must all tests be valid? If the term "valid" is not to be made synonymous with the term "good," if validity is a clearly defined concept which can be quantified by finding the correlation between test scores and criterion measures, then the answer is clearly "no," on the basis of the considerations discussed in this paper.

These views may be wrong. If so, and if the current conception of validity is philosophically sound and operationally useful, let us in the name of intellectual honesty, support this claim with some good solid evidence. The time is long past for lame apologies and prolix rationalization of failure to demonstrate that good tests have the quality we have said is more important than any other. Perhaps we should recognize the age-old alternatives so far as validity is concerned. Either put up the evidence or withdraw the claim. It is my view that in general, we have not and will not be able to put up satisfactory evidence. On the other hand we should not stop being concerned about test quality. What is proposed here is that we stop beating our heads against a stone wall and step back to look for a way over it or around it. There is one, I think, and this article has attempted to elucidate it.

Having followed the argument thus far some will say: "You still want valid tests. All you have done is to propose a different term, meaningfulness, to replace validity." This is surely not what I have been trying to do. I hope that your time has not been wasted in reading one side of a purely lexical debate. I hope that these efforts may contribute to the adoption of a more appropriate and productive procedure than validation has been for determining the quality of a test.

REFERENCES

American Educational Research Association, Committee on Test Standards. *Technical recommendations for achievement tests.* Washington, D. C.: AERA, 1955.

American Psychological Association. *Technical recommendations for psychological tests and diagnostic techniques.* Washington, D. C.: APA, 1954.

Anastasi, Anne. *Psychological testing.* New York: Macmillan, 1954.

Bridgman, P. W. *The logic of modern physics.* New York: Macmillan, 1927.

Buros, O. (Ed.) *The fifth mental measurements yearbook.* Highland Park, N. J.: Gryphon, 1959.

Campbell, D. T., & Fiske, D. W. Convergent and discriminant validation by the multitrait-multimethod matrix. *Psychol. Bull.*, 1959, **56,** 81–105.

Campbell, N. R. *Foundations of science.* (Originally published as *Physics: The elements.*) New York: Dover, 1957.

Cronbach, L. J. *Essentials of psychological testing.* (2nd ed.) New York: Harper, 1960. (a)

Cronbach, L. J. Validity. In C. W. Harris (Ed.), *Encyclopedia of educational research.* New York: Macmillan, 1960. (b)

Cureton, E. E. Validity. In E. F. Lindquist (Ed.), *Educational measurement.* Washington, D. C.: American Council on Education, 1951, Pp. 621–694.

Edgerton, H. A. The place of measuring instruments in guidance. In Wilma T. Donahue, C. H. Coombs, & R. M. W. Travers (Eds.), *The measurement of student adjustment and achievement.* Ann Arbor, Mich.: Univer. Michigan Press, 1949. Pp. 51–58.

Guilford, J. P. *Fundamental statistics in psychology and education.* (3rd ed.) New York: McGraw-Hill, 1956.

Gulliksen, H. Intrinsic validity. *Amer. Psychologist,* 1950, **5,** 511–517. (a)

Gulliksen, H. *Theory of mental tests.* New York: Wiley, 1950. (b)

Kaiser, H. F. Review of Virginia L. Senders, *Measurement and statistics. Psychometrika,* 1960, **25,** 411–413.

Lindquist, E. F. *A first course in statistics.* (Rev. ed.) Boston: Houghton Mifflin, 1942.

Mosier, C. I. A critical examination of the concepts of face validity. *Educ. psychol. Measmt.,* 1947, **7,** 191–205.

Mosier, C. I. Batteries and profiles. In E. F. Lindquist (Ed.), *Educational measurement.* Washington, D. C.: American Council on Education, 1951.

Ruch, G. M. Recent developments in statistical procedures. *Rev. educ. Res.,* 1933, **3,** 39–40.

Thorndike, E. L. Measurement in education. In, *Twenty-first yearbook of the National Society for the Study of Education.* Bloomington, Ill.: Public School Publishing Company, 1922.

Toops, H. A. The Criterion. *Educ. psychol. Measmt.,* 1944, **4,** 271–297.

24. Intrinsic Validity[1]

HAROLD O. GULLIKSEN

Aptitude tests are usually expected to have predictive validity. Achievement tests need content validity. But it is possible for aptitude test scores to correlate with criterion measures of achievement because of some superficial association of non-essential characteristics. Similarly, the subjective judgments on which the content validity of achievement tests usually rests may be superficial and faulty. They need not be accepted uncritically. They ought not to be made without regard for objective evidence.

These are some of the points the author of this article develops as he contends that less credence should be accorded to apparent validity and that more effort should be expended in the search for intrinsic validity. Gulliksen is one of the senior scientists in the field of psychometrics. His book, *The Theory of Mental Tests,* is a classic in the field.

When the early studies of psychological tests were made, the value of these tests was assessed by comparing the test results with expert judgment (*1, 2, 3, 5, 6, 14, 16, 27*). The judgment of a teacher or supervisor was regarded as a *criterion* which the psychological test should approximate as closely as possible. In the early stages of a science it is

Gulliksen, H. O. Intrinsic validity. *American Psychologist,* 1950, 5, 511–517. Reprinted with the permission of the publisher and author.

[1] The material in this article is adapted, with the permission of the Secretary-Treasurer of the National Council on Measurements Used in Education, from a talk given at the March 1949 Philadelphia regional meeting of the Council and published as "History of, and present trends in testing," pp. 1–20, in *The Sixth Yearbook of the N.C.M.U.E., 1948–1949,* 1949, pp. 72 + 43.

appropriate for the scientist to be certain that his measurements are at least as accurate as the results of skilled but non-scientific appraisal. Such comparisons of the results of accurate scientific measurement with non-scientific appraisals are also necessary to aid the scientist in determining the extent to which he is developing measures of aspects already recognized in the field or is measuring other, possibly new, aspects. For example, the physicists' precise definitions of mass, work, and energy do not now correspond to the non-scientific use of these terms.

In the development of the psychology of individual differences, it is appropriate to assess a given aptitude or achievement test by determining its agreement with a non-scientific appraisal of the "same" quality. In this stage of development, the psychologist is following—possibly feebly and imperfectly—the lead given by the non-scientific judgment of the expert. At some point in the advance of psychology as a science it would seem appropriate for the psychologist to lead the way in establishing good criterion measures, instead of just attempting to construct imperfect tests for attributes that are presumed to be assessed more accurately and more validly by the judgment of the experts.

INTRINSIC CONTENT VALIDITY

It seems relevant to ask: "How do we know that the expert has given us the correct criterion and the best method of measuring it?" Whenever one test has a correlational validity for a given criterion, this criterion has been accepted as correct without question. This criterion, then, must have some sort of intrinsic validity. It seems to me that psychologists must pay increasing attention to the problem of assessing the intrinsic validity of the criterion and must develop standard and recognized quantitative methods for this assessment. This problem has been discussed by Thorndike (*25,* pages 119–132) in terms of "ultimate, intermediate and immediate criteria." His solution, however, seems to be non-quantitative and to rely entirely on "a judgment of relevance" of the criterion.

Recently there has been some emphasis on the concept of "definitional validity" (*18*); and on the "obviously valid test" (*21*, *22*). The implication of this latter concept is that a test which is set up on the basis of expert judgment to cover material that is deemed important by the expert cannot be questioned; it is necessarily valid and serves as its own criterion. I should like to take issue with this point of view. While it seems to me possible to set up a test on the basis of expert judgment which cannot be validated by *correlating* it with something else, I would have a number of suggestions to make regarding the experimental technique which must be applied to such a test suggested by the expert in order to determine whether it is or is not an intrinsically valid test.

Use of factor analysis of criterion variables. In applying this assessment technique it is necessary to insist that the expert give a number of different methods of measuring the skill involved. Numerous possible types of criterion measures have been listed and discussed by Thorndike (*25,* pp. 132–159). An excellent study utilizing many measures of a given skill was published in 1932 by W. W. Cook (*9*) in which the problem of spelling was investigated. Factor methods were not used in this study, but the necessary basic data were gathered. It would be possible, of course, simply to define spelling as the ability to spell a specified list of words from dictation and let the matter go at that. Cook, however, went beyond this. His first step was to insist that many different methods of measuring spelling be used. He utilized dictation, dictation in context, spelling errors occurring in written compositions and various recognition-type spelling tests where the student was to select the correctly or incorrectly spelled words in a list, was given five spellings of each word to select the one correct, etc., etc. With all these different measures available, it is then possible to see if one has a one-factor system or not and to see which type of test involved the higher specifics.

If one has several experts, it is then possible to check the judgments of one expert against the judgment of another expert to see whether or not they are agreed in their judgments. Where several experts are involved, a factor study might show that we have two or three schools of thought involved in a particular field. Such an analysis of grades in English Composition has been given by Torgerson and Green (*26*). The expert judgment, then, can be checked by determining agreement with itself in various forms and by agreement with judgments of other experts. The results of such a study can then form the basis for a reconsultation with your experts to see whether or not they would wish to revise their opinions.

Use of validity coefficients. If only a single criterion measure is available this measure can frequently be assessed in terms of its correlations with various predictors. A common-sense notion of the nature of the criterion and an approximate idea of the appropriate magnitude of correlations with a set of predictors can be very illuminating. For example, when it was found that the U. S. Navy Reading Test correlated well with grades in Gunner's Mates Schools, steps were taken to introduce more practical work on assembling and disassembling the guns and to place less emphasis on a study of manuals in the training and testing of gunner's mates (*11, 12*).

Such a change in the criterion resulted in a decreased validity for the Reading Test and an increased validity for some of the mechanical type tests. A similar drop in the validity of the General Classification Test and the Reading Test and increase in the validity of the Mechanical

Knowledge Test followed the introduction of achievement tests in the Torpedoman School (*24*, page 308).

Another concrete illustration of the use of a set of validity coefficients for making an initial appraisal of a criterion is furnished by the Navy Basic Engineering School (*24*, pp. 305–309). The first eye-opener to an unsatisfactory situation was the fact that an arithmetical reasoning test gave the highest correlation with final grades in the Basic Engineering School. Mechanical knowledge and mechanical comprehension tests gave the lowest correlation with these final grades. This state of affairs was extremely peculiar in view of the fact that arithmetic constituted *one* seventh and shop work *four* sevenths of the curriculum. Investigation of grades showed that the standard deviation of the grades covering the one week of arithmetic was about 8.0; the standard deviation of grades for approximately four weeks devoted to shop work was about 2.5. Averaging one-seventh arithmetic (standard deviation 8.0) with four times as much shop work (standard deviation 2.5) gave a final grade which correlated in the high .80's with arithmetic and in the .50's with shop work. It, of course, would have been possible to suggest that grades in shop work be multiplied by a factor of 100 or so to increase their weight. However, a study among different instructors showed that the ratings of shop work intercorrelated from − .11 to .55. Clearly the problem was to develop more precise ratings before allowing them to determine the major portion of the grade. This was done in terms of better rating scales, and various gauges and calipers to measure accurately the precision of the product.[2] The result was a highly reliable set of ratings of shop performance which were judged by the chiefs to be ratings of important characteristics. A recheck on the correlation of various aptitude tests with grades after institution of this program showed that the mechanical knowledge tests had the highest correlations and the arithmetical reasoning tests the lowest correlations with final grades (*24*, page 307). Here we have a case where the interrelationships among part scores, the inspection of the curriculum, the judgment of the instructors, and the pattern of validity coefficients from selection tests all gave a consistent picture. The initial picture was strongly indicative of a *low intrinsic validity* of basic engineering grades. In the final picture all the evidence pointed toward a *higher intrinsic content validity* of basic engineering grades.

Comprehensive factor study of criterion and predictor variables. Putting together the ideas of the two previous sections we see that the most information about the criterion would be afforded if a comprehensive

[2] The major part of this work was done by Dr. Nicholas A. Fattu on NDRC Project N–106 of the Applied Psychology Panel. This project was conducted by the College Entrance Examination Board at the request of the Bureau of Naval Personnel.

matrix of intercorrelations including both criterion and predictor variables were available. A representative set of predictor variables should be included so that the investigator will be able to inspect both the high *and low* validity coefficients to be certain that this pattern is reasonable. Also a variety of methods for assessing different aspects of the criterion must be used in order to determine the dimensionality of the criterion variables and the extent to which the various expert judgments agree and disagree.

As yet there are very few studies which include an attempt both to analyze and to represent various *aspects* of the criterion and to include a representative list of a variety of predictor variables (*4, 8, 13, 23*). It seems to me that such studies are the major means now at the psychologist's disposal for evaluating the intrinsic validity of a criterion.

Use of pre-training and post-training tests. In case we are dealing with material which is taught in a course, it is possible to utilize parallel tests, one given before and one after training. Clearly the expert judgment is corroborated if the students do not know the material before training and do know it afterwards. However, if the material *is* known *before* the training or is *not* known *after* training, it would seem clear that the expert judgment would bear reconsideration.

The value of intrinsic content validity. In the present stage of development of psychological techniques, the psychologist is obligated to go much farther than the concept of definitional validity or the obviously valid test. An approach to assessing what may be termed "intrinsic content validity" may be made by the systematic use of many different measures for evaluating any given criterion, a representative set of possible predictor variables, and a study of the results from pre-training and post-training tests.

Such studies of intrinsic content validity would be a valuable contribution to the clarification of problems of selection and training techniques and of refining the judgments of the experts.

It is important, therefore, in the development of criteria to stress intrinsic validity, first, by utilizing items that are judged by experts to be directly relevant to the problems at hand; second, by assessing from a common-sense point of view the relationships among these items; and third, by studying their relationship to various other types of achievement and aptitude tests and investigating the effect of training on the items. In the light of such results it may be necessary to revise certain judgments and certain tests, and to proceed again until one secures a total picture of interrelationships that seems consistent and sensible. I would then tend to feel that one had probably succeeded in developing an intrinsically valid criterion which is the crucial problem in criterion development.

Currently the Educational Testing Service is considering a project which I might characterize as an investigation of intrinsic validity of various measures of English writing ability. A large number of aptitude tests, objective achievement tests, and essay achievement tests suggested by various experts in the field would be used and their interrelationships found. Such a study would give an indication of the basic complexity of the field of English writing. It will then be possible to utilize parallel tests in a pre-test-post-test English training series to determine whether or not certain types of training actually produce the changes they are designed to produce. The result of such a program should be the development of English writing tests with greater intrinsic content validity than those we now have.

Studies of this type, applied systematically to various areas of the school curriculum, might result in considerable reorganization of teaching so that differential types of learning ability would be recognized by teaching practices. The organization of teaching in terms of learning abilities of the students would thus be facilitated.

A test serves as a very powerful incentive both to the teacher and to the students if it has high intrinsic validity, in the sense that the material in the test is judged to be crucial by the teacher, that the material has been taught in class, and is recognized by the students as material they could have learned if they had applied themselves. In our work in Navy schools during the war, for example, the intensity of effort and seriousness of purpose exhibited after a revised testing program had been introduced was in marked contrast to the undirected effort exhibited by students in the classroom prior to the introduction of the tests.

In order to have this favorable effect on attitudes of teacher and student, the tests must deal directly with the material of that particular course. When the test is not closely related to the course work, the teacher may say, "It doesn't matter whether the students do well or poorly on this test because it isn't testing for the important things I taught them." In a similar vein one educator recently commented on standardized educational tests as follows: "Buy them therefore, and give them to your pupils. Look at their marks, too, if you will and if you can, interpret them. But stop there. Attach no significance to them or you are lost. Look instead at your pupils in the classroom, listen to what they say, read what they write, when the time comes give them an examination of your own, and then make up your mind about them on these human and personal bases instead of on the impersonal and mechanical basis of batteries of tests devised by theorizers" (*19*). When a course achievement test does not deal directly with the material of that course the students also are likely to feel that "the test is not fair" because it contains many items which they were never given a chance to learn. Such attitudes are detrimental to learning as contrasted with the favorable attitude when the course work is clearly directly related to the material in the examination. The tremendous growth in use of tests and test results over the past fifty years (*17, 20, 28*) puts an increased obligation on psychologists to develop tests with high intrinsic validity.

A special problem is presented by items requiring the examinee to apply his training to novel situations. Items which involve new applications of principles should be introduced in the tests only if the course work has included some practice in such novel applications. Introducing such items for the first time in the test has an unfavorable effect on attitudes if there has been no attention to such matters in the preparatory work.

Increasing intrinsic content validity for educational achievement tests. In order to develop achievement tests that are both well-constructed technically, and represent precisely the objectives of any given course, it is probably necessary to make specific training in item writing and examination evaluation an important part of the required teacher-training curriculum. Present requirements emphasize that the teacher must know the subject matter and must know how to present it at a level suitable for the students being trained with him. The educational requirements for teachers should also include knowing how to prepare good examination material; how to use a wide variety of item types; how to test for various sorts of educational objectives other than memorization of facts; how to interpret examination scores; and how to evaluate examination results quantitatively.

It might also be that the development of tests with high intrinsic validity would be aided if the national standardized achievement tests moved in the direction of a "basic skills" concept such as has been developed by Lindquist at Iowa. Perhaps it is possible to get national agreement easily on certain skills, such as spelling, reading comprehension, grammar, arithmetic, etc., and set up tests of these skills on a national basis. In addition, it might be desirable to insist on the development of a certain degree of local option by requiring that additional tests must be locally constructed and "passed" by the students on standards that are determined locally. By some provisions such as these, we might ensure that no control was exercised over the nature of certain of the local tests and also ensure that no school system could settle for simply passing the minimum national standards.

So much for the concept of intrinsic content validity as applied to achievement tests. I do not have, as can be seen, a coefficient of intrinsic validity to propose, but it seems to me that it is highly desirable to assess our tests along the lines which I have indicated in order to be certain that we are measuring factors which are important.

INTRINSIC CORRELATIONAL VALIDITY

I would like next to turn to a problem which I will designate as intrinsic correlational validity of an aptitude test. It seems to me dangerous to depend entirely on correlational validity to evaluate a test. One can, of course, cite various interesting correlational validities; for example, the reported correlation of about .90 between the number of storks' nests in Stockholm and the number of babies born in Stockholm over a period of years. The correlation is unquestionably there. Whether a census of stork nests made by helicopter could be made a legitimate substitute for a census of births is probably a question that no one would raise. Many examples of nonsense correlations have been cited (*7,* pp. 670–671; and *31*). Surprisingly, however, no attention has been paid, as far as I know, to the converse problem of detecting necessary or intrinsic correlations. It seems to me that the correlations which we obtain need to be inspected with an eye to whether or not they represent an intrinsic relationship among variables or a fortuitous relationship such as the various "nonsense correlations" that have attracted attention.

For example, if one wished to predict ability as a mechanic, a test of manual dexterity, a test of mechanical ingenuity, and a paper-pencil test of familiarity with mechanical terms might have equal correlational validities with a criterion of mechanical performance. However, if such tests are to be used over a period of years, there would be a temptation in this case to utilize the easily administered paper-pencil test and to abandon the more cumbersome tests of manual dexterity and mechanical ingenuity since they required apparatus and hence were "administratively impractical." However, in a depression when mechanics' jobs were at a premium, persons of high verbal aptitude might be coached and might pass the paper-pencil verbal test with flying colors, but perform poorly as mechanics. It might be, however, that if one made the *administratively* cumbersome decision to utilize the apparatus tests of manual dexterity and mechanical ingenuity, one might find that coaching for these tests would also increase the person's performance as a mechanic. If there is some direct and intrinsic causal relationship between the aptitude test and criterion, it is likely that efforts to improve one's aptitude test score will also improve criterion performance. This distinction is especially pertinent because of the tendency of some test constructors to stress the administrative convenience of paper-pencil tests as compared with apparatus tests, to utilize approximately equal validity coefficients for justifying the use of paper-pencil tests, and to neglect the possibility of differential effects of coaching. If the test has only an indirect, not an intrinsic correlational validity, then coaching will destroy test validity. A very good illustration of a test with intrinsic correlational validity would be a test of a genuine prerequisite. Suppose that the ability to *multiply* and to *subtract* is a genuine prerequisite to learning *long division.* One would then find that a person's ability to perform well in the classwork in long division might be predicted by his performance in multiplication and subtraction. If a person had a poor performance in multiplication and subtraction, one would recommend that he should go back and study this material whereupon his improved test performance on multiplication and subtraction would be accompanied by better performance in the work on long division. Similarly, if a calculus course is so taught that algebra and analytical geometry are essential, one could utilize scores in algebra and analytical geometry to predict performance in calculus and if persons did poorly on the algebra and analytical geometry tests, the recommendation would be a positive one. "Go back and study these two subjects, take the prerequisite tests again: whenever you do well on these two tests you are then ready to study calculus and can go ahead."

It is interesting to note that at present the psychological literature indicates a reasonably low relationship between intelligence as measured by tests, and learning ability as measured by laboratory experiments in learning or by improvement in school subjects (*29, 30*). To me this means a still unsatisfactory status of our knowledge of the various types of learning ability, and the various types of primary mental abilities.

I would hope that it would be ultimately possible to do a fair proportion of aptitude testing in terms of measures of learning ability as determined by laboratory tests of learning. It also seems to me that if we are able to use direct measures of learning ability, we may have measures more "culture-free" than tests so far developed. At present laboratory tests of learning cannot be utilized for predicting various types of achievement. However, it should be noted that in 1900, correlations only as high as .19 were found between college grades and predictive tests (*6, 14, 16, 27*). Such low validities are in marked contrast with validity coefficients as high as .50 to .70 reported thirty to fifty years later (*10, 17*). Perhaps in another fifty years laboratory learning tasks will be our best predictors of achievement in various fields. It is my hope that such measures would have a high *intrinsic* validity.

I think these illustrations suffice to show what might be meant by *intrinsic correlational validity* of an aptitude test. It seems to me that if we work for this type of validity we will be building on a much more certain foundation for the future. We will find that the validity of a test will maintain itself. We will not be concerned with minor problems of coaching. In fact, we will recommend coaching; and the subject-matter experts who survey this new material in the field of testing may well have much greater confidence in it because the relationships found are of a direct causal type that can be appreciated by the expert in the field. He will not be skeptical that something is being put over on him with an unfamiliar correlational technique, the meaning of which is not quite clear.

SUMMARY

It would be my hope then that the future development of aptitude and achievement testing will be in the direction of greater emphasis on a search for validities that may be fundamental and lasting as contrasted with those that are likely to be fortuitous or transient. It seems that this concept might be denoted by the term "intrinsic validity"—intrinsic *content* validity for achievement tests and intrinsic *correlational* validity for aptitude tests.

I hope that while we will continue to insist on high correlations between aptitude tests and criteria, we will also conduct studies on the transfer of learning and the effect of coaching that will enable us gradually to discard certain aptitude tests which have only a superficial correlational validity, and move gradually in the direction of tests that have intrinsic correlational validity.

Finally, I would suggest that we attempt to assess achievement tests more systematically in terms of the ideas I have tried to subsume under the concept of intrinsic content validity. As far as I can see, we have in the achievement testing field the judgment of the experts to rely upon, but we can do a much better and more intensive job of checking these expert judgments. If judgments are obtained from a number of persons, the techniques of factor analysis can give us some idea of the complexity of the system with which the experts are really dealing. Furthermore, a more intensive use of pre-training and post-training tests would probably be of very great value in sharpening the judgments of the experts regarding the relationships among different types of content. I would hope, then, for more intensive investigation directed toward determining the intrinsic correlational validity of aptitude tests and the intrinsic content validity of achievement tests.

REFERENCES

1. Binet, A. (1899). Attention et adaptation. *Année Psychol.,* **6,** 248–404.
2. Binet, A., and Henri, V. (1895). La psychologie individuelle. *Année Psychol.,* **2,** 411–465.
3. Bolton, T. L. (1892). Growth of memory in school children. *Amer. J. Psychol.,* **4,** 362–380.
4. Carroll, J. B. (1943). The factorial representation of mental ability and academic achievement. *Educ. & Psychol. Meas.,* **3,** 307–332.
5. Cattell, J. McK. (1890). Mental tests and measurements. *Mind,* **15,** 373–381.

6. Cattell, J. McK., and Farrand, L. (1896). Physical and mental measurements of the students of Columbia University. *Psychol. Rev.*, **3,** 618–648.
7. Cohen, J. B. (1938). The misuse of statistics. *J. Amer. Stat. Assn.*, **33,** 657–674.
8. Comrey, A. L. (1949). A factorial study of achievement in West Point courses. *Educ. and Psych. Meas.*, **9,** 193–209.
9. Cook, W. W. (1932). The measurement of general spelling ability involving controlled comparisons between techniques. *Univ. of Iowa Studies in Educ.*, **6,** No. 6, Iowa City, Iowa.
10. Crawford, A. B., and Burnham, P. S. (1946). *Forecasting college achievement,* Part I. New Haven, Conn.: Yale University Press, p. 291.
11. Frederiksen, Norman (1948). *Statistical Study of the Achievement Testing Program in Gunner's Mates Schools.* (Navpers 18079), Pp. iv. + 41.
12. Frederiksen, Norman, and Monroe, Lt. A. E. (1945). *The Development of Achievement Tests for Gunner's Mates Schools.* (OSRD Report No. 5259) (Project N–106, Report No. 17), Pp. vii + 253.
13. French, J. W. (1951). The description of aptitude and achievement tests in terms of rotated factors. *Psychometric Monograph No. 4.*
14. Gilbert, J. A. (1894). Researches on the mental and physical development of school children. *Stud. Yale Lab.*, **2,** 40–100.
15. Gulliksen, Harold (1949). "History of, and present trends in testing," pp. 1–22 in the *Sixth Yearbook of the National Council on Measurements Used in Education 1948–1949;* Fairmont, West Virginia. Frank S. White, Secretary-Treasurer, N.C.M.U.E. Pp. v + 72 + 43.
16. Jastrow, J., and Morehouse, G. W. (1892). Some anthropometric and psychologic tests on college students. *Amer. J. Psychol.*, **4,** 420–428.
17. Monroe, W. S. (1928). Ten years of educational research 1918–1927. *Bureau of Educational Research Bulletin,* College of Education, Univ. of Illinois, No. 42.
18. Mosier, C. I. (1947). A critical examination of the concepts of face validity. *Educ. and Psych. Meas.*, **7,** 191–205.
19. *New York Times* (Feb. 18, 1949). Page 25. "Dr. Carman assails college teaching."
20. Reavis, W. C. (1947). Testing is big business. *School Review,* **55,** 259–260.
21. Rulon, P. J. (1946). On the validity of educational tests. *Harvard Educ. Rev.*, **16,** 290–296.
22. Rulon, P. J. (1947). Validity of educational tests. Pp. 13–20 in *National Projects in Educational Measurement.* A report of the 1946 Invitational Conference on Testing Problems. Pp. vii + 80.
23. Sisk, H. L. (1939). A multiple factor analysis of mental abilities in the freshman engineering curriculum. *J. Psychol.*, **9,** 165–177.
24. Stuit, D. B. (1947). *Personnel research and test development in the Bureau of Naval Personnel.* Princeton, N. J.: Princeton University Press. Pp. xxiv + 513.
25. Thorndike, R. L. (1949). *Personnel selection, test and measurement techniques.* New York: John Wiley & Sons, Inc. Pp. viii + 358.
26. Torgerson, W. S., and Green, B. F., Jr. (1950). A factor analysis of English essay readers. *Research Bulletin No. RB–50–30,* Educational

Testing Service, Princeton, N. J., Feb. 16, 1950. (Abstract, *Amer. Psychologist,* **5,** 370.)

27. Wissler, Clark (1901). The correlation of mental and physical tests. *Psychol. Monogr.,* **3,** No. 16, pp. 1–62.
28. Wolfle, Dael (1947). Testing is big business. *Amer. Psychologist,* **2,** p. 26.
29. Woodrow, Herbert (1945). Intelligence and improvement in school subjects. *J. Educ. Psychol.,* **36,** 155–166.
30. Woodrow, Herbert (1946). The ability to learn. *Psychol. Rev.,* **53,** 147–158.
31. Yule, G. U. (1926). Why do we sometimes get nonsense correlations between time series? A study in sampling and the nature of time series. *J. Roy. Stat. Soc.,* **89,** 1–64.

25. Construct Validity in Psychological Tests

LEE J. CRONBACH
PAUL E. MEEHL[1]

A new term entered the vocabularies of test specialists in the 1950s—*construct validity*. Its purpose was to provide a rationale and a procedure for the validation of tests that purport to measure hypothetical psychological traits.

Claims for construct validity, like those for predictive validity, rest on correlation coefficients or some other measure of relationship. If psychological theory calls for authoritarian people to be egotistical, antisocial and uninterested in cultural activities, a test of authoritarianism is regarded as valid to the degree that scores on it correlate positively with measures of egotism and negatively with measures of social and cultural interests.

The concept of construct validity has won wide acceptance. This is partly attributable to the eminence of its sponsors, particularly Cronbach and Meehl. But, because of the current imperfections of psychological theory and the current vagueness of many psychological trait constructs, it has not yet led to many important advances toward more valid tests.

Cronbach, L. J., and Meehl, P. E. Construct validity in psychological tests. *Psychological Bulletin,* 1955, *52,* 281–302. Reprinted with the permission of the publisher and authors.

[1] The second author worked on this problem in connection with his appointment to the Minnesota Center for Philosophy of Science. We are indebted to the other members of the Center (Herbert Feigl, Michael Scriven, Wilfrid Sellars), and to D. L. Thistlethwaite of the University of Illinois, for their major contributions to our thinking and their suggestions for improving this paper.

Nevertheless, what the authors of this article have to say about the problems of validity in general and about the possibilities and limitations of construct validation in particular is fundamental and sound. Bechtoldt (1959) presents an opposing point of view that also merits study.

Validation of psychological tests has not yet been adequately conceptualized, as the APA Committee on Psychological Tests learned when it undertook (1950–54) to specify what qualities should be investigated before a test is published. In order to make coherent recommendations the Committee found it necessary to distinguish four types of validity, established by different types of research and requiring different interpretation. The chief innovation in the Committee's report was the term *construct validity*.[2] This idea was first formulated by a subcommittee (Meehl and R. C. Challman) studying how proposed recommendations would apply to projective techniques, and later modified and clarified by the entire Committee (Bordin, Challman, Conrad, Humphreys, Super, and the present writers). The statements agreed upon by the Committee (and by committees of two other associations) were published in the *Technical Recommendations* (59). The present interpretation of construct validity is not "official" and deals with some areas where the Committee would probably not be unanimous. The present writers are solely responsible for this attempt to explain the concept and elaborate its implications.

Identification of construct validity was not an isolated development. Writers on validity during the preceding decade had shown a great deal of dissatisfaction with conventional notions of validity, and introduced new terms and ideas, but the resulting aggregation of types of validity seems only to have stirred the muddy waters. Portions of the distinctions we shall discuss are implicit in Jenkins' paper, "Validity for what?" (33), Gulliksen's "Intrinsic validity" (27), Goodenough's distinction between tests as "signs" and "samples" (22), Cronbach's separation of "logical" and "empirical" validity (11), Guilford's "factorial validity" (25), and Mosier's papers on "face validity" and "validity generalization" (49, 50). Helen Peak (52) comes close to an explicit statement of construct validity as we shall present it.

FOUR TYPES OF VALIDATION

The categories into which the *Recommendations* divide validity studies are: predictive validity, concurrent validity, content validity, and construct validity. The first two of these may be considered together as *criterion-oriented* validation procedures.

[2] Referred to in a preliminary report (58) as *congruent validity*.

The pattern of a criterion-oriented study is familiar. The investigator is primarily interested in some criterion which he wishes to predict. He administers the test, obtains an independent criterion measure on the same subjects, and computes a correlation. If the criterion is obtained some time after the test is given, he is studying *predictive validity*. If the test score and criterion score are determined at essentially the same time, he is studying *concurrent validity*. Concurrent validity is studied when one test is proposed as a substitute for another (for example, when a multiple-choice form of spelling test is substituted for taking dictation), or a test is shown to correlate with some contemporary criterion (e.g., psychiatric diagnosis).

Content validity is established by showing that the test items are a sample of a universe in which the investigator is interested. Content validity is ordinarily to be established deductively, by defining a universe of items and sampling systematically within this universe to establish the test.

Construct validation is involved whenever a test is to be interpreted as a measure of some attribute or quality which is not "operationally defined." The problem faced by the investigator is, "What constructs account for variance in test performance?" Construct validity calls for no new scientific approach. Much current research on tests of personality (9) is construct validation, usually without the benefit of a clear formulation of this process.

Construct validity is not to be identified solely by particular investigative procedures, but by the orientation of the investigator. Criterion-oriented validity, as Bechtoldt emphasizes (3, p. 1245), "involves the *acceptance* of a set of operations as an adequate definition of whatever is to be measured." When an investigator believes that no criterion available to him is fully valid, he perforce becomes interested in construct validity because this is the only way to avoid the "infinite frustration" of relating every criterion to some more ultimate standard (21). In content validation, *acceptance* of the universe of content as defining the variable to be measured is essential. Construct validity must be investigated whenever no criterion or universe of content is accepted as entirely adequate to define the quality to be measured. Determining what psychological constructs account for test performance is desirable for almost any test. Thus, although the MMPI was originally established on the basis of empirical discrimination between patient groups and so-called normals (concurrent validity), continuing research has tried to provide a basis for describing the personality associated with each score pattern. Such interpretations permit the clinician to predict performance with respect to criteria which have not yet been employed in empirical validation studies (cf. 46, pp. 49–50, 110–111).

> We can distinguish among the four types of validity by noting that each involves a different emphasis on the criterion. In predictive or concurrent validity, the criterion behavior is of concern to the tester, and he may have no concern whatsoever with the type of behavior exhibited in the test. (An employer does not care if a worker can manipulate blocks, but the score on the block test may predict something he cares about.) Content validity is studied when the tester *is* concerned with the type of behavior involved in the test performance. Indeed, if the test is a work sample, the behavior represented in the test may be an end in itself. Construct validity is ordinarily studied when the tester has no definite criterion measure of the quality with which he is concerned, and must use indirect measures. Here the trait or quality underlying the test is of central importance, rather than either the test behavior or the scores on the criteria (59, p. 14).

Construct validation is important at times for every sort of psychological test: aptitude, achievement, interests, and so on. Thurstone's statement is interesting in this connection:

> In the field of intelligence tests, it used to be common to define validity as the correlation between a test score and some outside criterion. We have reached a stage of sophistication where the test-criterion correlation is too coarse. It is obsolete. If we attempted to ascertain the validity of a test for the second space-factor, for example, we would have to get judges [to] make reliable judgments about people as to this factor. Ordinarily their [the available judges'] ratings would be of no value as a criterion. Consequently, validity studies in the cognitive functions now depend on criteria of internal consistency . . . (60, p. 3).

Construct validity would be involved in answering such questions as: To what extent is this test of intelligence culture-free? Does this test of "interpretation of data" measure reading ability, quantitative reasoning, or response sets? How does a person with A in Strong Accountant, and B in Strong CPA, differ from a person who has these scores reversed?

Example of construct validation procedure. Suppose measure X correlates .50 with Y, the amount of palmar sweating induced when we tell a student that he has failed a Psychology I exam. Predictive validity of X for Y is adequately described by the coefficient, and a statement of the experimental and sampling conditions. If someone were to ask, "Isn't there perhaps another way to interpret this correlation?" or "What other kinds of evidence can you bring to support your interpretation?", we would hardly understand what he was asking because no interpretation has been made. These questions become relevant when the correlation is advanced as evidence that "test X measures anxiety proneness." Alternative interpretations are possible; e.g., perhaps the test measures "academic aspiration," in which case we will expect different results if we induce palmar sweating by economic threat. It is then reasonable to inquire about other *kinds* of evidence.

Add these facts from further studies: Test *X* correlates .45 with fraternity brothers' ratings on "tenseness." Test *X* correlates .55 with amount of intellectual inefficiency induced by painful electric shock, and .68 with the Taylor Anxiety scale. Mean *X* score decreases among four diagnosed groups in this order: anxiety state, reactive depression, "normal," and psychopathic personality. And palmar sweat under threat of failure in Psychology I correlates .60 with threat of failure in mathematics. Negative results eliminate competing explanations of the *X* score; thus, findings of negligible correlations between *X* and social class, vocational aim, and value-orientation make it fairly safe to reject the suggestion that *X* measures "academic aspiration." We can have substantial confidence that *X* does measure anxiety proneness if the current theory of anxiety can embrace the variates which yield positive correlations, and does not predict correlations where we found none.

KINDS OF CONSTRUCTS

At this point we should indicate summarily what we mean by a construct, recognizing that much of the remainder of the paper deals with this question. A construct is some postulated attribute of people, assumed to be reflected in test performance. In test validation the attribute about which we make statements in interpreting a test is a construct. We expect a person at any time to possess or not possess a qualitative attribute (amnesia) or structure, or to possess some degree of a quantitative attribute (cheerfulness). A construct has certain associated meanings carried in statements of this general character: Persons who possess this attribute will, in situation *X,* act in manner *Y* (with a stated probability). The logic of construct validation is invoked whether the construct is highly systematized or loose, used in ramified theory or a few simple propositions, used in absolute propositions or probability statements. We seek to specify how one is to defend a proposed interpretation of a test; *we are not recommending any one type of interpretation.*

The constructs in which tests are to be interpreted are certainly not likely to be physiological. Most often they will be traits such as "latent hostility" or "variable in mood," or descriptions in terms of an educational objective, as "ability to plan experiments." For the benefit of readers who may have been influenced by certain exegeses of MacCorquodale and Meehl (40), let us here emphasize: Whether or not an interpretation of a test's properties or relations involves questions of construct validity is to be decided by examining the entire body of evidence offered, together with what is asserted about the test in the context of this evidence. Proposed identifications of constructs allegedly measured by the test with constructs of other sciences (e.g., genetics, neuroanatomy, biochemistry) make up only *one* class of construct-validity claims, and a rather minor one at present. Space does not permit full analysis of the relation of the present paper to the MacCorquodale-Meehl distinction between hypothetical constructs and intervening variables. The philosophy of science pertinent to the present paper is set forth later in the section entitled, "The nomological network."

THE RELATION OF CONSTRUCTS TO "CRITERIA"

Critical View of the Criterion Implied

An unquestionable criterion may be found in a practical operation, or may be established as a consequence of an operational definition. Typically, however, the psychologist is unwilling to use the directly operational approach because he is interested in building theory about a generalized construct. A theorist trying to relate behavior to "hunger" almost certainly invests that term with meanings other than the operation "elapsed-time-since-feeding." If he is concerned with hunger as a tissue need, he will not accept time lapse as *equivalent* to his construct because it fails to consider, among other things, energy expenditure of the animal.

In some situations the criterion is no more valid than the test. Suppose, for example, that we want to know if counting the dots on Bender-Gestalt figure five indicates "compulsive rigidity," and take psychiatric ratings on this trait as a criterion. Even a conventional report on the resulting correlation will say something about the extent and intensity of the psychiatrist's contacts and should describe his qualifications (e.g., diplomate status? analyzed?).

Why report these facts? Because data are needed to indicate whether the criterion is any good. "Compulsive rigidity" is not really intended to mean "social stimulus value to psychiatrists." The implied trait involves a range of behavior-dispositions which may be very imperfectly sampled by the psychiatrist. Suppose dot-counting does not occur in a particular patient and yet we find that the psychiatrist has rated him as "rigid." When questioned the psychiatrist tells us that the patient was a rather easy, free-wheeling sort; however, the patient *did* lean over to straighten out a skewed desk blotter, and this, viewed against certain other facts, tipped the scale in favor of a "rigid" rating. On the face of it, counting Bender dots may be just as good (or poor) a sample of the compulsive-rigidity domain as straightening desk blotters is.

Suppose, to extend our example, we have four tests on the "predictor" side, over against the psychiatrist's "criterion," and find generally positive correlations among the five variables. Surely it is artificial and arbitrary to impose the "test-should-predict-criterion" pattern on such data. The psychiatrist samples verbal content, expressive pattern, voice, posture, etc. The psychologist samples verbal content, perception, expressive pattern, etc. Our proper conclusion is that, from this evidence, the four tests and the psychiatrist all assess some common factor.

The asymmetry between the "test" and the so-designated "criterion" arises only because the terminology of predictive validity has become a commonplace in test analysis. In this study where a construct is the central concern, any distinction between the merit of the test and criterion variables would be justified only if it had already been shown that the psychiatrist's theory and operations were excellent measures of the attribute.

INADEQUACY OF VALIDATION IN TERMS OF SPECIFIC CRITERIA

The proposal to validate constructual interpretations of tests runs counter to suggestions of some others. Spiker and McCandless (57) favor an operational approach. Validation is replaced by compiling statements as to how strongly the test predicts other observed variables of interest. To avoid requiring that each new variable be investigated completely by itself, they allow two variables to collapse into one whenever the properties of the operationally defined measures are the same: "If a new test is demonstrated to predict the scores on an older, well-established test, then an evaluation of the predictive power of the older test may be used for the new one." But accurate inferences are possible only if the two tests correlate so highly that there is negligible reliable variance in either test, independent of the other. Where the correspondence is less close, one must either retain all the separate variables operationally defined or embark on construct validation.

The practical user of tests must rely on constructs of some generality to make predictions about new situations. Test *X* could be used to predict palmar sweating in the face of failure without invoking any construct, but a counselor is more likely to be asked to forecast behavior in diverse or even unique situations for which the correlation of test *X* is unknown. Significant predictions rely on knowledge accumulated around the generalized construct of anxiety. The *Technical Recommendations* state:

> It is ordinarily necessary to evaluate construct validity by integrating evidence from many different sources. The problem of construct validation becomes especially acute in the clinical field since for many of the constructs dealt with it is not a question of finding an imperfect criterion but of finding any criterion at all. The psychologist interested in construct validity for clinical devices is concerned with making an estimate of a hypothetical internal process, factor, system, structure, or state and cannot expect to find a clear unitary be-

> havioral criterion. An attempt to identify any one criterion measure or any composite as *the* criterion aimed at is, however, usually unwarranted (59, p. 14–15).

This appears to conflict with arguments for specific criteria prominent at places in the testing literature. Thus Anastasi (2) makes many statements of the latter character: "It is only as a measure of a specifically defined criterion that a test can be objectively validated at all . . . To claim that a test measures anything over and above its criterion is pure speculation" (p. 67). Yet elsewhere this article supports construct validation. Tests can be profitably interpreted if we "know the relationships between the tested behavior . . . and other behavior samples, none of these behavior samples necessarily occupying the preeminent position of a criterion" (p. 75). Factor analysis with several partial criteria might be used to study whether a test measures a postulated "general learning ability." If the data demonstrate specificity of ability instead, such specificity is "useful in its own right in advancing our knowledge of behavior; it should not be construed as a weakness of the tests" (p. 75).

We depart from Anastasi at two points. She writes, "The validity of a psychological test should not be confused with an analysis of the factors which determine the behavior under consideration." We, however, regard such analysis as a most important type of validation. Second, she refers to "the will-o'-the-wisp of psychological processes which are distinct from performance" (2, p. 77). While we agree that psychological processes are elusive, we are sympathetic to attempts to formulate and clarify constructs which are evidenced by performance but distinct from it. Surely an inductive inference based on a pattern of correlations cannot be dismissed as "pure speculation."

Specific Criteria Used Temporarily: The "Bootstraps" Effect

Even when a test is constructed on the basis of a specific criterion, it may ultimately be judged to have greater construct validity than the criterion. We start with a vague concept which we associate with certain observations. We then discover empirically that these observations covary with some other observation which possesses greater reliability or is more intimately correlated with relevant experimental changes than is the original measure, or both. For example, the notion of temperature arises because some objects feel hotter to the touch than others. The expansion of a mercury column does not have face validity as an index of hotness. But it turns out that (*a*) there is a statistical relation between expansion and sensed temperature; (*b*) observers employ the mercury method with good interobserver agreement; (*c*) the regularity of observed relations is increased by using the thermometer (e.g., melting points of samples of the same material vary little on the thermometer; we obtain nearly linear relations between mercury measures and pressure of a gas). Finally, (*d*) a theoretical structure involving unobservable microevents—the kinetic theory—is worked out which explains the relation of mercury expansion to heat. This whole process of conceptual enrichment begins with what in retrospect we see as an extremely fallible "criterion"—the human temperature sense. That original criterion has now been relegated to a peripheral position. We have lifted ourselves by our bootstraps, but in a legitimate and fruitful way.

Similarly, the Binet scale was first valued because children's scores tended to agree with judgments by schoolteachers. If it had not shown this agreement, it would have been discarded along with reaction time and the other measures of ability previously tried. Teacher judgments once constituted the criterion against which the individual intelligence test was validated. But if today a child's IQ is 135 and three of his teachers complain about how stupid he is, we do not conclude that the test has failed. Quite to the contrary, if no error in test procedure can be argued, we treat the test score as a valid statement about an important quality, and define our task as that of finding out what other variables—personality, study skills, etc.—modify achievement or distort teacher judgment.

EXPERIMENTATION TO INVESTIGATE CONSTRUCT VALIDITY

Validation Procedures

We can use many methods in construct validation. Attention should particularly be drawn to MacFarlane's survey of these methods as they apply to projective devices (41).

Group differences. If our understanding of a construct leads us to expect two groups to differ on the test, this expectation may be tested directly. Thus Thurstone and Chave validated the Scale for Measuring Attitude Toward the Church by showing score differences between church members and nonchurchgoers. Churchgoing is not *the* criterion of attitude, for the purpose of the test is to measure something other than the crude sociological fact of church attendance; on the other hand, failure to find a difference would have seriously challenged the test.

Only coarse correspondence between test and group designation is expected. Too great a correspondence between the two would indicate that the test is to some degree invalid, because members of the groups are expected to overlap on the test. Intelligence test items are selected initially on the basis of a correspondence to age, but an item that correlates .95 with age in an elementary school sample would surely be suspect.

Correlation matrices and factor analysis. If two tests are presumed to measure the same construct, a correlation between them is predicted. (An exception is noted where some second attribute has positive loading in the first test and negative loading in the second test; then a low correlation is expected. This is a testable interpretation provided an external measure of either the first or the second variable exists.) If the obtained correlation departs from the expectation, however, there is no way to know whether the fault lies in test A, test B, or the formulation of the construct. A matrix of intercorrelations often points out profitable ways of dividing the construct into more meaningful parts, factor analysis being a useful computational method in such studies.

Guilford (26) has discussed the place of factor analysis in construct validation. His statements may be extracted as follows:

"The personnel psychologist wishes to know 'why his tests are valid.' He can place tests and practical criteria in a matrix and factor it to identify 'real dimensions of human personality.' A factorial description is exact and stable; it is economical in explanation; it leads to the creation of pure tests which can be combined to predict complex behaviors." It is clear that factors here function as constructs. Eysenck, in his "criterion analysis" (18), goes farther than Guilford, and shows that factoring can be used explicitly to test hypotheses about constructs.

Factors may or may not be weighted with surplus meaning. Certainly when they are regarded as "real dimensions" a great deal of surplus meaning is implied, and the interpreter must shoulder a substantial burden of proof. The alternative view is to regard factors as defining a working reference frame, located in a convenient manner in the "space" defined by all behaviors of a given type. Which set of factors from a given matrix is "most useful" will depend partly on predilections, but in essence the best construct is the one around which we can build the greatest number of inferences, in the most direct fashion.

Studies of internal structure. For many constructs, evidence of homogeneity within the test is relevant in judging validity. If a trait such as *dominance* is hypothesized, and the items inquire about behaviors subsumed under this label, then the hypothesis appears to require that these items be generally intercorrelated. Even low correlations, if consistent, would support the argument that people may be fruitfully described in terms of a generalized tendency to dominate or not dominate. The general quality would have power to predict behavior in a variety of situations represented by the specific items. Item-test correlations and certain reliability formulas describe internal consistency.

It is unwise to list uninterpreted data of this sort under the heading "validity" in test manuals, as some authors have done. High internal consistency may *lower* validity. Only if the underlying theory of the trait being measured calls for high item intercorrelations do the correlations support construct validity. Negative item-test correlations may support construct validity, provided that the items with negative correlations are believed irrelevant to the postulated construct and serve as suppressor variables (31, p. 431–436; 44).

Study of distinctive subgroups of items within a test may set an upper limit to construct validity by showing that irrelevant elements influence scores. Thus a study of the PMA space tests shows that variance can be partially accounted for by a response set, tendency to mark many figures as similar (12). An internal factor analysis of the PEA Interpretation of Data Test shows that in addition to measuring reasoning skills, the test score is strongly influenced by a tendency to say "probably true" rather than "certainly true," regardless of item content (17). On the other hand, a study of item groupings in the DAT Mechanical Comprehension Test permitted rejection of the hypothesis that knowledge about specific topics such as gears made a substantial contribution to scores (13).

Studies of change over occasions. The stability of test scores ("retest reliability," Cattell's "N-technique") may be relevant to construct validation. Whether a high degree of stability is encouraging or discouraging for the proposed interpretation depends upon the theory defining the construct.

More powerful than the retest after uncontrolled intervening experiences is the retest with experimental intervention. If a transient influence swings test scores over a wide range, there are definite limits on the extent to which a test result can be interpreted as reflecting the typical behavior of the individual. These are examples of experiments which have indicated upper limits to test validity: studies of differences associated with the examiner in projective testing, of change of score under alternative directions ("tell the truth" vs. "make yourself look good to an employer"), and of coachability of mental tests. We may recall Gulliksen's distinction (27): When the coaching is of a sort that improves the pupil's intellectual functioning in school, the test which is affected by the coaching has validity as a measure of intellectual functioning; if the coaching improves test taking but not school performance, the test which responds to the coaching has poor validity as a measure of this construct.

Sometimes, where differences between individuals are difficult to assess by any means other than the test, the experimenter validates by determining whether the test can detect induced intra-individual differences. One might hypothesize that the Zeigarnik effect is a measure of ego involvement, i.e., that with ego involvement there is more recall of incomplete tasks. To support such an interpretation, the investigator will try to induce ego involvement on some task by appropriate directions and compare subjects' recall with their recall for tasks where there was a contrary induction. Sometimes the intervention is drastic. Porteus finds (53) that brain-operated patients show disruption of performance on his maze, but do not show impaired performance on conventional verbal tests and argues therefrom that his test is a better measure of planfulness.

Studies of process. One of the best ways of determining informally what accounts for variability on a test is the observation of the person's process of performance. If it is supposed, for example, that a test measures mathematical competence, and yet observation of students' errors shows that erroneous reading of the question is common, the implications of a low score are altered. Lucas in this way showed that the Navy Relative Movement Test, an aptitude test, actually involved two different abilities: spatial visualization and mathematical reasoning (39).

Mathematical analysis of scoring procedures may provide important negative evidence on construct validity. A recent analysis of "empathy" tests is perhaps worth citing (14). "Empathy" has been operationally defined in many studies by the ability of a judge to predict what responses will be given on some questionnaire by a subject he has observed briefly. A mathematical argument has shown, however, that the scores depend on several attributes of the judge which enter into his perception of *any* individual, and that they therefore cannot be interpreted as evidence of his ability to interpret cues offered by particular others, or his intuition.

The Numerical Estimate of Construct Validity

There is an understandable tendency to seek a "construct validity coefficient." A numerical statement of the degree of construct validity would be a statement of the proportion of the test score variance that is attributable to the construct variable. This numerical estimate can sometimes be arrived at by a factor analysis, but since present methods of factor analysis are based on linear relations, more general methods will ultimately be needed to deal with many quantitative problems of construct validation.

Rarely will it be possible to estimate definite "construct saturations," because no factor corresponding closely to the construct will be available. One can only hope to set upper and lower bounds to the "loading." If "creativity" is defined as something independent of knowledge, then a correlation of .40 between a presumed test of creativity and a test of arithmetic knowledge would indicate that at least 16 per cent of the reliable test variance is irrelevant to creativity as defined. Laboratory performance on problems such as Maier's "hatrack" would scarcely be an ideal measure of creativity, but it would be somewhat relevant. If its correlation with the test is .60, this permits a tentative estimate of 36 per cent as a lower bound. (The estimate is tentative because the test might overlap with the irrelevant portion of the laboratory measure.) The saturation seems to lie between 36 and 84 per cent; a cumulation of studies would provide better limits.

It should be particularly noted that rejecting the null hypothesis does not finish the job of construct validation (35, p. 284). The problem is not to conclude that the test "is valid" for measuring the construct variable. The task is to state as definitely as possible the degree of validity the test is presumed to have.

THE LOGIC OF CONSTRUCT VALIDATION

Construct validation takes place when an investigator believes that his instrument reflects a particular construct, to which are attached certain meanings. The proposed interpretation generates specific testable hypotheses, which are a means of confirming or disconfirming the claim. The philosophy of science which we believe does most justice to actual scientific practice will now be briefly and dogmatically set forth. Readers interested in further study of the philosophical underpinning are referred to the works by Braithwaite (6, especially Chapter III), Carnap (7; 8, pp. 56–69), Pap (51), Sellars (55, 56), Feigl (19, 20), Beck (4), Kneale (37, pp. 92–110), Hempel (29; 30, Sec. 7).

The Nomological Net

The fundamental principles are these:

1. Scientifically speaking, to "make clear what something *is*" means to set forth the laws in which it occurs. We shall refer to the interlocking system of laws which constitute a theory as a *nomological network*.

2. The laws in a nomological network may relate (*a*) observable properties or quantities to each other; or (*b*) theoretical constructs to observables; or (*c*) different theoretical constructs to one another. These "laws" may be statistical or deterministic.

3. A necessary condition for a construct to be scientifically admissible is that it occur in a nomological net, at least *some* of whose laws involve observables. Admissible constructs may be remote from observation, i.e., a long derivation may intervene between the nomologicals which implicitly define the construct, and the (derived) nomologicals of type *a*. These latter propositions permit predictions about events. The construct is not "reduced" to the observations, but only combined with other constructs in the net to make predictions about observables.

4. "Learning more about" a theoretical construct is a matter of elab-

orating the nomological network in which it occurs, or of increasing the definiteness of the components. At least in the early history of a construct the network will be liimted, and the construct will as yet have few connections.

5. An enrichment of the net such as adding a construct or a relation to theory is justified if it generates nomologicals that are confirmed by observation or if it reduces the number of nomologicals required to predict the same observations. When observations will not fit into the network as it stands, the scientist has a certain freedom in selecting where to modify the network. That is, there may be alternative constructs or ways of organizing the net which for the time being are equally defensible.

6. We can say that "operations" which are qualitatively very different "overlap" or "measure the same thing" if their positions in the nomological net tie them to the same construct variable. Our confidence in this identification depends upon the amount of inductive support we have for the regions of the net involved. It is not necessary that a direct observational comparison of the two operations be made—we may be content with an intranetwork proof indicating that the two operations yield estimates of the same network-defined quantity. Thus, physicists are content to speak of the "temperature" of the sun and the "temperature" of a gas at room temperature even though the test operations are nonoverlapping because this identification makes theoretical sense.

With these statements of scientific methodology in mind, we return to the specific problem of construct validity as applied to psychological tests. The preceding guide rules should reassure the "toughminded," who fear that allowing construct validation opens the door to nonconfirmable test claims. *The answer is that unless the network makes contact with observations, and exhibits explicit, public steps of inference, construct validation cannot be claimed.* An admissible psychological construct must be behavior-relevant (59, p. 15). For most tests intended to measure constructs, adequate criteria do not exist. This being the case, many such tests have been left unvalidated, or a finespun network of rationalizations has been offered as if it were validation. Rationalization is not construct validation. One who claims that his test reflects a construct cannot maintain his claim in the face of recurrent negative results because these results show that his construct is too loosely defined to yield verifiable inferences.

A rigorous (though perhaps probabilistic) chain of inference is required to establish a test as a measure of a construct. To validate a claim that a test measures a construct, a nomological net surrounding the concept must exist. When a construct is fairly new, there may be few specifiable associations by which to pin down the concept. As research proceeds, the construct sends out roots in many directions, which attach it to more and more facts or other constructs. Thus the electron has more accepted properties than the neutrino; *numerical ability* has more than *the second space factor*.

"Acceptance," which was critical in criterion-oriented and content validities, has now appeared in construct validity. Unless substantially the same nomological net is accepted by the several users of the construct, public validation is impossible. If A uses *aggressiveness* to mean overt assault on others, and B's usage includes repressed hostile reactions, evidence which convinces B that a test measures *aggressiveness* convinces A that the test does not. Hence, the investigator who proposes to establish a test as a measure of a construct must specify his network or theory sufficiently clearly that others can accept or reject it (cf. 41, p. 406). A consumer of the test who rejects the author's theory cannot accept the author's validation. He must validate the test for himself, if he wishes to show that it represents the construct as *he* defines it.

Two general qualifications are in order with reference to the methodological principles 1–6 set forth at the beginning of this section. Both of them concern the amount of "theory," in any high-level sense of that word, which enters into a construct-defining network of laws or lawlike statements. We do not wish to convey the impression that one always has a very elaborate theoretical network, rich in hypothetical processes or entities.

Construct as inductive summaries. In the early stages of development of a construct or even at more advanced stages when our orientation is thoroughly practical, little or no theory in the usual sense of the word need be involved. In the extreme case the hypothesized laws are formulated entirely in terms of descriptive (observational) dimensions although not all of the relevant observations have actually been made.

The hypothesized network "goes beyond the data" only in the limited sense that it purports to *characterize* the behavior facets which belong to an observable but as yet only partially sampled cluster; hence, it generates predictions about hitherto unsampled regions of the phenotypic space. Even though no unobservables or high-order theoretical constructs are introduced, an element of inductive extrapolation appears in the claim that a cluster including some elements not-yet-observed has been identified. Since, as in any sorting or abstracting task involving a finite set of complex elements, several nonequivalent bases of categorization are available, the investigator may choose a hypothesis which generates erroneous predictions. The failure of a supposed, hitherto untried, member of the cluster to behave in the manner said to be characteristic of the group, or the finding that a nonmember of the postulated cluster does behave in this manner, may modify greatly our tentative construct.

For example, one might build an intelligence test on the basis of his background notions of "intellect," including vocabulary, arithmetic calculation, general information, similarities, two-point threshold, reaction time, and line bisection as subtests. The first four of these correlate, and he extracts a huge first factor. This becomes a second approximation of the intelligence construct, described by its pattern of loadings on the four tests. The other three tests have negligible loading on any common factor. On this evidence the investigator reinterprets intelligence as "manipulation of words." Subsequently it is discovered that test-stupid people are rated as unable to express their ideas, are easily taken in by fallacious arguments, and misread complex directions. These data support the "linguistic" definition of intelligence and the test's claim of validity *for* that construct. But then a block design test with pantomime instructions is found to be strongly saturated with the first factor. Immediately the purely "linguistic" interpretation of Factor I becomes suspect. This finding, taken together with our initial acceptance of the others as relevant to the background concept of intelligence, forces us to reinterpret the concept once again.

If we simply *list* the tests or traits which have been shown to be saturated with the "factor" or which belong to the cluster, no construct is employed. As soon as we even *summarize the properties* of this group of indicators—we are already making some guesses. Intensional characterization of a domain is hazardous since it selects (abstracts) properties and implies that new tests sharing those properties will behave as do the known tests in the cluster, and that tests not sharing them will not.

The difficulties in merely "characterizing the surface cluster" are strikingly exhibited by the use of certain special and extreme groups for purposes of construct validation. The P_d scale of MMPI was originally derived and cross-validated upon hospitalized patients diagnosed "Psychopathic personality, asocial and amoral type" (42). Further research shows the scale to have a limited degree of predictive and concurrent validity for "delinquency" more broadly defined (5, 28). Several studies show associations between P_d and very special "criterion" groups which it would be ludicrous to identify as "*the* criterion" in the traditional sense. If one lists these heterogeneous groups and tries to characterize them intensionally, he faces enormous conceptual difficulties. For example, a recent survey of hunting accidents in Minnesota showed that hunters who had "carelessly" shot someone were significantly elevated on P_d when compared with other hunters (48). This is in line with one's theoretical expectations; when you ask MMPI "experts" to predict for such a group they invariably predict P_d *or* M_a or both. The finding seems therefore to lend some slight support to the construct validity of the P_d scale. But of course it would be nonsense to *define* the P_d component "operationally" in terms of, say, accident proneness. We might try to subsume the original phenotype and the hunting-accident proneness under some broader category, such as "Disposition to violate society's rules, whether legal, moral, or just *sensible*." But now we have ceased to have a neat operational criterion, and are using instead a rather vague and wide-range class. Besides, there is worse to come. We want the class specification to cover a group trend that (nondelinquent) high school students judged by their peer group as least "responsible" score over a full sigma higher on P_d than those judged most "responsible" (23, p. 75). Most of the behaviors contributing to such sociometric choices fall well within the range of socially permissible action; the proffered criterion specification is still too restrictive. Again, any clinician familiar with MMPI lore would predict an elevated P_d on a sample of (nondelinquent) professional actors. Chyatte's confirmation of this prediction (10) tends to support *both:* (*a*) the theory sketch of "what the P_d factor is, psychologically"; and (*b*) the claim of the P_d scale to construct validity for this hypothetical factor. Let the reader try his hand at writing a brief phenotypic criterion specification that will cover both trigger-happy hunters and Broadway actors! And if he should be ingenious enough to achieve this, does his definition also encompass Hovey's report that high P_d predicts the judgments "not shy" and "unafraid of mental patients" made upon nurses by their supervisors (32, p. 143)? And then we have Gough's report that *low* P_d is associated with ratings as "good-natured" (24, p. 40), Roessell's data showing that high P_d is predictive of "dropping out of high school" (54). The point is that all seven of these "criterion" dispositions would be readily guessed by any clinician having even superficial familiarity with MMPI interpretation; but to mediate these inferences explicitly requires quite a few hypotheses about dynamics, constituting an admittedly sketchy (but far from vacuous) network defining the genotype *psychopathic deviate.*

Vagueness of present psychological laws. This line of thought leads directly to our second important qualification upon the network schema. The idealized picture is one of a tidy set of postulates which jointly entail the desired theorems; since some of the theorems are coordinated to the observation base, the system constitutes an implicit definition of the theoretical primitives and gives them an indirect empirical meaning. In practice, of course, even the most advanced physical sciences only approximate this ideal. Questions of "categoricalness" and the like, such as logicians raise about pure calculi, are hardly even statable for empirical networks. (What, for example, would be the desiderata of a "well-formed formula" in molar behavior theory?) Psychology works with crude, half-explicit formulations. We do not worry about such advanced formal questions as "whether all molar-behavior statements are decidable by appeal to the postulates" because we know that no existing theoretical network suffices to predict even the *known* descriptive laws. Nevertheless, the sketch of a network is there; if it were not, we would not be saying *anything* intelligible about our constructs. We do not have the rigorous implicit definitions of formal calculi (which still, be it noted, usually permit of a multiplicity of interpretations). Yet the vague, avowedly incomplete network still gives the constructs whatever meaning they do have. When the network is very incomplete, having many strands missing entirely and some constructs tied in only by tenuous threads, then the "implicit definition" of these constructs is disturbingly loose; one might say that the meaning of the constructs is underdetermined. *Since the meaning of theoretical constructs is set forth by stating the laws in which they occur, our incomplete knowledge of the laws of nature produces a vagueness in our constructs* (see Hempel, 30; Kaplan, 34; Pap, 51). We will be able to say "what anxiety is" when we know all of the laws involving it; meanwhile, since we are in the process of discovering these laws, we do not yet know precisely what anxiety is.

CONCLUSIONS REGARDING THE NETWORK AFTER EXPERIMENTATION

The proposition that x per cent of test variance is accounted for by the construct is inserted into the accepted network. The network then generates a testable prediction about the relation of the test scores to certain other variables, and the investigator gathers data. If prediction and result are in harmony, he can retain his belief that the test measures the construct. The construct is at best adopted, never demonstrated to be "correct."

We do not first "prove" the theory, and then validate the test, nor conversely. In any probable inductive type of inference from a pattern of observations, we examine the relation between the total network of theory and observations. The system involves propositions relating test to construct, construct to other constructs, and finally relating some of these constructs to observables. In ongoing research the chain of inference is very complicated. Kelly and Fiske (36, p. 124) give a complex diagram showing the numerous inferences required in validating a prediction from assessment techniques, where theories about the criterion situation are as integral a part of the prediction as are the test data. A predicted empirical relationship permits us to test all the propositions leading to that prediction. Traditionally the proposition claiming to interpret the test has been set apart as the hypothesis being tested, but actually the evidence is significant for all parts of the chain. If the prediction is not confirmed, any link in the chain may be wrong.

A theoretical network can be divided into subtheories used in making particular predictions. All the events successfully predicted through a subtheory are of course evidence in favor of that theory. Such a subtheory may be so well confirmed by voluminous and diverse evidence that we can reasonably view a particular experiment as relevant only to the test's validity. If the theory, combined with a proposed test interpretation, mispredicts in this case, it is the latter which must be abandoned. On the other hand, the accumulated evidence for a test's construct validity may be so strong that an instance of misprediction will force us to modify the subtheory employing the construct rather than deny the claim that the test measures the construct.

Most cases in psychology today lie somewhere between these extremes. Thus, suppose we fail to find a greater incidence of "homosexual signs" in the Rorschach records of paranoid patients. Which is more strongly disconfirmed—the Rorschach signs or the orthodox theory of paranoia? The negative finding shows the bridge between the two to be undependable, but this is all we can say. The bridge cannot be used unless one end is placed on solider ground. The investigator must decide which end it is best to relocate.

Numerous successful predictions dealing with phenotypically diverse "criteria" give greater weight to the claim of construct validity than do fewer predictions, or predictions involving very similar behaviors. In arriving at diverse predictions, the hypothesis of test validity is connected each time to a subnetwork largely independent of the portion previously used. Success of these derivations testifies to the inductive power of the test-validity statement, and renders it unlikely that an equally effective alternative can be offered.

Implications of Negative Evidence

The investigator whose prediction and data are discordant must make strategic decisions. His result can be interpreted in three ways:

1. The test does not measure the construct variable.
2. The theoretical network which generated the hypothesis is incorrect.
3. The experimental design failed to test the hypothesis properly. (Strictly speaking this may be analyzed as a special case of 2, but in practice the distinction is worth making.)

For further research. If a specific fault of procedure makes the third a reasonable possibility, his proper response is to perform an adequate study, meanwhile making no report. When faced with the other two alternatives, he may decide that his test does not measure the construct adequately. Following that decision, he will perhaps prepare and validate a new test. Any rescoring or new interpretative procedure for the original instrument, like a new test, requires validation *by means of a fresh body of data.*

The investigator may regard interpretation 2 as more likely to lead to eventual advances. It is legitimate for the investigator to call the network defining the construct into question, if he has confidence in the test. Should the investigator decide that some step in the network is unsound, he may be able to invent an alternative network. Perhaps he modifies the network by splitting a concept into two or more portions, e.g., by designating types of *anxiety,* or perhaps he specifies added conditions under which a generalization holds. When an investigator modifies the theory in such a manner, he is now required to *gather a fresh body of data* to test the altered hypotheses. This step should normally precede publication of the modified theory. If the new data are consistent with the modified network, he is free from the fear that his nomologicals were gerrymandered to fit the peculiarities of his first sample of observations. He can now trust his test to some extent, because his test results behave as predicted.

The choice among alternatives, like any strategic decision, is a gamble as to which course of action is the best investment of effort. Is it wise to modify the theory? That depends on how well the system is confirmed by prior data, and how well the modifications fit available observations. Is it worth while to modify the test in the hope that it will fit the construct? That depends on how much evidence there is—apart from this abortive experiment—to support the hope, and also on how much it is worth to the investigator's ego to salvage the test. The choice among alternatives is a matter of research planning.

For practical use of the test. The consumer can accept a test as a measure of a construct only when there is a strong positive fit between predictions and subsequent data. When the evidence from a proper investigation of a published test is essentially negative, it should be reported as a stop sign to discourage use of the test pending a reconciliation of test and construct, or final abandonment of the test. If the test has not been published, it should be restricted to research use until some degree of validity is established (1). The consumer can await the results of the investigator's gamble with confidence that proper application of the scientific method will ultimately tell whether the test has value. Until the evidence is in, he has no justification for employing the test as a basis for terminal decisions. The test may serve, at best, only as a source of suggestions about individuals to be confirmed by other evidence (15, 47).

There are two perspectives in test validation. From the viewpoint of the psychological practitioner, the burden of proof is on the test. A test should not be used to measure a trait until its proponent establishes that predictions made from such measures are consistent with the best available theory of the trait. In the view of the test developer, however, both the test and the theory are under scrutiny. He is free to say *to himself privately,* "If my test disagrees with the theory, so much the worse for the theory." This way lies delusion, unless he continues his research using a better theory.

Reporting of Positive Results

The test developer who finds positive correspondence between his proposed interpretation and data is expected to report the basis for his validity claim. Defending a claim of construct validity is a major task, not to be satisfied by a discourse without data. The *Technical Recommendations* have little to say on reporting of construct validity. Indeed, the only detailed suggestions under that heading refer to correlations of the test with other measures, together with a cross reference to some other sections of the report. The two key principles, however, call for the most comprehensive type of reporting. The manual for any test "should report all available information which will assist the user in determining what psychological attributes account for variance in test scores" (59, p. 27). And, "The manual for a test which is used primarily to assess postulated attributes of the individual should outline the theory on which the test is based and organize whatever partial validity data there are to show in what way they support the theory" (59, p. 28). It is recognized, by a classification as "very desirable" rather than "essential," that the latter recommendation goes beyond present practice of test authors.

The proper goals in reporting construct validation are to make clear (*a*) what interpretation is proposed, (*b*) how adequately the writer believes this interpretation is substantiated, and (*c*) what evidence and reasoning lead him to this belief. Without *a* the construct validity of the test is of no use to the consumer. Without *b* the consumer must carry the entire burden of evaluating the test research. Without *c* the consumer or reviewer is being asked to take *a* and *b* on faith. The test manual cannot always present an exhaustive statement on these points, but it should summarize and indicate where complete statements may be found.

To specify the interpretation, the writer must state what construct he has in mind, and what meaning he gives to that construct. For a construct which has a short history and has built up few connotations, it will be fairly easy to indicate the presumed properties of the construct, i.e., the nomologicals in which it appears. For a construct with a longer history, a summary of properties and references to previous theoretical discussions may be appropriate. It is especially critical to distinguish proposed interpretations from other meanings previously given the same construct. The validator faces no small task; he must somehow communicate a theory to his reader.

To evaluate his evidence calls for a statement like the conclusions from a program of research, noting what is well substantiated and what alternative interpretations have been considered and rejected. The writer must note what portions of his proposed interpretation are speculations, extrapolations, or conclusions from insufficient data. The author has an ethical responsibility to prevent unsubstantiated interpretations from appearing as truths. A claim is unsubstantiated unless the evidence for the claim is public, so that other scientists may review the evidence, criticize the conclusions, and offer alternative interpretations.

The report of evidence in a test manual must be as complete as any research report, except where adequate public reports can be cited. Reference to something "observed by the writer in many clinical cases" is worthless as evidence. Full case reports, on the other hand, may be a valuable source of evidence so long as these cases are representative and negative instances receive due attention. The report of evidence must be interpreted with reference to the theoretical network in such a manner that the reader sees why the author regards a particular correlation or experiment as confirming (or throwing doubt upon) the proposed interpretation. Evidence collected by others must be taken fairly into account.

VALIDATION OF A COMPLEX TEST "AS A WHOLE"

Special questions must be considered when we are investigating the validity of a test which is aimed to provide information about several constructs. In one sense, it is naive to inquire "Is this test valid?" One does not validate a test, but only a principle for making inferences. If a test yields many different types of inferences some of them can be valid and others invalid (cf. Technical Recommendation C2: "The manual should report the validity of each type of inference for which a test is recommended"). From this point of view, every topic sentence in the typical book on Rorschach interpretation presents a hypothesis requiring validation, and one should validate inferences about each aspect of the personality separately and in turn, just as he would want information on the validity (concurrent or predictive) for each scale of MMPI.

There is, however, another defensible point of view. If a test is purely empirical, based strictly on observed connections between response to an item and some criterion, then of course the validity of one scoring key for the test does not make validation for its other scoring keys any less necessary. But a test may be developed on the basis of a theory which in itself provides a linkage between the various keys and the various criteria. Thus, while Strong's Vocational Interest Blank is developed empirically, it also rests on a "theory" that a youth can be expected to be satisfied in an occupation if he has interests common to men now happy in the occupation. When Strong finds that those with high Engineering interest scores in college are preponderantly in engineering careers 19 years later, he has partly validated the proposed use of the Engineer score (predictive validity). Since the evidence is consistent with the theory on which all the test keys were built, this evidence alone increases the presumption that the *other* keys have predictive validity. How strong is this presumption? Not very, from the viewpoint of the traditional skepticism of science. Engineering interest may stabilize early, while interests in art or management or social work are still unstable. A claim cannot be made that the whole Strong approach is valid just because one score shows predictive validity. But if thirty interest scores were investigated longitudinally and all of them showed the type of validity predicted by Strong's theory, we would indeed be caviling to say that this evidence gives no confidence in the long-range validity of the thirty-first score.

Confidence in a theory is increased as more relevant evidence confirms it, but it is always possible that tomorrow's investigation will render the theory obsolete. The Technical Recommendations suggest a rule of reason, and ask for evidence for each *type* of inference for which a test is recommended. It is stated that no test developer can present predictive validities for all possible criteria; similarly, no developer can run all possible experimental tests of his proposed interpretation. But the recommendation is more subtle than advice that a lot of validation is better than a little.

Consider the Rorschach test. It is used for many inferences, made by means of nomological networks at several levels. At a low level are the simple unrationalized correspondences presumed to exist between certain signs and psychiatric diagnoses. Validating such a sign does nothing to substantiate Rorschach theory. For other Rorschach formulas an explicit a priori rationale exists (for instance, high *F%* interpreted as implying rigid control of impulses). Each time such a sign shows correspondence with criteria, its rationale is supported just a little. At a still higher level of abstraction, a considerable body of theory surrounds the general area of *outer control,* interlacing many different constructs. As evidence cumulates, one should be able to decide what specific inference-making chains within this system can be depended upon. One should also be able to conclude—or deny—that so much of the system has stood up under test that one has some confidence in even the untested lines in the network.

In addition to relatively delimited nomological networks surrounding *control* or *aspiration,* the Rorschach interpreter usually has an overriding theory of the test as a whole. This may be a psychoanalytic theory, a theory of perception and set, or a theory stated in terms of learned habit patterns. Whatever the theory of the interpreter, whenever he validates an inference from the system, he obtains some reason for added confidence in his overriding system. His total theory is not tested, however, by experiments dealing with only one limited set of constructs. The test developer must investigate far-separated, independent sections of the network. The more diversified the predictions the system is required to make, the greater confidence we can have that only minor parts of the system will later prove faulty. Here we begin to glimpse a logic to defend the judgment that the test and its whole interpretative system is valid at some level of confidence.

There are enthusiasts who would conclude from the foregoing paragraphs that since there is some evidence of correct, diverse predictions made from the Rorschach, the test as a whole can now be accepted as validated. This conclusion overlooks the negative evidence. Just one finding contrary to expectation, based on sound research, is sufficient to wash a whole theoretical structure away. Perhaps the remains can be salvaged to form a new structure. But this structure now must be exposed to fresh risks, and sound negative evidence will destroy it in turn. There is sufficient negative evidence to prevent acceptance of the Rorschach and its accompanying interpretative structures as a whole. So long as any aspects of the overriding theory stated for the test have been disconfirmed, this structure must be rebuilt.

Talk of areas and structures may seem not to recognize those who would interpret the personality "globally." They may argue that a test is best validated in matching studies. Without going into detailed questions of matching methodology, we can ask whether such a study validates the nomological network "as a whole." The judge does employ some network in arriving at his conception of his subject, integrating specific inferences from specific data. Matching studies, if successful, demonstrate only that each judge's interpretative theory has some validity, that it is not completely a fantasy. Very high consistency between judges is required to show that they are using the same network, and very high success in matching is required to show that the network is dependable.

If inference is less than perfectly dependable, we must know which aspects of the interpretative network are least dependable and which are most dependable. Thus, even if one has considerable confidence in a test "as a whole" because of frequent successful inferences, one still returns as an ultimate aim to the request of the Technical Recommendation for separate evidence on the validity of each type of inference to be made.

RECAPITULATION

Construct validation was introduced in order to specify types of research required in developing tests for which the conventional views on validation are inappropriate. Personality tests, and some tests of ability, are interpreted in terms of attributes for which there is no adequate criterion. This paper indicates what sorts of evidence can substantiate such an interpretation, and how such evidence is to be interpreted. The following points made in the discussion are particularly significant.

1. A construct is defined implicitly by a network of associations or propositions in which it occurs. Constructs employed at different stages of research vary in definiteness.

2. Construct validation is possible only when some of the statements in the network lead to predicted relations among observables. While some observables may be regarded as "criteria," the construct validity of the criteria themselves is regarded as under investigation.

3. The network defining the construct, and the derivation leading to the predicted observation, must be reasonably explicit so that validating evidence may be properly interpreted.

4. Many types of evidence are relevant to construct validity, including content validity, interitem correlations, intertest correlations, test-"criterion" correlations, studies of stability over time, and stability under experimental intervention. High correlations and high stability may constitute either favorable or unfavorable evidence for the proposed interpretation, depending on the theory surrounding the construct.

5. When a predicted relation fails to occur, the fault may lie in the proposed interpretation of the test or in the network. Altering the network so that it can cope with the new observations is, in effect, redefining the construct. Any such new interpretation of the test must be validated by a fresh body of data before being advanced publicly. Great care is required to avoid substituting a posteriori rationalizations for proper validation.

6. Construct validity cannot generally be expressed in the form of a single simple coefficient. The data often permit one to establish upper and lower bounds for the proportion of test variance which can be attributed to the construct. The integration of diverse data into a proper interpretation cannot be an entirely quantitative process.

7. Constructs may vary in nature from those very close to "pure description" (involving little more than extrapolation of relations among observation-variables) to highly theoretical constructs involving hypothesized entities and processes, or making identifications with constructs of other sciences.

8. The investigation of a test's construct validity is not essentially different from the general scientific procedures for developing and confirming theories.

Without in the least *advocating* construct validity as preferable to the other three kinds (concurrent, predictive, content), we do believe it imperative that psychologists make a place for it in their methodological thinking, so that its rationale, its scientific legitimacy, and its dangers may be explicit and familiar. This would be preferable to the widespread current tendency to engage in what actually amounts to construct validation research and use of constructs in practical testing, while talking an "operational" methodology which, if adopted, would force research into a mold it does not fit.

REFERENCES

1. American Psychological Association. *Ethical standards of psychologists.* Washington, D.C.: American Psychological Association, Inc., 1953.
2. Anastasi, Anne. The concept of validity in the interpretation of test scores. *Educ. psychol. Measmt.,* 1950, **10,** 67–78.
3. Bechtoldt, H. P. Selection. In S. S. Stevens (Ed.), *Handbook of experimental psychology.* New York: Wiley, 1951. Pp. 1237–1267.
4. Beck, L. W. Constructions and inferred entities. *Phil. Sci.,* 1950, 17. Reprinted in H. Feigl and M. Brodbeck (Eds.), *Readings in the philosophy of science.* New York: Appleton-Century-Crofts, 1953. Pp. 368–381.
5. Blair, W. R. N. A comparative study of disciplinary offenders and non-offenders in the Canadian Army. *Canad. J. Psychol.,* 1950, **4,** 49–62.
6. Braithwaite, R. B. *Scientific explanation.* Cambridge: Cambridge Univer. Press, 1953.
7. Carnap, R. Empiricism, semantics, and ontology. *Rev. int. de Phil.,* 1950, II, 20–40. Reprinted in P. P. Wiener (Ed.), *Readings in philosophy of science,* New York: Scribner's, 1953. Pp. 509–521.
8. Carnap, R. *Foundations of logic and mathematics. International encyclopedia of unified science,* I, No. 3. Pages 56–69 reprinted as "The interpretation of physics" in H. Feigl and M. Brodbeck (Eds.), *Readings in the philosophy of science.* New York: Appleton-Century-Crofts, 1953. Pp. 309–318.
9. Child, I. L. Personality. *Annu. Rev. Psychol.,* 1954, **5,** 149–171.
10. Chyatte, C. Psychological characteristics of a group of professional actors. *Occupations,* 1949, **27,** 245–250.
11. Cronbach, L. J. *Essentials of psychological testing.* New York: Harper, 1949.
12. Cronbach, L. J. Further evidence on response sets and test design. *Educ. psychol. Measmt,* 1950, **10,** 3–31.
13. Cronbach, L. J. Coefficient alpha and the internal structure of tests. *Psychometrika,* 1951, **16,** 297–335.
14. Cronbach, L. J. Processes affecting scores on "understanding of others" and "assumed similarity." *Psychol. Bull.,* 1955, **52,** 177–193.
15. Cronbach, L. J. The counselor's problems from the perspective of communication theory. In Vivian H. Hewer (Ed.), *New perspectives in counseling.* Minneapolis: Univer. of Minnesota Press, 1955.
16. Cureton, E. E. Validity. In E. F. Lindquist (Ed.), *Educational measurement.* Washington, D. C.: American Council on Education, 1950. Pp. 621–695.
17. Damrin, Dora E. A. comparative study of information derived from a diagnostic problem-solving test by logical and factorial methods of scoring. Unpublished doctor's dissertation, Univer. of Illinois, 1952.
18. Eysenck, H. J. Criterion analysis—an application of the hypothetico-deductive method in factor analysis. *Psychol. Rev.,* 1950, **57,** 38–53.
19. Feigl, H. Existential hypotheses. *Phil. Sci.,* 1950, **17,** 35–62.

20. Feigl, H. Confirmability and confirmation. *Rev. int. de Phil.*, 1951, **5,** 1–12. Reprinted in P. P. Wiener (Ed.), *Readings in philosophy of science*. New York: Scribner's, 1953. Pp. 522–530.
21. Gaylord, R. H. Conceptual consistency and criterion equivalence: a dual approach to criterion analysis. Unpublished manuscript (PRB Research Note No. 17). Copies obtainable from ASTIA-DSC, AD-21 440.
22. Goodenough, Florence L. *Mental testing*. New York: Rinehart, 1950.
23. Gough, H. G., McClosky, H., & Meehl, P. E. A personality scale for social responsibility. *J. abnorm. soc. Psychol.*, 1952, **47,** 73–80.
24. Gough, H. G., McKee, M. G., & Yandell, R. J. Adjective check list analyses of a number of selected psychometric and assessment variables. Unpublished manuscript. Berkeley: IPAR, 1953.
25. Guilford, J. P. New standards for test evaluation. *Educ. psychol. Measmt*. 1946, **6,** 427–439.
26. Guilford, J. P. Factor analysis in a test-development program. *Psychol. Rev.*, 1948, **55,** 79–94.
27. Gulliksen, H. Intrinsic validity. *Amer. Psychologist,* 1950, **5,** 511–517.
28. Hathaway, S. R., & Monachesi, E. D. *Analyzing and predicting juvenile delinquency with the MMPI*. Minneapolis: Univer. of Minnesota Press, 1953.
29. Hempel, C. G. Problems and changes in the empiricist criterion of meaning. *Rev. int. de Phil.*, 1950, **4,** 41–63. Reprinted in L. Linsky, *Semantics and the philosophy of language*. Urbana: Univer. of Illinois Press, 1952. Pp. 163–185.
30. Hempel, C. G. *Fundamentals of concept formation in empirical science*. Chicago: Univer. of Chicago Press, 1952.
31. Horst, P. The prediction of personal adjustment. *Soc. Sci. Res. Council Bull.*, 1941. No. 48.
32. Hovey, H. B. MMPI profiles and personality characteristics. *J. consult. Psychol.*, 1953, **17,** 142–146.
33. Jenkins, J. G. Validity for what? *J. consult. Psychol.*, 1946, **10,** 93–98.
34. Kaplan, A. Definition and specification of meaning. *J. Phil.*, 1946, **43,** 281–288.
35. Kelly, E. L. Theory and techniques of assessment. *Annu. Rev. Psychol.*, 1954, **5,** 281–311.
36. Kelly, E. L., & Fiske, D. W. *The prediction of performance in clinical psychology*. Ann Arbor: Univer. of Michigan Press, 1951.
37. Kneale, W. *Probability and induction*. Oxford: Clarendon Press, 1949. Pages 92–110 reprinted as "Induction, explanation, and transcendent hypotheses" in H. Feigl and M. Brodbeck (Eds.), *Readings in the philosophy of science*. New York: Appleton-Century-Crofts, 1953. Pp. 353–367.
38. Lindquist, E. F. *Educational measurement*. Washington, D. C.: American Council on Education, 1950.
39. Lucas, C. M. Analysis of the relative movement test by a method of individual interviews. *Bur. Naval Personnel Res. Rep.*, Contract Nonr-694 (00), NR 151–13, Educational Testing Service, March 1953.
40. MacCorquodale, K., & Meehl, P. E. On a distinction between hypothetical constructs and intervening variables. *Psychol. Rev.*, 1948, **55,** 95–107.

41. Macfarlane, Jean W. Problems of validation inherent in projective methods. *Amer. J. Orthopsychiat.,* 1942, **12,** 405–410.
42. McKinley, J. C., & Hathaway, S. R. The MMPI: V. Hysteria, hypomania, and psychopathic deviate. *J. appl. Psychol.,* 1944, **28,** 153–174.
43. McKinley, J. C., Hathaway, S. R., & Meehl, P. E. The MMPI: VI. The K scale. *J. consult. Psychol.,* 1948, **12,** 20–31.
44. Meehl, P. E. A simple algebraic development of Horst's suppressor variables. *Amer. J. Psychol.,* 1945, **58,** 550–554.
45. Meehl, P. E. An investigation of a general normality or control factor in personality testing. *Psychol. Monogr.,* 1945, **59,** No. 4 (Whole No. 274).
46. Meehl, P. E. *Clinical vs. statistical prediction.* Minneapolis: Univer. of Minnesota Press, 1954.
47. Meehl, P. E., & Rosen, A. Antecedent probability and the efficiency of psychometric signs, patterns or cutting scores. *Psychol. Bull.,* 1955, **52,** 194–216.
48. *Minnesota Hunter Casualty Study.* St. Paul: Jacob Schmidt Brewing Company, 1954.
49. Mosier, C. I. A critical examination of the concepts of face validity. *Educ. psychol. Measmt,* 1947, **7,** 191–205.
50. Mosier, C. I. Problems and designs of cross-validation. *Educ. psychol. Measmt,* 1951, **11,** 5–12.
51. Pap, A. Reduction-sentences and open concepts. *Methodos,* 1953, **5,** 3–30.
52. Peak, Helen. Problems of objective observation. In L. Festinger and D. Katz (Eds.), *Research methods in the behavioral sciences.* New York: Dryden Press, 1953. Pp. 243–300.
53. Porteus, S. D. *The Porteus maze test and intelligence.* Palo Alto: Pacific Books, 1950.
54. Roessel, F. P. MMPI results for high school drop-outs and graduates. Unpublished doctor's dissertation, Univer. of Minnesota, 1954.
55. Sellars, W. S. Concepts as involving laws and inconceivable without them. *Phil. Sci.,* 1948, **15,** 287–315.
56. Sellars, W. S. Some reflections on language games. *Phil. Sci.* 1954, **21,** 204–228.
57. Spiker, C. C., & McCandless, B. R. The concept of intelligence and the philosophy of science. *Psychol. Rev.,* 1954, **61,** 255–267.
58. Technical recommendations for psychological tests and diagnostic techniques: preliminary proposal. *Amer. Psychologist,* 1952, **7,** 461–476.
59. Technical recommendations for psychological tests and diagnostic techniques, *Psychol. Bull. Supplement,* 1954, **51,** 2, Part 2, 1–38.
60. Thurstone, L. L. The criterion problem in personality research. *Psychometric Lab. Rep.,* No. 78. Chicago: Univer. of Chicago, 1952.

26. Validity, Reliability, and Baloney[1]

EDWARD E. CURETON

Test items are frequently selected, and tests are often specially weighted so as to maximize the correlation of the test scores or battery composites with some criterion measure. But if the test constructor then uses the same data that led to the item or test selection as a basis for estimating the validity of the resulting test or battery, his estimate may be seriously inflated. Cureton illustrates this point dramatically.

To avoid errors of this kind, the test constructor should always use different test responses to validate his test than he used to select the elements for inclusion in it. That is, he should cross-validate.

Other discussions of cross-validation are found in the articles by Cureton (1951), Katzel (1951), Mosier (1951), Wherry (1951), and Langmuir (1954).

It is a generally accepted principle that if a test has demonstrated validity for some given purpose, considerations of reliability are secondary. The statistical literature also informs us that a validity coefficient cannot exceed the square root of the reliability coefficient of either the predictor or the criterion. This paper describes the construction and validation of a new test which seems to call in question these accepted principles. Since the technique of validation is the crucial point, I shall discuss the validation procedures before describing the test in detail.

Briefly, the test uses a new type of projective technique which appears to reveal controllable variations in psychokinetic force as applied in certain particular situations. In the present study the criterion is college scholarship, as given by the usual grade-point average. The subjects were 29 senior and graduate students in a course in Psychological Measurements. These students took Forms Q and R of the *Cooperative Vocabulary Test,* Form R being administered about two weeks after Form Q. The correlation between grade-point average and the combined score on both forms of this test was .23. The reliability of the test, estimated by the Spearman-Brown formula from the correlation between the two forms, was .90.

Cureton, E. E. Validity, reliability, and baloney. *Educational and Psychological Measurement,* 1950, *10,* 94–96. Reprinted with the permission of the publisher and author.

[1] This paper was presented in Denver, Colorado, September 7, 1949, at a meeting sponsored jointly by the Division on Evaluation and Measurement of the American Psychological Association and the Psychometric Society.

The experimental form of the new test, which I have termed the "B – Projective Psychokinesis Test," or Test B, was also applied to the group. This experimental form contained 85 items, and there was a reaction to every item for every student. The items called for unequivocal "plus" or "minus" reactions, but in advance of data there is no way to tell which reaction to a given item may be valid for any particular purpose. In this respect Test B is much like many well-known interest and personality inventories. Since there were no intermediate reactions, all scoring was based on the "plus" reactions alone.

I first obtained the mean grade-point average of all the students whose reaction to each item was "plus." Instead of using the usual technique of biserial correlation, however, I used an item-validity index based on the significance of the difference between the mean grade-point average of the whole group, and the mean grade-point average of those who gave the "plus" reaction to any particular item. This is a straightforward case of sampling from a finite universe. The mean and standard deviation of the grade-point averages of the entire group of 29 are the known parameters. The null hypothesis to be tested is the hypothesis that the subgroup giving the "plus" reaction to any item is a random sample from this population. The mean number giving the "plus" reaction to any item was 14.6. I therefore computed the standard error of the mean for independent samples of 14.6 drawn from a universe of 29, with replacement. If the mean grade-point average of those giving the "plus" reaction to any particular item was more than one standard error *above* the mean of the whole 29, the item was retained with a scoring weight of *plus one*. If it was more than one standard error *below* this general mean, the item was retained with a scoring weight of *minus one*.

By this procedure, 9 positively weighted items and 15 negatively weighted items were obtained. A scoring key for all 24 selected items was prepared, and the "plus" reactions for the 29 students were scored with this key. The correlations between the 29 scores on the revised Test B and the grade-point averages was found to be .82. In comparison with the Vocabulary Test, which correlated only .23 with the same criterion, Test B appears to possess considerable promise as a predictor of college scholarship. However, the authors of many interest and personality tests, who have used essentially similar validation techniques, have warned us to interpret high validity coefficients with caution when they are derived from the same data used in making the item analysis.

The correlation between Test B and the Vocabulary Test was .31, which is .08 higher than the correlation between the Vocabulary Test and the grade-point averages. On the other hand, the reliability of Test B, by the Kuder-Richardson Formula 20, was −.06. Hence it would appear that the accepted principles previously mentioned are called in question rather severely by the findings of this study. The difficulty may be explained, however, by a consideration of the structure of the B – Projective Psychokinesis Test.

The items of Test B consisted of 85 metal-rimmed labelling tags. Each tag bore an item number, from 1 to 85, on one side only. To derive a score for any given student, I first put the 85 tags in a cocktail shaker and shook them up thoroughly. Then I looked at the student's grade-point average. If it was B or above, I projected into the cocktail shaker a wish that the student should receive a high "plus" reaction score. If his grade-point average was below B, I projected a wish that he should receive a low score. Then I threw the tags on the table. To obtain the student's score, I counted as "plus" reactions all the tags which lit with the numbered side up. The derivation of the term "B – Projective Psychokinesis Test" should now be obvious.

The moral of this story, I think, is clear. When a validity coefficient is computed from the same data used in making an item analysis, this coefficient cannot be interpreted uncritically. And, contrary to many statements in the literature, it cannot be interpreted "with caution" either. There is one clear interpretation for all such validity coefficients. This interpretation is—

"Baloney!"

27. Convergent and Discriminant Validation by the Multitrait-Multimethod Matrix[1]

DONALD T. CAMPBELL
DONALD W. FISKE

A hypothetical human trait can seldom, if ever, be measured directly. Instead, one must infer how the hypothesized trait might make a person behave, look for instances in which he does or does not behave that way,

Campbell, D. T., and Fiske, D. W. Convergent and discriminant validation by the multitrait-multimethod matrix. *Psychological Bulletin,* 1959, *56,* 81–105. Reprinted with the permission of the publisher and authors.

[1] The new data analyses reported in this paper were supported by funds from the Graduate School of Northwestern University and by the Department of Psychology of the University of Chicago. We are also indebted to numerous colleagues for their thoughtful criticisms and encouragement of an earlier draft of this paper, especially Benjamin S. Bloom, R. Darrell Bock, Desmond S. Cartwright, Loren J. Chapman, Lee J. Cronbach, Carl P. Duncan, Lyle V. Jones, Joe Kamiya, Wilbur L. Layton, Jane Loevinger, Paul E. Meehl, Marshall H. Segall, Thornton B. Roby, Robert C. Tryon, Michael Wertheimer, and Robert F. Winch.

and from the nature of his behavior estimate the strength or weakness of the trait that contributed to it.

Now, if only one kind of behavior is observed—that is, if only one method of measurement is used—as a basis for estimating trait strength, there is no check on the validity of the original inference relating trait to behavior. But if more than one method of measurement is used, and if the estimates of trait strength from these different methods are consistent, confidence in the trait concept and in the methods for measuring it increases. The various methods of measurement *converge* on a single trait.

But methods of measurement must also *discriminate* among different traits. If the same kinds of behavior observations are used as bases for estimating the strength of different traits, different measurements should result. If not, there is reason to suspect that it was the method, not the trait, that primarily determined the measures obtained.

These insights and this approach to the measurement of hypothetical traits are developed in the present article by Campbell and Fiske. The article raises, and provides answers to, some fundamental questions of the validity of trait measures.

In the cumulative experience with measures of individual differences over the past 50 years, tests have been accepted as valid or discarded as invalid by research experiences of many sorts. The criteria suggested in this paper are all to be found in such cumulative evaluations, as well as in the recent discussions of validity. These criteria are clarified and implemented when considered jointly in the context of a multitrait-multimethod matrix. Aspects of the validational process receiving particular emphasis are these:

1. Validation is typically *convergent,* a confirmation by independent measurement procedures. Independence of methods is a common denominator among the major types of validity (excepting content validity) insofar as they are to be distinguished from reliability.

2. For the justification of novel trait measures, for the validation of test interpretation, or for the establishment of construct validity, *discriminant* validation as well as convergent validation is required. Tests can be invalidated by too high correlations with other tests from which they were intended to differ.

3. Each test or task employed for measurement purposes is a *trait-method unit,* a union of a particular trait content with measurement procedures not specific to that content. The systematic variance among test scores can be due to responses to the measurement features as well as responses to the trait content.

4. In order to examine discriminant validity, and in order to estimate the relative contributions of trait and method variance, *more than one trait* as well as *more than one method* must be employed in the validation process. In many instances it will be convenient to achieve this through a multitrait-multimethod matrix. Such a matrix presents all of

the intercorrelations resulting when each of several traits is measured by each of several methods.

To illustrate the suggested validational process, a synthetic example is presented in Table 1. This illustration involves three different traits, each measured by three methods, generating nine separate variables. It will be convenient to have labels for various regions of the matrix, and such have been provided in Table 1. The reliabilities will be spoken of in terms of three *reliability diagonals,* one for each method. The reliabilities could also be designated as the monotrait-monomethod values. Adjacent to each reliability diagonal is the *heterotrait-monomethod* triangle. The reliability diagonal and the adjacent heterotrait-monomethod triangle make up a *monomethod block*. A *heteromethod block* is made up of a *validity* diagonal (which could also be designated as monotrait-heteromethod values) and the two *heterotrait-heteromethod* triangles lying on each side of it. Note that these two heterotrait-heteromethod triangles are not identical.

In terms of this diagram, four aspects bear upon the question of validity. In the first place, the entries in the validity diagonal should be significantly different from zero and sufficiently large to encourage further examination of validity. This requirement is evidence of con-

TABLE 1. A Synthetic Multitrait-Multimethod Matrix

		Method 1			Method 2			Method 3		
	Traits	A_1	B_1	C_1	A_2	B_2	C_2	A_3	B_3	C_3
Method 1	A_1	(.89)								
	B_1	.51	(.89)							
	C_1	.38	.37	(.76)						
Method 2	A_2	*.57*	.22	.09	(.93)					
	B_2	.22	*.57*	.10	.68	(.94)				
	C_2	.11	.11	*.46*	.59	.58	(.84)			
Method 3	A_3	*.56*	.22	.11	*.67*	.42	.33	(.94)		
	B_3	.23	*.58*	.12	.43	*.66*	.34	.67	(.92)	
	C_3	.11	.11	*.45*	.34	.32	*.58*	.58	.60	(.85)

Note:—The validity diagonals are the three sets of italicized values. The reliability diagonals are the three sets of values in parentheses. Each heterotrait-monomethod triangle is enclosed by a solid line. Each heterotrait-heteromethod triangle is enclosed by a broken line.

vergent validity. Second, a validity diagonal value should be higher than the values lying in its column and row in the heterotrait-heteromethod triangles. That is, a validity value for a variable should be higher than the correlations obtained between that variable and any other variable having neither trait nor method in common. This requirement may seem so minimal and so obvious as to not need stating, yet an inspection of the literature shows that it is frequently not met, and may not be met even when the validity coefficients are of substantial size. In Table 1, all of the validity values meet this requirement. A third common-sense desideratum is that a variable correlate higher with an independent effort to measure the same trait than with measures designed to get at different traits which happen to employ the same method. For a given variable, this involves comparing its values in the validity diagonals with its values in the heterotrait-monomethod triangles. For variables A_1, B_1, and C_1, this requirement is met to some degree. For the other variables, A_2, A_3 etc., it is not met and this is probably typical of the usual case in individual differences research, as will be discussed in what follows. A fourth desideratum is that the same pattern of trait interrelationship be shown in all of the heterotrait triangles of both the monomethod and heteromethod blocks. The hypothetical data in Table 1 meet this requirement to a very marked degree, in spite of the different general levels of correlation involved in the several heterotrait triangles. The last three criteria provide evidence for discriminant validity.

Before examining the multitrait-multimethod matrices available in the literature, some explication and justification of this complex of requirements seems in order.

Convergence of independent methods: the distinction between reliability and validity. Both reliability and validity concepts require that agreement between measures be demonstrated. A common denominator which most validity concepts share in contradistinction to reliability is that this agreement represent the convergence of independent approaches. The concept of independence is indicated by such phrases as "external variable," "criterion performance," "behavioral criterion" (American Psychological Association, 1954, pp. 13–15) used in connection with concurrent and predictive validity. For construct validity it has been stated thus: "Numerous successful predictions dealing with phenotypically diverse 'criteria' give greater weight to the claim of construct validity than do . . . predictions involving very similar behavior" (Cronbach & Meehl, 1955, p. 295). The importance of independence recurs in most discussions of proof. For example, Ayer, discussing a historian's belief about a past event, says "if these sources are numerous and independent, and if they agree with one another, he will be reasonably confident that their account of the matter is correct" (Ayer, 1954, p. 39). In discussing the manner in which abstract scientific concepts are tied to operations, Feigl speaks of their being "fixed" by "triangulation in logical space" (Feigl, 1958, p. 401).

Independence is, of course, a matter of degree, and in this sense, reliability and validity can be seen as regions on a continuum. (Cf. Thurstone, 1937, pp. 102–103.) Reliability is the agreement between two efforts to measure the same trait through maximally similar methods. Validity is represented in the agreement between two attempts to measure the same trait through maximally different methods. A split-half reliability is a little more like a validity coefficient than is an immediate test-retest reliability, for the items are not quite identical. A correlation between dissimilar subtests is probably a reliability measure, but is still closer to the region called validity.

Some evaluation of validity can take place even if the two methods are not entirely independent. In Table 1, for example, it is possible that Methods 1 and 2 are not entirely independent. If underlying Traits A and B are entirely independent, then the .10 minimum correlation in the heterotrait-heteromethod triangles may reflect method covariance. What if the overlap of method variance were higher? All correlations in the heteromethod block would then be elevated, including the validity diagonal. The heteromethod block involving Methods 2 and 3 in Table 1 illustrates this. The degree of elevation of the validity diagonal above the heterotrait-heteromethod triangles remains comparable and relative validity can still be evaluated. The interpretation of the validity diagonal in an absolute fashion requires the fortunate coincidence of both an independence of traits and an independence of methods, represented by zero values in the heterotrait-heteromethod triangles. But zero values could also occur through a combination of negative correlation between traits and positive correlation between methods, or the reverse. In practice, perhaps all that can be hoped for is evidence for relative validity, that is, for common variance specific to a trait, above and beyond shared method variance.

Discriminant validation. While the usual reason for the judgment of invalidity is low correlations in the validity diagonal (e.g., the Downey Will-Temperament Test [Symonds, 1931, p. 337ff]) tests have also been invalidated because of too high correlations with other tests purporting to measure different things. The classic case of the social intelligence tests is a case in point. (See below and also [Strang, 1930; R. Thorndike, 1936].) Such invalidation occurs when values in the heterotrait-heteromethod triangles are as high as those in the validity diagonal, or even where within a monomethod block, the heterotrait values are as high as the reliabilities. Loevinger, Gleser, and DuBois (1953) have emphasized this requirement in the development of maximally discriminating subtests.

When a dimension of personality is hypothesized, when a construct is proposed, the proponent invariably has in mind distinctions between the new dimension and other constructs already in use. One cannot define without implying distinctions, and the verification of these distinctions is an important part of the validational process. In discussions of construct validity, it has been expressed in such terms as "from this point of view, a low correlation with athletic ability may be just as important and encouraging as a high correlation with reading comprehension" (APA, 1954, p. 17).

The test as a trait-method unit. In any given psychological measuring device, there are certain features or stimuli introduced specifically to represent the trait that it is intended to measure. There are other features which are characteristic of the method being employed, features which could also be present in efforts to measure other quite different traits. The test, or rating scale, or other device, almost inevitably elicits systematic variance in response due to both groups of features. To the extent that irrelevant method variance contributes to the scores obtained, these scores are invalid.

This source of invalidity was first noted in the "halo effects" found in ratings (Thorndike, 1920). Studies of individual differences among laboratory animals resulted in the recognition of "apparatus factors," usually more dominant than psychological process factors (Tryon, 1942). For paper-and-pencil tests, methods variance has been noted under such terms as "test-form factors" (Vernon: 1957, 1958) and "response sets" (Cronbach: 1946, 1950; Lorge, 1937). Cronbach has stated the point particularly clearly: "The assumption is generally made . . . that what the test measures is determined by the content of the items. Yet the final score . . . is a composite of effects resulting from the content of the item and effects resulting from the form of the item used" (Cronbach, 1946, p. 475). "Response sets always lower the logical validity of a test. . . . Response sets interfere with inferences from test data" (p. 484).

While E. L. Thorndike (1920) was willing to allege the presence of halo effects by comparing the high obtained correlations with common sense notions of what they ought to be (e.g., it was unreasonable that a teacher's intelligence and voice quality should correlate .63) and while much of the evidence of response set variance is of the same order, the clear-cut demonstration of the presence of method variance requires both several traits and several methods. Otherwise, high correlations between tests might be explained as due either to basic trait similarity or to shared method variance. In the multitrait-multimethod matrix, the presence of method variance is indicated by the difference in level of correlation between the parallel values of the monomethod block and the heteromethod blocks, assuming comparable reliabilities among all tests. Thus the contribution of method variance in Test A_1 of

Table 1 is indicated by the elevation of $r_{A_1B_1}$ above $r_{A_1B_2}$, i.e., the difference between .51 and .22, etc.

The distinction between trait and method is of course relative to the test constructor's intent. What is an unwanted response set for one tester may be a trait for another who wishes to measure acquiescence, willingness to take an extreme stand, or tendency to attribute socially desirable attributes to oneself (Cronbach: 1946, 1950; Edwards, 1957; Lorge, 1937).

MULTITRAIT-MULTIMETHOD MATRICES IN THE LITERATURE

Multitrait-multimethod matrices are rare in the test and measurement literature. Most frequent are two types of fragment: two methods and one trait (single isolated values from the validity diagonal, perhaps accompanied by a reliability or two), and heterotrait-monomethod triangles. Either type of fragment is apt to disguise the inadequacy of our present measurement efforts, particularly in failing to call attention to the preponderant strength of methods variance. The evidence of test validity to be presented here is probably poorer than most psychologists would have expected.

One of the earliest matrices of this kind was provided by Kelley and Krey in 1934. Peer judgments by students provided one method, scores on a word-association test the other. Table 2 presents the data for the four most valid traits of the eight he employed. The picture is one of strong method factors, particularly among the peer ratings, and almost total invalidity. For only one of the eight measures, School Drive, is

TABLE 2. Personality Traits of School Children from Kelley's Study ($N = 311$)

		Peer Ratings				*Association Test*			
		A_1	B_1	C_1	D_1	A_2	B_2	C_2	D_2
Peer Ratings									
Courtesy	A_1	(.82)							
Honesty	B_1	.74	(.80)						
Poise	C_1	.63	.65	(.74)					
School Drive	D_1	.76	.78	.65	(.89)				
Association Test									
Courtesy	A_2	*.13*	.14	.10	.14	(.28)			
Honesty	B_2	.06	*.12*	.16	.08	.27	(.38)		
Poise	C_2	.01	.08	*.10*	.02	.19	.37	(.42)	
School Drive	D_2	.12	.15	.14	*.16*	.27	.32	.18	(.36)

the value in the validity diagonal (.16!) higher than all of the heterotrait-heteromethod values. The absence of discriminant validity is further indicated by the tendency of the values in the monomethod triangles to approximate the reliabilities.

An early illustration from the animal literature comes from Anderson's (1937) study of drives. Table 3 presents a sample of his data. Once again, the highest correlations are found among different constructs from the same method, showing the dominance of apparatus or method factors so typical of the whole field of individual differences. The validity diagonal for hunger is higher than the heteroconstruct-heteromethod values. The diagonal value for sex has not been *italicized* as a validity coefficient since the obstruction box measure was pre-sex-

TABLE 3. Measures of Drives from Anderson's Data
($N = 50$)

		Obstruction Box			Activity Wheel		
		A_1	B_1	C_1	A_2	B_2	C_2
Obstruction Box							
Hunger	A_1	(.58)					
Thirst	B_1	.54	( )				
Sex	C_1	.46	.70	( )			
Activity Wheel							
Hunger	A_2	*.48*	.31	.37	(.83)		
Thirst	B_2	.35	*.33*	.43	.87	(.92)	
Post Sex	C_2	.31	.37	.44	.69	.78	( )

Note.—Empty parentheses appear in this and subsequent tables where no appropriate reliability estimates are reported in the original paper.

opportunity, the activity wheel post-opportunity. Note that the high general level of heterotrait-heteromethod values could be due either to correlation of methods variance between the two methods, or to correlated trait variance. On a priori grounds, however, the methods would seem about as independent as one would be likely to achieve. The predominance of an apparatus factor for the activity wheel is evident from the fact that the correlation between hunger and thirst (.87) is of the same magnitude as their test-retest reliabilities (.83 and .92 respectively).

R. L. Thorndike's study (1936) of the validity of the George Washington Social Intelligence Test is the classic instance of invalidation by high correlation between traits. It involved computing all of the intercorrelations among five subscales of the Social Intelligence Test and five subscales of the George Washington Mental Alertness Test. The model of the present paper would demand that each of the traits, social intelligence and mental alertness, be measured by at least two methods. While this full symmetry was not intended in the study, it can be so interpreted without too much distortion. For both traits, there were subtests employing acquisition of knowledge during the testing period (i.e., learning or memory), tests involving comprehension of prose passages, and tests that involved a definitional activity. Table 4 shows six of Thorndike's 10 variables arranged as a multitrait-multimethod matrix. If the three subtests of the Social Intelligence Test are viewed as three methods of measuring social intelligence, then their intercorrelations (.30, .23, and .31) represent validities that are not only lower than their corresponding monomethod values, but also lower than the heterotrait-heteromethod correlations, providing a picture which totally fails to establish social intelligence as a separate dimension. The Mental Alertness validity diagonals (.38, .58, and .48) equal or exceed the monomethod values in two out of three cases, and exceed all heterotrait-heteromethod control values. These results illustrate the general conclusions reached by Thorndike in his factor analysis of the whole 10×10 matrix.

The data of Table 4 could be used to validate specific forms of cognitive functioning, as measured by the different "methods" represented by usual intelligence test content on the one hand and social content

TABLE 4. Social Intelligence and Mental Alertness Subtest Intercorrelations from Thorndike's Data

($N = 750$)

		Memory		Comprehension		Vocabulary	
		A_1	B_1	A_2	B_2	A_3	B_3
Memory							
Social Intelligence (Memory for Names & Faces)	A_1	( )					
Mental Alertness (Learning Ability)	B_1	.31	( )				
Comprehension							
Social Intelligence (Sense of Humor)	A_2	*.30*	.31	( )			
Mental Alertness (Comprehension)	B_2	*.29*	*.38*	.48	( )		
Vocabulary							
Social Intelligence (Recog. of Mental State)	A_3	*.23*	.35	*.31*	.35	( )	
Mental Alertness (Vocabulary)	B_3	.30	*.58*	.40	*.48*	.47	( )

on the other. Table 5 rearranges the 15 values for this purpose. The monomethod values and the validity diagonals exchange places, while the heterotrait-heteromethod control coefficients are the same in both tables. As judged against these latter values, comprehension (.48) and vocabulary (.47), but not memory (.31), show some specific validity. This transmutability of the validation matrix argues for the comparisons within the heteromethod block as the most generally relevant validation data, and illustrates the potential interchangeability of trait and method components.

Some of the correlations in Chi's (1937) prodigious study of halo effect in ratings are appropriate to a multitrait-multimethod matrix in which each rater might be regarded as representing a different method. While the published report does not make these available in detail be-

TABLE 5. Memory, Comprehension, and Vocabulary Measured with Social and Abstract Content

		Social Content			Abstract Content		
		A_1	B_1	C_1	A_2	B_2	C_2
Social Content							
Memory (Memory for Names and Faces)	A_1	( )					
Comprehension (Sense of Humor)	B_1	.30	( )				
Vocabulary (Recognition of Mental State)	C_1	.23	.31	( )			
Abstract Content							
Memory (Learning Ability)	A_2	*.31*	.31	.35	( )		
Comprehension	B_2	.29	*.48*	.35	.38	( )	
Vocabulary	C_2	.30	.40	*.47*	.58	.48	( )

cause it employs averaged values, it is apparent from a comparison of his Tables IV and VIII that the ratings generally failed to meet the requirement that ratings of the same trait by different raters should correlate higher than ratings of different traits by the same rater. Validity is shown to the extent that of the correlations in the heteromethod block, those in the validity diagonal are higher than the average heteromethod-heterotrait values.

A conspicuously unsuccessful multitrait-multimethod matrix is provided by Campbell (1953, 1956) for rating of the leadership behavior of officers by themselves and by their subordinates. Only one of 11 variables (Recognition Behavior) met the requirement of providing a validity diagonal value higher than any of the heterotrait-heteromethod values, that validity being .29. For none of the variables were the validities higher than heterotrait-monomethod values.

A study of attitudes toward authority and nonauthority figures by Burwen and Campbell (1957) contains a complex multitrait-multimethod matrix, one symmetrical excerpt from which is shown in Table 6. Method variance was strong for most of the procedures in this study. Where validity was found, it was primarily at the level of validity diagonal values higher than heterotrait-heteromethod values. As illustrated in Table 6, attitude toward father showed this kind of validity, as did attitude toward peers to a lesser degree. Attitude toward boss showed no validity. There was no evidence of a generalized attitude toward authority which would include father and boss, although such values as the .64 correlation between father and boss as measured by interview

TABLE 6. Attitudes toward Father, Boss, and Peer, as Measured by Interview and Check-List of Descriptive Traits

		Interview			Trait Check-List		
		A_1	B_1	C_1	A_2	B	C_2
Interview ($N = 57$)							
Father	A_1	( )					
Boss	B_1	.64	( )				
Peer	C_1	.65	.76	( )			
Trait Check-List ($N = 155$)							
Father	A_2	*.40*	.08	.09	(.24)		
Boss	B_2	.19	*−.10*	−.03	.23	(.34)	
Peer	C_2	.27	.11	*.23*	.21	.45	(.55)

might have seemed to confirm the hypothesis had they been encountered in isolation.

Borgatta (1954) has provided a complex multimethod study from which can be extracted Table 7, illustrating the assessment of two traits by four different methods. For all measures but one, the highest correlation is the apparatus one, i.e., with the other trait measured by the same method rather than with the same trait measured by a different method. Neither of the traits finds any consistent validation by the requirement that the validity diagonals exceed the heterotrait-heteromethod control values. As a most minimal requirement, it might be asked if the sum of the two values in the validity diagonal exceeds the sum of the two control values, providing a comparison in which differences in reliability or communality are roughly partialled out. This condition is achieved at the purely chance level of three times in the six tetrads. This matrix

TABLE 7. Multiple Measurement of Two Sociometric Traits
($N = 125$)

		Sociometric				Observation			
		by Others		by Self		Group Interaction		Role Playing	
		A_1	B_1	A_2	B_2	A_3	B_3	A_4	B_4
Sociometric by Others									
Popularity	A_1	( )							
Expansiveness	B_1	.47	( )						
Sociometric by Self									
Popularity	A_2	*.19*	.18	( )					
Expansiveness	B_2	.07	*.08*	.32	( )				
Observation of Group Interaction									
Popularity	A_3	*.25*	.18	*.26*	.11	( )			
Expansiveness	B_3	.21	*.12*	.28	*.15*	.84	( )		
Observation of Role Playing									
Popularity	A_4	*.24*	.14	*.18*	.01	*.66*	.58	( )	
Expansiveness	B_4	.25	*.12*	.26	*.05*	.66	*.76*	.73	( )

provides an interesting range of methodological independence. The two "Sociometric by Others" measures, while representing the judgments of the same set of fellow participants, come from distinct tasks: Popularity is based upon each participant's expression of his own friendship preferences, while Expansiveness is based upon each participant's guesses as to the other participant's choices, from which has been computed each participant's reputation for liking lots of other persons, i.e., being "expansive." In line with this considerable independence, the evidence for a method factor is relatively low in comparison with the observational procedures. Similarly, the two "Sociometric by Self" measures represent quite separate tasks, Popularity coming from his estimates of the choices he will receive from others, Expansiveness from the number of expressions of attraction to others which he makes on the sociometric task. In contrast, the measures of Popularity and Expansiveness from the observations of group interaction and the role playing not only involve the same specific observers, but in addition the observers rated the pair of variables as a part of the same rating task in each situation. The apparent degree of method variance within each of the two observational situations, and the apparent sharing of method variance between them, is correspondingly high.

In another paper by Borgatta (1955), 12 interaction process variables were measured by quantitative observation under two conditions, and by a projective test. In this test, the stimuli were pictures of groups, for which the *S* generated a series of verbal interchanges; these were then scored in Interaction Process Analysis categories. For illustrative purposes, Table 8 presents the five traits which had the highest mean communalities in the over-all factor analysis. Between the two highly similar observational methods, validation is excellent: trait variance runs higher than method variance; validity diagonals are in general higher than heterotrait values of both the heteromethod and monomethods blocks, most unexceptionably so for Gives Opinion and Gives Orientation. The pattern of correlation among the traits is also in general confirmed.

Of greater interest because of the greater independence of methods are the blocks involving the projective test. Here the validity picture is much poorer. Gives Orientation comes off best, its projective test validity values of .35 and .33 being bested by only three monomethod values and by no heterotrait-heteromethod values within the projective blocks. All of the other validities are exceeded by some heterotrait-heteromethod value.

The projective test specialist may object to the implicit expectations of a one-to-one correspondence between projected action and overt action. Such expectations should not be attributed to Borgatta, and are not necessary to the method here proposed. For the simple symmetrical model of this paper, it has been assumed that the measures are labeled in correspondence with the correlations expected, i.e., in correspondence with the traits that the tests are alleged to diagnose. Note that in Table 8, Gives Opinion is the best projective test predictor of both free behavior and role playing Shows Disagreement. Were a proper theoretical rationale available, these values might be regarded as validities.

Mayo (1956) has made an analysis of test scores and ratings of effort and intelligence, to estimate the contribution of halo (a kind of methods variance) to ratings. As Table 9 shows, the validity picture is ambiguous. The method factor or halo effect for ratings is considerable although the correlation between the two ratings (.66) is well below their reliabilities (.84 and .85). The objective measures share no appreciable apparatus overlap because they were independent operations. In spite of Mayo's argument that the ratings have some valid trait variance, the .46 heterotrait-heteromethod value seriously depreciates the otherwise impressive .46 and .40 validity values.

TABLE 8. Interaction Process Variables in Observed Free Behavior, Observed Role Playing and a Projective Test
($N = 125$)

		Free Behavior					Role Playing					Projective Test				
		A_1	B_1	C_1	D_1	E_1	A_2	B_2	C_2	D_2	E_2	A_3	B_3	C_3	D_3	E_3
Free Behavior																
Shows solidarity	A_1	( )														
Gives suggestion	B_1	.25	( )													
Gives opinion	C_1	.13	.24	( )												
Gives orientation	D_1	—.14	.26	.52	( )											
Shows disagreement	E_1	.34	.41	.27	.02	( )										
Role Playing																
Shows solidarity	A_2	*.43*	.43	.08	.10	.29	( )									
Gives suggestion	B_2	.16	*.32*	.00	.24	.07	.37	( )								
Gives opinion	C_2	.15	.27	*.60*	.38	.12	.01	.10	( )							
Gives orientation	D_2	—.12	.24	.44	*.74*	.08	.04	.18	.40	( )						
Shows disagreement	E_2	.51	.36	.14	—.12	*.50*	.39	.27	.23	—.11	( )					
Projective Test																
Shows solidarity	A_3	*.20*	.17	.16	.12	.08	*.17*	.12	.30	.17	.22	( )				
Gives suggestion	B_3	.05	*.21*	.05	.08	.13	.10	*.19*	—.02	.06	.30	.32	( )			
Gives opinion	C_3	.31	.30	*.13*	—.02	.26	.25	.19	*.15*	—.04	.53	.31	.63	( )		
Gives orientation	D_3	—.01	.09	.30	*.35*	—.05	.03	.00	.19	*.33*	.00	.37	.29	.32	( )	
Shows disagreement	E_3	.13	.18	.10	.14	*.19*	.22	.28	.02	.04	*.23*	.27	.51	.47	.30	( )

TABLE 9. Mayo's Intercorrelations between Objective and Rating Measures of Intelligence and Effort
($N = 166$)

		Peer Ratings		Objective	
		A_1	B_1	A_2	B_2
Peer Rating					
Intelligence	A_1	(.85)			
Effort	B_1	.66	(.84)		
Objective Measures					
Intelligence	A_2	*.46*	.29	( )	
Effort	B_2	.46	*.40*	.10	( )

Cronbach (1949, p. 277) and Vernon (1957, 1958) have both discussed the multitrait-multimethod matrix shown in Table 10, based upon data originally presented by H. S. Conrad. Using an approximative technique, Vernon estimates that 61% of the systematic variance is due to a general factor, that 21½% is due to the test-form factors specific to verbal or to pictorial forms of items, and that but 11½% is due to the content factors specific to electrical or to mechanical contents. Note that for the purposes of estimating validity, the interpretation of the general factor, which he estimates from the .49 and .45 heterotrait-heteromethod values, is equivocal. It could represent desired competence variance, representing components common to both electrical and mechanical skills—perhaps resulting from general industrial shop experience, common ability components, overlapping learning situations, and the like. On the other hand, this general factor could represent overlapping method factors, and be due to the presence in both tests of multiple choice item format, IBM answer sheets, or the heterogeneity of the *S*s in conscientiousness, test-taking motivation, and test-taking

TABLE 10. Mechanical and Electrical Facts Measured by Verbal and Pictorial Items

		Verbal Items		Pictorial Items	
		A_1	B_1	A_2	B_2
Verbal Items					
Mechanical Facts	A_1	(.89)			
Electrical Facts	B_1	.63	(.71)		
Pictorial Items					
Mechanical Facts	A_2	*.61*	.45	(.82)	
Electrical Facts	B_2	.49	*.51*	.64	(.67)

sophistication. Until methods that are still more different and traits that are still more independent are introduced into the validation matrix, this general factor remains uninterpretable. From this standpoint it can be seen that 21½% is a very minimal estimate of the total test-form variance in the tests, as it represents only test-form components specific to the verbal or the pictorial items, i.e., test-form components which the two forms do *not* share. Similarly, and more hopefully, the 11½% content variance is a very minimal estimate of the total true trait variance of the tests, representing only the true trait variance which electrical and mechanical knowledge do *not* share.

Carroll (1952) has provided data on the Guilford-Martin Inventory of Factors STDCR and related ratings which can be rearranged into the matrix of Table 11. (Variable R has been inverted to reduce the number of negative correlations.) Two of the methods, Self Ratings and Inventory scores, can be seen as sharing method variance, and thus as having an inflated validity diagonal. The more independent heteromethod blocks involving Peer Ratings show some evidence of discriminant and convergent validity, with validity diagonals averaging .33 (Inventory×Peer Ratings) and .39 (Self Ratings×Peer Ratings) against heterotrait-heteromethod control values averaging .14 and .16. While not intrinsically impressive, this picture is nonetheless better than most of the validity matrices here assembled. Note that the Self Ratings show slightly higher validity diagonal elevations than do the Inventory scores, in spite of the much greater length and undoubtedly higher reliability of the latter. In addition, a method factor seems almost totally lacking for the Self Ratings, while strongly present for the Inventory, so that the Self Ratings come off much the best if true trait variance is expressed as a proportion of total reliable variance (as Vernon [1958] suggests). The method factor in the STDCR Inventory is undoubtedly enhanced by scoring the same item in several scales, thus contributing correlated error variance, which could be reduced without loss of reliability by the simple expedient of adding more equivalent items and scoring each item in only one scale. It should be noted that Carroll makes explicit use of the comparison of the validity diagonal with the heterotrait-heteromethod values as a validity indicator.

RATINGS IN THE ASSESSMENT STUDY OF CLINICAL PSYCHOLOGISTS

The illustrations of multitrait-multimethod matrices presented so far give a rather sorry picture of the validity of the measures of individual differences involved. The typical case shows an excessive amount of method variance, which usually exceeds the amount of trait variance. This picture is certainly not as a result of a deliberate effort to select

TABLE 11. Guilford-Martin Factors STDCR and Related Ratings
($N = 110$)

	Inventory					Self Ratings					Peer Ratings				
	S	T	D	C	-R	S	T	D	C	-R	S	T	D	C	-R
Inventory															
S	(.92)														
T	.27	(.89)													
D	.62	.57	(.91)												
C	.36	.47	.90	(.91)											
-R	.69	.32	.28	—.06	(.89)										
Self Ratings															
S	*.57*	.11	.19	—.01	.53	( )									
T	.28	*.65*	.42	.26	.37	.26	( )								
D	.44	.25	*.53*	.45	.29	.31	.32	( )							
C	.31	.20	.54	*.52*	.13	.11	.21	.47	( )						
-R	.15	.30	.12	.04	*.34*	.10	.12	.04	.06	( )					
Peer Ratings															
S	*.37*	.08	.10	—.01	.38	*.42*	.02	.08	.08	.31	(.81)				
T	.23	*.32*	.15	.04	.40	.20	*.39*	.40	.21	.31	.37	(.66)			
D	.31	.11	*.27*	.24	.25	.17	.09	*.29*	.27	.30	.49	.38	(.73)		
C	.08	.15	.20	*.26*	—.05	.01	.06	.14	*.30*	.07	.19	.16	.40	(.75)	
-R	.21	.20	—.03	—.16	*.45*	.28	.17	.08	.01	*.56*	.55	.56	.34	—.07	(.76)

shockingly bad examples: these are ones we have encountered without attempting an exhaustive coverage of the literature. The several unpublished studies of which we are aware show the same picture. If they seem more disappointing than the general run of validity data reported in the journals, this impression may very well be because the portrait of validity provided by isolated values plucked from the validity diagonal is deceptive, and uninterpretable in isolation from the total matrix. Yet it is clear that few of the classic examples of successful measurement of individual differences are involved, and that in many of the instances, the quality of the data might have been such as to magnify apparatus factors, etc. A more nearly ideal set of personality data upon which to illustrate the method was therefore sought in the multiple application of a set of rating scales in the assessment study of clinical psychologists (Kelly & Fiske, 1951).

In that study, "Rating Scale A" contained 22 traits referring to "behavior which can be directly observed on the surface." In using this scale the raters were instructed to "disregard any inferences about underlying dynamics or causes" (p. 207). The *S*s, first-year clinical psychology students, rated themselves and also their three teammates with whom they had participated in the various assessment procedures and with whom they had lived for six days. The median of the three teammates' ratings was used for the Teammate score. The *S*s were also rated on these 22 traits by the assessment staff. Our analysis uses the Final Pooled ratings, which were agreed upon by three staff members after discussion and review of the enormous amount of data and the many other ratings on each *S*. Unfortunately for our purposes, the staff members saw the ratings by Self and Teammates before making theirs, although presumably they were little influenced by these data because they had so much other evidence available to them. (See Kelly & Fiske, 1951, especially p. 64.) The Self and Teammate ratings represent entirely separate "methods" and can be given the major emphasis in evaluating the data to be presented.

In a previous analysis of these data (Fiske, 1949), each of the three heterotrait-monomethod triangles was computed and factored. To provide a multitrait-multimethod matrix, the 1452 heteromethod correlations have been computed especially for this report.[2] The full 66×66 matrix with its 2145 coefficients is obviously too large for presentation here, but will be used in analyses that follow. To provide an illustrative sample, Table 12 presents the interrelationships among five variables,

[2] We are indebted to E. Lowell Kelly for furnishing the V.A. assessment date to us, and to Hugh Lane for producing the matrix of intercorrelations.

In the original report the correlations were based upon 128 men. The present analyses were based on only 124 of these cases because of clerical errors. This reduction in *N* leads to some very minor discrepancies between these values and those previously reported.

TABLE 12. Ratings from Assessment Study of Clinical Psychologists

($N = 124$)

		Staff Ratings					Teammate Ratings					Self Ratings				
		A_1	B_1	C_1	D_1	E_1	A_2	B_2	C_2	D_2	E_2	A_3	B_3	C_3	D_3	E_3
Staff Ratings																
Assertive	A_1	(.89)														
Cheerful	B_1	.37	(.85)													
Serious	C_1	—.24	—.14	(.81)												
Unshakable Poise	D_1	.25	.46	.08	(.84)											
Broad Interests	E_1	.35	.19	.09	.31	(.92)										
Teammate Ratings																
Assertive	A_2	*.71*	.35	—.18	.26	.41	(.82)									
Cheerful	B_2	.39	*.53*	—.15	.38	.29	.37	(.76)								
Serious	C_2	—.27	—.31	*.43*	—.06	.03	—.15	—.19	(.70)							
Unshakable Poise	D_2	.03	—.05	.03	*.20*	.07	.11	.23	.19	(.74)						
Broad Interests	E_2	.19	.05	.04	.29	*.47*	.33	.22	.19	.29	(.76)					
Self Ratings																
Assertive	A_3	*.48*	.31	—.22	.19	.12	*.46*	.36	—.15	.12	.23	( )				
Cheerful	B_3	.17	*.42*	—.10	.10	—.03	.09	.24	—.25	—.11	—.03	.23	( )			
Serious	C_3	—.04	—.13	*.22*	—.13	—.05	—.04	—.11	*.31*	.06	.06	—.05	—.12	( )		
Unshakable Poise	D_3	.13	.27	—.03	*.22*	—.04	.10	.15	.00	*.14*	—.03	.16	.26	.11	( )	
Broad Interests	E_3	.37	.15	—.22	.09	*.26*	.27	.12	—.07	.05	*.35*	.21	.15	.17	.31	( )

selecting the one best representing each of the five recurrent factors discovered in Fiske's (1949) previous analysis of the monomethod matrices. (These were chosen without regard to their validity as indicated in the heteromethod blocks. Assertive—No. 3 reflected—was selected to represent Recurrent Factor 5 because Talkative had also a high loading on the first recurrent factor.)

The picture presented in Table 12 is, we believe, typical of the best validity in personality trait ratings that psychology has to offer at the present time. It is comforting to note that the picture is better than most of those previously examined. Note that the validities for Assertive exceed heterotrait values of both the monomethod and heteromethod triangles. Cheerful, Broad Interests, and Serious have validities exceeding the heterotrait-heteromethod values with two exceptions. Only for Unshakable Poise does the evidence of validity seem trivial. The elevation of the reliabilities above the heterotrait-monomethod triangles is further evidence for discriminant validity.

A comparison of Table 12 with the full matrix shows that the procedure of having but one variable to represent each factor has enhanced the appearance of validity, although not necessarily in a misleading fashion. Where several variables are all highly loaded on the same factor, their "true" level of intercorrelation is high. Under these conditions, sampling errors can depress validity diagonal values and enhance others to produce occasional exceptions to the validity picture, both in the heterotrait-monomethod matrix and in the heteromethod-heterotrait triangles. In this instance, with an *N* of 124, the sampling error is appreciable, and may thus be expected to exaggerate the degree of invalidity.

Within the monomethod sections, errors of measurement will be correlated, raising the general level of values found, while within the heteromethods block, measurement errors are independent, and tend to lower the values both along the validity diagonal and in the heterotrait triangles. These effects, which may also be stated in terms of method factors or shared confounded irrelevancies, operate strongly in these data, as probably in all data involving ratings. In such cases, where several variables represent each factor, none of the variables consistently meets the criterion that validity values exceed the corresponding values in the monomethod triangles, when the full matrix is examined.

To summarize the validation picture with respect to comparisons of validity values with other heteromethod values in each block, Table 13 has been prepared. For each trait and for each of the three heteromethod blocks, it presents the value of the validity diagonal, the highest heterotrait value involving that trait, and the number out of the 42 such heterotrait values which exceed the validity diagonal in magnitude. (The number 42 comes from the grouping of the 21 other column values

TABLE 13. Validities of Traits in the Assessment Study of Clinical Psychologists, as Judged by the Heteromethod Comparisons

	Staff-Teammate			*Staff-Self*			*Teammate-Self*		
	Val.	Highest Het.	No. Higher	Val.	Highest Het.	No. Higher	Val.	Highest Het.	No. Higher
1. Obstructiveness*	.30	.34	2	.16	.27	9	.19	.24	1
2. Unpredictable	.34	.26	0	.18	.24	3	.05	.19	29
3. Assertive*	.71	.65	0	.48	.45	0	.46	.48	1
4. Cheerful*	.53	.60	2	.42	.40	0	.24	.38	5
5. Serious*	.43	.35	0	.22	.27	2	.31	.24	0
6. Cool, Aloof	.49	.48	0	.20	.46	10	.02	.34	36
7. Unshakable Poise	.20	.40	16	.22	.27	4	.14	.19	10
8. Broad Interests*	.47	.46	0	.26	.37	6	.35	.32	0
9. Trustful	.26	.34	5	.08	.25	19	.11	.17	9
10. Self-centered	.30	.34	2	.17	.27	6	—.07	.19	36
11. Talkative*	.82	.65	0	.47	.45	0	.43	.48	1
12. Adventurous	.45	.60	6	.28	.30	2	.16	.36	14
13. Socially Awkward	.45	.37	0	.06	.21	28	.04	.16	30
14. Adaptable*	.44	.40	0	.18	.23	10	.17	.29	8
15. Self-sufficient*	.32	.33	1	.13	.18	5	.18	.15	0
16. Worrying, Anxious*	.41	.37	0	.23	.33	5	.15	.16	1
17. Conscientious	.26	.33	4	.11	.32	19	.21	.23	2
18. Imaginative*	.43	.46	1	.32	.31	0	.36	.32	0
19. Interest in Women*	.42	.43	2	.55	.38	0	.37	.40	1
20. Secretive, Reserved*	.40	.58	5	.38	.40	2	.32	.35	3
21. Independent Minded	.39	.42	2	.08	.25	19	.21	.30	3
22. Emotional Expression*	.62	.63	1	.31	.46	5	.19	.34	10

Note.—Val. = value in validity diagonal; Highest Het. = highest heterotrait value; No. Higher = number of heterotrait values exceeding the validity diagonal.

* Trait names which have validities in all three heteromethod blocks significantly greater than the heterotrait-heteromethod values at the .001 level.

and the 21 other row values for the column and row intersecting at the given diagonal value.)

On the requirement that the validity diagonal exceed all others in its heteromethod block, none of the traits has a completely perfect record, although some come close. Assertive has only one trivial exception in the Teammate-Self block. Talkative has almost as good a record, as does Imaginative. Serious has but two inconsequential exceptions and Interest in Women three. These traits stand out as highly valid in both self-description and reputation. Note that the actual validity coefficients of these four traits range from but .22 to .82, or, if we concentrate on the Teammate-Self block as most certainly representing independent methods, from but .31 to .46. While these are the best traits, it seems that most of the traits have far above chance validity. All those having 10 or fewer exceptions have a degree of validity significant at the .001 level as crudely estimated by a one-tailed sign test.[3] All but one of the variables meet this level for the Staff-Teammate block, all but four for the Staff-Self block, all but five for the most independent block, Teammate-Self. The exceptions to significant validity are not parallel from column to column, however, and only 13 of 22 variables have .001 significant validity in all three blocks. These are indicated by the asterisk in Table 13.

This highly significant general level of validity must not obscure the meaningful problem created by the occasional exceptions, even for the best variables. The excellent traits of Assertive and Talkative provide a case in point. In terms of Fiske's original analysis, both have high loadings on the recurrent factor "Confident self-expression" (represented by Assertive in Table 12). Talkative also had high loadings on the recurrent factor of Social Adaptability (represented by Cheerful in Table 12). We would expect, therefore, both high correlation between them and significant discrimination as well. And even at the common sense level, most psychologists would expect fellow psychologists to discriminate validly between assertiveness (nonsubmissiveness) and talkativeness. Yet in the Teammate-Self block, Assertive rated by self correlates .48 with Talkative by teammates, higher than either of their validities in this block, .43 and .46.

In terms of the average values of the validities and the frequency of exceptions, there is a distinct trend for the Staff-Teammate block to show the greatest agreement. This can be attributed to several factors. Both represent ratings from the external point of view. Both are averaged over three judges, minimizing individual biases and undoubtedly increasing reliabilities. Moreover, the Teammate ratings were available to the Staff in making their ratings. Another effect contributing to the less adequate convergence and discrimination of Self ratings was a response set toward the favorable pole which greatly reduced the range of these measures (Fiske, 1949, p. 342). Inspection of the details of the instances of invalidity summarized in Table 13 shows that in most instances the effect is attributable to the high specificity and low communality for the self-rating trait. In these instances, the column and

[3] If we take the validity value as fixed (ignoring its sampling fluctuations), then we can determine whether the number of values larger than it in its row and column is less than expected on the null hypothesis that half the values would be above it. This procedure requires the assumption that the position (above or below the validity value) of any one of these comparison values is independent of the position of each of the others, a dubious assumption when common methods and trait variance are present.

row intersecting at the low validity diagonal are asymmetrical as far as general level of correlation is concerned, a fact covered over by the condensation provided in Table 13.

The personality psychologist is initially predisposed to reinterpret self-ratings, to treat them as symptoms rather than to interpret them literally. Thus, we were alert to instances in which the self ratings were not literally interpretable, yet nonetheless had a diagnostic significance when properly "translated." By and large, the instances of invalidity of self-descriptions found in this assessment study are not of this type, but rather are to be explained in terms of an absence of communality for one of the variables involved. In general, where these self descriptions are interpretable at all, they are as literally interpretable as are teammate descriptions. Such a finding may, of course, reflect a substantial degree of insight on the part of these *S*s.

The general success in discriminant validation coupled with the parallel factor patterns found in Fiske's earlier analysis of the three intramethod matrices seemed to justify an inspection of the factor pattern validity in this instance. One possible procedure would be to do a single analysis of the whole 66×66 matrix. Other approaches focused upon separate factoring of heteromethods blocks, matrix by matrix, could also be suggested. Not only would such methods be extremely tedious, but in addition they would leave undetermined the precise comparison of factor-pattern similarity. Correlating factor loadings over the population of variables was employed for this purpose by Fiske (1949) but while this provided for the identification of recurrent factors, no single over-all index of factor pattern similarity was generated. Since our immediate interest was in confirming a pattern of interrelationships, rather than in describing it, an efficient short cut was available: namely to test the similarity of the sets of heterotrait values by correlation coefficients in which each entry represented the size values of the given heterotrait coefficients in two different matrices. For the full matrix, such correlations would be based upon the *N* of the 22×21/2 or 231 specific heterotrait combinations. Correlations were computed between the Teammate and Self monomethods matrices, selected as maximally independent. (The values to follow were computed from the original correlation matrix and are somewhat higher than that which would be obtained from a reflected matrix.) The similarity between the two monomethods matrices was .84, corroborating the factor-pattern similarity between these matrices described more fully by Fiske in his parallel factor analyses of them. To carry this mode of analysis into the heteromethod block, this block was treated as though divided into two by the validity diagonal, the above diagonal values and the below diagonal representing the maximally independent validation of the heterotrait correlation pattern. These two correlated .63, a value which, while lower, shows an impressive degree of confimation. There remains the question as to whether this pattern upon which the two heteromethod-heterotrait triangles agree is the same one found in common between the two monomethod triangles. The intra-Teammate matrix correlated with the two heteromethod triangles .71 and .71. The intra-Self matrix correlated with the two .57 and .63. In general, then, there is evidence for validity of the intertrait relationship pattern.

DISCUSSION

Relation to construct validity. While the validational criteria presented are explicit or implicit in the discussions of construct validity (Cronbach & Meehl, 1955; APA, 1954), this paper is primarily concerned with the adequacy of tests as measures of a construct rather than with the adequacy of a construct as determined by the confirmation of theoretically predicted associations with measures of other constructs. We believe that before one can test the relationships between a specific trait and other traits, one must have some confidence in one's measures of that trait. Such confidence can be supported by evidence of convergent and discriminant validation. Stated in different words, any conceptual formulation of trait will usually include implicitly the proposition that this trait is a response tendency which can be observed under more than one experimental condition and that this trait can be meaningfully differentiated from other traits. The testing of these two propositions must be prior to the testing of other propositions to prevent the acceptance of erroneous conclusions. For example, a conceptual framework might postulate a large correlation between Traits A and B and no correlation between Traits A and C. If the experimenter then measures A and B by one method (e.g., questionnaire) and C by another method (such as the measurement of overt behavior in a situation test), his findings may be consistent with his hypotheses solely as a function of method variance common to his measures of A and B but not to C.

The requirements of this paper are intended to be as appropriate to the relatively atheoretical efforts typical of the tests and measurements field as to more theoretical efforts. This emphasis on validational criteria appropriate to our present atheoretical level of test constuction is not at all incompatible with a recognition of the desirability of increasing the extent to which all aspects of a test and the testing situation are determined by explicit theoretical considerations, as Jessor and Hammond have advocated (Jessor & Hammond, 1957).

Relation to operationalism. Underwood (1957, p. 54) in his effective presentation of the operationalist point of view shows a realistic awareness of the amorphous type of theory with which most psychologists work. He contrasts a psychologist's "literary" conception with the latter's operational definition as represented by his test or other measuring instrument. He recognizes the importance of the literary definition in communicating and generating science. He cautions that the operational definition "may not at all measure the process he wishes to measure; it may measure something quite different" (1957, p. 55). He does not, however, indicate how one would know when one was thus mistaken.

The requirements of the present paper may be seen as an extension of the kind of operationalism Underwood has expressed. The test constructor is asked to generate from his literary conception or private construct not one operational embodiment, but two or more, each as different in research vehicle as possible. Furthermore, he is asked to make explicit the distinction between his new variable and other variables, distinctions which are almost certainly implied in his literary definition. In his very first validational efforts, before he ever rushes into print, he is asked to apply the several methods and several traits jointly. His literary definition, his conception, is now best represented in what his independent measures of the trait hold *distinctively* in common. The multitrait-multimethod matrix is, we believe, an important practical first step in avoiding "the danger . . . that the investigator will fall into the trap of thinking that because he went from an artistic or literary conception . . . to the construction of items for a scale to measure it, he has validated his artistic conception" (Underwood, 1957, p. 55). In contrast with the *single operationalism* now dominant in psychology, we are advocating a *multiple operationalism,* a *convergent operationalism* (Garner, 1954; Garner, Hake, & Eriksen, 1956), a *methodological triangulation* (Campbell: 1953, 1956), an *operational delineation* (Campbell, 1954), a *convergent validation.*

Underwood's presentation and that of this paper as a whole imply moving from concept to operation, a sequence that is frequent in science, and perhaps typical. The same point can be made, however, in inspecting a transition from operation to construct. For any body of data taken from a single operation, there is a subinfinity of interpretations possible; a subinfinity of concepts, or combinations of concepts, that it could represent. Any single operation, as representative of concepts, is equivocal. In an analogous fashion, when we view the Ames distorted room from a fixed point and through a single eye, the data of the retinal pattern are equivocal, in that a subinfinity of hexahedrons could generate the same pattern. The addition of a second viewpoint, as through binocular parallax, greatly reduces this equivocality, greatly limits the constructs that could jointly account for both sets of data. In Garner's (1954) study, the fractionation measures from a single method were equivocal—they could have been a function of the stimulus distance being fractionated, or they could have been a function of the comparison stimuli used in the judgment process. A multiple, convergent operationalism reduced this equivocality, showing the latter conceptualization to be the appropriate one, and revealing a preponderance of methods variance. Similarly for learning studies: in identifying constructs with the response data from animals in a specific operational setup there is equivocality which can operationally be reduced by introducing transposition tests, different operations so designed as to put to comparison the rival conceptualizations (Campbell, 1954).

Garner's convergent operationalism and our insistence on more than one method for measuring each concept depart from Bridgman's early position that "if we have more than one set of operations, we have more than one concept, and strictly there should be a separate name to correspond to each different set of operations" (Bridgman, 1927, p. 10). At the current stage of psychological progress, the crucial requirement is the demonstration of some convergence, not complete congruence, between two distinct sets of operations. With only one method, one has no way of distinguishing trait variance from unwanted method variance. When psychological measurement and conceptualization become better developed, it may well be appropriate to differentiate conceptually between Trait-Method Unit A_1 and Trait-Method Unit A_2, in which Trait A is measured by different methods. More likely, what we have called method variance will be specified theoretically in terms of a set of constructs. (This has in effect been illustrated in the discussion above in which it was noted that the response set variance might be viewed as trait variance, and in the rearrangement of the social intelligence matrices of Tables 4 and 5.) It will then be recognized that measurement procedures usually involve several theoretical constructs in joint application. Using obtained measurements to estimate values for a single construct under this condition still requires comparison of complex measures varying in their trait composition, in something like a multitrait-multimethod matrix. Mill's joint method of similarities and differences still epitomizes much about the effective experimental clarification of concepts.

The evaluation of a multitrait-multimethod matrix. The evaluation of the correlation matrix formed by intercorrelating several trait-method units must take into consideration the many factors which are known to affect the magnitude of correlations. A value in the validity diagonal must be assessed in the light of the reliabilities of the two measures involved: e.g., a low reliability for Test A_2 might exaggerate the apparent method variance in Test A_1. Again, the whole approach assumes adequate sampling of individuals: the curtailment of the sample with respect to one or more traits will depress the reliability coefficients and intercorrelations involving these traits. While restrictions of range over all traits produces serious difficulties in the interpretation of a multitrait-multimethod matrix and should be avoided whenever possible, the presence of different degrees of restriction on different traits is the more serious hazard to meaningful interpretation.

Various statistical treatments for multitrait-multimethod matrices might be developed. We have considered rough tests for the elevation of a value in the validity diagonal above the comparison values in its row and column. Correlations between the columns for variables measuring the same trait, variance analyses, and factor analyses have been proposed to us. However, the development of such statistical methods is beyond the scope of this paper. We believe that such summary statistics are neither necessary nor appropriate at this time. Psychologists today should be concerned not with evaluating tests as if the tests were fixed and definitive, but rather with developing better tests. We believe that a careful examination of a multitrait-multimethod matrix will indicate to the experimenter what his next steps should be: it will indicate which methods should be discarded or replaced, which concepts need sharper delineation, and which concepts are poorly measured because of excessive or confounding method variance. Validity judgments based on such a matrix must take into account the stage of development of the constructs, the postulated relationships among them, the level of technical refinement of the methods, the relative independence of the methods, and any pertinent characteristics of the sample of *S*s. We are proposing that the validational process be viewed as an aspect of an ongoing program for improving measuring procedures and that the "validity coefficients" obtained at any one stage in the process be interpreted in terms of gains over preceding stages and as indicators of where further effort is needed.

The design of a multitrait-multimethod matrix. The several methods and traits included in a validational matrix should be selected with care. The several methods used to measure each trait should be appropriate to the trait as conceptualized. Although this view will reduce the range of suitable methods, it will rarely restrict the measurement to one operational procedure.

Wherever possible, the several methods in one matrix should be completely independent of each other: there should be no prior reason for believing that they share method variance. This requirement is necessary to permit the values in the heteromethod-heterotrait triangles to approach zero. If the nature of the traits rules out such independence of methods, efforts should be made to obtain as much diversity as possible in terms of data-sources and classification processes. Thus, the classes of stimuli *or* the background situations, the experimental contexts, should be different. Again, the persons providing the observations should have different roles *or* the procedures for scoring should be varied.

Plans for a validational matrix should take into account the difference between the interpretations regarding convergence and discrimination. It is sufficient to demonstrate convergence between two clearly distinct methods which show little overlap in the heterotrait-heteromethod triangles. While agreement between several methods is desirable, convergence between two is a satisfactory minimal requirement. Discriminative validation is not so easily achieved. Just as it is impossible to prove the null hypothesis, or that some object does not exist, so one can never establish that a trait, as measured, is differentiated from all other traits. One can only show that this measure of Trait A has little overlap with those measures of B and C, and no dependable generalization beyond B and C can be made. For example, social poise could probably be readily discriminated from aesthetic interests, but it should also be differentiated from leadership.

Insofar as the traits are related and are expected to correlate with each other, the monomethod correlations will be substantial and heteromethod correlations between traits will also be positive. For ease of interpretation, it may be best to include in the matrix at least two traits, and preferably two sets of traits, which are postulated to be independent of each other.

In closing, a word of caution is needed. Many multitrait-multimethod matrices will show no convergent validation: no relationship may be found between two methods of measuring a trait. In this common situation, the experimenter should examine the evidence in favor of several alternative propositions: (*a*) Neither method is adequate for measuring the trait; (*b*) One of the two methods does not really measure the trait. (When the evidence indicates that a method does not measure the postulated trait, it may prove to measure some other trait. High correlations in the heterotrait-heteromethod triangles may provide hints to such possibilities.) (*c*) The trait is not a functional unity, the response tendencies involved being specific to the nontrait attributes of each test. The failure to demonstrate convergence may lead to conceptual developments rather than to the abandonment of a test.

SUMMARY

This paper advocates a validational process utilizing a matrix of intercorrelations among tests representing at least two traits, each measured by at least two methods. Measures of the same trait should correlate higher with each other than they do with measures of different traits involving separate methods. Ideally, these validity values should also be higher than the correlations among different traits measured by the same method.

Illustrations from the literature show that these desirable conditions, as a set, are rarely met. Method or apparatus factors make very large contributions to psychological measurements.

The notions of convergence between independent measures of the same trait and discrimination between measures of different traits are compared with previously published formulations, such as construct validity and convergent operationalism. Problems in the application of this validational process are considered.

REFERENCES

American Psychological Association. Technical recommendations for psychological tests and diagnostic techniques. *Psychol. Bull., Suppl.,* 1954, **51,** Part 2, 1–38.

Anderson, E. E. Interrelationship of drives in the male albino rat. I. Intercorrelations of measures of drives. *J. comp. Psychol.,* 1937, **24,** 73–118.

Ayer, A. J. *The problem of knowledge.* New York: St. Martin's Press, 1956.

Borgatta, E. F. Analysis of social interaction and sociometric perception. *Sociometry,* 1954, **17,** 7–32.

Borgatta, E. F. Analysis of social interaction: Actual, role-playing, and projective. *J. abnorm. soc. Psychol.,* 1955, **51,** 394–405.

Bridgman, P. W. *The logic of modern physics.* New York: Macmillan, 1927.

Burwen, L. S., & Campbell, D. T. The generality of attitudes toward authority and nonauthority figures. *J. abnorm. soc. Psychol.,* 1957, **54,** 24–31.

Campbell, D. T. *A study of leadership among submarine officers.* Columbus: Ohio State Univer. Res. Found., 1953.

Campbell, D. T. Operational delineation of "what is learned" via the transposition experiment. *Psychol. Rev.,* 1954, **61,** 167–174.

Campbell, D. T. *Leadership and its effects upon the group.* Monogr. No. 83. Columbus: Ohio State Univer. Bur. Business Res., 1956.

Carroll, J. B. Ratings on traits measured by a factored personality inventory. *J. abnorm. soc. Psychol.,* 1952, **47,** 626–632.

Chi, P.-L. Statistical analysis of personality rating. *J. exp. Educ.,* 1937, **5,** 229–245.

Cronbach, L. J. Response sets and test validity. *Educ. psychol. Measmt,* 1946, **6,** 475–494.

Cronbach, L. J. *Essentials of psychological testing.* New York: Harper, 1949.

Cronbach, L. J. Further evidence on response sets and test design. *Educ. psychol. Measmt,* 1950, **10,** 3–31.

Cronbach, L. J., & Meehl, P. E. Construct validity in psychological tests. *Psychol. Bull.,* 1955, **52,** 281–302.

Edwards, A. L. *The social desirability variable in personality assessment and research.* New York: Dryden, 1957.

Feigl, H. The mental and the physical. In H. Feigl, M. Scriven, & G. Maxwell (Eds.), *Minnesota studies in the philosophy of science.* Vol. II. *Concepts, theories and the mind-body problem.* Minneapolis: Univer. Minnesota Press, 1958.

Fiske, D. W. Consistency of the factorial structures of personality ratings from different sources. *J. abnorm. soc. Psychol.,* 1949, **44,** 329–344.

Garner, W. R. Context effects and the validity of loudness scales. *J. exp. Psychol.,* 1954, **48,** 218–224.

Garner, W. R., Hake, H. W., & Eriksen, C. W. Operationism and the concept of perception. *Psychol. Rev.,* 1956, **63,** 149–159.

Jessor, R., & Hammond, K. R. Construct validity and the Taylor Anxiety Scale. *Psychol. Bull.,* 1957, **54,** 161–170.

Kelley, T. L., & Krey, A. C. *Tests and measurements in the social sciences.* New York: Scribner, 1934.

Kelly, E. L., & Fiske, D. W. *The prediction of performance in clinical psychology.* Ann Arbor: Univer. Michigan Press, 1951.

Loevinger, J., Gleser, G. C., & DuBois, P. H. Maximizing the discriminating power of a multiple-score test. *Psychometrika,* 1953, **18,** 309–317.

Lorge, I. Gen-like: Halo or reality? *Psychol. Bull.,* 1937, **34,** 545–546.

Mayo, G. D. Peer ratings and halo. *Educ. psychol. Measmt,* 1956, **16,** 317–323.

Strang, R. Relation of social intelligence to certain other factors. *Sch. & Soc.,* 1930, **32,** 268–272.

Symonds, P. M. *Diagnosing personality and conduct.* New York: Appleton-Century, 1931.

Thorndike, E. L. A constant error in psychological ratings. *J. appl. Psychol.,* 1920, **4,** 25–29.

Thorndike, R. L. Factor analysis of social and abstract intelligence. *J. educ. Psychol.,* 1936, **27,** 231–233.

Thurstone, L. L. *The reliability and validity of tests.* Ann Arbor: Edwards, 1937.

Tryon, R. C. Individual differences. In F. A. Moss (Ed.), *Comparative Psychology.* (2nd ed.) New York: Prentice-Hall, 1942. Pp. 330–365.

Underwood, B. J. *Psychological research.* New York: Appleton-Century-Crofts, 1957.

Vernon, P. E. Educational ability and psychological factors. Address given to the Joint Education-Psychology Colloquium, Univer. of Illinois, March 29, 1957.

Vernon, P. E. *Educational testing and test-form factors.* Princeton: Educational Testing Service, 1958. (Res. Bull. RB-58-3.)

28. Incremental Validity: A Recommendation[1]

LEE SECHRIST

In the preceding article Campbell and Fiske argued that the validity of a method for measuring a trait should be judged on the basis of its correspondence, or convergence, with measures of the same trait and on the basis of its distinction from measures of different traits. In the present article Sechrist adds another criterion. He suggests that the validity of a test should be judged on the basis of what useful information it provides that is not readily available from other simpler, more familiar methods of measurement. Cronbach and Gleser (1957) do an excellent job discussing this in more detail in their book.

The enthusiasm sometimes expressed for new methods of measurement that show limited but "promising" validity might be dampened somewhat if Sechrist's suggestion were to be generally followed. Another desirable consequence might be a substantial reduction in the needless size and apparent diversity of the psychometrist's kit of measurement tools.

The 1954 APA publication *Technical Recommendations for Psychological Tests and Diagnostic Techniques* established minimum standards to be met in the production and promotion of psychometric instruments. Since that time there have appeared a considerable number of articles elaborating or extending the considerations involved in developing tests (e.g., Cronbach & Meehl, 1955; Jessor & Hammond, 1957; Loevinger, 1957; Campbell & Fiske, 1959; Bechtoldt, 1959; Campbell, 1960). In one of the most recent developments, Campbell and Fiske (1959) have suggested that a crucial distinction is to be made between convergent and discriminant validity. It is necessary to demonstrate not only that a measure covaries with certain other connotatively similar variables, but that its covariance with other connotatively dissimilar variables is limited.

Campbell (1960) has suggested several possible additions to recommended validity indicators, all of which focus on the problem of *discriminant* validity, i.e., the demonstration that a test construct is not completely or even largely redundant with other better established or

---

Sechrist, L. Incremental validity: a recommendation. *Educational and Psychological Measurement,* 1963, *23,* 153–158. Reprinted with the permission of the publisher and author.

[1] The writer wishes to thank Donald T. Campbell and Douglas N. Jackson for helpful suggestions on an earlier version of this manuscript.

more parsimonious constructs. He has suggested, for example, that correlations with intelligence, social desirability and self-ratings should be reported since these variables are likely to be conceptually and theoretically simpler than most of our constructs. If a new test proves to be reducible to an intelligence or social desirability measure, its *raison d'etre* probably vanishes.

It is the purpose of this note to suggest an additional validity construct and evidence which should be presented in the basic publications concerning *any test which is intended for applied, predictive use.*

Incremental Validity

Almost without exception evidence which is presented to support the validity of a psychological test is presented in the form of some improvement over results which would be expected by chance. However, in *clinical* situations, at least, tests are rarely, if ever, used in a manner consistent with the chance model. Almost always Rorschachs are interpreted after interviews, reading of case reports, conferences and the like. The meaning of a report that some Rorschach variable will predict better than chance becomes obscure under those circumstances. It seems clear that validity must be claimed for a test in terms of some *increment* in predictive efficiency over the information otherwise easily and cheaply available.

Cronbach and Gleser (1957, pp. 30–32) and, as they point out, Conrad (1950), have both discussed the problem of the base against which the predictive power of a test is to be evaluated. Cronbach and Gleser declare, "Tests should be judged on the basis of their contribution over and above the best strategy available, making use of prior information" (1957, p. 31). They do indicate that tests may be valuable in spite of low correlations if they tap characteristics either unobservable or difficult to observe by other means. Shaffer (1950, p. 76) also suggested, "One can . . . study the degree to which the clinician is valid with and without the aid of a certain technique, and thereby assess the value of the test indirectly." We are not so sure that such an assessment is completely indirect.

In light of the above argument it is proposed that the publications adduced as evidence for the utility of a test in a clinical situation—and probably for most other uses—should include evidence that the test will *add to* or *increase* the validity of predictions made on the basis of data which are usually available. At a minimum it would seem that a test should have demonstrated incremental validity beyond that of brief case histories, simple biographical information and brief interviews. A strong case can also be made to demand that a test contribute beyond the level of simpler, e.g., paper and pencil, tests. As a matter of fact,

Campbell's recommendation that new tests be correlated with self-ratings is quite akin to some aspects of incremental validity.

Adequate Statistical Evidence

When a test is added to a battery, the usual way to express its contribution is either by a partial correlation or by an increment to a zero order or multiple correlation. There is, perhaps, one objection to the partial or multiple correlation as a demonstration of incremental validity. That is, the increase, even if significant, is of somewhat undetermined origin and obscures the exact nature of the increment achieved.

Consider the matrix of correlations:

	1	2	0
1		60	40
2			40
0			

in which 1 and 2 are predictors of criterion 0. The multiple $R_{12.0} = .45$ and the partial $r_{20.1} = .22$. Both values might be considered to represent improvements over the zero order correlations. And yet, without knowing the reliabilities of 1 and 2 we will be unable to discern whether 2 contributes to the prediction of 0 because it represents a theoretical variable distinct from 1 or whether 2 has only the same, and informationally redundant, effect of increasing the length and, hence, the reliability of Test 1. It will often be important to know whether an increment results from a Spearman-Brown prophecy operation or from some contribution of theoretical importance. Kelley (1927) suggested quite a number of years ago that when correlations between intelligence and achievement measures are properly treated the two measures prove to be almost completely overlapping. Thus, in his view, the two kinds of measures only combine to form a longer and more reliable measure of a single variable.

One solution to the problem might be the correction of inter-test correlations for attenuation. If the reliabilities are so low that the corrected correlation approaches unity, no increment to R nor a significant partial correlation will ensue. In the above example, given reliabilities for 1 and 2 of only .60, the correlation between them would become unity, the multiple would be .40, and the partial r .00. On the other hand, if both variables had reliability coefficients of .90, the correction for attenuation would have little effect on either R or partial correlation.[2]

[2] It is to be noted that correction for attenuation of the validity values is *not* suggested and should not be done.

Exemplary Instances of Incremental Validity Research

Demonstrations of incremental validity are not common in research literature except in prediction of academic performance. Unfortunately, where they occur the data often are discouraging. Winch and More (1956) used a multiple correlation technique in an attempt to determine the increment produced by TAT protocols over a semi-structured interview and case history material. Their results provide no basis for concluding that the TAT contributes anything beyond what is given by interviews or case histories. Sines (1959) discovered that the Rorschach apparently did yield better than chance predictions, but it seemingly not only did not add to other information obtained from interviews and a biographical data sheet, but it actually produced a net *decrement* in predictive accuracy. This in spite of *better than chance* "validity." Kostlan (1954) found that judges made better than chance inferences about patients' behavior from only "minimal data" (age, occupation, education, marital status and source of referral). When test results were used to make the same judgments, only the social history yielded more accurate inferences than those made from simple biographical facts.

In the general area of prediction of academic success, data are widely available indicating the increment over previous grades afforded by predictions based on psychometric data. Even in predicting academic performance, however, it is not always clear that the use of test data accomplishes anything beyond increasing the reliability of the ability measure based on grades. If treated as suggested above, it might be possible to determine whether a test contributes anything beyond maximizing the reliability of the general ability measure afforded by grades. Ford (1950) has presented data concerning the prediction of grades in nursing school making use of, among other measures, the Cooperative General Science Test (CGST) and high school point average (HSPA). The correlation matrix between these variables is:

	CGST	HSPA	Grades
1. CGST		.33	.57
2. HSPA			.51
0. Grades			

The multiple correlation $R_{12.0}$ is .66 and the partial $r_{10.2}$ is .50. The split-half reliability of the CGST has been reported to be .88. While no reliability estimate for HSPA is known to the writer, several researchers have reported reliabilities for colleges grades (Anderson, 1953; Bendig, 1953; Wallace, 1951). If we take the median value of the three reported values of .78, .80, and .90 as a likely estimate for HSPA and then correct the r_{12} for attenuation, the .33 becomes .40. The multiple correlation then drops only to .65 and the partial correlation only to .46. It is obvious that for the prediction of grades in nursing courses the use of the Cooperative General Science Test results in an *increment* in validity over high school grades and that the increment may be regarded as more than a contribution to reliable measurement of a single factor.

Summary

It is proposed that in addition to demonstrating the *convergent* and *discriminant* validity of tests intended for use in clinical situations, evidence should be produced for *incremental* validity. It must be demonstrable that the addition of a test will produce better predictions than are made on the basis of information other than the test ordinarily available. Reference to published research indicates that situations may well occur in which, in spite of better than chance validity, tests may not contribute to, or may even detract from, predictions made on the basis of biographical and interview information. It is further suggested that, when correlations for a given test are entered into a multiple correlation or partial correlation, the inter-predictor correlations be corrected for attenuation to determine whether an increase in the multiple or partial correlations is to be attributed to a mere increase in reliability of measurement of the predictor variable.

REFERENCES

American Council on Education: The Cooperative Test Service. "A Booklet on Norms." New York: 1938.

American Psychological Association, Committee on Psychological Tests. *Technical Recommendations for Psychological Tests and Diagnostic Techniques*. Washington, D. C.: APA, 1954. (Reprinted from: Psychological Bulletin Supplement, LI (1954), 619–629.

Anderson, Scarvia B. "Estimating Grade Reliability." *Journal of Applied Psychology,* XXXVII (1953), 461–464.

Bechtoldt, H. P. "Construct Validity: A Critique." *American Psychologist,* XIV (1959), 619–629.

Bendig, A. W. "The Reliability of Letter Grades." EDUCATIONAL AND PSYCHOLOGICAL MEASUREMENT, XIII (1953), 311–321.

Campbell, D. T. "Recommendations for APA Test Standards Regarding Construct, Trait, or Discriminant Validity." *American Psychologist,* XV (1960), 546–553.

Campbell, D. T. and Fiske, D. W. "Convergent and Discriminant Validation by the Multitrait-Multimethod Matrix." *Psychological Bulletin,* LVI (1959), 81–105.

Conrad, H. "Information Which Should Be Provided by Test Publishers and Testing Agencies on the Validity and Use of Their Tests." In *Proceedings, 1949, Invitational Conference on Testing Problems*. Princeton, N. J.: Educational Testing Service, 1950, 63–68.

Cronbach, L. J. and Gleser, Goldine C. *Psychological Tests and Personnel Decisions*. Urbana: University of Illinois Press, 1957.

Cronbach, L. J. and Meehl, P. E. "Construct Validity in Psychological Tests." *Psychological Bulletin,* LII (1955), 281–302.
Ford, A. H. "Prediction of Academic Success in Three Schools of Nursing." *Journal of Applied Psychology,* XXXIV (1950), 186–189.
Jessor, R. and Hammond, K. R. "Construct Validity and the Taylor Anxiety Scale." *Psychological Bulletin,* LIV (1957), 161–170.
Kelley, T. L. *Interpretation of Educational Measurements.* New York: World Book Company, 1927.
Kostlan, A. "A Method for the Empirical Study of Psychodiagnosis." *Journal of Consulting Psychology,* XVIII (1954), 83–88.
Loevinger, Jane. "Objective Tests as Instruments of Psychological Theory." *Psychological Reports,* III (1957), 635–694. Monograph Supplement 9.
Shaffer, L. "Information Which Should Be Provided by Test Publishers and Testing Agencies on the Validity and Use of Their Tests. Personality Tests." In *Proceedings, 1949, Invitational Conference on Testing Problems.* Princeton, N. J.: Educational Testing Service, 1950.
Sines, L. K. "The Relative Contribution of Four Kinds of Data to Accuracy in Personality Assessment." *Journal of Consulting Psychology,* XXIII (1959), 483–492.
Wallace, W. L. "The Prediction of Grades in Specific College Courses." *Journal of Educational Research,* XLIV (1951), 587–595.
Winch, R. F. and More, D. M. "Does TAT Add Information to Interviews? Statistical Analysis of the Increments." *Journal of Clinical Psychology,* XII (1956), 316–321.

29. Antecedent Probability and the Efficiency of Psychometric Signs, Patterns, or Cutting Scores[1]

PAUL E. MEEHL
ALBERT ROSEN

A clinician uses a test to aid him in identifying, in a certain population, those who have some talent, defect, or other special characteristic. Suppose his test has only moderate validity. Is it possible that he may actually make

Meehl, P. E., and Rosen, A. Antecedent probability and the efficiency of psychometric signs, patterns or cutting scores. *Psychological Bulletin,* 1955, *52,* 194–216. Reprinted with the permission of the publisher and authors.

[1] From the Neuropsychiatric Service, VA Hospital, Minneapolis, Minnesota, and the Divisions of Psychiatry and Clinical Psychology of the University of Minnesota Medical School. The senior author carried on his part of this work in connection with his appointment to the Minnesota Center for the Philosophy of Science.

more wrong identifications with the "help" of his test than he would be likely to make without it? Meehl and Rosen point out in this article that such an unfortunate outcome is quite possible if the incidence of the special characteristic in the population is very small, or very large. They also discuss probabilities of correct decisions, optimum cutting scores, and selection ratios.

In clinical practice, psychologists frequently participate in the making of vital decisions concerning the classification, treatment, prognosis, and disposition of individuals. In their attempts to increase the number of correct classifications and predictions, psychologists have developed and applied many psychometric devices, such as patterns of test responses as well as cutting scores for scales, indices, and sign lists. Since diagnostic and prognostic statements can often be made with a high degree of accuracy purely on the basis of actuarial or experience tables (referred to hereinafter as *base rates*), a psychometric device, to be efficient, must make possible a greater number of correct decisions than could be made in terms of the base rates alone.

The efficiency of the great majority of psychometric devices reported in the clinical psychology literature is difficult or impossible to evaluate for the following reasons:

a. Base rates are virtually never reported. It is, therefore, difficult to determine whether or not a given device results in a greater number of correct decisions than would be possible solely on the basis of the rates from previous experience. When, however, the base rates can be estimated, the reported claims of efficiency of psychometric instruments are often seen to be without foundation.

b. In most reports, the distribution data provided are insufficient for the evaluation of the probable efficiency of the device in other settings where the base rates are markedly different. Moreover, the samples are almost always too small for the determination of optimal cutting lines for various decisions.

c. Most psychometric devices are reported without cross-validation data. If a psychometric instrument is applied solely to the criterion groups from which it was developed, its reported validity and efficiency are likely to be spuriously high, especially if the criterion groups are small.

d. There is often a lack of clarity concerning the type of population in which a psychometric device can be effectively applied.

e. Results are frequently reported only in terms of significance tests for differences between groups rather than in terms of the number of correct decisions for individuals within the groups.

The purposes of this paper are to examine current methodology in studies of predictive and concurrent validity (1), and to present some methods for the evaluation of the efficiency of psychometric devices as well as for the improvement in the interpretations made from such devices. Actual studies reported in the literature will be used for illustration wherever possible. It should be emphasized that these particular illustrative studies of common practices were chosen simply because they contained more complete data than are commonly reported, and were available in fairly recent publications.

IMPORTANCE OF BASE RATES

Danielson and Clark (4) have reported on the construction and application of a personality inventory which was devised for use in military induction stations as an aid in detecting those men who would not complete basic training because of psychiatric disability or AWOL recidivism. One serious defect in their article is that it reports cutting lines which have not been cross validated. Danielson and Clark state that inductees were administered the Fort Ord Inventory within two days after induction into the Army, and that all of these men were allowed to undergo basic training regardless of their test scores.

Two samples (among others) of these inductees were selected for the study of predictive validity: (*a*) A group of 415 men who had made a good adjustment (Good Adjustment Group), and (*b*) a group of 89 men who were unable to complete basic training and who were sufficiently disturbed to warrant a recommendation for discharge by a psychiatrist (Poor Adjustment Group). The authors state that "the most important task of a test designed to screen out misfits is the detection of the (latter) group" (4, p. 139). The authors found that their most effective scale for this differentiation picked up, at a given cutting point, 55% of the Poor Adjustment Group (valid positives) and 19% of the Good Adjustment Group (false positives). The overlap between these two groups would undoubtedly have been greater if the cutting line had been cross validated on a random sample from the *entire population* of inductees, but for the purposes of the present discussion, let us assume that the results were obtained from cross-validation groups. There is no mention of the percentage of all inductees who fall into the Poor Adjustment Group, but a rough estimate will be adequate for the present discussion. Suppose that in their population of soldiers, as many as 5% make a poor adjustment and 95% make a good adjustment. The results for 10,000 cases would be as depicted in Table 1.

Efficiency in detecting poor adjustment cases. The efficiency of the scale can be evaluated in several ways. From the data in Table 1 it can be seen that if the cutting line given by the authors were used at Fort Ord, the scale could not be used directly to "screen out misfits." If all those predicted by the scale to make a poor adjustment were screened

TABLE 1. Number of Inductees in the Poor Adjustment and Good Adjustment Groups Detected by a Screening Inventory
(55% valid positives; 19% false positives)

Predicted Adjustment	Actual Adjustment				Total Predicted
	Poor		Good		
	No.	%	No.	%	
Poor	275	55	1,805	19	2,080
Good	225	45	7,695	81	7,920
Total actual	500	100	9,500	100	10,000

out, the number of false positives would be extremely high. Among the 10,000 potential inductees, 2080 would be predicted to make a poor adjustment. Of these 2080, only 275, or 13%, would actually make a poor adjustment, whereas the decisions for 1805 men, or 87% of those screened out, would be incorrect.

Efficiency in prediction for all cases. If a prediction were made for every man on the basis of the cutting line given for the test, 275 + 7695, or 7970, out of 10,000 decisions would be correct. Without the test, however, every man would be predicted to make a good adjustment, and 9500 of the predictions would be correct. Thus, use of the test has yielded a drop from 95% to 79.7% in the total number of correct decisions.

Efficiency in detecting good adjustment cases. There is one kind of decision in which the Inventory can improve on the base rates, however. If only those men are accepted who are predicted by the Inventory to make a good adjustment, 7920 will be selected, and the outcome of 7695 of the 7920, or 97%, will be predicted correctly. This is a 2% increase in hits among predictions of "success." The decision as to whether or not the scale improves on the base rates sufficiently to warrant its use will depend on the cost of administering the testing program, the administrative feasibility of rejecting 21% of the men who passed the psychiatric screening, the cost to the Army of training the 225 maladaptive recruits, and the intangible human costs involved in psychiatric breakdown.

Populations to which the scale is applied. In the evaluation of the efficiency of any psychometric instrument, careful consideration must be given to the types of populations to which the device is to be applied. Danielson and Clark have stated that "since the final decision as to disposition is made by the psychiatrist, the test should be classified as a screening adjunct" (4, p. 138). This statement needs clarification, however, for the efficiency of the scale can vary markedly according to the different ways in which it might be used as an adjunct.

It will be noted that the test was administered to men who were already in the Army, and not to men being examined for induction. The reported validation data apply, therefore, specifically to the population of *recent inductees*. The results might have been somewhat different if the population tested consisted of *potential inductees*. For the sake of illustration, however, let us assume that there is no difference in the test results of the two populations.

An induction station psychiatrist can use the scale cutting score in one or more of the following ways, i.e., he can apply the scale results to a variety of populations. (*a*) The psychiatrist's final decision to accept or reject a potential inductee may be based on both the test score and his usual interview procedure. The population to which the test scores are applied is, therefore, *potential inductees interviewed by the usual procedures for whom no decision was made.* (*b*) He may evaluate the potential inductee according to his usual procedures, and then consult the test score *only if* the tentative decision is to reject. That is, a decision to accept is final. The population to which the test scores are applied is *potential inductees tentatively rejected by the usual interview procedures.* (*c*) An alternative procedure is for the psychiatrist to consult the test score only if the tentative decision is to accept, the population being *potential inductees tentatively accepted by the usual interview procedures*. The decision to reject is final. (*d*) Probably the commonest proposal for the use of tests as screening adjuncts is that the more skilled and costly psychiatric evaluation should be made only upon the test positives, i.e., inductees classified by the test as good risks are not interviewed, or are subjected only to a very short and superficial interview. Here the population is *all potential inductees,* the test being used to make either a *final* decision to "accept" or a decision to "examine."

Among these different procedures, how is the psychiatrist to achieve maximum effectiveness in using the test as an adjunct? There is no answer to this question from the available data, but it can be stated definitely that the data reported by Danielson and Clark apply only to the third procedure described above. The test results are based on a selected group of men *accepted* for induction and not on a random sample of potential inductees. If the scale is used in any other way than the third procedure mentioned above, the results may be considerably inferior to those reported, and, thus, to the use of the base rates without the test.[2]

The principles discussed thus far, although illustrated by a single study, can be generalized to any study of predictive or concurrent validity. It can be seen that many considerations are involved in determining the efficiency of a scale at a given cutting score, especially the base

[2] Goodman (8) has discussed this same problem with reference to the supplementary use of an index for the prediction of parole violation.

rates of the subclasses within the population to which the psychometric device is to be applied. In a subsequent portion of this paper, methods will be presented for determining cutting points for maximizing the efficiency of the different types of decisions which are made with psychometric devices.

Another study will be utilized to illustrate the importance of an explicit statement of the base rates of population subgroups to be tested with a given device. Employing an interesting configural approach, Thiesen (18) discovered five Rorschach patterns, each of which differentiated well between 60 schizophrenic adult patients and a sample of 157 gainfully employed adults. The best differentiator, considering individual patterns or number of patterns, was Pattern A, which was found in 20% of the patients' records and in only .6% of the records of normals. Thiesen concludes that if these patterns stand the test of cross validation, they might have "clinical usefulness" in early detection of a schizophrenic process or as an aid to determining the gravity of an initial psychotic episode (18, p. 369). If by "clinical usefulness" is meant efficiency in a clinic or hospital for the diagnosis of schizophrenia, it is necessary to demonstrate that the patterns differentiate a higher percentage of schizophrenic patients from *other diagnostic groups* than could be correctly classified without any test at all, i.e., solely on the basis of the rates of various diagnoses in any given hospital. If a test is to be used in differential diagnosis among psychiatric patients, evidence of its efficiency for this function cannot be established solely on the basis of discrimination of diagnostic groups from normals. If by "clinical usefulness" Thiesen means that his data indicate that the patterns might be used to detect an early schizophrenic process among nonhospitalized gainfully employed adults, he would do better to discard his patterns and use the base rates, as can be seen from the following data.

Taulbee and Sisson (17) cross validated Thiesen's patterns on schizophrenic patient and normal samples, and found that Pattern A was the best discriminator. Among patients, 8.1% demonstrated this pattern and among normals, none had this pattern. There are approximately 60 million gainfully employed adults in this country, and it has been estimated that the rate of schizophrenia in the general population is approximately .85% (2, p. 558). The results for Pattern A among a population of 10,000 gainfully employed adults would be as shown in Table 2. In order to detect 7 schizophrenics, it would be necessary to test 10,000 individuals.

In the Neurology service of a hospital a psychometric scale is used which is designed to differentiate between patients with psychogenic and organic low back pain (9). At a given cutting point, this scale was found to classify each group with approximately 70% effectiveness upon cross validation, i.e., 70% of cases with no organic findings scored

TABLE 2. Number of Persons Classified as Schizophrenic and Normal by a Test Pattern Among a Population of Gainfully Employed Adults

(8.1% valid positives; 0.0% false positives)

Classification by Test	Criterion Classification				Total Classified by Test
	Schizophrenia		Normal		
	No.	%	No.	%	
Schizophrenia	7	8.1	0	0	7
Normal	78	91.9	9,915	100	9,993
Total in class	85	100	9,915	100	10,000

above an optimal cutting score, and 70% of surgically verified organic cases scored below this line. Assume that 90% of all patients in the Neurology service with a primary complaint of low back pain are in fact "organic." Without any scale at all the psychologist can say every case is organic, and be right 90% of the time. With the scale the results would be as shown in Section A of Table 3. Of 10 psychogenic cases, 7 score above the line; of 90 organic cases, 63 score below the cutting line. If every case above the line is called psychogenic, only 7 of 34 will be classified correctly or about 21%. Nobody wants to be right only one out of five times in this type of situation, so that it is obvious that it would be imprudent to call a patient psychogenic on the basis of this scale. Radically different results occur in prediction for cases below the cutting line. Of 66 cases 63, or 95%, are correctly classified as organic. Now the psychologist has increased his diagnostic hits from 90 to 95%

TABLE 3. Number of Patients Classified as Psychogenic and Organic on a Low Back Pain Scale Which Classifies Correctly 70% of Psychogenic and Organic Cases

Classification by Scale	Actual Diagnosis		Total Classified by Scale
	Psychogenic	Organic	
A. Base Rates in Population Tested: 90% Organic; 10% Psychogenic			
Psychogenic	7	27	34
Organic	3	63	66
Total diagnosed	10	90	100
B. Base Rates in Population Tested: 90% Psychogenic; 10% Organic			
Psychogenic	63	3	66
Organic	27	7	34
Total diagnosed	90	10	100

on the condition that he labels only cases falling below the line, and ignores the 34% scoring above the line.

In actual practice, the psychologist may not, and most likely will not, test every low back pain case. Probably those referred for testing will be a select group, i.e., those who the neurologist believes are psychogenic because neurological findings are minimal or absent. This fact changes the population from "all patients in Neurology with a primary complaint of low back pain," to "all patients in Neurology with a primary complaint of low back pain *who are referred for testing*." Suppose that a study of past diagnoses indicated that of patients with minimal or absent findings, 90% were diagnosed as psychogenic and 10% as organic. Section B of Table 3 gives an entirely different picture of the effectiveness of the low back pain scale, and new limitations on interpretation are necessary. Now the scale correctly classifies 95% of all cases above the line as psychogenic (63 of 66), and is correct in only 21% of all cases below the line (7 of 34). In this practical situation the psychologist would be wise to refrain from interpreting a low score.

From the above illustrations it can be seen that the psychologist in interpreting a test and in evaluating its effectiveness must be very much aware of the population and its subclasses and the base rates of the behavior or event with which he is dealing at any given time.

It may be objected that no clinician relies on just one scale but would diagnose on the basis of a configuration of impressions from several tests, clinical data and history. We must, therefore, emphasize that the preceding single-scale examples were presented for simplicity only, but that the main point is not dependent upon this "atomism." *Any complex configurational procedure in any number of variables, psychometric or otherwise, eventuates in a decision.* Those decisions have a certain objective success rate in criterion case identification; and for present purposes we simply treat the decision function, whatever its components and complexity may be, as a single variable. It should be remembered that the literature does not present us with cross-validated methods having hit rates much above those we have chosen as examples, regardless of how complex or configural the methods used. So that even if the clinician approximates an extremely complex configural function "in his head" before classifying the patient, for purposes of the present problem this complex function is treated as the scale. In connection with the more general "philosophy" of clinical decision making see Bross (3) and Meehl (12).

APPLICATIONS OF BAYES' THEOREM

Many readers will recognize the preceding numerical examples as essentially involving a principle of elementary probability theory, the so-called "Bayes' Theorem." While it has come in for some opprobrium on account of its connection with certain pre-Fisherian fallacies in statistical inference, as an algebraic statement the theorem has, of course, nothing intrinsically wrong with it and it does apply in the present case. One form of it may be stated as follows:

If there are k antecedent conditions under which an event of a given kind may occur, these conditions having the antecedent probabilities P_1, $P_2, \cdots, P_k$ of being realized, and the probability of the event upon each of them is $p_1, p_2, p_3, \cdots, p_k$; then, given that the event is observed to occur, the probability that it arose on the basis of a specified one, say j, of the antecedent conditions is given by

$$P_{j(o)} = \frac{P_j p_j}{\sum_{i=1}^{k} P_i p_i}.$$

The usual illustration is the case of drawing marbles from an urn. Suppose we have two urns, and the urn-selection procedure is such that the probability of our choosing the first urn is 1/10 and the second 9/10. Assume that 70% of the marbles in the first urn are black, and 40% of those in the second urn are black. I now (blindfolded) "choose" an urn and then, from it, I choose a marble. The marble turns out to be black. What is the probability that I drew from the first urn?

$$P_1 = .10 \qquad P_2 = .90$$

$$p_1 = .70 \qquad p_2 = .40$$

Then

$$P_{1(b)} = \frac{(.10)(.70)}{(.10)(.70)+(.90)(.40)} = .163.$$

If I make a practice of inferring under such circumstances that an observed black marble arose from the first urn, I shall be correct in such judgments, in the long run, only 16.3% of the time. Note, however that the "test item" or "sign" *black marble* is correctly "scored" in favor of Urn No. 1, since there is a 30% difference in black marble rate between it and Urn No. 2. But this considerable disparity in symptom rate is overcome by the very low base rate ("antecedent probability of choosing from the first urn"), so that inference to first-urn origin of black marbles will actually be wrong some 84 times in 100. In the clinical analogue, the urns are identified with the subpopulations of patients to be discriminated (their antecedent probabilities being equated to their base rates in the population to be examined), and the black marbles are test results of a certain ("positive") kind. The proportion of black marbles in one urn is the valid positive rate, and in the other is the false positive rate. Inspection and suitable manipulations of the formula for the common two-category case, viz.,

$$P_{(o)} = \frac{Pp_1}{Pp_1 + Qp_2}$$

$P_{d(o)}$ = Probability that an individual is diseased, given that his observed test score is positive
P = Base rate of actual positives in the population examined
$P + Q = 1$
p_1 = Proportion of diseased identified by test ("valid positive" rate)
$q_1 = 1 - p_1$
p_2 = Proportion of nondiseased misidentified by test as being diseased ("false positive" rate)
$q_2 = 1 - p_2$

yields several useful statements. Note that in what follows we are operating entirely with exact population parameter values; i.e., sampling errors are not responsible for the dangers and restrictions set forth. See Table 4.

1. In order for a positive diagnostic assertion to be "more likely true than false," the ratio of the positive to the negative base rates in the examined population must exceed the ratio of the false positive rate to the valid positive rate. That is,

$$\frac{P}{Q} > \frac{p_2}{p_1}.$$

If this condition is not met, the attribution of pathology on the basis of the test is more probably in error than correct, *even though the sign being used is valid* (i.e., $p_1 \neq p_2$).

TABLE 4. Definition of Symbols

Diagnosis from Test	Actual Diagnosis	
	Positive	Negative
Positive	p_1 Valid positive rate (Proportion of positives called positive)	p_2 False positive rate (Proportion of negatives called positive)
Negative	q_1 False negative rate (Proportion of positives called negative)	q_2 Valid negative rate (Proportion of negatives called negative)
Total with actual diagnosis	$p_1 + q_1 = 1.0$ (Total positives)	$p_2 + q_2 = 1.0$ (Total negatives)

Note.—For simplicity, the term "diagnosis" is used to denote the classification of any kind of pathology, behavior, or event being studied, or to denote "outcome" if a test is used for prediction. Since horizontal addition (e.g., $p_1 + p_2$) is meaningless in ignorance of the base rates, there is no symbol or marginal total for these sums. *All values are parameter values.*

Example: If a certain cutting score identifies 80% of patients with organic brain damage (high scores being indicative of damage) but is also exceeded by 15% of the nondamaged sent for evaluation, in order for the psychometric decision "brain damage present" to be more often true than false, the ratio of actually brain-damaged to nondamaged cases among all seen for testing must be at least one to five (.19).

Piotrowski has recommended that the presence of 5 or more Rorschach signs among 10 "organic" signs is an efficient indicator of brain damage. Dorken and Kral (5), in cross validating Piotrowski's index, found that 63% of organics and 30% of a mixed, nonorganic, psychiatric patient group had Rorschachs with 5 or more signs. Thus, our estimate of $p_2/p_1 = .30/.63 + .48$, and in order for the decision "brain damage present" to be correct more than one-half the time, the proportion of positives (P) in a given population must equal or exceed .33 (i.e., $P/Q > .33/.67$). Since few clinical populations requiring this clinical decision would have such a high rate of brain damage, especially among psychiatric patients, the particular cutting score advocated by Piotrowski will produce an excessive number of false positives, and the positive diagnosis will be more often wrong than right. Inasmuch as the base rates for any given behavior or pathology differ from one clinical setting to another, *an inflexible cutting score should not be advocated for any psychometric device.* This statement applies generally—thus, to indices recommended for such diverse purposes as the classification or detection of deterioration, specific symptoms, "traits," neuroticism, sexual aberration, dissimulation, suicide risk, and the like. When P is small, it may be advisable to explore the possibility of dealing with a restricted population within which the base rate of the attribute being tested is higher. This approach is discussed in an article by Rosen (14) on the detection of suicidal patients in which it is suggested that an attempt might be made to apply an index to subpopulations with higher suicide rates.

2. If the base rates are equal, the probability of a positive diagnosis being correct is the ratio of valid positive rate to the sum of valid and false positive rates. That is,

$$P_{d(o)} = \frac{p_1}{p_1 + p_2} \quad \text{if} \quad P = Q = \tfrac{1}{2}.$$

Example: If our population is evenly divided between neurotic and psychotic patients the condition for being "probably right" in diagnosing psychosis by a certain method is simply that the psychotics exhibit the pattern in question more frequently than the neurotics. This is the intuitively obvious special case; it is often misgeneralized to justify use of the test in those cases where base-rate asymmetry ($P \neq Q$) counteracts the $(p_1 - p_2)$ discrepancy, leading to the paradoxical consequence that *deciding on the basis of more information can actually worsen the chances of a correct decision.* The apparent absurdity of such an idea has often misled psychologists into behaving as though the establishment of "validity" or "discrimination," i.e., that $p_1 \neq p_2$, indicates that a procedure should be used in decision making.

Example: A certain test is used to select those who will continue in outpatient psychotherapy (positives). It correctly identifies 75% of these good cases but the same cutting score picks up 40% of the poor risks who subsequently terminate against advice. Suppose that in the past experience of the clinic 50% of the patients terminated therapy prematurely. Correct selection of patients can be made with the given cutting score on the test 65% of the time, since $p_1/(p_1 + p_2) = .75/(.75 + .40) = .65$. It can be seen that the efficiency of the test would be exaggerated if the base rate for continuation in therapy were actually .70, but the efficiency were evaluated solely on the basis of a research study containing equal groups of continuers and noncontinuers, i.e., if it were assumed that $P = .50$.

3. In order for the hits in the entire population which is under consideration to be increased by use of the test, the base rate of the more numerous class (called here positive) must be less than the ratio of the valid negative rate to the sum of valid negative and false negative rates. That is, unless

$$P < \frac{q_2}{q_1 + q_2},$$

the making of decisions on the basis of the test will have an adverse effect. An alternative expression is that $(P/Q) < (q_2/q_1)$ when $P > Q$, i.e., the ratio of the larger to the smaller class must be less than the ratio of the valid negative rate to the false negative rate. When $P < Q$, the conditions for the test to improve upon the base rates are:

$$Q < \frac{p_1}{p_1 + p_2}$$

and

$$\frac{Q}{P} < \frac{p_1}{p_2}.$$

Rotter, Rafferty, and Lotsof (15) have reported the scores on a sentence completion test for a group of 33 "maladjusted" and 33 "adjusted" girls. They report that the use of a specified cutting score (not cross validated) will result in the correct classification of 85% of the maladjusted girls and the incorrect classification of only 15% of the adjusted girls. It is impossible to evaluate adequately the efficiency of the test unless one knows the base rates of maladjustment (P) and adjustment (Q) for the population of high school girls, although there would be general agreement that $Q > P$. Since $p_1/(p_1 + p_2) = .85/(.85 + .15)$

= .85, the overall hits in diagnosis with the test will not improve on classification based solely on the base rates unless the proportion of adjusted girls is less than .85. Because the reported effectiveness of the test is spuriously high, the proportion of adjusted girls would no doubt have to be considerably less than .85. Unless there is good reason to believe that the base rates are similar from one setting to another, it is impossible to determine the efficiency of a test such as Rotter's when the criterion is based on ratings unless one replicates his research, including the criterion ratings, with a representative sample of each new population.

4. In altering a sign, improving a scale, or shifting a cutting score, the increment in valid positives per increment in valid positive *rate* is proportional to the positive base rate; and analogously, the increment in valid negatives per increment in valid negative *rate* is proportional to the negative base rate. That is, if we alter a sign the net improvement in over-all hit rate is

$$H'_T - H_T = \Delta p_1 P + \Delta q_2 Q,$$

where H_T = original proportion of hits (over-all) and H'_T = new proportion of hits (over-all).

5. A corollary of this is that altering a sign or shifting a cut will improve our decision making if, and only if, the ratio of *improvement* Δp_1 in valid positive rate to *worsening* Δp_2 in false negative rate exceeds the ratio of actual negatives to positives in the population.

$$\frac{\Delta p_1}{\Delta p_2} > \frac{Q}{P}.$$

Example: Suppose we improve the intrinsic validity of a certain "schizophrenic index" so that it now detects 20% more schizophrenics than it formerly did, at the expense of only a 5% increase in the false positive rate. This surely looks encouraging. We are, however, working with an outpatient clientele only 1/10th of whom are actually schizophrenic. Then, since

$$\Delta p_1 = .20 \qquad P = .10$$

$$\Delta p_2 = .05 \qquad Q = .90$$

applying the formula we see that

$$\frac{.20}{.05} \ngtr \frac{.90}{.10}$$

i.e., the required inequality does not hold, and the routine use of this "improved" index will result in an increase in the proportion of erroneous diagnostic decisions.

In the case of any pair of unimodal distributions, this corresponds to the principle that the optimal cut lies at the intersection of the two distribution envelopes (11, pp. 271–272).

MANIPULATION OF CUTTING LINES FOR DIFFERENT DECISIONS

For any given psychometric device, no one cutting line is maximally efficient for clinical settings in which the base rates of the criterion groups in the population are different. Furthermore, different cutting lines may be necessary for various decisions within the same population. In this section, methods are presented for manipulating the cutting line of any instrument in order to maximize the efficiency of a device in the making of several kinds of decisions. Reference should be made to the scheme presented in Table 5 for understanding of the discussion which follows. This scheme and the methods for manipulating cutting lines are derived from Duncan, Ohlin, Reiss, and Stanton (6).

TABLE 5. Symbols to Be Used in Evaluating the Efficiency of a Psychometric Device in Classification or Prediction

Diagnosis from Test	Actual Diagnosis		Total Diagnosed from Test
	Positive	Negative	
Positive	NPp_1 (Number of valid positives)	NQp_2 (Number of false positives)	$NPp_1 + NQp_2$ (Number of test positives)
Negative	NPq_1 (Number of false negatives)	NQq_2 (Number of valid negatives)	$NPq_1 + NQq_2$ (Number of test negatives)
Total with actual diagnosis	NP (Number of actual positives)	NQ (Number of actual negatives)	N (Total number of cases)

Note.—For simplicity, the term "diagnosis" is used to denote the classification of any kind of pathology, behavior, or event studied, or to denote "outcome" if a test is used for prediction. "Number" means *absolute frenquency*, not *rate* or probability.

A study in the prediction of juvenile delinquency by Glueck and Glueck (7) will be used for illustration. Scores on a prediction index for 451 delinquents and 439 nondelinquents (7, p. 261) are listed in Table 6. If the Gluecks' index is to be used in a population with a given juvenile delinquency rate, cutting lines can be established to maximize the efficiency of the index for several decisions. In the following illustration, a delinquency rate of .20 will be used. From the data in Table 6, optimal cutting lines will be determined for maximizing the proportion of correct predictions, or hits, for all cases (H_T), and for maximizing the proportion of hits (H_P) among those called delinquent (positives) by the index.

TABLE 6. Prediction Index Scores for Juvenile Delinquents and Nondelinquents and Other Statistics for Determining Optimal Cutting Lines for Certain Decisions in a Population with a Delinquency Rate of .20*

Prediction Index Score	Delinquents			Nondelinquents									
			$\frac{cf}{451}$			$\frac{cf}{439}$	$1 - p_2$	$.2p_1$	$.8p_2$	$.8q_2$	$Pp_1 + Qq_2$	$Pp_1 + Qp_2$	$\frac{Pp_1}{R_P}$
	(1)	(2)	(3)	(4)	(5)	(6)	(7)	(8)	(9)	(10)	(11)	(12)	(13)
	f	cf	p_1	f	cf	p_2	q_2	Pp_1	Qp_2	Qq_2	H_T	R_P	H_P
400 +	51	51	.1131	1	1	.0023	.9977	.0226	.0018	.7982	.821	.024	.926
350–399	73	124	.2749	8	9	.0205	.9795	.0550	.0164	.7836	.839	.071	.770
300–349	141	265	.5876	23	32	.0729	.9271	.1175	.0583	.7417	.859	.176	.668
250–299	122	387	.8581	70	102	.2323	.7677	.1716	.1858	.6142	.786	.357	.480
200–249	40	427	.9468	68	170	.3872	.6128	.1894	.3098	.4902	.680	.499	.379
150–199	19	446	.9889	102	272	.6196	.3804	.1978	.4957	.3043	.502	.694	.285
< 150	5	451	1.0000	167	439	1.0000	.0000	.2000	.8000	.0000	.200	1.000	.200

* Frequencies in columns 1 and 4 are from Glueck and Glueck (7, p. 261).

In the first three columns of Table 6, "*f*" denotes the number of delinquents scoring in each class interval, "*cf*" represents the cumulative frequency of delinquents scoring above each class interval (e.g., 265 score above 299), and p_1 represents the proportion of the total group of 451 delinquents scoring above each class interval. Columns 4, 5, and 6 present the same kind of data for the 439 nondelinquents.

Maximizing the number of correct predictions or classifications for all cases. The proportion of correct predictions or classifications (H_T) for any given cutting line is given by the formula, $H_T = Pp_1 + Qq_2$. Thus, in column 11 of Table 6, labelled H_T, it can be seen that the best cutting line for this decision would be between 299 and 300, for 85.9% of all predictions would be correct if those above the line were predicted to become delinquent and all those below the line nondelinquent. Any other cutting line would result in a smaller proportion of correct predictions, and, in fact, any cutting line set lower than this point would make the index inferior to the use of the base rates, for if all cases were predicted to be nondelinquent, the total proportion of hits would be .80.

Maximizing the number of correct predictions or classifications for positives. The primary use of a prediction device may be for *selection* of (*a*) students who will succeed in a training program, (*b*) applicants who will succeed in a certain job, (*c*) patients who will benefit from a certain type of therapy, etc. In the present illustration, the index would most likely be used for detection of those who are likely to become delinquents. Thus, the aim might be to maximize the number of hits only within the group predicted by the index to become delinquents (predicted positives $= NPp_1 + NQp_2$). The proportion of correct predictions for this group by the use of different cutting lines is given in column 13, labelled H_P. Thus, if a cutting line is set between 399 and 400, one will be correct over 92 times in 100 if predictions are made *only* for persons scoring above the cutting line. The formula for determining the efficiency of the test when only positive predictions are made is $H_P = Pp_1/(Pp_1 + Qp_2)$.

One has to pay a price for achieving a very high level of accuracy with the index. Since the problem is to select potential delinquents so that some sort of therapy can be attempted, the proportion of this selected group in the total sample may be considered as a selection ratio. The selection ratio for positives is $R_P = Pp_1 + Qp_2$, that is, predictions are made only for those above the cutting line. The selection ratio for each possible cutting line is shown in column 12 of Table 6, labelled R_P. It can be seen that to obtain maximum accuracy in selection of delinquents (92.6%), predictions can be made for only 2.4% of the population. For other cutting lines, the accuracy of selection and the corresponding selection ratios are given in Table 6. The worker applying the index must use his own judgment in deciding upon the level of accuracy and the selection ratio desired.

Maximizing the number of correct predictions or classifications for negatives. In some selection problems, the goal is the selection of negatives rather than positives. Then, the proportion of hits among all predicted negative for any given cutting line is $H_N = Qq_2/(Qq_2 + Pq_1)$, and the selection ratio for negatives is $R_N = Pq_1 + Qq_2$.

In all of the above manipulations of cutting lines, it is essential that there be a large number of cases. Otherwise, the percentages about any given cutting line would be so unstable that very dissimilar results would be obtained on new samples. For most studies in clinical psychology, therefore, it would be necessary to establish cutting lines according to the decisions and methods discussed above, and then to cross validate a specific cutting line on new samples.

The amount of shrinkage to be expected in the cross validation of cutting lines cannot be determined until a thorough mathematical and statistical study of the subject is made. It may be found that when criterion distributions are approximately normal and large, cutting lines should be established in terms of the normal probability table rather than on the basis of the observed p and q values found in the samples. In a later section dealing with the selection ratio we shall see that it is sometimes the best procedure to select all individuals falling above a cerain cutting line and to select the others needed to reach the selection ratio by choosing at random below the line; or in other cases to establish several different cuts defining *ranges* within which one or the opposite decision should be made.

Decisions based on score intervals rather than cutting lines. The Gluecks' data can be used to illustrate another approach to psychometric classification and prediction when scores for large samples are available with a relatively large number of cases in each score interval. In Table 7 are listed frequencies of delinquents and nondelinquents for prediction index score intervals. The frequencies for delinquents are the same as those in Table 6, whereas those for nondelinquents have been corrected for a base rate of .20 by multiplying each frequency in column 4 of Table 6[3] by

$$4.11 = \frac{(.80)}{(.20)} \frac{(451)}{(439)}.$$

Table 7 indicates the proportion of delinquents and nondelinquents among all juveniles who fall within a given score interval when the base

[3] The Gluecks' Tables XX-2, 3, 4, 5, (7, pp. 261–262) and their interpretations therefrom are apt to be misleading because of their exclusive consideration of approximately equal base rates of delinquency and nondelinquency. Reiss (13), in his review of the Gluecks' study, has also discussed their use of an unrepresentative rate of delinquency.

TABLE 7. Percentage of Delinquents (D) and Nondelinquents (ND) in Each Prediction Index Score Interval in a Population in Which the Delinquency Rate is .20*

Prediction Index Score Interval	No. of D	No. of ND	Total of D and ND	% of D in Score Interval	% of ND in Score Interval	% of D and ND in Score Interval
400 +	51	4	55	92.7	7.3	100
350–399	73	33	106	68.9	31.1	100
300–349	141	95	236	59.7	40.3	100
250–299	122	288	410	29.8	70.2	100
200–249	40	279	319	12.5	87.5	100
150–199	19	419	438	4.3	95.7	100
< 150	5	686	691	.7	99.3	100
Total	451	1804	2255			

* Modification of Table XX-2, p. 261, from Glueck and Glueck (7).

rate of delinquency is .20. It can be predicted that of those scoring 400 or more, 92.7% will become delinquent, of those scoring between 350 and 399, 68.9% will be delinquent, etc. Likewise, of those scoring between 200 and 249, it can be predicted that 87.5% will not become delinquent. Since 80% of predictions will be correct without the index if all cases are called nondelinquent, one would not predict nondelinquency with the index in score intervals over 249. Likewise, it would be best not to predict delinquency for individuals in the intervals under 250 because 20% of predictions will be correct if the base rate is used.

It should be emphasized that there are different ways of quantifying one's clinical errors, and they will, of course, not all give the same evaluation when applied in a given setting. "Per cent valid positives" ($= p_1$) is rarely if ever meaningful without the correlated "per cent false positives" ($= p_2$), and clinicians are accustomed to the idea that we pay for an increase in the first by an increase in the second, whenever the increase is achieved not by an improvement in the test's intrinsic validity but by a shifting of the cutting score. But the two quantities p_1 and p_2 do not define our over-all hit frequency, which depends also upon the base rates P and Q. The three quantities p_1, p_2, and P do, however, contain all the information needed to evaluate the test with respect to any given sign or cutting score that yields these values. Although p_1, p_2, and P contain the relevant information, other forms of it may be of greater importance. No two of these numbers, for example, answer the obvious question most commonly asked (or vaguely implied) by psychiatrists when an inference is made from a sign, viz., "How sure can you be on the basis of that sign?" The answer to this eminently practical query involves a probability different from any of the above, namely, the *inverse* probability given by Bayes' formula:

$$H_P = \frac{Pp_1}{Pp_1 + Qp_2}.$$

Even a small improvement in the hit frequency to $H'_T = Pp_1 + Qq_2$ over the $H_T = P$ attainable without the test may be adjudged as worth while when the increment ΔH_T is multiplied by the N examined in the course of one year and is thus seen to involve a dozen lives or a dozen curable schizophrenics. On the other hand, the simple fact that an actual *shrinkage* in total hit rate may occur seems to be unappreciated or tacitly ignored by a good deal of clinical practice. One must keep constantly in mind that numerous diagnostic, prognostic, and dynamic statements can be made about almost all neurotic patients (e.g., "depressed," "inadequate ability to relate," "sexual difficulties") or about very few patients (e.g., "dangerous," "will act in therapy," "suicidal," "will blow up into a schizophrenia"). A psychologist who uses a test sign that even cross validates at $p_1 = q_2 = 80\%$ to determine whether "depression" is present or absent, working in a clinical population where practically everyone is fairly depressed except a few psychopaths and old-fashioned hysterics, is kidding himself, the psychiatrist, and whoever foots the bill.

"SUCCESSIVE-HURDLES" APPROACH

Tests having low efficiency, or having moderate efficiency but applied to populations having very unbalanced base rates ($P \ll Q$) are sometimes defended by adopting a "crude initial screening" frame of reference, and arguing that certain other procedures (whether tests or not) can be applied to the subset identified by the screener ("successive hurdles"). There is no question that in some circumstances (e.g., military induction, or industrial selection with a large labor market) this is a thoroughly defensible position. However, as a general rule one should examine this type of justification critically, with the preceding considerations in mind. Suppose we have a test which distinguishes brain-tumor from non-brain-tumor patients with 75% accuracy and no differential bias ($p_1 = q_2 = .75$). Under such circumstances the test hit rate H_T is .75 regardless of the base rate. If we use the test in making our judgments, we are correct in our diagnoses 75 times in 100. But suppose only one patient in 10 actually has a brain tumor, we will drop our over-all "success" from 90% (attainable by diagnosing "No tumor" in all cases) to 75%. We do, however, identify 3 out of 4 of the real brain tumors, and in such a case it seems worth the price. The "price" has two aspects to it: We take time to give the test, and, having given it, we call many "tumorous" who are not. Thus, suppose that in the course of a year we see 1000 patients. Of these, 900 are non-tumor, and we erroneously call 225 of these "tumor." To pick up (100) (.75) = 75 of the tumors, *all* 100 of whom would have been called tumor-free using the base rates alone, we are willing to mislabel 3 times this many as tumorous who are actually not. Putting it another way, whenever we say "tumor" on the basis of the test, the chances are 3 to 1 that we are mistaken. When we "rule out" tumor by the test, we are correct 96% of the time, an improvement of only 6% in the confidence attachable to a negative finding over the confidence yielded by the base rates.[4]

Now, picking up the successive-hurdles argument, suppose a major decision (e.g., exploratory surgery) is allowed to rest upon a second test which is infallible but for practically insuperable reasons of staff, time, etc., cannot be routinely given. We administer Test 2 only to "positives" on (screening) Test 1. By this tactic we eliminate all 225 false positives left by Test 1, and we verify the 75 valid positives screened in by Test 1. The 25 tumors that slipped through as false negatives on Test 1 are, of course, not picked up by Test 2 either, because it is not applied to them. Our total hit frequency is now 97.5%, since the only cases ultimately misclassified out of our 1000 seen are these 25 tumors which escaped through the initial sieve Test 1. We are still running only 7½% above the base rate. We have had to give our short-and-easy test to 1000 individuals and our cumbersome, expensive test to 300 individuals, 225 of whom turn out to be free of tumor. But we have located 75 patients with tumor who would not otherwise have been found.

Such examples suggest that, except in "life-or-death" matters, the successive-screenings argument merely tends to soften the blow of Bayes' Rule in cases where the base rates are very far from symmetry. Also, if Test 2 is not assumed to be infallible but only highly effective, say 90% accurate both ways, results start looking unimpressive again. Our net false positive rate rises from zero to 22 cases miscalled "tumor," and we operate 67 of the actual tumors instead of 75. The total hit frequency drops to 94.5%, only 4½% above that yielded by a blind guessing of the modal class.

THE SELECTION RATIO

Straightforward application of the preceding principles presupposes that the clinical decision maker is free to adopt a policy solely on the

[4] Improvements are expressed throughout this article as *absolute* increments in percentage of hits, because: (*a*) This avoids the complete arbitrariness involved in choosing between original hit rate and miss rate as starting denominator; and (*b*) for the clinician, the person is the most meaningful unit of gain, rather than a proportion *of* a proportion (especially when the reference proportion is very small).

basis of maximizing hit frequency. Sometimes there are external constraints such as staff time, administrative policy, or social obligation which further complicate matters. It may then be impossible to make all decisions in accordance with the base rates, and the task given to the test is that of selecting a subset of cases which are decided in the direction opposite to the base rates but will still contain fewer erroneous decisions than would ever be yielded by opposing the base rates without the test. If 80% of patients referred to a Mental Hygiene Clinic are recoverable with intensive psychotherapy, we would do better to treat everybody than to utilize a test yielding 75% correct predictions. But suppose that available staff time is limited so that we *can* treat only half the referrals. The Bayes-type injunction to "follow the base rates when they are better than the test" becomes pragmatically meaningless, for it directs us to make decisions which we cannot implement. The imposition of an *externally* imposed selection ratio, not determined on the basis of any maximizing or minimizing policy but by nonstatistical considerations, renders the test worth while.

Prior to imposition of any arbitrary selection ratio, the fourfold table for 100 referrals might be as shown in Table 8. If the aim were simply

TABLE 8. Actual and Test-Predicted Therapeutic Outcome

Test Prediction	Therapeutic Outcome		
	Good	Poor	Total
Good	60	5	65
Poor	20	15	35
Total	80	20	100

to minimize total errors, we would predict "good" for each case and be right 80 times in 100. Using the test, we would be right only 75 times in 100. But suppose a selection ratio of .5 is externally imposed. We are then forced to predict "poor" for half the cases, even though this "prediction" is, in any given case, likely to be wrong. (More precisely, we handle this subset *as if* we predicted "poor," by refusing to treat.) So we now select our 50 to-be-treated cases from among those 65 who fall in the "test-good" array, having a frequency of $60/65 = 92.3\%$ hits among those selected. This is better than the 80% we could expect (among those selected) by choosing half the total referrals at random. Of course we pay for this, by making many "false negative" decisions; but these are necessitated, whether we use the test or not, by the fact that the selection ratio was determined without regard for hit maximization but by external considerations. Without the test, our false negative rate q_1 is 50% (i.e., 40 of the 80 "good" cases will be called "poor");

the test reduces the false negative rate to 42.5% (= 34/80), since 15 cases from above the cutting line must be selected at random for inclusion in the not-to-be-treated group below the cutting line [i.e., 20 + (60/65) 15 = 34]. Stated in terms of correct decisions, without the test 40 out of 50 selected for therapy will have a good therapeutic outcome; with the test, 46 in 50 will be successes.

Reports of studies in which formulas are developed from psychometrics for the prediction of patients' continuance in psychotherapy have neglected to consider the relationship of the selection ratio to the specific population to which the prediction formula is to be applied. In each study the population has consisted of individuals who were *accepted for therapy* by the usual methods employed at an outpatient clinic, and the prediction formula has been evaluated *only* for such patients. It is implied by these studies that the formula would have the same efficiency if it were used for the *selection* of "continuers" from all those *applying* for therapy. Unless the formula is tested on a random sample of applicants who are allowed to enter therapy without regard to the test scores, its efficiency for selection purposes is unknown. The reported efficiency of the prediction formula in the above studies pertains only to its use in a population of patients who have already been selected for therapy. There is little likelihood that the formula can be used in any practical way for further selection of patients unless the clinic's therapists are carrying a far greater load than they plan to carry in the future.

The use of the term "selection" (as contrasted with "prediction" or "placement") ought not to blind us to the important differences between industrial selection and its clinical analogue. The incidence of false negatives—of potential employees screened out by the test who would actually have made good on the job if hired—is of little concern to management except as it costs money to give tests. Hence the industrial psychologist may choose to express his aim in terms of minimizing the false positives, i.e., of seeing to it that the job success *among those hired* is as large a rate as possible. When we make a clinical decision to treat or not to treat, we are withholding something from people who have a claim upon us in a sense that is much stronger than the "right to work" gives a job applicant any claim upon a particular company. So, even though we speak of a "selection ratio" in clinical work, it must be remembered that those cases *not selected* are patients about whom a certain kind of important negative decision is being made.

For any *given* selection ratio, maximizing total hits is always equivalent to maximizing the hit rate for either type of decision (or minimizing the errors of either, or both, kinds), since cases shifted from one cell of the table have to be exactly compensated for. If *m* "good" cases that were correctly classified by one decision method are incorrectly classified by another, maintenance of the selection ratio entails that m cases correctly called "poor" are also miscalled "good" by the new method. Hence an externally imposed selection ratio eliminates the often troublesome value questions about the relative seriousness of the two kinds of errors, since they are unavoidably increased or decreased at exactly the same rate.

If the test yields a score or a continuously varying index of some kind, the values of p_1 and p_2 are not fixed, as they may be with "patterns" or "signs." Changes in the selection ratio, R, will then suggest shifting the cutting scores or regions on the basis of the relations obtaining among R, P, and the p_1, p_2 combinations yielded by various cuts. It is worth special comment that, in the case of continuous distributions, the optimum procedure is *not* always to move the cut until the total area truncated $= NR$, selecting all above that cut and rejecting all those below. Whether this "obvious" rule is wise or not depends upon the distribution characteristics. We have found it easy to construct pairs of distributions such that the test is "discriminating" throughout, in the sense that the associated cumulative frequencies q_1 and q_2 maintain the same direction of their inequality everywhere in the range.

$$\left(\text{i.e., } \frac{1}{N_2}\int_{-\infty}^{x_i} f_2(x)\,dx > \frac{1}{N_1}\int_{-\infty}^{x_i} f_1(x)\,dx \text{ for all } x_i\right);$$

yet in which the hit frequency given by a single cut at R is inferior to that given by first selecting with a cut which yields $N_c < NR$, and then picking up the remaining $(NR - N_c)$ cases at random below the cut. Other more complex situations may arise in which different types of decisions should be made in different regions, actually reversing the policy as we move along the test continuum. Such numerical examples as we have constructed utilize continuous, unimodal distributions, and involve differences in variability, skewness, and kurtosis not greater than those which arise fairly often in clinical practice. Of course the utilization of any very complicated pattern of regions requires more stable distribution frequencies than are obtainable from the sample sizes ordinarily available to clinicians.

It is instructive to contemplate some of the moral and administrative issues involved in the practical application of the preceding ideas. It is our impression that a good deal of clinical research is of the "So—what?" variety, not because of defects in experimental design such as inadequate cross validation but because it is hard to see just what are the useful changes in decision making which could reasonably be expected to follow. Suppose, for example, it is shown that "duration of psychotherapy" is 70% predictable from a certain test. Are we prepared to propose that those patients whose test scores fall in a certain range should not receive treatment? If not, then is it of any real advantage therapeutically to "keep in mind" that the patient has 7 out of 10 chances of staying longer than 15 hours, and 3 out of 10 chances of staying less than that? We are not trying to poke fun at research, since presumably almost any lawful relationship stands a chance of being valuable to our total scientific comprehension some day. But many clinical papers are ostensibly inspired by practical aims, and can be given theoretical interpretation or fitted into any larger framework only with great difficulty if at all. It seems appropriate to urge that such "practical"-oriented investigations should be really *practical,* enabling us to see how our clinical decisions could rationally be modified in the light of the findings. It is doubtful how much of current work could be justified in these terms.

Regardless of whether the test validity is capable of improving on the base rates, there are some prediction problems which have practical import only because of limitations in personnel. What other justification is there for the great emphasis in clinical research on "prognosis," "treatability," or "stayability"? The very formulation of the predictive task as "maximizing the number of hits" already presuppose that we intend *not* to treat some cases; since if we treat all comers, the ascertainment of a bad prognosis score has no practical effect other than to discourage the therapist (and thus hinder therapy?). If intensive psychotherapy could be offered to all veterans who are willing to accept referral to a VA Mental Hygiene Clinic, would it be licit to refuse those who had the poorest outlook? Presumably not. It is interesting to contrast the emphasis on prognosis in clinical psychology with that in, say, cancer surgery, where the treatment *of choice* may still have a very low probability of "success," but is nevertheless carried out on the basis of that low probability. Nor does this attitude seem unreasonable, since no patient would refuse the best available treatment on the ground that even it was only 10% effective. Suppose a therapist, in the course of earning his living, spends 200 hours a year on nonimprovers by following a decision policy that also results in his unexpected success with one 30-year-old "poor bet." If this client thereby gains $16 \times 365 \times 40 = 233{,}600$ hours averaging 50% less anxiety during the rest of his natural life, it was presumably worth the price.

These considerations suggest that, with the expansion of professional facilities in the behavior field, the prediction problem will be less like that of industrial *selection* and more like that of *placement.* "To treat or not to treat" or "How treatable" or "How long to treat" would be replaced by "What *kind* of treatment?" But as soon as the problem is formulated in this way, the external selection ratio is usually no longer imposed. Only if we are deciding between such alternatives as classical analysis and, say, 50-hour interpretative therapy would such personnel limitations as can be expected in future years impose an arbitrary R.

But if the decision is between such alternatives as short-term interpretative therapy, Rogerian therapy, Thorne's directive therapy, hypnotic retraining, and the method of tasks (10, 16, 19), we could "follow the base rates" by treating every patient with the method known to have the highest success frequency among patients "similar" to him. The criteria of similarity (class membership) will presumably be multiple, both phenotypic and genotypic, and will have been chosen because of their empirically demonstrated prognostic relevance rather than by guesswork, as is current practice. Such an idealized situation also presupposes that the selection and training of psychotherapists will have become socially realistic so that therapeutic personnel skilled in the various methods will be available in some reasonable proportion to the incidence with which each method is the treatment of choice.

How close are we to the upper limit of the predictive validity of personality tests, such as was reached remarkably early in the development of academic aptitude tests? If the now-familiar ⅔ to ¾ proportions of hits against even-split criterion dichotomies are already approaching that upper limit, we may well discover that for many decision problems the search for tests that will significantly better the base rates is a rather unrewarding enterprise. When the criterion is a more circumscribed trait or symptom ("depressed," "affiliative," "sadistic," and the like), the difficulty of improving upon the base rates is combined with the doubtfulness about how valuable it is to have such information with 75% confidence anyhow. But this involves larger issues beyond the scope of the present paper.

AVAILABILITY OF INFORMATION ON BASE RATES

The obvious difficulty we face in practical utilization of the preceding formulas arises from the fact that actual quantitative knowledge of the base rates is usually lacking. But this difficulty must not lead to a dismissal of our considerations as clinically irrelevant. In the case of many clinical decisions, chiefly those involving such phenotypic criteria as overt symptoms, formal diagnosis, subsequent hospitalization, persistence in therapy, vocational or marital adjustment, and the numerous "surface" personality traits which clinicians try to assess, *the chief reason for our ignorance of the base rates is nothing more subtle than our failure to compute them.* The file data available in most installations having a fairly stable source of clientele would yield values sufficiently accurate to permit minimum and maximum estimates which might be sufficient to decide for or against use of a proposed sign. It is our opinion that this rather mundane taxonomic task is of much greater importance than has been realized, and we hope that the present paper will impel workers to more systematic efforts along these lines.

Even in the case of more subtle, complex, and genotypic inferences, the situation is far from hopeless. Take the case of some such dynamic attribution as "strong latent dependency, which will be anxiety-arousing as therapy proceeds." If this is so difficult to discern *even during intensive therapy* that a therapist's rating on it has too little reliability for use as a criterion, it is hard to see just what is the value of guessing it from psychometrics. If a skilled therapist cannot discriminate the personality characteristic after considerable contact with the patient, it is at least debatable whether the characteristic makes any practical difference. On the other hand, if it can be reliably judged by therapists, the determination of approximate base rates again involves nothing more complex than systematic recording of these judgments and subsequent tabulation. Finally, "clinical experience" and "common sense" must be invoked when there is nothing better to be had. Surely if the q_1/q_2 ratio for a test sign claiming validity for "difficulty in accepting inner drives" shows from the formula that the base rate must not exceed .65 to justify use of the sign, we can be fairly confident in discarding it for use with *any* psychiatric population! Such a "backward" use of the formula to obtain a maximum useful value of P, in conjunction with the most tolerant common-sense estimates of P from daily experience, will often suffice to answer the question. If one is really in complete ignorance of the limits within which P lies, then obviously no rational judgment as to the probable efficiency of the sign can be made.

ESTIMATION VERSUS SIGNIFICANCE

A further implication of the foregoing thinking is that the exactness of certain small sample statistics, or the relative freedom of certain nonparametric methods from distribution assumptions, has to be stated with care lest it mislead clinicians into an unjustified confidence. When an investigator concludes that a sign, item, cutting score, or pattern has "validity" on the basis of small sample methods, he has rendered a certain very broad null hypothesis unplausible. To decide, however, whether this "validity" warrants clinicians in using the test is (as every statistician would insist) a further and more complex question. To answer this question, we require more than knowledge that $p_1 \neq p_2$. We need in addition to know, with respect to each decision for which the sign is being proposed, whether the appropriate inequality involving p_1, p_2, and P is fulfilled. More than this, since we will usually be extrapolating to a somewhat different clinical population, we need to know whether altered base rates P' and Q' will falsify these inequalities. To do this demands *estimates* of the test parameters p_1 and p_2, the setting up of confidence belts for their difference $p_1 - p_2$ rather than the mere proof of their nonidentity. Finally, if the sign is a cutting score, we will want to consider shifting it so as to *maintain* optimal hit frequency with new base rates. The effect upon p_1 and p_2 of a contemplated movement of a critical score or band requires a knowledge of distribution form such as only a large sample can give.

As is true in all practical applications of statistical inference, nonmathematical considerations enter into the use of the numerical patterns that exist among P, p_1, p_2, and R. But "pragmatic" judgments initially require a separation of the several probabilities involved, some of which may be much more important than others in terms of the human values associated with them. In some settings, over-all hit rate is all that we care about. In others, a redistribution of the hits and misses even without much total improvement may concern us. In still others, the proportions p_1 and q_2 are of primary interest; and, finally, in some instances the confrontation of a certain increment in the absolute frequency (NPp_1) of one group identified will outweigh all other considerations.

Lest our conclusions seem unduly pessimistic, what constructive suggestions can we offer? We have already mentioned the following: (*a*) Searching for subpopulations with different base rates; (*b*) successive-hurdles testing; (*c*) the fact that even a very small *percentage* of improvement may be worth achieving in certain crucial decisions; (*d*) the need for systematic collection of base-rate data so that our several equations can be applied. To these we may add two further "constructive" comments. First, test research attention should be largely concentrated upon behaviors having base rates nearer a 50–50 split, since it is for these that it is easiest to improve on a base-rate decision policy by use of a test having moderate validity. There are, after all, a large number of clinically important traits which do not occur "almost always" or "very rarely." Test research might be slanted more toward them; the current popularity of *Q*-sort approaches should facilitate the growth of such an emphasis, by directing attention to items having a reasonable "spread" in the clinical population. Exceptions to such a research policy will arise, in those rare domains where the pragmatic consequences of the alternative decisions justify focusing attention almost wholly on maximizing Pp_1, with relative neglect of Qp_2. Secondly, we think the injunction "quit wasting time on noncontributory psychometrics" is really constructive. When the clinical psychologist sees the near futility of predicting rare or near-universal events and traits from test validities incapable of improving upon the base rates, his clinical time is freed for more economically defensible activities, such as research which will improve the parameters p_1 and p_2; and for *treating* patients rather than uttering low-confidence prophecies or truisms about them (in this connection see 12, pp. vii, 7, 127–128). It has not been our intention to be dogmatic about "what is worth finding out, how often." We do suggest that the clinical use of patterns, cutting scores, and signs, or research efforts devoted to the discovery of such, should always be evaluated in the light of the simple algebraic fact discovered in 1763 by Mr. Bayes.

SUMMARY

1. The practical value of a psychometric sign, pattern, or cutting score depends jointly upon its intrinsic validity (in the usual sense of its discriminating power) and the distribution of the criterion variable (base rates) in the clinical population. Almost all contemporary research reporting neglects the base-rate factor and hence makes evaluation of test usefulness difficult or impossible.

2. In some circumstances, notably when the base rates of the criterion classification deviate greatly from a 50 per cent split, use of a test sign having slight or moderate validity will result in an *increase* of erroneous clinical decisions.

3. Even if the test's parameters are precisely known, so that ordinary cross-validation shrinkage is not a problem, application of a sign within a population having these same test parameters but a different base rate may result in a marked change in the proportion of correct decisions. For this reason validation studies should present trustworthy information respecting the criterion distribution in addition to such test parameters as false positive and false negative rates.

4. Establishment of "validity" by exact small statistics, since it does not yield accurate information about the test parameters (a problem of estimation rather than significance), does not permit trustworthy judgments as to test usefulness in a new population with different or unknown base rates.

5. Formulas are presented for determining limits upon relations among (*a*) the base rates, (*b*) false negative rate, and (*c*) false positive rate which must obtain if use of the test sign is to improve clinical decision making.

6. If, however, external constraints (e.g., available staff time) render it administratively unfeasible to decide all cases in accordance with the base rates, a test sign may be worth applying even if following the base rates *would* maximize the total correct decisions, were such a policy possible.

7. Trustworthy information as to the base rates of various patient characteristics can readily be obtained by file research, and test development should (other things being equal) be concentrated on those characteristics having base rates nearer .50 rather than close to .00 or 1.00.

8. The basic rationale is that of Bayes' Theorem concerning the calculation of so-called "inverse probability."

REFERENCES

1. American Psychological Association, American Educational Research Association, and National Council on Measurements Used in Education, Joint Committee. Technical recommendations for psychological tests and diagnostic techniques. *Psychol. Bull.*, 1954, **51,** 201–238.
2. Anastasi, Anne, & Foley, J. P. *Differential psychology*. (Rev. Ed.) New York: Macmillan, 1949.
3. Bross, I. D. J. *Design for decision*. New York: Macmillan, 1953.
4. Danielson, J. R., & Clark, J. H. A personality inventory for induction screening. *J. clin. Psychol.*, 1954, **10,** 137–143.
5. Dorken, H., & Kral, A. The psychological differentiation of organic brain lesions and their localization by means of the Rorschach test. *Amer. J. Psychiat.*, 1952, **108,** 764–770.
6. Duncan, O. D., Ohlin, L. E., Reiss, A. J., & Stanton, H. R. Formal devices for making selection decisions. *Amer. J. Sociol.*, 1953, **58,** 573–584.
7. Glueck, S., & Glueck, Eleanor. *Unraveling juvenile delinquency*. Cambridge, Mass.: Harvard Univer. Press, 1950.
8. Goodman, L. A. The use and validity of a prediction instrument. I. A reformulation of the use of a prediction instrument. *Amer. J. Sociol.*, 1953, **58,** 503–509.
9. Hanvik, L. J. Some psychological dimensions of low back pain. Unpublished doctor's thesis, Univer. of Minnesota, 1949.
10. Herzberg, A. *Active psychotherapy*. New York: Grune & Stratton, 1945.
11. Horst, P. (Ed.) The prediction of personal adjustment. *Soc. Sci. Res. Coun. Bull.*, 1941, No. 48, 1–156.
12. Meehl, P. E. *Clinical versus statistical prediction*. Minneapolis: Univer. of Minnesota Press, 1954.
13. Reiss, A. J. Unraveling juvenile delinquency. II. An appraisal of the research methods. *Amer. J. Sociol.*, 1951, **57,** 115–120.
14. Rosen, A. Detection of suicidal patients: an example of some limitations in the prediction of infrequent events. *J. consult. Psychol.*, 1954, **18,** 397–403.
15. Rotter, J. B., Rafferty, J. E., & Lotsof, A. B. The validity of the Rotter Incomplete Sentences Blank: high school form. *J. consult. Psychol.*, 1954, **18,** 105–111.
16. Salter, A. *Conditioned reflex therapy*. New York: Creative Age Press, 1950.
17. Taulbee, E. S., & Sisson, B. D. Rorschach pattern analysis in schizophrenia: a cross-validation study. *J. clin. Psychol.*, 1954, **10,** 80–82.
18. Thiesen, J. W. A pattern analysis of structural characteristics of the Rorschach test in schizophrenia. *J. consult. Psychol.*, 1952, **16,** 365–370.
19. Wolpe, J. Objective psychotherapy of the neuroses. *S. African Med. J.*, 1952, **26,** 825–829.

30. Validity and Reliability: A Proposed More Basic Set of Concepts[1]

RAYMOND B. CATTELL

Cattell, in the final article of this unit, raises some penetrating criticisms of conventional ways of viewing reliability and validity. He suggests that mathematical psychometricians have "seemed lost in their labyrinthine fastnesses from logic, from common sense, and certainly from psychological perspective." His restructuring of the concepts is a reaction to that perceived limitation.

This article has probably not had as much impact on psychometricians as it deserves. Perhaps they have not seen the practical advantages of using his structure. Cattell's views are expressed more fully in some of his other works to which references are made at the end of this article. The one by Cattell and Tsjuioka (1964) is particularly valuable for readers with a factor analytic background.

By introducing more basic concepts, the miscellany of validities and reliabilities is reducible. Validity has 3 parameters—direct to circumstantial, concrete to conceptual, and natural to artifactual—generating 2^3 types. Factor (conceptual) validity is distinguishable by formula from factor trueness. Consistency, as a generic term, covers reliability, homogeneity, and transferability, respectively, across time, items, and people in the covariation chart. Reliability, formulable like validity in direct or indirect forms, gives a series of coefficients according to error sources controlled. Homogeneity likewise has several formulas distinguishing, e.g., test and factor homogeneity. Transferability, like other consistencies, requires both a correlation and an index of variance. Ideal tests have highest validity, reliability rivaling stability, but homogeneity at whatever lowly value maximizes validity and transferability.

NEED FOR REDEFINITION

So great has the variety of tests become—in regard to intelligence, achievement, personality, and motivation—that the chances of unsuitable choice are now disastrously high unless the psychologist obtains a high degree of clarity and sophistication in his conceptions of validity,

Cattell, R. B. Validity and reliability: A proposed more basic set of concepts. *Journal of Educational Psychology,* 1964, *55,* 1–22. Reprinted with the permission of the publisher and author.

[1] This investigation was supported by Public Health Service Research Grant MH 01723–17 from the National Institutes of Mental Health.

reliability, and other universal parameters by which tests are evaluated. The way in which these parameters were defined 20 years ago and the present habitual usages which derive from those definitions are now increasingly recognized to be misleading and provocative of inconsistent conclusions. This inadequacy and confusion becomes especially evident as testing extends from ability and achievement areas to the more subtle concepts required in personality and motivation measurement. The present article raises some basic issues, suggests powerful criticisms of conventional concepts, and gives the briefest possible summary of certain restructurings already partly developed elsewhere (Cattell, 1957a; Cattell & Butcher, in press).

The extraordinarily massive literature on this topic, running back 50 years and illuminated by such writers as Burt (1921, 1941), Spearman (1904, 1927), Kelley (1935), Thurstone (1945), Gulliksen (1950), Thorndike (1949), Guilford (1954), Coombs (1958), Edwards (1954), Woodrow (1932), Kuder and Richardson (1937), Cronbach and Gleser (1957), Loevinger (1947), Humphreys (1956), Lord (1953, 1959), Torgerson (1958), and Vernon (1953)—to mention just a few highlights—has never lacked statistical finesse and mathematical virtuosity. But to the general practicing psychologist, mathematical psychometricians have sometimes seemed lost in their labyrinthine fastnesses from logic, from common sense, and certainly from psychological perspective. In the interests of a return to perspective Cureton (1950) wrote, "Validity, reliability, and baloney," and the American Psychological Association (1954) set up a committee to stabilize definitions. The well-chosen eclectic character of this committee certainly avoided any failure to stabilize nomenclature at a popular, common denominator of meaning. Indeed, in the present writer's opinion it succeeded too well in stabilizing too soon a relatively naive stage of psychological opinion. Certain radical changes have accordingly now become necessary, as suggested below.

BASIC DIMENSIONS OF VALIDITY

Validity, in its broadest sense, will be defined by a widely accepted but penetrating phrase as the capacity of a test to predict some specified behavioral measure (or set of measures) other than itself. It is contended here that this test property admits always of further analysis along precisely three independent parameters or dimensions as follows.

Degree of Abstraction of the Referent Criterion. This dimension extends from *concrete* (or particular) at one pole to *conceptual* at the other. Correlation with a job skill, such as operating a lathe, illustrates the former; and concept validity as a measure of intelligence, anxiety, etc., illustrates the latter. It is particularly to meet the latter case that the expression "a set of measures" is included in the above definition. For a concept can usually only be defined by a whole pattern of measures (taken under defined conditions). This and the remaining two parameters are to be discussed more fully in separate sections below.

Degree of Naturalness of the Criterion. This extends from *natural* or in situ validity, as when correlations are made with some behavior (concrete) or abstraction from behavior (conceptual) which naturally occurs in or derives from our existing culture and environment, to *artifactual* validity at the other pole. Artifactual validity is validity against a criterion which would not naturally exist in our culture, but arises only among the instruments of psychologists, e.g.—in validating an intelligence test against the Binet—or some artificial, prescribed laboratory performance. The means of determining such a continuum is discussed below.

Degree of Directness of Validation. This extends from *direct* to *circumstantial* or *indirect*. In the simplest sense the validity of Test x as a good measure of Criterion X might seem sufficiently evidenced by the magnitude of its direct correlation with X. But in a deeper philosophical sense it depends also on x behaving toward "the not-X" universe in the same way as X does. Even at a simple statistical level it is evident that two (or more) tests might show exactly the same correlation with X and yet correlate in very different patterns from each other with the not-X variables. These differences affect the degree and kind of error which will follow when x is allowed to stand for X.

These validity dimensions will be discussed more fully in a moment. Meanwhile, one should note that, as in Figure 1, they are independent and thus create, if considered in their dichotomous bipolar nature, $2^3 = 8$ varieties or types of validity coefficients which must be exhaustive of all possibilities.

However, if the following discussion on the nature of the natural-artifactual dimension is correct, it is sufficiently less important (in the sense of being less relevant to most issues and more arbitrary) to justify basing the main classification on the other two. We thus have four main varieties of validity coefficient, for which the following nomenclature and denotation are suggested (see Figure 1).

1. Concrete-direct (or particular-direct) validity coefficient $r_{v(pd)}$
2. Conceptual-direct validity coefficient $r_{v(cd)}$
3. Conceptual-circumstantial (or indirect) validity coefficient $r_{v(ci)}$
4. Concrete-circumstantial validity coefficient $r_{v(pi)}$

If one wishes to include the natural-artifactual distinction too, an *n* or an *a* can be added as third letter in the above subscripts.

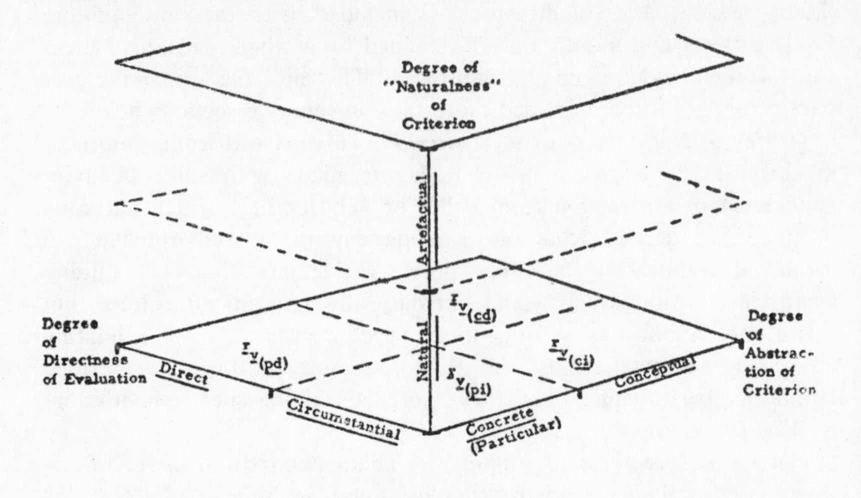

FIGURE 1. The eight validity coefficients from three dichotomous dimensions of validation.

FULLER IMPLICATIONS OF DIMENSIONS

Some further discussion is now necessary to bring out more fully the basic nature of these logical divisions.

Concrete versus Abstract or Particular versus Conceptual. The concrete-abstract continuum is so well known to philosophy, and so readily given operational reality, e.g., by a Spearman hierarchy of concrete fundaments with increasingly general relations built upon them, that minimal illustration is necessary. The correlation of a test with success as a lathe operator, or number of traffic parking offenses, or degree of stuttering, is a concrete particular validity. To assert that a test measures intelligence, or anxiety, on the other hand, is to claim for it an abstract or conceptual validity.

Concrete validities have perhaps hitherto had greater appeal, especially to practitioners, for two reasons. First, they appear more immediately useful; secondly, they can be calculated with lesser demands on theoretical and statistical sophistication. Despite a serious inferiority in concrete validities, shortly to be mentioned, one can actually sympathize with the educational and industrial psychologists' preference for a concrete or "particular" validity, as one contemplates the vague, verbal, and evasive nature of many definitions of conceptual validity. The latter situation has led some psychologists, unfortunately, to conclude that one must abandon operations in accepting concept or construct[2] validity. This is by no means an inevitable conclusion. Indeed any concept worthy of the name, in the domain of psychological theory, *must* be reducible to operations. Commonly it will be reducible, however, to a *pattern* of operations, not to a single measurement operation. Such a pattern is most commonly made available, e.g., as a set of factor loadings, such as defines the weighting of battery components in an intelligence or anxiety test, or in the weights of a discriminant function maximally distinguishing two known types.

Indeed, the very popularity of concrete validities is liable to bring confusion in its train, for different psychologists will often use a particular test with an eye to quite different criteria, e.g., the Rorschach is preferred by one for diagnosing schizophrenia and by another as an indicator of suicidal tendencies. Most tests correlate significantly with several concrete criteria which are then perhaps better called "referents" until psychologists agree to call *one* the criterion. Otherwise it does not make sense to talk about *the* validity of a test (as a concrete validity; as a concept validity there is no problem). And it makes sense to talk about a *single and concrete* criterion only for *special* purpose and not *general* purpose tests (Cattell, 1957a). (Indeed, a special purpose test is *defined* by its being oriented to one concrete criterion.) But a general purpose test, e.g., an intelligence or personality test, is not intended to correlate exclusively with any one of the millions of possible concrete criteria, but strictly with a concept which naturally relates to *many* concrete expressions. The operational, experimental definition of concept validity is taken up in the following section.

Natural versus Artifactual. This also needs little discussion, except to point out that the cheapness of validating one test against another has made artifactual (and concrete) validation altogether too prevalent. Although we have agreed here, in the interests of comprehensiveness, to admit that "criterion" can be applied to an artificial test or specific laboratory situation performance, let us not forget that psychological testing has its very raison d'être in predicting real-life behavior! Some may raise the objection to this dimension, *as* a dimension, that there may be arbitrariness in deciding what is natural and what artificial, since the whole of culture may be called "art," and psychology is a part of it. A clear line can nevertheless be drawn if we remember that the artifact we are talking about here is psychology. The rest of culture is as much a part of nature to us as it is to the anthropologist or the

[2] Concept and construct validity are used interchangeably here. The reasons for ultimately preferring concept validity for the more common "construct" validity are given below.

sociologist. "Ability to adjust in the classroom," or "freedom from automobile accidents" are natural criteria belonging to the natural history of our general culture. Correlation with the AB Inventory of Self-Derogation or the Picayune Intelligence Scale, on the other hand, is an artificial, though well-fixed, criterion.

Except as an academic gain, or as a preliminary check, or as an unavoidable short cut to avoid the greater labor of going to real-life criteria, concrete artifactual validity, against a concept "surrogate," is surely something which the research minded psychologist will commonly avoid. Furthermore, it has actually tended to bring reverence for a false "apostolic succession," as when a new intelligence test, say, is validated against the Wechsler Adult Intelligence Scale, which was validated against the Stanford, which was validated against the Binet. One does not validate a modern caesium clock against Big Ben, and Big Ben against a medieval water clock! Concept validity avoids this excessive reverence for the past, demanding in each field an onward movement with the increasing accuracy of the concept per se. This criticism obviously does not suggest, therefore, rejecting the convenience of transferring a concept from behavior actually in situ in the life environment if it can be accurately re-represented, as a *factor,* in some defined laboratory behavior. Hence artifactual conceptual validity, with proper proof of the factor, is on a different footing.

Direct versus Circumstantial. Until recently (Beloff & Cattell, 1962) all validation definitions had been conceived only in the "direct" sense. Some philosophical reflection will show that there exists also a neglected realm of indirect or circumstantial validation which has the virtue of being independent of, and supplementary to, the familiar realm of direct validation. Circumstantial, incidentally, is probably a better term than indirect, for it connotes the positive aspect of the procedure: the operational relating of the test to *many* required anchors in the surroundings instead of one. It also reminds us of its generic affiliation to "circumstantial evidence" in the law courts.

Its definition can best be approached by an actual illustration. In the task of validating the 14 personality source trait scales in the High School Personality Questionnaire (HSPQ; Beloff & Cattell, 1962). In HSPQ, as well as the Child Personality Questionnaire (Porter & Cattell, 1960), both direct and circumstantial validities were calculated. The former consisted of determining the correlation of the actual scale for, say, intelligence, ego strength, or surgency, with the pure factor measure for each, as discussed a few paragraphs below, and in accordance with the usual theory of validation. The latter consisted in asking, "How far do the correlations of the (say) Surgency scale with a representative array of other dimensions from the personality realm (in this case 13 other factors) match the correlations of the *pure surgency factor* with these other factors in the realm?" The validity calculation thus requires that we compare, by a suitable statistic, one pattern of 13 correlations with another pattern of 13 correlations. (Actually the pattern similarity coefficient, r_p, was the statistic preferred by us here to any simple correlation of the two series of correlations.)

The rationale of such a procedure can be shown by reference to legal procedure; procedures in other sciences; and, last but not least, symbolic logic. If Mr. X in this country is suspected to be identical with a Mr. Y who disappeared from another country, one not only compares the fingerprints and photographs for a direct match, but also seeks the circumstantial evidence of a disappearance in one place corresponding to an appearance in another, of a similarity in size of bank accounts, of a similar occupation, size of family, and of role relation to this and that. Or the identity of two chemicals independently isolated may be tested not only by similarity of crystalline form, melting point, and molecular weight, but also by the fact that they can be derived from Substance A, converted by similar operations into B, and made to interact with C, D, etc., in similar ways. In bare logic we are saying that the proof of degree of resemblance of Y to X resides not only in direct similarity measures but also in measures of similarity of their relation to the universe of not-X. Naturally, one will want strategically to *sample* the landmarks of the not-X to make such a calculation.

The correlations of Scale A with the pure Factor A, Scale B with B, etc., should theoretically run parallel to the magnitudes of their indirect validities as calculated from the similarities of their patterns of correlations with other factors. When the validity reaches unity by one it will be unity by the other, and although any given direct validity short of unity is compatible with a whole set of different correlations with other factors, the degree of agreement of the criterion set and the test scale set should, with a proper statistic, remain roughly parallel. The value of circumstantial validity does not lie in contributing algebraic independence—indeed one would not want algebraic independence rather than a proper functional relation of the formulas for the concepts—but in the *experimental* independence of the evidence, and, very secondarily, in a computational independence. It is implied in a good circumstantial validity that the surrounding universe is systematically sampled, in a defined way; for example, *all* other known personality factors were used in the above HSPQ validation. This first use yielded what had been theoretically expected, namely, a good agreement of indirect and direct validity evaluations. The assumptions about the reliability of the pure factor used in these calculations are discussed at the end of the following section.

NEW ORGANIZATION OF CONCEPTS VIEWED IN RELATION TO CURRENT TERMS

As indicated above, the notion of concept validity is approximately the same as APA (1954) committee's construct validity. Let us examine what advantages are claimed for reformulating as concept validity, both as a theoretical element in terms of assumptions and of operations for its measurement.

First, there is an unnecessary limitation and inaptness in the term construct. Most commonly, in epistemology and logic the latter becomes synonymous with an "empirical construct." As such it dares not have theoretical parentage or be enriched by an ideational content or extra meaning beyond that given by its derivation as a complex of relationships among a set of empirical observations. When a psychologist speaks of, say, intelligence, anxiety, neuroticism, or the self-sentiment, he is generally interested in a whole set of theoretical relations which go therewith, in virtue of which it is properly called a concept. To deny him the right to operate with this concept in the measurement field and to insist that he deal with a mere construct is to perpetuate that divorce of psychological theory from psychometric practice which has so long been unquestionably disastrous to both. On the one hand it has permitted a rank growth of spurious theory, too vague and overelaborated to be useful as scientific theory (see Wepman & Heine, 1963), and, on the other, it has left us with a purely statistical psychometry too dryly pointless to grip the attention of a psychologist with broad conceptual interests.

If theory and experiment are to get together, we should better be talking about concept validity, for indeed, no theoretical concept worthy of the name need lack translation into measurement operations, if they are sufficiently imaginative. Any concept of course is still a man-made model not "something in nature," but hopefully it can yield a pretty close fit to something in nature. What has been lacking hitherto has been the discipline and ingenuity to recognize that nearly all concepts (*a*) *can* be expressed as measurement derivatives, and (*b*) *cannot* be defined by any single operation, but require a whole pattern of measurement and control operations.

It behoves us to make a closer examination of the ways in which a concept may be brought into the measurement field. The concepts used by psychologists, or, indeed most scientists, are tied down in any of four ways:

1. By a pattern of stated conditions either of logical, theoretical, or an inductive empirical nature. However, especially with the former, it is easily possible to define something which does not exist—like the medieval unicorn—or could not exist. For example, a geographical theorist

could, like Columbus, define his concept of a land 2,000 miles west of Spain and 1,000 miles east of India—an impossible position—or define a long sought island as having four straight sides, five headlands, a tropical climate, and a latitude of 80° south. Many psychological concepts, e.g., of anxiety, the authoritarian personality, the self-realized personality, etc., etc., against which the definers would validate a test, are not demonstratedly better than these.

2. By type concepts. These are essentially empirical constructs. Once types are demonstrated to exist as real person-clusters in test hyperspace, such devices as the multiple-discriminant function or Eysenck's (1950) criterion rotation can be used to find how validly a given test measures the type difference. (For a fuller definition see Cronbach & Gleser, 1953; McQuitty, 1954; Rao, 1952; Tsujioka & Cattell, in press.)

3. By homogeneous clusters. As in Method 2 the concept has the status of an empirical construct. A correlation cluster or surface trait, though often popularly used as a criterion, suffers from the intrinsic disability, long recognized (Cattell, 1946), that cluster "identity" is impossible to establish, changing with choice of variables, positions of other clusters, changing variance of factors across samples, etc.

4. By a factor concept when the factor is uniquely revealed (by simple structure, Thurstone, 1947; or confactor rotation, Cattell, 1962) as a single influence. In Methods 1, 2, and 3 the danger is very real that one's concept, whatever other defects it may have, will also have the defect of being a mixture of two or more entities. For example, validating an anxiety scale by Method 2 as "that which most distinguishes neurotics from normals" produces a mixture of anxiety with characterological peculiarities of neurotics (Cattell & Scheier, 1961). The great majority of psychological concepts can, provided one thinks out a suitable experimental design, be tied down as unitary simple-structure factors. (Parenthetically, one should note that a factor is not only from correlating across people, but may be a pattern concept across all manner of entries in the basic data relation matrix—Cattell, in press b.) From cross reference among experiments a factor normally has additional meaning beyond the immediate construct, and correlation of test with factor thus constitutes quite the best basis for concept validation.

It is sometimes objected to a conceptual, as opposed to a concrete, criterion that it is not itself perfectly reliable. There are two misunderstandings in this comparison. (*a*) A concrete criterion is also rarely completely reliable—e.g., a 1-week output on a lathe is particular enough, and could be considered perfectly reliable as such, but it is rarely that what we are really interested in is the output specifically for the week beginning January 4, 1959. Our criterion is an average week's output, and this we have only estimated, *not* accurately measured, as the criterion. (*b*) A factor (and, *mutatis mutandem,* any other operational root of a concept) is unreliable if it is *estimated*, but not if the test-factor correlation is ascertained by an actual factor analysis. In the latter we deal with the unit length (full variance) factor, and this is a perfect measure even when the actual sample of tests used is not capable of perfectly estimating it. True, there may remain the unreliability of imperfect rotation, but if the rotation position is accepted, our conceptual criterion is fully reliable.

The above argument for an ensuing better integration of psychometrics with personality theory and general psychological theory is the main basis for preferring the concept of concept validity to that of construct validity, proposed as a label by the APA committee. However, the points just made about superior stability, consistency, etc., of factor concepts also have their weight. Moreover, the whole recent trend of psychometrics, away from merely itemetric standards, e.g., of homogeneity, etc., and from artificial scales, to scales based on structural psychometrics (Cattell & Tsujioka, in press) is in line with this development toward concept validities as opposed to narrow, concrete validities.

Now in the APA committee report and elsewhere a motley list of "validity" terms is in use over and above the basic senses given above. The objection to these is that some of them are not validity at all, while others are better and more accurately conceived as *utility* coefficients (Cattell, in press a) than validity coefficients. In this list one finds face validity, content validity, predictive versus concurrent validity, fiat validity, semantic validity, and many more.

Face validity would perhaps require nothing but a requiem and a sigh of relief were it not that wishful thinking is too deep in psychologists' reasoning to be so easily eradicated. For example, the belief that by looking at tests you can tell what they measure has recently cropped up again in Campbell and Fiske's (1959) multitrait-multimethod conception and Guttman's "facet analysis." (An open-minded search for distinguishable instrument factors, Cattell, 1961, and real factors is the present writer's alternative to these current assumptions. It is merely setting up a straw problem if one decides, by choosing tests for face validity, what facets, respectively corresponding to alleged traits and methods, shall be *made* to appear in the structural analysis.) Face validity is part of the callow denial that "there are more things in heaven and earth than are dreamt of in our philosophy." What element of truth exists in this general area really belongs to a logical, distinct, and usable procedure of allocating *semantic* validity (see below). In some trivial sense face or faith validity perhaps still has a role, but in diplomacy rather than psychology, as when an industrial psychologist is pressured to make tests which a chief executive will, from the depths of his ignorance, commend or sanction as measuring what he conceives to be this or that trait. From the standpoint of good test construction, on the other hand, the less face validity one leaves in the items the less fakable the test.

Content validity surely scarcely deserves a separate term, being a special case of face validity in the achievement or interest field. The idea that an achievement test must be valid if its items have the right content looks at first like an objective foundation, but without other validity criteria one is still on shifting sands. This will be evident if one asks what the content of a history test would be when variously made up by, say, H. G. Wells, Toynbee, Karl Marx, and Henry Ford. A concrete validity against a specific, named textbook or curriculum is perhaps the only firm meaning immediately available for validity here. Fiat validity, a term more used by test critics than test constructors, is also a form of face validity, but rightly distinguishes the face validity which is self-evident only to the one or two people who made the test. It is exemplified when a psychologist tells us that "need for achievement," or "creativity," etc., are measured by this particular uncorrelated, unfactored, open-ended test which only specially, locally trained people can score correctly.

If by semantic validity we mean that it is appropriate to attach the term "intelligence" or "anxiety" to a clearly defined factor or set of factors found among many behaviors which, *according to the dictionary,* fall in the general area of intelligent or anxious manifestations, one need take no exception to it. It is purely a matter of suitability of name when the identity of the concept is already fixed by a factor or related real pattern, and is better called semantic appropriateness rather than validity. However, since language shifts, it is always best to tie such a clearly located pattern concept also to an index number in an appropriate series (Cattell, 1957a, 1957b). This proposal for a universal index, to escape semantic contamination and drift, is still not taken seriously by as high a proportion of psychologists as, say, chemists and physicists. This is why discussion on theory by the latter succeeds in being brief and to the point, being tied to exact symbols and indexes. Without embarking on the vast sea presented by the philosophy of meaning one can, however, recognize that rating studies, for example, are from the beginning floating on a tide of cultural drift, unless carefully operationalized. This is a second, distinct sense of semantic validity, again perhaps better thought of merely as defining the semantic referent of a behavior.

Still in the service of pruning away unnecessary verbiage in validity terms let us examine the APA proposal for assigning distinct values (and meanings) for what it is suggested we call the concurrent and predictive validities of any particular test. Information regarding the relative power of tests to give us future prediction is of interest, but it is confused thinking which considers this a property of the test rather than of the trait. It is an unfortunate terminology also because the term "predictive" has long ceased in science to apply specifically to a calculation projected into the future. (Can you predict from the atomic weight of an element its impermeability to X rays?) But, even if we are referring to the future, the correlation of a test now with a criterion next year has a host of determinants among which the properties of the test may well be insignificant. The terms repeat the same mistake of confusing test and trait properties, which is made in the reliability field (see below), when a stability coefficient is not distinguished from a dependability coefficient.

Let us suggest that the capacity of a test to help in an estimate of remote future behavior is better conceived under the broader notion of the *scientific utility* (Cattell, in press a) of a test. It is certainly not the test property of validity as such. For example, the trait Surgency versus Desurgency—F in the Sixteen Personality Factor Questionnaire—is known to change rapidly with age (rising to a high level in adolescence) and to fluctuate with daily success and failure, etc. The trait of Cyclothymia versus Schizothymia (Factor A), on the other hand, is more stable. The predictive validity of the Surgency versus Desurgency (F) scale could, therefore, easily be raised by contaminating it with Factor A, which happens to have several specific behaviors, e.g., sociability, in common with it. *Future* prediction, after all, requires knowledge of the natural history of the trait, the laws of psychology, and (not least!) the changing life situations, e.g., the stock exchange, which will affect the individual in the interim. If only, say, a tenth, of the variance in estimates of that future behavior is tied to test validity variance, it is absurd to use that behavior to calculate an alleged property of predictive validity in a test.

THREE PILLARS OF TEST CONSISTENCY

It will be evident in a moment that reversing the usual order of discussing reliability before validity is not mere whimsy. In what is generally called reliability the innovations to be proposed cover first that involved by the introduction of the generic, supraordinate term—*test consistency*—to express the test's *total consistency along all dimensions of the covariation chart*. Within this we recognize the three distinct forms of consistency presented by *reliability, homogeneity,* and *transferability*. Let us examine these separately leaving until later the derivation and definition of some single index corresponding to a test's total consistency.

The covariation chart (Cattell, 1946) was proposed as a comprehensive scheme to bring order into the handling of the sources of variance commonly combined in any actual psychological measurements, regardless of whether the further statistical treatment of these measures is to be by correlation, analysis of variance, or less common methods. Its function has been to remind one of the diversity of sources of variance and therefore of the full diversity of possible relational concepts. (For example, in the present context of interest it reminds one that reliabilities are possible also for stimuli, persons, administrators, scorers, etc., as well as tests.) In its first form (Cattell, 1946) Cartesian coordinates were erected for three sets only, consisting of (*a*) people, (*b*) tests, and (*c*) occasions (or conditions). On this basis, the possible variance analyses and the possible correlational techniques (*P, Q, R,* etc.) were systematically examined. It turned out that in the light of the total number of relations possible in this parallelopiped, several possible kinds of analyses had never been experimentally realized. Since then the notion has been generalized more widely in the concept of the basic data relation matrix (BDRM or "data box") to include, at a first argument (Cattell, 1957a), 5 coordinates (namely, people, stimuli, responses, observers, and background conditions) and, on deeper analysis (Cattell, in press b), 10, made up by adding "states" for each of the 5 original patterns. But the simplified three-dimensional system seems still to suffice for the *main* problems of psychological test analysis and is best used for illustration here.

Just as the covariation chart performed the service in factor analysis of bringing out research designs (*P, O, S,* and *T* techniques) not previously tried, so here it reveals that there are really *three* possible senses

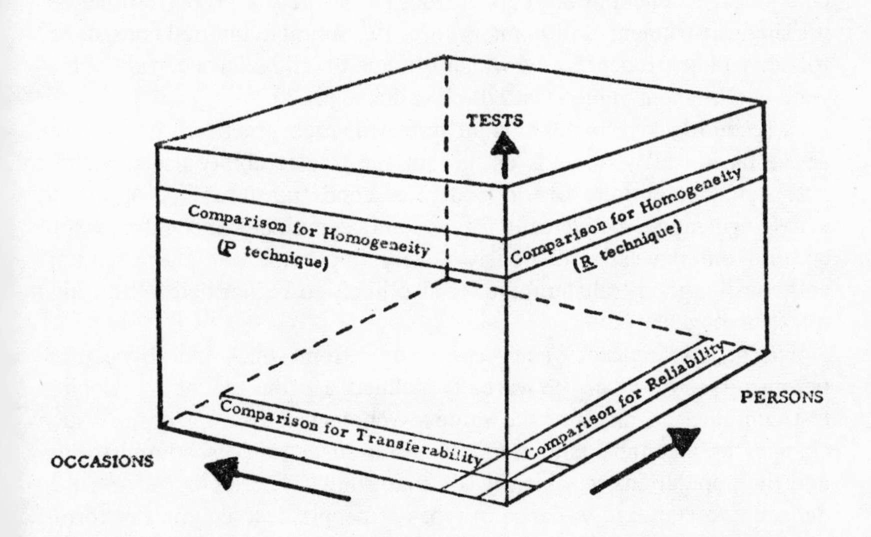

FIGURE 2. Derivation of forms of consistency from BDRM. (A *P* technique reliability and a transferability in the second sense of the text cannot be shown in this diagram without elaborations.)

in which the consistency or generalizability of a test needs to be evaluated, viz.:

1. Across occasions. The agreement of scores on the same test applied to the same people on different occasion conditions. This we shall call its reliability.

2. Across tests. The agreement on the same occasion and the same people of different subsets (or, commonly, single items) in the same test. This agreement among parts of a test (or battery) designed to measure some one thing we shall call its homogeneity.

3. Across people. The agreement in score meaning of the same test applied (on the same kind of occasion condition) to different sets of people we shall call its transferability (or *hardiness,* in the sense of a plant withstanding changes of climate).

Before proceeding to infer the proper operations for measuring these, a word can be said in a general way about their relations. In the first place we pay a heavy price, in terms of testing inefficiency, for mistaking homogeneity for reliability. Indeed, it is frequently indifferently *designated* reliability. A high reliability is almost always desirable, but homogeneity should be low or high depending on purpose and test structure. A good test, like a good engine, may perform its function best when its parts are differentiated. Whether water is better raised by a homogeneous sponge or a nonhomogeneous pump depends on the specific purpose. The aim of good test design is surely a properly functioning single instrument, and in many cases the optimum internal consistency for such an instrument is one which is made to fall *below* a certain homogeneity coefficient value (Cattell & Tsujioka, 1963).

A second lack in much current test evaluation practice, of which the above basic trinity reminds us, is that the transferability aspect of test consistency is entirely overlooked. Yet good transferability of a test, across age ranges convenient for use and commonly encountered subcultural differences, is obviously a very important test property. Parenthetically, good transferability is also likely to be harmed by too high a test homogeneity.

The generic concept of *test consistency* from which the above three parameters derive can be verbally defined as: the extent to which a test continues to measure the same psychological concept despite such changes as inevitably and normally occur in a test, its administration and the populations to which it is administered. These changes must be defined as a standard variance in types of people, test lengths and forms, and common conditions of administration and scoring. It will be noted that the word "normally," and the added clause, define a distribution and sigma for each of the universe parameters—people, tests, and circumstances. In other words, published consistency values, to be helpful, must be known to apply to a defined, typical variability in populations of people, test elements, and occasion conditions *not* to some egregious, artificial, laboratory changes of condition or to inflated ranges of performance, etc., such as often determine published test parameters in handbooks.

Since it is usual to consider the value of test reliability (in the older sense, which we are now proposing should more broadly be called *consistency*) in terms of the effect of an error variance contribution, let us note that the same *experimental error of measurement* would be considered in relation to each of the three distinct real variances in the covariation chart if we were talking of reliability over people, over occasions, and over tests. However, the concept of test consistency does not have this unity of reference; it refers to error of measurement in reliability, difference of test parts in homogeneity, and population-structural differences in transferability. Furthermore, the sampling error of obtained coefficients will arise in each of the three forms of consistency from a different source, and require principles peculiar to each. Thus our estimate of the true *reliability* will be affected by a sampling *of people and occasions;* of the true *homogeneity* by sampling of *items* (or *test elements*) and *people,* and of the true *transferability* across populations by the sampling of *people* from various cultures and occasions.

OPERATIONAL MEASUREMENT OF THE CHIEF RELIABILITY COEFFICIENTS

Although it has been usual to think of consistency as the agreement of a test *with itself,* when two series of measures are taken, one should consider the possibility that a theoretically better (if practically more difficult) notion is the agreement of both testings with a third, external standard. We might then ask "How far does the test continue to measure the same psychological concept?" instead of the familiar "How far does it literally continue to agree with itself in score?" This integrates consistency more closely with validity, which is our reason for here inverting, as stated, the usual order of presentation, by considering validity before reliability instead of vice versa.

Numerically we should, in any case, get somewhat different results from such a shift, because the degree to which a test agrees with itself is not necessarily exactly parallel to the extent to which it retains constancy of validity, though it is roughly parallel. Magnitude of change of factor composition and measured departure from perfect self-correlation are exactly parallel only *if we include within the factor composition change, the change on the contaminating, unwanted factors as well as the wanted, validating factor.* But validity, as such, definitely refers only to the test's amount of the wanted factor and takes no account of the nature of the contamination. Consequently, it is a matter for choice in definition whether, when we come to consistency, we want to ask about consistency only in the amount of the wanted factor but also in the nature and amounts of the unwanted common and specific factors. Since the treatment here is only an introduction to the new concepts and has no space for these special issues, our first treatment of reliability handles the "third referent" approach to consistency in terms of the usual concept of self-agreement, i.e., of both wanted and unwanted factors remaining constant.

With this statement of principle the present section will now develop specifically the reliability aspect of consistency. At the outset let us be reminded that although psychologists commonly think of *correlation coefficients* as expressing validity and reliability, the full evaluation of consistency should actually include three indexes, respectively, to express the retention (across whatever change of testing is involved) of, (*a*) rank order of subjects (or occasions) by correlation, (*b*) the mean score, and (*c*) the standard deviation of scores. If indexes are to be used, the last two are most simply expressed as reciprocals of the variance across groups of the mean and sigma in standard score units. Completely ignoring the last two, as is commonly done with reliability coefficients, is surely justifiable only in quite special circumstances. If one wishes, however, to take cognizance of all three in a single index rather than with separate precision, then the use of the pattern similarity coefficient, r_p (Cattell, 1949), with ipsatized scores would avoid some of the inadequacy of the correlation coefficient, r.[3]

Reliability is a subconcept within consistency. But it can itself be divided into several subtypes, and in practical psychological test evaluation it is extremely important to recognize their differences and to refer to them correctly by specific terms. The types derive from inclusion of varying combinations of conceivable sources of error variances. Actually, there is little point, however, in employing ideationally conceivable sources of error when we cannot also operationally isolate them. On this basis of operational realism some six different reliability coefficients (and corresponding mean and sigma constancy measures) have been defined elsewhere (Cattell, 1957a) with a suggestion for

[3] In passing, let us glance back at the covariation chart and notice that consistency in its reliability and homogeneity senses will obviously always have a double basis of evaluation. For example, the correlation among parts of a test (or items) can be carried out for one occasion over a series of people, or for one person over a series of occasions. Commonly the former is alone implied and calculated, yet it is also an essential feature of the concept of homogeneity that the parts shall cohere over different settings and occasions and ideally we should publish two homogeneity coefficients and similar twin coefficients for other consistencies. Figure 2 can conveniently show this double sense only for homogeneity, but reliability can also be calculated for *P* technique, as when one readministers a test to the subject within a few minutes, each day, for 100 days and correlates the two series obtained over 100 occasions (see Equation 8).

specific titles. But these are only a few of the possible, even if we restrict to the *R* technique relation alone. However, if one confines consideration to what are in factual experience the main sources of retest variability, one can perhaps advantageously cut down to even three, namely, (*a*) that which estimates unreliability due to having different test administrators; (*b*) that evaluating unreliability due to different scorers; and (*c*) that expressing the unreliability due to the remaining, unknown and uncontrollable conditions of the subjects' decision in the test and its situation. This is the unreliability remaining when the same administrator and same scorer handle the retesting.

From considering these three sources of error, in relation to the true score variance, one issues with a total of five conceptual variances as symbolized in Equation 1. Actually the three error terms could be combined in ${}^3C_3 + {}^3C_2 + {}^3C_1 = 7$ ways, each defining a distinct and worthwhile type of reliability coefficient. However, probably only three of these—which can be called the *dependability* (immediate retest), *administrative* reliability (across administrators), and the *conspection* (across scorers) coefficients—are of major importance and justify sufficient description and definition here. Let us first state the basic model of uncorrelated true and error variances, as follows:

$$\sigma_o^2 = \sigma_t^2 + \sigma_s^2 + \sigma_a^2 + \sigma_e^2 \qquad [1]$$

where,

σ_o^2 = variance of observed scores
σ_t^2 = variance of true scores
σ_s^2 = variance due to errors by scorers
σ_a^2 = variance due to errors by administrators
σ_e^2 = variance due to other, unassignable and ineradicable errors.

The *dependability* reliability coefficient just listed, has been defined as that obtained by an essentially *immediate* retest (using the same administrator and scorer).

$$r_{r(d)} = 1 - \frac{\sigma_e^2}{\sigma_o^2} = 1 - \frac{\sigma_e^2}{\sigma_t^2 + \sigma_e^2} \qquad [2]$$

Obviously this is a correct statement of the meaning of the immediate test-retest coefficient only if there are no learning, no error in scoring and no difference in administration. That is to say, we assume the test is a perfectly *conspect reliable* test, i.e., without scoring error, as obtainable, e.g., through using selective answer, key scored designs. Otherwise, the *actual* immediate retest coefficient (the test allowing no learning) would result from σ_s^2 being added to both numerator and denominator at the right.

The *conspection reliability coefficient* has been defined as the agreement usually found between two different scorers (from *con* and *spectare,* to observe together). If we choose to define it as that obtained when they are given the *same* batch of completed tests (from a single administrator, of course), then the observed variance nevertheless already contains experimental error, and the coefficient is written:

$$r_{r(c)} = 1 - \frac{\sigma_s^2}{\sigma_o^2} = 1 - \frac{\sigma_s^2}{\sigma_t^2 + \sigma_s^2 + \sigma_e^2} \quad [3]$$

The value obtained for $r_{r(c)}$ would typically be unity for a *fully* conspective test, e.g., a multiple-choice, carefully stencil marked test, but much less for tests like the Rorschach and the Thematic Apperception Test.

The administrative reliability coefficient shows the extent of agreement between two different administrators (and like the conspection coefficient would best be averaged over several typical pairs of administrators). Its value is:

$$r_{r(a)} = 1 - \frac{\sigma_a^2}{\sigma_o^2} = 1 - \frac{\sigma_a^2}{\sigma_t^2 + \sigma_a^2 + \sigma_e^2} \quad [4]$$

Like Equation 3 it can only be obtained by secondary calculation, not directly, because we wish to isolate the error due to σ_a^2 from that due also to σ_e^2. The manner in which these derived coefficients can be secondarily calculated from the directly experimentally calculated administrative and dependability coefficients will be readily seen from the algebra necessary to isolate the variance components.

A fourth coefficient which is frequently classed with the reliability coefficients, but does not actually belong there, or, indeed, with the true test consistency coefficients *at all,* is the *stability* coefficient. Measured simply as the correlation between a test and itself, readministered (same administrator and scorer) after an appreciable time interval, it may be called the *uncorrected* stability coefficient and has the constitution in Equation 5.

$$r_{s(r)} = 1 - \frac{\sigma_f^2 + \sigma_e^2}{\sigma_o^2} = 1 - \frac{\sigma_f^2 + \sigma_e^2}{\sigma_t^2 + \sigma_e^2} \quad [5]$$

(Re the denominator, see Equation 6.) It will be noted that we have refrained from symbolizing this as a reliability coefficient, $r_{(r)}$, because what is usually the greater part of its "unreliability" (namely, σ_f^2) is a *function fluctuation* (or what Woodrow, 1932, called "quotidian variability"—when diurnal) of the trait itself, *not* unreliability of the test. In fact, since the uncorrected stability coefficient reflects a mixture of trait and test qualities it would be quite fallacious to conclude that a low stability value shows a test to be of poor consistency.[4]

[4] An illustration of the substantial difference may be given in connection with what is known to be a relatively factor-pure anxiety scale (Scheier & Cattell, 1963). With this IPAT scale the $r_{s(r)}$ for medical students retested after a 2-year interval equals .60, but the dependability coefficient, $r_{r(d)}$, equals .93. Thus the trait stability for anxiety over this interval is relatively low, as might well be expected on psychological grounds, but the reliability of the test as such is all that could reasonably be desired for a 9-minute test.

Correct reasoning in this area would be aided by properly formulating the true score component always by *two* symbols, one for a *constant,* unchanging, trait contribution, S_c, and one for a trait state or *fluctuant* contribution score, S_f, such that S_f is the diurnal or, at least, reversible deviation from the central trait level S_c. This S_f component in the true score, i.e., nonerror score, is an appreciable fraction of the interperson difference in personality traits, especially in dynamic traits, but should not have been neglected even in evaluating ability traits and tests. Assuming $S_t = S_c + S_f$ and that the two last are uncorrelated, then:

$$\sigma_t^2 = \sigma_c^2 + \sigma_f^2 \qquad [6]$$

(This may be substituted in Equation 5, for clarity, as in Equation 9.) Consequently, a true coefficient of trait stability can be written:

$$r_s = 1 - \frac{\sigma_f^2}{\sigma_c^2 + \sigma_f^2} \qquad [7]$$

and derived from the dependability and uncorrected stability coefficients actually measured.

This same division into (*a*) constant trait and (*b*) trait fluctuation true scores reminds us why, even in the best experiments, the dependability coefficient of a test should run decidedly lower in *P* technique than *R* technique experiments. For in the correlation within one person of two measures made at about the same time each day over a series of days, in *P* technique, the dependability coefficient (written with a subscript *P* to indicate *P* technique) becomes:

$$r_{r(d)_P} = 1 - \frac{\sigma_e^2}{\sigma_f^2 + \sigma_e^2} \qquad [8]$$

whereas the expression for *R* technique, in Equation 2, written out fully would be:

$$r_{r(d)_R} = 1 - \frac{\sigma_e^2}{\sigma_c^2 + \sigma_f^2 + \sigma_e^2} \qquad [9]$$

Since σ_c^2 (the interpersonal trait variance) is almost invariably larger than σ_f^2 and σ_e^2 together, while σ_e^2 (error of measurement) is essentially the *same magnitude and nature* in the "over person" and "over time" repetitions of the act of measurement, the *P* technique reliability is at least twice as far from unity as the *R* technique value, for the same accuracy of experimental work.

Beyond the three main and one spurious (stability) reliability coefficients just designated, some four other coefficients are theoretically possible, from the totality of variance combinations, as stated at the opening of this section. They require some manipulative control of other sources of variance and/or an algebraic derivation from directly obtainable coefficients. For example, Cattell and Butcher (in press) define coefficients of *circumstance* reliability, and *sophistication* reliability (this latter expressing the effects of experience or test sophistication on a test), etc.

Consistent with the terminology and concepts here adopted, it is suggested that the notation for a reliability coefficient be r_r (as in Equations 2, 3, 8, and 9; avoided in Equations 5 and 7); for a homogeneity coefficient, r_h; and for a transferability coefficient, r_t. Subvarieties within these can be indicated by subscripts in parentheses as we have done for the main three (retest) reliability coefficients, $r_{r(d)}$, dependability, $r_{r(a)}$, administrative reliability, and $r_{r(c)}$ the scoring reliability or conspection coefficient among reliabilities. Not to lose sight of the fact that reliability *also* deals with differences of means and sigmas between two administrations, corresponding subscripts can be attached to the m_r and the s_r indexes defining the freedom of test means and sigmas from change.

As indicated above, space precludes our pursuit of the above formulas into the forms they would take when we define reliability, etc., in the more basic sense of "constancy of validity" proposed here. It will be noted that logically and formally "constancy of validity" has the same relation to "agreement of a test with itself" that "indirect validity" has to "direct validity." The same notion is thus consistently being introduced into both reliability and validity. As stated introductorily, two different answers will be obtained on "validity reliability" according to whether we deal only with one "wanted" factor or consider validity to cover several factors. (See for a fuller discussion, Cattell & Radcliffe, 1963.) In the first case, if s_x is the loading (correlation) of Test x on the one wanted factor (and let us for simplicity consider orthogonal factors), the highest reliability will be obtained if the retest loading $s_{x'}$ is the same as s_x. A possible expression for such a single-criterion-factor validity-reliability $r_{rv(1)}$ is, therefore:

$$r_{rv(1)} = 1 - (s_{x'}^2 - s_x^2) \qquad [10a]$$

where the sign of the parenthesis term is always treated as positive.

If we choose, instead, to consider agreement of meaning with respect to several, k, common factors, a suitable multiple-criterion-factor validity-reliability, $r_{rv(m)}$, would be:

$$r_{rv(m)} = 1 - \frac{(s_{1'}^2 - s_1^2) + (s_{2'}^2 - s_2^2) \ . \ . \ . + (s_{k'}^2 - s_k^2)}{s_{1'}s_1 + s_{2'}s_2 \ . \ . \ . + s_{k'}s_k} \qquad [10b]$$

where each expression in parentheses is again entered as a positive difference, regardless of the immediate sign obtained. This has a meaning: "relative to the common factor variance" not present in Equation 10a; and it could go negative.

When *all* common factors *and* specific factors are considered the validity-reliability (indirect reliability) becomes the same as the direct reliability, just as the indirect validity becomes algebraically identical with the direct validity.

OPERATIONAL MEASUREMENT OF HOMOGENEITY AND TRANSFERABILITY

The operational measurement of homogeneity (despite a fairly widespread semantic and even logical confusion with reliability) has been so competently treated by a succession of expert writers (Gulliksen, 1950; Kuder & Richardson, 1937; Loevinger, 1948) culminating in the generalized alpha coefficient of Cronbach (1951) that little requires to be added except relationships. Also some very recent additional modifications have been proposed by Cattell and Radcliffe (1963) and Cattell and Tsujioka (1964). In Figure 2's necessarily brief schematic representation only two tests, subtests, or items—the ultimate reduction—are used to represent the calculation of homogeneity, though of course more would usually be involved. What Figure 2 is intended to bring out is that homogeneity, as stated above, has a *P* technique, "over-time-occasion" meaning, *beyond* the usually exclusively considered *R* technique meaning. No experimental data appear yet to have been obtained to ascertain empirically how far the *R* and *P* technique examinations of a test's homogeneity would normally agree.

A second aspect of homogeneity discussion which needs new concepts concerns the drawing of a distinction between the *factor* homogeneity of a test (Cattell, 1957a) and the *test* homogeneity, per se. One can have a perfectly correlationally homogeneous test which is factorially quite heterogeneous (complex). Also it is possible to have a unifactor scale, in Lumsden's (1957) sense, i.e., of a set of items giving a Rank I intercorrelation matrix, or in Guttman's (1944) sense of a pure scale, which is yet very mixed (composite) in the sense of measuring a miscellany of psychological primary factors. Indeed, neither Rank I, nor Guttman scale, nor correlational homogeneity guarantees a factor homogeneous (pure) scale.

As mentioned initially, there has been an uncritical tendency in test reviewers to criticize low homogeneity in a test as if it were a form of unreliability. A more complete analysis than can be given here has recently been made by Cattell and Tsujioka (1964) bringing out certain radical shifts in the evaluation of homogeneity, based on the algebraic demonstrations that: (*a*) If the items in two tests have the same *mean* correlation with their factor criterion (of validity), then the less homogeneous test will have a higher final validity for the test as a whole. (*b*) There is a high probability that high homogeneity is being achieved in many current tests by causing items to share what are really *specific* factors, over and above the general personality or ability factor which they claim to measure. (*c*) A highly "inbred," homogeneous test would be expected to show poorer transferability or hardiness across subcultures, age ranges, etc.

Among the varieties of homogeneity coefficients—the genus being symbolized as r_h—one may especially recognize four as of main importance. They are the familiar random split-half coefficient, $r_{h(h)}$; the generalized homogeneity coefficient, $r_{h(g)}$ (Cronbach's, 1957, alpha); the symmetrical or "herring-bone" homogeneity coefficient, $r_{h(s)}$; and the equivalence coefficient, $r_{h(e)}$. The two last are special cases of the notion of a *structured* homogeneity coefficient, differing from the generalized or *unstructured* homogeneity evaluation as in the Kuder-Richardson and Cronbach coefficients (split-half and generalized homogeneities).

In the symmetrical homogeneity coefficient each person's score on, say, a total school achievement would be split in a special, structured way. One half of the items for arithmetic, for English, for social studies, etc., would score on one side and half on the other—hence the "herring-bone" title. Similarly, the equivalence coefficient, between two forms of a test, A and B, which are deliberately constructed for equivalence, will generally belong with the structured homogeneity coefficients. For in most modern tests there is in some sense an organic structure introduced in the construction of any unit or form to give a single score. The agreement between any two deliberately, organically constructed forms is therefore something different from any random split-half or general homogeneity coefficient, taken *within* one form. The design of construction may be such that the internal homogeneity of a broken form runs much lower than the equivalence coefficient between two forms that are designed and intended to measure the same thing. This is true, for example, of HSPQ, where normally a Spearman-Brown correction or the correlation between two random parts of, say Form B, will not reach the equivalence coefficient between Forms A and B. This situation is generally due to maximum validity within any one form being sought by arranging *suppressor* action among items on unwanted factors, which reduces homogeneity *within* scales.

For this and other reasons a number of new concepts and formulas in homogeneity measurement have recently been developed (Cattell & Tsujioka, 1964), such as the structured homogeneity coefficients calculable separately on wanted (criterion) and unwanted factors. With this there goes an associated development, in the validity field, of a distinction between the factor *trueness* and the factor *validity* of a scale. Since it is much harder in some fields than others to find items simultaneously of high validity and high mutual correlation (homogeneity), there comes a point in such areas where even a psychologist habituated to think of homogeneity as a virtue must recognize that he ought to sacrifice it to validity. Formulas have therefore been developed (Cattell & Tsujioka, 1964) to evaluate the optimum desirable homogeneity for maximum validity, and also to ask how far an experimenter has succeeded in maximizing the desirable properties of his test in relation to the density of available items in that field. Throughout these formulas the essential meaning of *homogeneity* remains the extent to which those subdivisions of a test which contribute to the same score are alike in factor composition. For the sake of control and understanding it is always desirable to *know* what the homogeneity of any given scale or battery may be, but provided the total test score behaves as it should, i.e., has good validity and reasonable equivalence with another form, low homogeneity should never be considered a defect. In a good test such low homogeneity, or even an equivalence below what could be attained by concentrating on equivalence, has probably been deliberately arranged for certain advantages in construction and use.

Turning lastly to the measurement of transferability, we encounter a pioneer area concerning which a little more space must be given to concepts and fundamental principles. For the sake of symmetry with reliability and homogeneity the transferability calculation in Figure 3 has been indicated as the correlation between two persons from the application of the same test over a series of occasions where they are

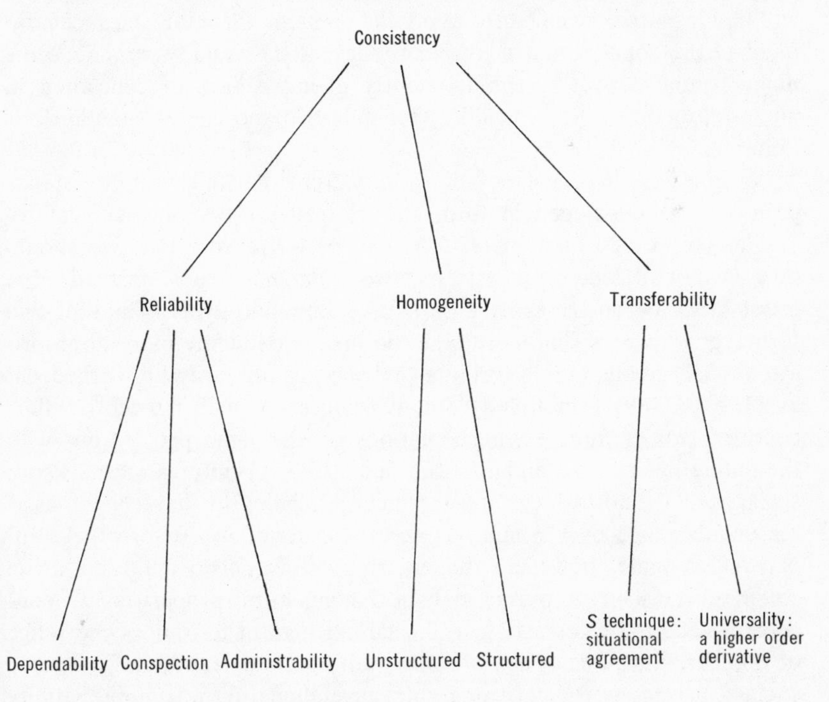

FIGURE 3. Forms of consistency.

experiencing exposure to exactly the same series of stimuli. (This is conceptually a transferability in terms of the *P* technique situation. Among basic experimental correlation designs—Cattell, 1946—it is in fact *S* technique.) This is, of course, a schematic indication of what would commonly be arranged, instead, as the application to two *groups* of persons (subcultures, for example) whose mean score could be so compared.

While this is one theoretically satisfactory way (using r_p instead of r) of evaluating the extent to which a test retains its properties over different people and groups, namely, with respect to the effects of a varied set of stimulus occasions, it is not the only or the best evaluation of transferability. In fact, what is conceptually the most *essential* form of transferability measurement transcends this *P* technique form, and departs from this simple symmetry to the reliability and homogeneity measurement operations. *Transferability* is essentially defined as the degree to which a test retains its properties constant across an agreed, standard range of reference populations.

Although transferability is here introduced as a new psychometric parameter, it is obviously one which, though unmeasured, has always been of first importance to both the practicing and research psychologist. Experience must henceforth decide, however, whether psychologists will find it more convenient to apply the common meaning and measurement of the concept to (*a*) the constancy of the validity, or (*b*) some higher order derivative simultaneously giving weight to constancy in all test properties, viz.: validity, reliability, homogeneity, standardization, etc.

An index of the constancy of validity from the transferability standpoint can be developed in form strictly analogous to the indirect reliability index of Equations 10(a) and 10(b), except that we should now deal with factor analysis on two *different* groups, instead of a retest factoring on the same group. Like Equation 10 it admits of two forms, of which we shall here take the first as definitely more appropriate, though a comparable formula to 10(b) could easily be worked out as 11(b). Unlike Equation 10 it is not concerned with the score differences of two or more testing situations on the same people, but with the difference over a standard, stratified set of subcultures (ages, sexes, social levels, national cultures) which psychologists have fixed as a reasonable range over which to expect transferability. Before the comparison is made, however, the entering coefficients should be made comparable as far as purely statistical noncultural properties are concerned, notably by correction to the same length of test and same range of population sample. Then we may write a transferability consistency coefficient r_t to appear in comparable correlational form to the reliability and homogeneity coefficients, thus:

$$r_t = 1 - \frac{\sum_{j=1}^{j=k} \sum_{a/b=1}^{a/b=n} (S_{ja}^2 - S_{jb}^2)}{\sum_{j=1}^{j=k} \sum_{a/b=1}^{a/b=n} S_{ja}S_{jb}} \qquad [11]$$

where there are k factors involved in the test and n cultures of which a and b are any two and the expression in parentheses is always treated as a positive value.

Any attempt to use the second sense—the degree of constancy of *all* properties of a test across cultures—would involve one in a value judgment regarding the weighting to be given each parameter, which we shall not attempt. However, we would argue that the first sense, (Equation 11), should suffice since surely reliability and homogeneity are important only to the extent that they yield or qualify validity. Parenthetically, though high transferability is surely desirable if other things are equal, it is probable that it will commonly be gained at the expense of validity in one preferred group, so that a compromise between it and other properties will generally be desirable.

A weighting problem which cannot so easily be avoided is that involved in combining r_r (reliability), r_h (homogeneity), and r_t (transferability) to give a single index of a test's *consistency*. It can well be objected to any single index that consistency is a logical not a functional concept, and that homogeneity and reliability, for example, are functionally and correlationally independent, bound only by being, generically, aspects of a concept of consistency. Two alternatives therefore present themselves: (*a*) to give equal weight, i.e., calculate a single total consistency coefficient as a (z transformed) mean of the three coefficients; (*b*) to name some specific purpose for which their relevance is being examined, e.g., obtaining maximum agreement with teachers' judgments, over several school systems, on which children need special class instruction (battery validities being initially equal). This latter, and more defensible "specific purpose" use would take the form of determining weights in the ordinary way in a multiple correlation, such that:

$$R = ar_r + br_h + cr_t \qquad [12]$$

maximizes R with the desired specific purpose.

SUMMARY

1. A logical and psychological reexamination of the concepts of validity and reliability has been made with a view to arriving at more fundamental, and practically effective, parameters for evaluating tests.

2. *Validity* appears to have three bipolar (dichotomous or continuous) dimensions: *abstract to concrete,* or particular; *direct to cir-*

cumstantial; and *cultural to artifactual,* which yield eight types of coefficients (23) of which 4 deserve, by importance, distinguishing titles.

3. *Conceptual* validity hinges on four ways of operationalizing a theoretical or empirical construct, viz.: as an entity fitting a defined set of conditions (which may yield something real *or* imaginary), as a correlation cluster, as a natural type difference, and as a simple structure factor across several studies. The last combines measurement precision which unitary character, as well as a meaning enriched beyond that of an empirical construct.

4. It is suggested that several existing popular uses of validity are either unfruitful (the use of "construct" instead of concept validity) or superfluous (face, predictive, concurrent, content, etc., validity).

5. A generic term for the total constancy of a test—quite apart from validity—is proposed as *test consistency.* This generic term covers *reliability, homogeneity,* and *transferability,* for which distinct formulas are proposed. They derive from consideration of the contribution of error to entries along the three main dimensions of the covariation chart or basic data relation matrix and are thus exhaustive.

6. If one considers experimental error as most aptly divided into error due to (*a*) different administrators or observers, (*b*) different scores, and (c) other sources, seven *reliability coefficients* exist from the possible different combinations of these. Again, in practical importance, however, a restricted set of three reliability coefficients stand out, namely, *dependability*, *conspection*, and *administrative* reliability. The stability coefficient is not a reliable coefficient, depending more on trait than test.

Coefficients are given for those which may sometimes need to be algebraically derived from directly measurable and calculable coefficients. Reliabilities can be either direct, as a comparison of two testings, or indirect as a reliability of validity measurement. The reliability of a test includes constancy of mean and sigma as well as of the rank order of second administration scores, i.e., the value given by the usual *coefficient,* so that two *indexes* need also to be calculated for these, presenting three values altogether for a test reliability statement. Alternatively, an r_p will give a single value evaluating combined agreement on rank, mean, and deviation.

7. *Homogeneity* in a test is conceivable either as test homogeneity or factor homogeneity. As test homogeneity it needs to be differently evaluated for unstructured tests (by split-half, Kuder-Richardson, Cronbach alpha, etc.) and for structured tests (symmetrical, equivalence, etc., coefficients).

8. *Transferability* (hardiness, durability) is a test's constancy across the typical range of age, subculture, status, etc., a test is likely to en-

counter. Formulas are proposed for constancy of validity not for constancy of all properties.

9. Whereas high reliability is almost always desirable, and high transferability is desirable if other qualities are not lost, an optimum rather than a high homogeneity is commonly desired. Sufficient suppressor action, validity against a broad as opposed to a narrow factor, and adequate transferability are all likely to be impaired by too high a homogeneity, in degrees partly derivable from formulas.

10. A single index for consistency may be obtained by giving equal summation weight to the three logically, and largely correlationally, independent coefficients; but it is probably more meaningful to calculate a "special purpose consistency" weighting for each of the three according to the multiple correlation possible with the special criterion for which consistency is desired.

REFERENCES

American Psychological Association, Committee on Test Standards. Technical recommendations for psychological tests and diagnostic techniques. *Psychol. Bull.*, 1954, **51** (2, Pt. 2).

Beloff, H., & Cattell, R. B. *The High School Personality Questionnaire.* Champaign, Ill.: Institute for Personality and Ability Testing, 1962.

Burt, C. L. *Mental and scholastic tests.* London: P. S. King, 1921.

Burt, C. L. *The factors of the mind: An introduction to factor analysis in psychology.* New York: Macmillan, 1941.

Campbell, D. T., & Fiske, D. W. Convergent and discriminant validation by the multitrait-multimethod matrix. *Psychol. Bull.*, 1959, **56**, 82–105.

Cattell, R. B. *The description and measurement of personality.* New York: World Book, 1946.

Cattell, R. B. r_p and other coefficients of pattern similarity. *Psychometrika,* 1949, **14**, 279–298.

Cattell, R. B. *Personality and motivation structure and measurement.* New York: Harcourt, Brace & World, 1957. (a)

Cattell, R. B. A universal index for psychological factors. *Psychologia,* 1957, **1**, 74–85. (b)

Cattell, R. B. *Handbook to the Culture Fair Intelligence Tests.* Champaign, Ill.: Institute for Personality and Ability Testing, 1958.

Cattell, R. B. Theory of situational, instrument, second order, and refraction factors in personality structure research. *Psychol. Bull.,* 1961, **56**, 160–174.

Cattell, R. B. *The confactor method of unique factor resolution: Its present status.* (Advanced Publ. No. 19) Urbana: Laboratory of Personality Assessment, University of Illinois, 1962.

Cattell, R. B. The theory of fluid and crystallized intelligence: A critical experiment. *J. educ. Psychol.,* 1963, **54**, 1–22.

Cattell, R. B. Beyond reliability and validity: Some further concepts and coefficients for evaluating tests. *J. educ. Res.,* in press. (a)

Cattell, R. B. (Ed.) *Handbook of multivariate experimental psychology.* Chicago: Rand McNally. In press. (b)

Cattell, R. B., & Butcher, J. *The dynamic prediction of achievement.* Indianapolis: Bobbs Merrill, in press.

Cattell, R. B., & Radcliffe, J. A. Reliabilities and validities of simple and extended, weighted and buffered unifactor scales. *Brit. J. statist. Psychol.,* 1963, **15**, 113–128.

Cattell, R. B., & Scheier, I. H. *The meaning and measurement of neuroticism and anxiety.* New York: Ronald Press, 1961.

Cattell, R. B., & Tsujioka, B. Orthogonality, homogeneity and other test evils: A plea for structural psychometric concepts and evaluative formulae in personality test design. *Educ. psychol. Measmt.,* 1964, **24**, 1–28.

Coombs, C. H. Inconsistency of preferences in psychological measurement. *J. exp. Psychol.,* 1958, **55**, 1–7.

Cronbach, L. J. Coefficient alpha and the internal structure of tests. *Psychometrika,* 1951, **16**, 297–334.

Cronbach, L. J., & Gleser, G. C. Assessing similarity between profiles. *Psychol. Bull.,* 1953, **50**, 456–473.

Cronbach, L. J., & Gleser, G. C. *Psychological tests and personnel decisions.* Urbana: Univer. Illinois Press, 1957.

Cureton, E. E. Validity, reliability and baloney. *Educ. psychol. Measmt.,* 1950, **10**, 94–96.

Edwards, W. The reliability of probability preferences. *Amer. J. Psychol.,* 1954, **57**, 380–417.

Eysenck, H. J. Criterion rotation: An application of the hypothetico-deductive method to factor analysis. *Psychol. Rev.,* 1950, **57**, 38–53.

Guilford, J. P. *Psychometric methods.* New York: McGraw-Hill, 1954.

Gulliksen, H. *Theory of mental tests.* New York: Wiley, 1950.

Guttman, L. A basis for scaling qualitative data. *Amer. sociol. Rev.,* 1944, **9**, 139–150.

Humphreys, L. G. The normal curve and the attenuation paradox in test theory. *Psychol. Bull.,* 1956, **53**, 472–476.

Kelley, T. L. Essential traits of mental life. *Harvard Stud. Educ.,* 1935, **26**, 146.

Kuder, G. F., & Richardson, M. W. The theory of estimation of test reliability. *Psychometrika,* 1937, **2**, 151–160.

Loevinger, J. A. A systematic approach to the construction and evaluation of tests of ability. *Psychol. Monogr.,* 1947, **61** (4, Whole No. 285).

Loevinger, J. A. The technic of homogeneous tests compared with some aspects of "scale analysis" and factor analysis. *Psychol. Bull.,* 1948, **45**, 507–529.

Lord, F. M. The relation of test score to the trait underlying the test. *Educ. psychol. Measmt.,* 1953, **13**, 517–549.

Lord, F. M. Statistical inferences about true score. *Psychometrika,* 1959, **24**, 1–17.

Lumsden, J. A factorial approach to unidimensionability. *Aust. J. Psychol.,* 1957, **78**, 41–54.

McQuitty, L. L. Pattern analysis illustrated in classifying patients and normals. *Educ. psychol. Measmt.,* 1954, **14**, 598–604.

Porter, R. B., & Cattell, R. B. *The Child Personality Questionnaire.* Champaign, Ill.: Institute for Personality and Ability Testing, 1960.

Rao, C. R. *Advanced statistical methods in biometric research.* New York: Wiley, 1952.

Scheier, I. H., & Cattell, R. B. *The IPAT Anxiety Scale Questionnaire.* Champaign, Ill.: Institute for Personality and Ability Testing, 1963.
Spearman, C. General intelligence objectively determined and measured. *Amer. J. Psychol.*, 1904, **15**, 201–293.
Spearman, C. *The abilities of man: Their nature and measurement.* London: Macmillan, 1927.
Thorndike, R. L. *Personnel selection: Test Measurement and techniques.* New York: Wiley, 1949.
Thurstone, L. L. The prediction of choice. *Psychometrika*, 1945, **10**, 237–253.
Thurstone, L. L. *Multiple factor analysis.* Chicago: Univer. Chicago Press, 1947.
Torgerson, W. S. *Theory and methods of scaling.* New York: Wiley, 1958.
Tsujioka, B., & Cattell, R. B. The definition and location of types. In R. B. Cattell (Ed.), *Handbook of multivariate experimental psychology.* Chicago: Rand McNally, In press. Chap. 12.
Vernon, P. E. *Personality tests and assessments.* London: Methuen, 1953.
Wepman, J. M., & Heine, R. W. (Eds.) *Concepts of personality.* Chicago: Aldine, 1963.
Woodrow, H. Quotidian variability. *Psychol. Rev.*, 1932, **39**, 245–256.

UNIT FOUR: VALIDITY
ADDITIONAL READINGS

Bechtoldt, H. P. Construct validity: A critique. *American Psychologist,* 1959, *14*, 619–629.
Brogden, H. E. On the interpretation of the correlation coefficient as a measure of predictive efficiency. *Journal of Educational Psychology,* 1946, *37*, 65–76.
Campbell, D. T. Recommendations for APA test standards regarding construct, trait, or discriminant validity. *American Psychologist,* 1960, *15*, 546–553.
Cattell, R. B., and Tsujioka, B. The importance of factor-trueness and validity, versus homogeneity and orthogonality, in test scales. *Educational and Psychological Measurement,* 1964, *24*, 3–30.
Cronbach, L. J. Response sets and test validity. *Educational and Psychological Measurement,* 1946, *6*, 475–494.
Cronbach, L. J. New light on test strategy from decision theory. *Proceedings of the 1954 Invitational Conference on Testing Problems, Educational Testing Service*, 1955, 30–36.
Cronbach, L. J., and Gleser, Goldine C. *Psychological Tests and Personnel Decisions.* Urbana, Illinois: University of Illinois Press, 1957, 165 pp.
Cureton, E. E. Symposium: The need and means of cross-validation, II. Approximate linear restraints and best predictor weights. *Educational and Psychological Measurement,* 1951, *11*, 12–15.
Cureton, E. E. Recipe for a cookbook. *Psychological Bulletin,* 1957, *54*, 494–497.

Dawes, R. M. A note on base rates and psychometric efficiency. *Journal of Consulting Psychology*, 1962, *26*, 422–424.

Ebel, R. L. Obtaining and reporting evidence on content validity. *Educational and Psychological Measurement*, 1956, *16*, 269–282.

Frederiksen, N. O., and Melville, S. D. Differential predictability in the use of test scores. *Educational and Psychological Measurement*, 1954, *14*, 647–656.

French, J. W. The logic of and assumptions underlying differential testing. *Proceedings of the 1955 Invitational Conference on Testing Problems, Educational Testing Service*, 1956, 40–48.

Jenkins, J. G. Validity for what? *Journal of Consulting Psychology*, 1946, *10*, 93–98.

Katzell, R. A. Symposium: The need and means of cross-validation, III. Cross-validation in item analyses. *Educational and Psychological Measurement*, 1951, *11*, 16–22.

Langmuir, C. R. Cross-validation. *Test Service Bulletin*, 1954, *47*, 1–4.

Lord, F. M. Formula scoring and validity. *Educational and Psychological Measurement*, 1963, *23*, 663–672.

Manning, W. H., and DuBois, P. H. Gain in proficiency as a criterion in test validation. *Journal of Applied Psychology*, 1958, *42*, 191–194.

Mosier, C. I. Symposium: The need and means of cross-validation, I. Problems and designs of cross-validation. *Educational and Psychological Measurement*, 1951, *11*, 5–11.

Richardson, M. W. The interpretation of a test validity coefficient in terms of increased efficiency of a selected group of personnel. *Psychometrika*, 1944, *9*, 245–248.

Rulon, P. J. On the validity of educational tests. *Harvard Educational Review*, 1946, *16*, 290–296.

Wherry, R. J. Symposium: The need and means of cross-validation, IV. Comparison of cross-validation with statistical inference of betas and multiple R from a single sample. *Educational and Psychological Measurement*, 1951, *11*, 23–28.

Unit Five:

ITEM ANALYSIS AND SELECTION

31. General Considerations in the Selection of Test Items and a Short Method of Estimating the Product-Moment Coefficient from Data at the Tails of the Distribution[1]

JOHN C. FLANAGAN

An objective test usually consists of a set of more or less similar test items. The characteristics of these items determine the characteristics of the whole test. Very early in the development of objective testing, the test specialists discovered the value of item analysis as a tool for item selection and revision. In particular, they learned to pay attention to item difficulty and item discrimination.

Most indices of item discrimination express the relation between that which the item measures and that which is measured by the test in which it appears. A vast array of indices has been invented and advocated. One of the more popular ones, over the years, has been an estimate of the product-moment coefficient of correlation between scores on the item and scores on the test, such as Flanagan presents in the following paper.

Dr. Flanagan has for many years been one of this country's, and one of the world's, outstanding test specialists. He has been a leader not only in the development of psychometric techniques, as exemplified in the present article, but also in the application of tests to the problems of education, government, and business.

This paper is essentially a progress report concerning a series of studies of the procedures for the selection of test items. The present discussion will review briefly the arguments for the use of statistical criteria in the selection of test items, point out fallacies in previous studies and discussions of these statistical considerations, and present a short method of obtaining validity coefficients.

Unless the author of a number of test items writes only items of an

---

Flanagan, J. C. General considerations in the selection of test items and a short method of estimating the product-moment coefficient from data at the tails of the distribution. *Journal of Educational Psychology,* 1939, *30,* 674–680. Reprinted with the permission of the publisher and author.

[1] Read before the Eastern Psychological Association, March 31, 1939, at Bryn Mawr, Pennsylvania.

entirely uniform degree of excellence, in which case, of course, no improvement by any method of selection would be possible, the refinement and improvement of a test usually requires the use of empirically obtained statistical indices of the characteristics of the item. The importance of such statistical indices may be illustrated by quoting from a previous report by the present writer[2] " . . . the reliability coefficient of a test composed of one hundred items having item intercorrelations of .15 would be .95. If another group of one hundred items having intercorrelations of .03 and measuring the same general function are added to this test, the reliability coefficient for the total test composed of two hundred items is slightly less than the previous value." A table is being prepared which will provide a simple means of determining which ones of a group of experimental items should be included in the final form to obtain the maximum reliability coefficient for the finished test. The proportion of items which should be used would depend on the degree of excellence and heterogeneity of the original items. It appears quite obvious that some published tests would have been improved had half of the items not been included. The resulting increase in efficiency appears very desirable at the present time when so many demands are being made on the students' time.

In selecting items, there are two primary considerations: First, "Is the item valid?" That is, does it discriminate between persons having much of the quality being measured and persons having only a relatively small amount of this quality? This question is usually answered in terms of some statistical index of the validity of the test item. The second consideration is, "Is the difficulty level of the item suited to the group for which it is intended?" It has frequently been pointed out that items which either all students or no students get correct are performing no measuring function in the test.

Although much time and energy have been spent on empirical studies in an effort to discover the most satisfactory procedure for selecting the best items for inclusion in a final form of a particular test, these studies have produced conflicting results, and have conspicuously failed to settle the issue. A favorite type of empirical study has been the comparison of several methods of obtaining validity coefficients. Most of these studies are of little practical value because the experimenters have failed to control the effect of item difficulty on test validity. It should be emphasized that these are two separate considerations. As will be mentioned later, items of fifty per cent difficulty tend in certain situations to provide the most valid test. Therefore, a method which combines a rough measure of validity or discriminating value with a

---

[2] Flanagan, John C.: "A Proposed Procedure for Increasing the Efficiency of Objective Tests." *J. Educ. Psychol.*, Vol. XXVIII, 1937, pp. 17–21.

device which will favor items of fifty per cent difficulty will tend to appear to be superior to a method which provides a more valid index of item validity unaffected by difficulty. Obviously, in a practical situation, these two factors of item validity and item difficulty should be given separate consideration, and an index which obscures the estimate of validity by combining it with a difficulty characteristic is to be avoided. Similarly, empirical studies of the effect on test validity of item difficulty have neglected the factor of item validity.

In addition to these empirical studies, there have been several logical discussions of statistical criteria for selecting test items. Several investigators have brought forth logical proofs to show that a test should be composed of items of fifty per cent difficulty. Here, again, the proofs are based on assumptions which are artificial and fallacious in representing typical conditions. It can easily be shown that, to obtain the maximum amount of discrimination between the individuals in a particular group, a test should be composed of items all of which are of fifty per cent difficulty for that group, provided the intercorrelations of all the items are zero. This situation obviously never exists. It can also be shown that a rectangular distribution of item difficulties extending from the level of ability of the highest individual in a group to the level of the lowest individual in the group is necessary to obtain maximum discrimination among the members of the group, provided the intercorrelations between all of the items are unity. This situation also must be regarded as a purely hypothetical one. The practical situation is one which is intermediate between these extremes. Therefore, we may dismiss the notion that all items should be of fifty per cent difficulty as one based on a hypothetical situation which is contrary to fact. The decision concerning the most desirable distribution of item difficulties for a particular test should be based on the accuracy of measurement desired at various levels and the intercorrelations of the items affecting scores at these levels.

Although the two factors which have been mentioned are usually regarded as the primary considerations in the selection of test items, they are by no means the only considerations. For example, item intercorrelations, although shown to be of only minor importance for certain types of tests, may, in particular situations, be of paramount importance. Some statistical methods have been devised for taking item intercorrelations into account, such as the approximation procedures devised by the present writer in 1934 and 1936.[3] However, the typical method of

---

[3] Flanagan, John C.: *Factor Analysis in the Study of Personality.* Stanford University Press, Stanford University, California, 1935.

Flanagan, John C.: "A Short Method for Selecting the Best Combination of Test Items for a Particular Purpose." *Psychol. Bull.,* Vol. XXXIII, 1936, pp. 603–604.

controlling item intercorrelations has been some relatively crude method such as the selection of items with respect to various logical categories. This procedure is commonly known as one of obtaining adequate sampling.

Two other considerations of importance in particular situations are length of time required per item, and objectivity of scoring. It need hardly be said that a test of one hundred items requiring only twenty minutes of testing time would, in general, be definitely superior to one of fifty items requiring the same amount of testing time, even though the average of the item validities in the first case was somewhat lower. Objectivity of scoring is almost entirely a practical consideration, but becomes of great importance in certain situations.

The final pair of criteria which will be mentioned are illustrated by such competitive examinations as those given by Civil Service Commissions. These criteria are "face-validity" and defensibility or authoritativeness of the correct answer. By "face-validity" is meant the requirement that examinations appear to measure what is popularly understood from the title. By defensibility or authoritativeness is meant the ability of the examiners to convince interested parties that the answer given by the examiners is the correct answer. Although these are definitely secondary considerations from the measurement point of view, they frequently are of great practical importance.

Although it is clear that these secondary considerations can rarely be neglected, the major considerations in most situations remain those considered above; namely, item validity and item difficulty.

It follows from the definition given above for item validity that the best index of validity is one which provides an index of the extent to which an item will predict the criterion. Such an index is provided by the product-moment correlation coefficient and its various modifications. The most common situation is one in which the biserial correlation coefficient applies. These coefficients have been widely used and various procedures have been developed for reducing the relatively large amount of time and effort required for their computation. Even though these procedures have materially decreased the labor involved, many individuals feel that the time expended in obtaining these coefficients is frequently not justifiable. Such individuals have made considerable use of the upper- and lower-groups method. T. L. Kelley reported a number of years ago that, if upper and lower groups were to be used, the certainty with which the means of the upper and lower groups are differentiated is a maximum when the two tails of the normal distribution each contain twenty-seven per cent of the cases. Kelley[4] has recently

---

[4] Kelley, T. L.: "The Selection of Upper and Lower Groups for the Validation of Test Items." *J. Educ. Psychol.*, Vol. XXX, 1939, pp. 17–24.

amplified this statement showing that in certain situations a slightly smaller proportion of all cases appears desirable. He concludes, however, that "Upper and lower groups consisting of twenty-seven per cent from the extremes of the criterion score distribution are optimal for the study of test items, provided the differences in criterion scores among the members of each group are not utilized."[5]

The upper- and lower-groups method has been quite extensively used in connection with a chart which provides a graphic indication of the separation, in terms of quarter-sigma units, of the means of the upper and lower groups on the particular item. In many situations, it appears advantageous to have the index in terms of the degree of relationship shown between the item and the criterion. For example, such coefficients facilitate thinking in terms of the relation between item validity and test validity. The writer, therefore, has prepared a chart based on Tables VIII and IX in *Tables for Statisticians and Biometricians,* Part II, edited by Karl Pearson. Pearson's tables give volumes of the normal bivariate surface included in any cell whose lower limit is 0.0, 0.1, 0.2, . . . 2.6 standard deviations, and whose upper limit runs to infinity, for specified correlations at intervals of .05 from -1.00 to $+1.00$.

The derived chart (Fig. 1) shows the values of the product-moment coefficient of correlation corresponding to given proportions of success in the upper and lower twenty-seven per cent of the criterion group.

A project to determine the standard error of a correlation coefficient obtained by the use of this and similar charts is now in progress. It is clear that such a chart, utilizing as it does the information from only about half of the cases and lumping these cases together into only two groups, will give much less accurate results than does the more usual biserial correlation coefficient. However, the results obtained from this chart have been found to be satisfactory approximations to the biserial coefficients in the comparisons which have been made by the writer.

In practice, it appears that frequently it is satisfactory to use the values obtained from this chart together with an index of difficulty found by averaging the difficulties for the upper and lower groups.

In conclusion, it should be mentioned that such a procedure as that just described provides a very rapid method of obtaining difficulty and validity indices for items when the tests have been administered with answer sheets for the International test-scoring machine. The item analysis unit tabulates the number of correct responses to ninety items for a group of one hundred papers in about fifteen minutes. Thus a simple item analysis of the type herein described for about four hundred cases on a one hundred fifty item test would require only a couple of hours after the tests had been scored. The scoring itself should require a little more than an hour under these circumstances.

[5] *Ibid.,* p. 24.

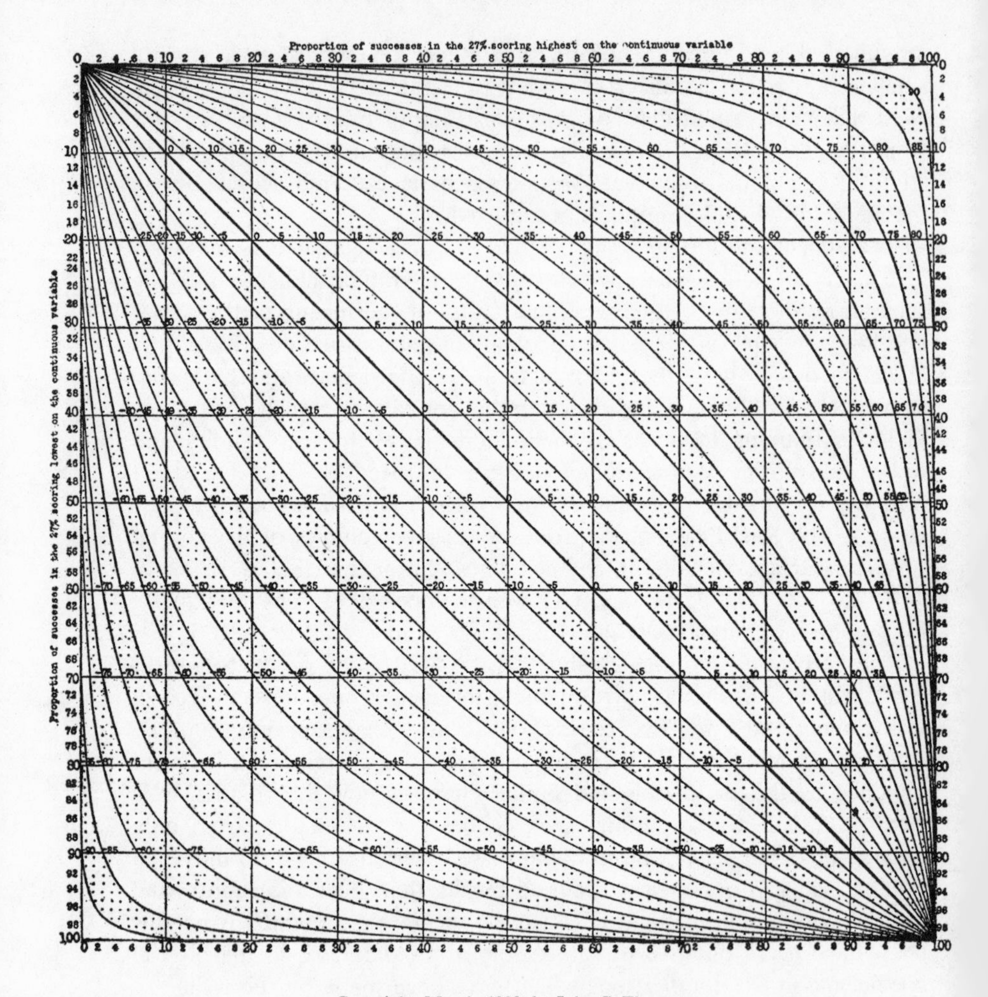

FIGURE 1. Chart showing the values of the product-moment coefficient of correlation in a normal bivariate population corresponding to given proportions of successes.

Example: The correlation coefficient between the continuous variable and an item on which 56% of the group achieving scores in the highest 27% for the continuous variable succeed and on which 23% of the group achieving scores in the lowest 27% for the continuous variable succeed is .35.

SUMMARY

Most recent discussions of the various techniques which have been proposed for the selection of test items have contained major fallacies. Empirical studies have, in general, overlooked the fact that there are *two* very important considerations involved in any selection of test items. The first consideration is item validity or discriminating power, and the second one is item difficulty. The empirical selection of items by means of a single index of item validity overlooks the necessity for separate consideration of these two criteria, and any comparison of methods on this basis is, therefore, of only trivial value.

Logical discussions concerning the optimum distribution of item difficulties have invariably overlooked the very important bearing of item validities on this function. Therefore, these discussions may also be regarded as having little practical significance.

In certain special situations, secondary considerations such as item intercorrelations, length of time required for a response, objectivity of scoring, "face-validity," and defensibility or authoritativeness are important factors in determining which items should be chosen.

A short method of obtaining item validity and item difficulty indices was presented. The chart utilized in this procedure was based on Kelley's finding that upper and lower groups containing twenty-seven per cent of the cases were optimum for certain related estimations. Pearson's *Tables for Statisticians and Biometricians* was used in obtaining the charted values.

Though the method does not in any way depend on any particular type of item or method of scoring, its brevity is probably best illustrated by stating that within three or four hours of the time four hundred tests of one hundred fifty items are received in the office, a simple item analysis including the necessary scoring and checking may be obtained if the International test-scoring machine is used.

32. Notes on a Suggested Index of Item Validity: The U-L Index

A. PEMBERTON JOHNSON

In the preceding article Flanagan argued that a valid index of discrimination would be unaffected by item difficulty and advocated separate consideration of discrimination and difficulty in item selection. He did recognize that in certain situations items of fifty per cent difficulty may provide the most valid test and that certain indices of discrimination tend to favor such items.

The index described in Johnson's article is such an index. It is strongly biased in favor of items of fifty per cent difficulty. The situations in which such items, if they discriminate well, produce highly reliable tests are very common in educational testing of aptitude and achievement. For this reason and because of its simplicity of conception and calculation, the U-L index has become popular in recent years.

In 1935 Long, Sandiford, et al.,* reported an empirical comparative study of the effectiveness of thirteen validity techniques in selecting from among four hundred eighty-two six-choice vocabulary items that set of fifty and that set of one hundred items which correlated highest with criterion scores based on all four hundred eighty-two items. For this situation they concluded, among other things, that those validity techniques which tend to discriminate in favor of items of fifty per cent difficulty appear to be superior to the techniques such as bi-serial *r,* Kelley and Vincent which make no discrimination in favor of median difficulty items. Considering both effectiveness and ease of computation, they concluded that among those techniques tending to select items of fifty per cent difficulty (percentage passing), the upper vs. lower (group) technique was to be preferred. They stated that item validities derived by the upper vs. lower technique tend to reach maximum reliability when the proportion of cases in each of these groups is twenty-seven per cent.† Numerically the item validities were expressed in this technique by the difference between number of correct responses for the highest twenty-seven per cent (or by the highest third) and the

---

Johnson, A. P. Notes on a suggested index of item validity: the U-L index. *Journal of Educational Psychology,* 1951, *42,* 499–504. Reprinted with the permission of the publisher and author.

* John A. Long, Peter Sandiford, and Others. *The Validation of Test Items.* Bulletin No. 3, Dept. of Ed. Res., University of Toronto, Toronto, 1935, pp. 94–5.

† See also T. L. Kelley, "The Selection of Upper and Lower Groups for the Validation of Test Items," *J. Educ. Psychol.,* XXX, January, 1939, pp. 17–24.

number of correct responses for the lowest twenty-seven per cent (or the lowest third) of the cases as arrayed on the criterion scale.

This paper proposes the U-L Index, a simple modification of the upper-lower twenty-seven per cent technique. This index proved extremely useful during World War II as a basis for selecting items to be included in Army Air Forces bombardier knowledge tests. The U-L Index effectively tends to select items of moderate difficulty which show good separation between upper and lower twenty-seven per cent groups. It is more easily computed and interpreted than any conventional item validity index known to the author. For many practical test construction situations where expensive item analysis cannot be justified, it is believed to be quite useful.

This modification possibly has been used by other investigators before, but is believed not to have been. It requires the difference between the groups in number of correct responses to be divided by the number of cases in each group. Symbolically, if

R_u = number correct responses in the upper group of twenty-seven per cent

R_l = number correct responses in the lower group of twenty-seven per cent

N = number of cases

$f = .27N$

$$\text{U-L Index} = \frac{R_u - R_l}{.27N} = \frac{R_u - R_l}{f} \tag{1}$$

This index can theoretically vary from + 1 through 0 to − 1. These proportions are independent of the N of the population sample and similar in magnitude though not strictly in meaning to conventional correlation coefficients.

Long, Sandiford, et al., found in their empirical study that (1) the average difficulty of a group of items shown to be least valid by the bi-serial r technique was about equal to the average difficulty of the group of items indicated to be least valid by the upper-lower thirds technique, but (2) that the bi-serial r tended to eliminate items indiscriminately throughout the entire range of item difficulty whereas the upper-lower thirds technique tended to eliminate items farthest removed from the fifty per cent level of difficulty (percentage passing).*

In a table of intercorrelations among the validity values obtained for one hundred items by the thirteen methods which they studied, Long, Sandiford, et al., report a correlation of .65 between bi-serial r and upper-lower thirds validities. This finding strongly suggests the need

---

* Ibid., p. 114.

to interpret the proposed U-L Index in somewhat different fashion than the conventional bi-serial r.

The standard error of the U-L Index may be derived from the conventional formula for the standard error of the difference of two proportions, when the data are uncorrelated.

Guilford* gives the following generalized formulae:

$$\#34 \qquad \sigma_{dp} = \sqrt{\sigma_{p_1}{}^2 + \sigma_{p_2}{}^2 - 2r\sigma_{p_1}\sigma_{p_2}}$$

$$\#28 \qquad \sigma_p = \sqrt{\frac{pq}{N}}$$

where: σ_{dp} = S.E. of a difference between two proportions
σ_p = S.E. of a proportion
p_1 = 1st proportion
p_2 = 2nd proportion
$q = 1 - p$
N = number of cases
r = coefficient of intercorrelation of the two sets of data.

Using the previously mentioned symbols for the U-L Index:

$$\sigma_{p_1} = \sqrt{\frac{p_1q_1}{N}} = \sqrt{\frac{\left(\frac{R_u}{f}\right)\left(1 - \frac{R_u}{f}\right)}{f}} = \frac{1}{f}\sqrt{\frac{R_u(f - R_u)}{f}}$$

$$= \frac{1}{f}\sqrt{R_u - \frac{R_u{}^2}{f}}$$

Similarly $$\sigma_{p_2} = \frac{1}{f}\sqrt{R_l - \frac{R_l{}^2}{f}}$$

In Guilford's formula #34 for σ_{dp}, the most conservative estimate of r is 0. That formula then reduces to $\sigma_{dp} = \sqrt{\sigma_{p_1}{}^2 + \sigma_{p_2}{}^2}$

By substitution:

$$\text{SE U-L Index} = \frac{1}{f}\sqrt{R_u - \frac{R_u{}^2}{f} + R_l - \frac{R_l{}^2}{f}}$$

$$= \frac{1}{f}\sqrt{R_u + R_l - \left(\frac{R_u{}^2 + R_l{}^2}{f}\right)}$$

The formula for the standard error of the U-L Index is such that the maximum value of the standard error occurs in the fifty per cent passing situation where the true index equals zero. Table I below gives the 5% and 1% "t" significance levels of the SE of the U-L Index in that situation.

---

* J. P. Guilford. *Fundamental Statistics in Psychology and Education,* New York: McGraw-Hill, 1942, pp. 133 and 142.

TABLE I.—5% and 1% "t" Test Significance Levels for the SE of U-L Index When the U-L Index = 0 and 50% Pass the Item*

N	$f = .27N$	SE of the U-L Index	5% Level	1% Level
100	27	.136	.273	.364
148	40	.112	.223	.295
200	54	.096	.190	.252
248	67	.087	.172	.227
300	81	.079	.156	.206
348	94	.073	.144	.190
400	108	.068	.134	.177
500	135	.061	.120	.159
1000	270	.043	.084	.111

* For example, only 1 per cent of obtained values would be expected to exceed $\pm .364$ were the true index zero for a sample of one hundred cases. In this table the degrees of freedom have been taken as equal to $2(f\text{-}1)$ since f is defined as the number in each of the two contrasted groups.

A quite serviceable index of item difficulty (percentage passing) for each item can be obtained from the values for R_u and R_l by use of the following formula:

$$\text{Difficulty level (percentage passing)} = \frac{100\ (R_u + R_l)}{2f}$$

$$= \frac{50(R_u + R_l)}{f} \qquad (3)$$

Since this is based on only the extreme fifty-four per cent of the cases, it does not give exactly the value for the index of item difficulty which would be obtained from all of the cases. In practice however the discrepancy usually is not appreciable.

Formula (1) for the U-L Index provides no specific correction for omissions, although it is necessary sometimes to item analyze speeded tests in which the number of omissions among later items is appreciable.

Omissions on speeded tests are usually of two types: (a) those by persons who read the item but fail to mark any choice and (b) those by persons who have not read as far in the test as the end of that item. Davis* in a communication to the writer suggests a method of determining the 'non-reads' directly. The test papers are scored and arranged in rank order according to the criterion score. The group which includes the top twenty-seven per cent of papers is segregated as is the group which comprises the bottom twenty-seven per cent of test papers. Next the papers of the upper group are gone through to determine which item on each paper is the last one marked. A tally is then made opposite

* Dr. Frederick B. Davis, formerly with the Cooperative Test Service and the Aviation Psychology Program of the Army Air Forces, now at Hunter College.

the number of the next item for that one is presumably the first item not read by the subject. This tally is the basis for a cumulative frequency table of the number of cases within the upper group who have not read each particular item. A similar count is made of the 'non-reads' in the lower group or the bottom twenty-seven per cent of the test papers.

By graphic item count on the International Test Scoring machine, or by other means, the number of right responses and the number of wrong responses in the upper group to each item is found. The omits may be obtained, if desired, by subtracting from the number of papers within the upper group the rights plus wrongs plus 'non-reads.' Similarly the omits among the lower group may be obtained, if desired.

Where the 'non-reads' represent an appreciable proportion of either criterion group the following formula for the U-L Index is suggested:

$$\frac{R_u}{(f - \text{'non-reads'}_u)} - \frac{R_l}{(f - \text{'non-reads'}_l)} \tag{4}$$

where R_u = number of right responses in the upper group
R_l = number of right responses in the lower group
$f = .27N$
'non-reads'$_u$ = 'non-reads' in the lower group
'non-reads'$_l$ = 'non-reads' in the upper group

The proportion $\frac{R_u}{(f - \text{'non-reads'}_u)}$ is the proportion of right responses in the upper group to the number in that group who read the item. The proportion $\frac{R_l}{(f - \text{'non-reads'}_l)}$ may be similarly interpreted for the lower group.

The U-L Index is proposed as a useful means of selecting items either to increase the internal consistency (odd-even reliability) of a test or to increase its correlation with a given criterion. Some advantages of the U-L Index are: (1) the demonstrated effectiveness of the upper vs. lower twenty-seven per cent technique on which it is based, (2) its ease of computation, and (3) the readiness with which its level of significance may be approximated.

33. A Rationale for Evaluation of Item Discrimination Statistics

WARREN G. FINDLEY

In this article Findley shows that the value of Johnson's U-L Index, here designated as D, is directly proportional to the number of correct discriminations made by the item. Acknowledging its dependence on item difficulty, he argues that this is usually advantageous rather than detrimental. He also suggests that useful guidance in item revision can be obtained from these simple upper-lower differences, especially when they are recorded for all possible responses to the item.

Evaluation specialists are accustomed to using complicated statistical measures of difficulty and discriminating power in assessing the worth of individual items in a test. In helping subject-matter specialists build achievement tests, however, they have learned to use simplified item statistics for several reasons: to reduce the computational chore, because the small numbers of cases often involved will not justify elaborate techniques, and to make the measures more comprehensible to the uninitiated. It is the thesis of this paper that one type of simplified technique lends itself to a rationale that should commend it not only as an aid for the unsophisticated, but as directly useful to the statistically sophisticated test specialist in evaluating test materials.

The type of simplified technique of item analysis in question is the broad general type in which the number right on the item in an upper fraction of the group with respect to criterion score (usually total score on the test itself) is compared with the number right in the corresponding lower fraction of the group. The comparison groups may be upper and lower halves, upper and lower thirds, upper and lower quarters, upper and lower 27 per cents, or whatever. For use with classroom or end-of-course tests prepared by instructors, upper and lower thirds are probably to be recommended to conserve cases while providing a clear cut on the criterion between upper and lower groups. For tests for large-scale use made by evaluation specialists, the magic upper and lower 27 per cents may be preferred in order to take advantage of tables and statistical relations derived for such groups.

Ebel (1) has argued that it is sufficient for purposes of guiding class-

Findley, W. G. A rationale for evaluation of item discrimination statistics. *Educational and Psychological Measurement,* 1956, *16,* 175–180. Reprinted with the permission of the publisher and author.

room instructors in the improvement of their tests to report for each item of a test the difference in the number right in the upper group and the number right in the lower group as a measure of the relative effectiveness of the item in achieving desired discriminations. However, Ebel (2) and Johnson (3) suggest dividing such differences by their maximum possible value, the number in each group, in order to have an abstract number that is independent of the size of the group involved.

Consider the following logic for such statistics. The optimal item would be one on which all in the upper group obtained the right answer and none in the lower group obtained the right answer. For simplicity of illustration, let us assume we have 100 in the upper group and 100 in the lower group. The ideal item would then distinguish each of the 100 individuals in the top group from each of the 100 individuals in the bottom group in the proper sense, and thus achieve 100×100, or 10,000, correct discriminations. Consider now an item on which 90 of the top group obtain the right answer, but only 40 of the bottom group get it. In this case we may say that the 90 in the top group who got the item right are distinguished correctly from the 60 in the bottom group who got it wrong, a total of 5400 correct discriminations. On the other hand, the 10 in the top group that got the item wrong are distinguished in the wrong sense from the 40 in the bottom group who got it right, a total of 400 incorrect discriminations. The difference, $5400 - 400 = 5000$, is the net amount of effective discrimination achieved by the item. This amount is 50 per cent of the 10,000 maximum possible correct discriminations achievable and entitles the item to an index of .50.

Note now that the simple difference between the number right in the top group and the number right in the bottom group, $90 - 40 = 50$, is also 50 per cent of the maximum possible value of this difference, 100. That this relation is direct and completely general may be shown by the brief algebraic derivation below.

Let $U =$ the number in the upper group who get the item right.
$L =$ the number in the lower group who get the item right.
$n =$ the number in each group.

Then $n - U =$ the number in the upper group who get the item wrong.
$n - L =$ the number in the lower group who get the item wrong.
$n \times n = n^2 =$ the maximum number of correct discriminations achievable when all the upper group get the item right and none of the lower group get it right $= D_{max.}$.
$U(n - L) =$ number of correct discriminations $= D_{+}$.
$L(n - U) =$ number of incorrect discriminations $= D_{-}$.

Then
$$\frac{D_+ - D_-}{D_{\max}} = \frac{U(n-L) - L(n-U)}{n^2}$$
$$= \frac{Un - UL - Ln + UL}{n^2}$$
$$= \frac{Un - Ln}{n^2} = \frac{n(U-L)}{n^2} = \frac{U-L}{n}$$

Table 1 presents an illustration of the generality of this relation for a set of items having the same difference (20) between number right in upper and lower groups, but differing in difficulty. The middle column of Neutral *D*'s accounts for the two other undiscriminated groups necessary to complete the total of 10,000 possible correct discriminations. In the case of each item, those in the upper group getting the item right are undifferentiated by that item from those in the lower group who get it right; similarly, those in the two groups who get the item wrong are undifferentiated by that item.

Finally, note that the bi-serial coefficients of correlation in the last column give higher values at the extremes of difficulty for items of equal discriminating power as measured by the index thus far discussed. It may be that such coefficients are more invariant in passing from one population to another of greater or lesser ability, but for the original group and similar groups, to which we ordinarily intend to apply the results of our item statistics, the "net discrimination achieved" has a more direct and comprehensible meaning.

As a subjective check on the relative merits of *D* and bi-serial *r* as indexes of item discriminating power, consider the data of Table 2. Items 1 and 2 are from the same test. *D* indicates item 2 has more discriminating power than item 1, while *r* indicates item 1 is more discriminating than item 2. Items 3 and 4 are from a second test. *D* indicates item 3 is far more discriminating than item 4, while *r* indicates they are almost equally discriminating. Finally, items 7 and 8 are from a third test. *D* indicates they are equally discriminating, but *r* indicates item 7 to be far more discriminating than item 8. Note in this last case that the below-chance frequency of choice of the right answer in the lower group on item 7 is dependent on the very large frequency of omissions by the lower group. Any shift in the direction of marking answers to all questions would tend to undermine the discriminating power of this item. In all three comparisons, I feel sure, most test specialists would feel better guided by the values of *D* than by the corresponding values of *r*.

Another virtue of these simple item statistics deserves mention. The difference between numbers right in top and bottom groups is inversely related to the numbers choosing the other options in the top and bottom groups. Consider again the item data presented in Table 2. For item 3,

TABLE 1. Discriminating Power of Items with Equal Difference Values (Groups of 100; Upper and Lower 27 Per Cent of Population of 370)

Correct Top-Bottom	Positive D	Neutral D	Negative D	Net D	Per Cent D	r
100–80	100 × 20 = 2000	(100 × 80) + (0 × 20) = 8,000	(0 × 80) = 0	2000	20	.54+
90–70	90 × 30 = 2700	(90 × 70) + (10 × 30) = 6,600	(10 × 70) = 700	2000	20	.30
80–60	80 × 40 = 3200	(80 × 60) + (20 × 40) = 5,600	(20 × 60) = 1200	2000	20	.24
70–50	70 × 50 = 3500	(70 × 50) + (30 × 50) = 5,000	(30 × 50) = 1500	2000	20	.21
60–40	60 × 60 = 3600	(60 × 40) + (40 × 60) = 4,800	(40 × 40) = 1600	2000	20	.20
50–30	50 × 70 = 3500	(50 × 30) + (50 × 70) = 5,000	(50 × 30) = 1500	2000	20	.21
40–20	40 × 80 = 3200	(40 × 20) + (60 × 80) = 5,600	(60 × 20) = 1200	2000	20	.24
30–10	30 × 90 = 2700	(30 × 10) + (70 × 90) = 6,600	(70 × 10) = 700	2000	20	.30
20–0	20 × 100 = 2000	(20 × 0) + (80 × 100) = 8,000	(80 × 0) = 0	2000	20	.54+

TABLE 2. Item Analysis—Comparative Data
(Groups of 100; Upper and Lower 27 Per Cent of Population of 370)

	Options							
Item	0	*a*	*b*	*c*	*d*	*e*	*D*	*r*
1	2–12	0–1	0–3	0–4	*98–77*	0–3	21	.48
2	16–23	2–11	6–10	4–10	5–10	*67–36*	31	.31
3	0–9	4–9	*77–34*	10–19	8–21	1–8	43	.44
4	0–0	0–3	0–1	*99–87*	1–6	0–6	12	.45
5	3–14	20–32	2–11	4–6	*71–26*	0–3	45	.45
6	6–21	*52–14*	35–13	4–26	0–5	3–12	38	.42
7	22–44	6–6	2–10	29–26	12–12	*29–2*	27	.54
8	8–11	11–17	5–14	*59–31*	12–17	5–10	28	.29
9	7–20	11–14	2–7	1–9	2–8	*67–39*	28	.28
10	2–8	*43–22*	34–40	4–12	5–7	2–11	21	.24

the difference of 43 shown by the underlined values for the right answer may be considered to have been produced by the distractive power of the several options in the amounts shown by the negative differences of 5 for option *a*, 9 for option *c*, 13 for option *d*, 7 for option *e*, and 9 for the option 0 for omits. This becomes helpful in guiding item revisions where one frequently has to choose between substituting for the option that attracts a few low scorers and substituting for an option chosen by many with a more nearly average score. Thus, in item 3, if revision were attempted, option *a* would be better to change than option *c* in terms of item statistics; in item 9, option *a* might better be changed than any other option; in item 10, option *d* might better be changed than option *b*. In all this, of course, the subject-matter specialist would be involved and might well adduce subject-matter considerations that would make statistical considerations secondary. But, within the realm of statistical interpretation, the upper-lower difference permits a precise measure of the distractive power of each option that cannot be achieved, except approximately by crude estimation, when the statistics for distractors are in the form of mean criterion scores and total numbers selecting each option.

The data of Table 2 incidentally illustrate the value of item statistics showing responses to *all* options. Note that item 6 might have passed muster about as well as item 5 on the basis of the right answer alone, while the statistics for option *b* clearly indicate need for a careful review. Item 7 is clearly marked out as having only one properly discriminating distractor, option *b*.

Conclusion

A logical analysis and mathematical derivation have been presented that justify interpreting simple differences between upper and lower groups as reflecting precisely the relative effectiveness of discrimination achieved by items in a test. Also, it has been pointed out one may interpret the negative differences on wrong options in an item as measures reflecting precisely the relative contributions made by the distractive power of the several options to the positive difference found for the correct option. It is felt that these interpretations help clarify item analysis for the sophisticated test specialist as well as for the generally less sophisticated subject-matter specialists who are responsible in whole or in part for constructing classroom and standardized achievement tests.

REFERENCES

1. Ebel, Robert L. "Procedures for the Analysis of Classroom Tests." *Educational and Psychological Measurement,* XIV (1954), 352–363.
2. Ebel, Robert L. "How an Examination Service Helps College Teachers to Give Better Tests" *Proceedings of the 1953 Invitational Conference on Testing Problems*. Princeton: Educational Testing Service, 1954.
3. Johnson, A. Pemberton. "Notes on a Suggested Index of Item Validity: The U-L Index" *Journal of Educational Psychology,* XLII (1951), 499–504.

34. A Comparison of Several Item Discrimination Indices[1]

MAX D. ENGELHART

The availability of a wide variety of different indices of discrimination has naturally raised questions about their relative merits and limitations and about the circumstances in which each may be most appropriate to use. A number of experimental studies, designed to answer some of these questions, have been undertaken and published. A good recent example is reported in the following article. But this is much more than a report of experimental data, for Engelhart contributes to an understanding of the indices he compares by discussing the definitions and derivations of the various indices.

The data reported show a high degree of agreement among the various indices and lead Engelhart to recommend use of the upper-lower index *D* on the ground of its simplicity of conception and calculation.

The item discrimination indices compared in this study include tetrachoric coefficients of correlation, phi or fourfold point correlation coefficients, biserial coefficients, point biserial coefficients, Davis discrimination indices, and simple differences in proportions of correct response between upper and lower groups given the symbol "D." The tetrachoric coefficients, the phi coefficients, and the D indices were secured for test samples both divided at the median total score and into highest and lowest thirds in terms of total scores. These subgroups were also used in obtaining the Davis indices. Use of subgroups comprising highest and lowest 27 per cents of the test sample in terms of total scores was shown by Kelley (1939) to yield the most sensitive item indices. In this study, highest and lowest thirds were used because the test samples were relatively small and it seemed that such subgroups would be more meaningful to instructors to whom item data are reported since they more nearly approximate the proportions of students earning

Engelhart, M. D. A comparison of several item discrimination indices. *Journal of Educational Measurement,* 1965, *2,* 69–76. Reprinted with the permission of the publisher and author.

[1] Paper read at the Annual Meeting of the National Council on Measurement in Education, Chicago, Illinois, February 1965. Material supplementary to this article has been deposited as Document No. 8356 with the ADI Auxiliary Publications Project, Photoduplication Service, Library of Congress, Washington 25, D.C. A copy may be secured by citing the Document number and by remitting $2.50 for photoprints, or $1.75 for 35 mm. microfilm. Advance payment is required. Make checks or money orders payable to: Chief, Photoduplication Service, Library of Congress.

A and B and D and F course marks. In any case, use of highest and lowest thirds does not materially affect the comparisons made in this study. Had highest and lowest 27 per cents been used, the indices concerned would have generally been slightly higher.

The sources of data were two samples of 210 answer sheets used with Forms A and B of the 60-item Constitution Test used in the Illinois State High School Equivalency Testing Program. In these tests, series of key-list and multiple-choice exercises assess examinee knowledge of the Illinois Constitution, the United States Constitution, the Declaration of Independence, and flag etiquette. The tests have no time limit and no correction is made for guessing. The total scores of the Form A sample have a mean of 30.10 and a standard deviation of 7.67. The Kuder-Richardson 20 reliability coefficient obtained from the sample data is .80. The Form A total scores correlated .70 with the average standard scores of the GED tests taken by the same examinees. For the Form B sample, the mean and standard deviation are respectively 30.42 and 7.74. The Kuder-Richardson reliability is .81 and the correlation with GED average standard scores is .72. Item analysis data obtained in this study have been used in the revision of both forms.

A tetrachoric coefficient of correlation whether obtained from samples split at the median total score or divided into highest and lowest 27 per cents is an estimate of the Pearson product-moment coefficient. It can be thought of as an estimate of the correlation coefficient which would appear in the equation of the normal correlation surface best fitting the per cents or proportions in a fourfold table. Imagine a normal bivariate distribution given in a table of 25 rows and 25 columns from which a product-moment coefficient of +.60 can be computed, changing the proportions in each cell to equivalent frequencies. Then suppose that this table is divided at the means or medians of both variables to give four quadrants containing the per cents of frequencies 30 and 70 in the left and right upper quadrants and 70 and 30 in the left and right lower quadrants. These per cents when used to estimate a tetrachoric r will yield a coefficient of +.60. In the case of the tetrachoric coefficient it is assumed that the variables dichotomized are continuous and normally distributed. Many regard this as a reasonable assumption with reference to the abilities measured by single test items scored 1 or 0, but some authorities do not.

The equation for tetrachoric r derived by Pearson is extremely long and complex although less complicated approximation formulas are available. If not calculated by computer, tetrachoric coefficients are usually obtained through use of computing diagrams or abacs or from tables. Such abacs or tables are derived from tables of normal bivariate frequency distributions corresponding to various values of product-moment *r*. In item analysis, one enters such an abac or table with the per cents (or proportions) of examinees in the upper and lower groups responding correctly to the given item, identifying the per cents in the top and left margins. In an abac one then notes the intersect of horizontal and vertical lines from the per cents. (Such lines are not actually drawn, nor the intersect marked. It may be located through use of edges of cards.) The intersect just mentioned may fall on a curve labeled, for example, +.40 or it may fall between two such labeled curves and interpolation is required. When a table is used, the per cents are also identified in the top and left margins while the corresponding tetrachoric coefficient appears within the table in the corresponding row and column. The abac prepared by Mosier and McQuitty (1940) was used to obtain the tetrachoric coefficients (r_{t_1}) from the median split data while the table produced by Chung-Teh Fan (1952) was used to obtain tetrachoric coefficients (r_{t_2}) from the highest and lowest thirds data. The Fan table yields coefficients corresponding to those which may be obtained from an abac introduced by Flanagan (1939) or from a table also prepared by Flanagan (Thorndike, 1949, p. 348–351 or Walker and Lev, 1953, p. 472–475). The Fan table is especially convenient since no interpolation is required and very effective difficulty indices are also listed.

Phi coefficients, or fourfold point correlation coefficients, are actually product-moment correlation coefficients. Their formula can be derived from the usual product-moment formula. The phi coefficient differs from the tetrachoric coefficient, however, in that it does not similarly estimate the degree of correlation or strength of relationship. For example, where upper and lower per cents of correct response equal 70 and 30, phi equals .40 where tetrachoric *r* equals .60. Phi tends to favor test items of moderate difficulty when used as a basis of item selection, a characteristic it shares with the point biserial coefficient and the simple index, *D*. Where upper and lower groups contain equal numbers of tests whether upper and lower halves, highest and lowest thirds, or highest and lowest 27 per cents, phi coefficients can be computed by means of the formula:

$$\phi = \frac{p_u - p_l}{2\sqrt{pq}}$$

Given a list of reciprocals of $2\sqrt{pq}$ for values of p or q from .50 to .99, values of ϕ can be quickly computed by multiplying each $p_u - p_l$ with a desk calculator or a slide rule. The values of $\sqrt{pq}$ needed can be found in Guilford (1950, p. 614).

Where p, or the proportion of correct response in the total sample, equals the average of p_u and p_l expressed as proportions, the same values of the phi coefficient can be obtained from an abac developed by Guilford (1950 and 1954) and very conveniently from the table produced by Jurgensen (1947) to obtain the phi coefficients (ϕ_1 and ϕ_2).

The discrimination indices D_1 and D_2 are the simple differences between the proportions of correct response in upper and lower groups. In the case of D_1 the split was at the median, and, in the case of D_2, highest and lowest thirds were used. The discrimination indices D_1 and D_2 are direct measures of the numbers of discriminations made by an item. Like phi, but to a greater extent, this index favors items of moderate difficulty. As will be seen from the data reported in later pages, D_1 and D_2 may decrease in size for very easy or very difficult items while the correlation-type indices increase in magnitude. According to the correlation-type index such an item may have considerable discriminating power, but according to D it is discriminating among relatively few examinees. For further discussion of this index see Bridgman (1964), Ebel (1954 a and b), Findley (1956), and Johnson (1951).

Biserial coefficients (r_b) and point biserial coefficients (r_{pb}) are estimates of the correlation between one variable measured finely along a continuum, for example, total test scores, while the other variable is measured dichotomously, for example, 1 or 0 on a test item. In the case of the biserial coefficient the trait or ability underlying the dichotomous variable is assumed to be normally distributed. In the case of the point biserial coefficient, no such assumption need be made. Both of these indices were obtained through use of the standard formulas presented in most texts on statistical method. A major disadvantage of both is the labor of obtaining the means of the total test scores of those examinees responding correctly to each item—as many means as there are items in the test.

Davis index values are conversions of tetrachoric coefficients for the highest and lowest 27 per cent split to a scale of equal units based on Fisher's *z*. (As everyone knows, a difference between correlations of .20 and .25 is not comparable to a difference between coefficients of .85 and .90.) The Davis difficulty indices are also based on a scale of equal units. The Davis chart (1946) is similar to the Fan and Jurgensen tables, but interpolation is required where one or both per cents are odd.

Tables 1 and 2 report the intercorrelations between the various item discrimination indices and the means and standard deviations of the indices. The last line of each of these tables reports as "*g*" the correlations between each index and the first centroid factor of each matrix of correlations. The values of "*g*" are a measure of what the various indices have in common. While all of the correlations and the values of "*g*" are impressively high, those for the *D*'s are among the lower ones. This reflects some amount of curvilinear relationship with indices which tend to increase for items of low or high difficulty.

TABLE 1. Intercorrelations Between the Various Item Discrimination Indices, the Means and Standard Deviations of the Indices and the Values of "*g*"—Form A[2]

	r_{t_1}	ϕ_1	D_1	r_{t_2}	ϕ_2	D_2	r_b	r_{pb}	Davis Index
r_{t_1}	—	.967	.889	.945	.906	.846	.939	.924	.931
ϕ_1		—	.974	.947	.956	.933	.917	.945	.943
D_1			—	.896	.949	.964	.841	.908	.897
r_{t_2}				—	.979	.932	.948	.954	.992
ϕ_2					—	.985	.911	.951	.976
D_2						—	.848	.917	.933
r_b							—	.982	.934
r_{pb}								—	.943
Davis Index									—
M	38.1	22.9	20.6	32.3	29.6	27.2	38.1	28.4	21.3
s	20.8	13.0	12.6	17.7	16.8	16.6	17.8	13.4	12.9
"*g*"	.953	.981	.951	.985	.986	.957	.952	.975	.979

[2] The correlations, means, and standard deviations, were computed in the Bureau of Data Processing of the Chicago Public Schools.

TABLE 2. Intercorrelations Between the Various Item Discrimination Indices, the Means and Standard Deviations of the Indices and the Values of "*g*"—Form B

	r_{t_1}	ϕ_1	D_1	r_{t_2}	ϕ_2	D_2	r_b	r_{pb}	Davis Index
r_{t_1}	—	.984	.943	.949	.932	.901	.925	.923	.940
ϕ_1		—	.985	.939	.951	.941	.909	.931	.929
D_1			—	.905	.947	.959	.867	.913	.900
r_{t_2}				—	.985	.950	.957	.962	.991
ϕ_2					—	.990	.938	.967	.978
D_2						—	.901	.949	.945
r_b							—	.987	.948
r_{pb}								—	.954
Davis Index									—
M	36.1	22.2	20.4	32.5	30.8	28.6	37.6	28.3	21.5
s	19.2	12.2	12.1	16.4	16.3	16.2	17.4	13.4	11.4
"*g*"	.968	.976	.959	.984	.990	.973	.960	.978	.978

Although ϕ_1 correlates most highly with D_1 and ϕ_2 correlates most highly with D_2 and, in general, both ϕ_1 and ϕ_2 have most in common with other indices as shown by the values of "*g*", for four items ϕ_1 disagrees with D_1 and for one item, ϕ_2 disagrees with D_2. In all five of the quite difficult or easy items it is the D_1 or D_2 which indicates the discrimination as unsatisfactory according to the standards listed in Table 3. Although it is probably safest to conclude that both ϕ_1 and ϕ_2 (and ϕ_2 especially) are as efficient as D_1 and D_2 in identifying unsatisfactory items, the former exhibit some tendency to increase for very difficult or very easy items. The obtaining of ϕ_1 or ϕ_2 requires more effort than the obtaining of D_1 or D_2 and the latter are more readily explained to teachers.

TABLE 3. Equivalent Item Discrimination Indices

For the median split:			
(a) Where $p_t = 50$, $p_u = 60$, $p_l = 40$;	$r_{t_1} = .30$	$\phi_1 = .20$	$D_1 = .20$
(b) Where $p_t = 70$, $p_u = 79$, $p_l = 62$;	$r_{t_1} = .30$	$\phi_1 = .19$	$D_1 = .17$
(c) Where $p_t = 85$, $p_u = 90$, $p_l = 78$;	$r_{t_1} = .30$	$\phi_1 = .16$	$D_1 = .12$
For the highest 27 per cent—lowest 27 per cent split:			
(a) Where $p_t = 50$, $p_u = 65$, $p_l = 35$;	$r_{t_2} = .30$	$\phi_2 = .30$	$D_2 = .30$
	$r_b = .30$	$r_{pb} = .24$	Davis Index = 19
(b) Where $p_t = 70$, $p_u = 83$, $p_l = 58$;	$r_{t_2} = .30$	$\phi_2 = .27$	$D_2 = .25$
	$r_b = .30$	$r_{pb} = .23$	Davis Index = 19
(c) Where $p_t = 85$, $p_u = 93$, $p_l = 76$;	$r_{t_2} = .30$	$\phi_2 = .24$	$D_2 = .17$
	$r_b = .30$	$r_{pb} = .20$	Davis Index = 19

It is claimed that biserial coefficients and other estimates of correlation are more stable from population to population. If so, this is probably of greater importance with reference to standardized or other tests widely used than with reference to tests locally constructed and used with comparable populations.

In Table 3 are listed values of the various discrimination indices occurring for items of 50, 70, and 85 per cent correct response (or 50, 30, and 15 per cent correct response) where the differences in per cents for upper and lower groups (p_u and p_l) are such as to yield tetrachoric coefficients of +.30. The indices listed were obtained as earlier explained, except that the biserial coefficients were estimated by means of an abac produced by Dingman and quoted by Guilford (1954, p. 428) and the point biserial coefficients computed from the equation relating them to biserial coefficients. An item-test correlation of less than +.30 is often regarded as indicative of items of dubious discriminating power —items which should be eliminated or revised. The values listed in Table 3, including the correlation coefficients, may all be used as approximately equivalent critical values for certain suggested ranges of item difficulty.

The indices in the lines labeled (*a*) may be used as critical values for the p_t range 30–70, those in the lines labeled (*b*) for the ranges 15–29 or 71–85, and those in the lines labeled (*c*) for items of less than 15 or more than 85 per cent correct response.

Application of the standards in Table 3 to the data obtained for the 120 items in the two forms of the test revealed 92 items unequivocally classified as satisfactory or unsatisfactory by all of the indices, 6 items with one index exceptional, 11 items with two indices exceptional, and 11 items with three or four indices reversing the others. For 8 of the 120 items, D_1 was exceptional to a majority of the other indices, but 6 of the 8 were quite difficult or relatively easy items. For 10 of the 120 items D_2 was similarly exceptional, but 7 of the 10 were either very difficult or comparatively easy. Five of the 6 items and all of the 7 items just noted were identified as unsatisfactory by D_1 or D_2 though correlation-type indices supported them as discriminating.

These data support the conclusion that the simple discrimination indices D_1 and D_2 are remarkably effective in identifying relatively poor items for elimination or revision. It should be recalled in this connection that D_1 and D_2 are more indicative of actual numbers of discriminations made by items than indices of the correlation type. In this connection, see especially Findley (1956).

For items of moderate difficulty a D_1 of +.20 of a D_2 of +.30 may be regarded as the critical values. For relatively easy or relatively difficult items these critical values may be lowered as described above where a wide range of difficulties is desired. See Davis (1946, p. 21–26 and 1951, p. 308–312) and Guilford (1950, p. 489–492 and 1954, p. 390–391) for excellent discussions of the merit of seeking a range of difficulties in tests designed to discriminate among students of varying levels of ability rather than at some given level of ability.

Where item-analysis data are obtained largely for use by teachers and for tests locally constructed, the indices D_1 or D_2 should suffice, especially if they can be obtained for *all* answers to each item.

REFERENCES

Bridgman, C. S. The relation of the upper-lower item discrimination index, *D*, to the bivariate normal correlation coefficient. *Educational and Psychological Measurement*, 1964, **24**, 85–90.

Davis, F. B. Item-analysis data: their computation, interpretation, and use in test construction. *Harvard Education Papers, No. 2*. Cambridge: Graduate School of Education, Harvard University, 1946.

Davis, F. B. Item selection techniques. Chapter 9 in E. F. Lindquist (Ed.), *Educational Measurement*, Washington, D.C.: American Council on Education, 1951.

Ebel, R. L. How an examination service helps college teachers to give better tests. *Proceedings of the 1953 Invitational Conference on Testing Problems*. Princeton: Educational Testing Service, 1954a.

Ebel, R. L. Procedures for the analysis of classroom tests. *Educational and Psychological Measurement*, 1954, **14**, 352–363, b.

Fan, Chung-Teh. *Item-Analysis table*. Princeton: Educational Testing Service, 1952.

Findley, W. G. A rationale for evaluation of item discrimination statistics. *Educational and Psychological Measurement*, 1956, **16**, 175–180.

Flanagan, J. C. General considerations in the selection of test items and a short method of estimating the product-moment coefficient from data at the tails of the distribution. *Journal of Educational Psychology*, 1939, **30**, 674–680.

Guilford, J. P. *Fundamental Statistics in Psychology and Education*. New York: McGraw-Hill, 1950.

Guilford, J. P. *Psychometric methods*. New York: McGraw-Hill, 1954.

Johnson, A. P. Notes on a suggested index of item validity: the U-L Index. *Journal of Educational Psychology*, 1951, **42**, 499–504.

Jurgensen, C. E. Table for determining phi coefficients. *Psychometrika*, 1947, **12**, 17–29.

Kelley, T. L. The selection of upper and lower groups for the validation of test items. *Journal of Educational Psychology*, 1939, **30**, 17–24.

Mosier, C. I., & McQuitty, J. V. Methods of item validation and abacs for item-test correlation and critical ratio of upper-lower differences. *Psychometrika*, 1940, **5**, 57–65.

Thorndike, R. L. *Personnel selection test and measurement techniques*. New York: John Wiley and Sons, 1949.

Walker, H., & Lev, J. *Statistical inference*. New York: Henry Holt and Company, 1953.

35. Notes on the Rationale of Item Analysis

MARION W. RICHARDSON

As long ago as 1936, some test specialists were expressing concern over the possibility that ". . . the ingenuity displayed in the invention of new indices has outstripped the critical examination of the logical foundation for item analysis." The following article was written to help understanding catch up with computation. It was written by a test specialist whose rational and inventive mind contributed enormously to the development of psychometric science. Dr. Richardson used algebra as a tool to develop practical principles of test construction that can be expressed, as they are expressed here, in non-algebraic language.

Richardson, M. W. Notes on the rationale of item analysis. *Psychometrika*, 1936, *1*, 69–76. Reprinted with the permission of the publisher.

Mosier (1936) examines the implications of the article in the light of multiple-factor theory.

Item Validity

There is increasing use of item analysis procedures for the improvement of objective examinations. The development of the procedures of item analysis has consisted chiefly of the invention of various forms of an index of association between the test item and the total test score. At least ten indices of item validity have appeared in various articles, which have been chiefly concerned with the relative effectiveness of the indices as devices for the improvement of tests. (4, 5, 6, 10). Since these indices of "item validity" are substitutes for or approximations to the ordinary coefficient of correlation between the item and the total test score, it may be useful to present certain deductions from simple correlational algebra. The present writer is of the opinion that the ingenuity displayed in the invention of new indices has outstripped the critical examination of the logical foundation for item analysis. The subsequent discussion is therefore concerned only with the underlying rationale of item analysis.

The first step in the description of item analysis procedures is to express the item-test coefficient in terms of the item intercorrelations. A test score t is defined by the equation

$$t \equiv x_1 + x_2 + x_3 + \cdots + x_n\,, \qquad (1)$$

where t is the deviate score on the test, and the x's are the deviate scores on the items, which are n in number. This definition embodies, of course, the usual practice of summing the unit or zero scores on the separate objective items to obtain the total test score. Let us take r_{it}, the correlation between any item i and the test t as a measure of item validity.

Then

$$r_{it} \equiv \frac{\sum x_i t}{N\sigma_i\sigma_t} \qquad (2)$$

where σ_i is the standard deviation of item i, and σ_t is the standard deviation of the test scores. The general subscript i means that the formula applies to any item of a given test. The summation is over the population N. Substituting in (2) the value of t from (1), we have

$$r_{it} \equiv \frac{\sum x_i\,(x_1 + x_2 + \cdots + x_n)}{N\sigma_i\sigma_t} \qquad (3)$$

$$= \frac{\sum x_i x_1 + \sum x_i x_2 + \cdots + \sum x_i x_n}{N\sigma_i\sigma_t}$$

$$= \frac{N\,r_{i1}\sigma_i\sigma_1 + N\,r_{i2}\sigma_i\sigma_2 + \cdots + N\,r_{in}\sigma_i\sigma_n}{N\sigma_i\sigma_t}$$

If we now assume that

$$\sigma_i = \sigma_1 = \sigma_2 = \sigma_3 = \cdots \sigma_n \,,$$

which is rigidly true when all items are of the same difficulty as measured by the percentage of correct response, and approximately true for a wide range of difficulty, we have

$$r_{it} = \frac{N\,\sigma_i^2 \sum_{k=1}^{n} r_{ik}}{N\sigma_i\sigma_t} = \frac{\sigma_i \sum_{k=1}^{n} r_{ik}}{\sigma_t}\,, \tag{4}$$

in which the summation is over the n correlations of item i with each of the n items in turn. In order to further simplify equation (4), the standard deviation of test scores σ_t will be expressed in terms of the test elements. Squaring (1), and summing, we have

$$\Sigma t^2 = \Sigma x_1^2 + \Sigma x_2^2 + \cdots + \Sigma x_n^2 + 2\,\Sigma x_1x_2 + \cdots + 2\,\Sigma x_1x_n$$
$$+ \cdots + 2\,\Sigma x_{n-1}x_n = N\sigma_t^2 = N\sigma_i^2 \sum_{i=1}^{n}\sum_{k=1}^{n} r_{ik}. \tag{5}$$

The double summation indicates that all item intercorrelations are taken. We can simplify (5) to

$$\sigma_t = \sigma_i \sqrt{\sum_{i=1}^{n}\sum_{k=1}^{n} r_{ik}}\,, \tag{6}$$

Substituting this value of σ_t in equation (4), we may write

$$r_{it} = \frac{\sum_{k=1}^{n} r_{ik}}{+\sqrt{\sum_{i=1}^{n}\sum_{k=1}^{n} r_{ik}}}\,. \tag{7}$$

Equation (7) expresses any item-test correlation as a function of the item intercorrelations. As applied to any item i of a test homogeneous in difficulty, the item-test correlation is equal to the sum of the correlations of that item with all items of the test, divided by the positive square root of the sum of all item intercorrelations. (In any actual test, the denominator of (7) will not be imaginary). Since the denominator is constant in any situation where item analysis procedures are employed, it can be concluded that:

In a test of uniform difficulty, the correlation of an item with the test is proportional to the average correlation of that item with each item of the test.

Since the item intercorrelation coefficients themselves form a distribution, it may be concluded that:

The rejection of items whose correlations with the test are relatively low raises the average intercorrelations of the remaining items.

The formal similarity of equation (7) to Thurstone's expression for the first factor loading for the Centroid Method is not accidental. (9). The first factor loading on the centroid is a measure of the correlation between a test and the sum or average of the tests in the battery. A similar interpretation may be made in the item analysis situation. The item-test coefficient measures the correlation between a variable (the item) and the sum or average of many such variables. In this context, the item-test coefficient is the "factor" loading of the item with an arbitrary test variable which is the sum of the items. These considerations make it possible to conclude that:

The item-test cofficient gives an indication of the extent to which the item measures what the test as a whole measures. The item-test coefficient merely tells whether or not an item is in step with other items of the test.

Item Validity and Test Reliability

If we assume, as in the foregoing, equal difficulty of items, the Spearman-Brown Formula might be used to estimate the reliability of a test of n items from $\bar{r}_{ik}$, the (average) correlation between two items. This is significant in connection with the effect of rejection of items with low item intercorrelations upon the reliability of the test. Let us take $\bar{r}_{ik}$, the average item intercorrelation as a measure of item reliability. Equation (7) gives the expression for any item-test coefficient. If we now add the n item-test coefficients we have

$$\sum_{i=1}^{n} r_{it} = \frac{\sum_{i=1}^{n}\sum_{k=1}^{n} r_{ik}}{+\sqrt{\sum_{i=1}^{n}\sum_{k=1}^{n} r_{ik}}} = +\sqrt{\sum_{i=1}^{n}\sum_{k=1}^{n} r_{ik}}\,. \tag{8}$$

The sum of the item-test coefficients is simply the positive square root of the sum of the item intercorrelations.

Writing equation (8) in terms of the respective average coefficients we have

$$n\,\bar{r}_{it} = +\sqrt{n^2\,\bar{r}_{ik}}\;,$$

where $\bar{r}$ means the average of the respective r's.
This is simplified to

$$\bar{r}_{it} = +\sqrt{\bar{r}_{ik}}\;,$$

or

$$\bar{r}_{it}{}^2 = \bar{r}_{ik}\,. \tag{9}$$

Substituting $\bar{r}_{ik}$ in the Spearman-Brown Formula, we may write

$$R = \frac{n\,\bar{r}_{ik}}{1 + (n-1)\bar{r}_{ik}}\,, \tag{10}$$

where R is the reliability coefficient. Solving for $\bar{r}_{ik}$, we have

$$\bar{r}_{ik} = \frac{R}{n-nR+R}\,. \tag{11}$$

Also, from (9) and (11), we may write

$$\bar{r}_{it} = \sqrt{\frac{R}{n-nR+R}}\,. \tag{12}$$

Equation (12) gives a direct solution for the mean item-test coefficient. Either the mean item-test coefficient or its square may be used as a measure of the cohesiveness or purity of the test. If equation (10) is used to compute the reliability coefficient from the mean item-test coefficient and the number of items, the estimate of the reliability coefficient will not be subject to the fluctuations in the value of R which are due to the arbitrary samplings of items to get the two split-halves. These fluctuations may be considerable in magnitude for different split-halves when the test is short. (2).

From the foregoing equation, it is possible to conclude that:

The rejection of items with low item-test correlations raises the reliability of a test, if the number of items is held constant. Whether the reliability coefficient will be raised absolutely, even with a reduced number of items, depends upon the dispersion of the original item intercorrelations. If this dispersion is great, extending to a number of negative values, it is theoretically possible to attain a higher reliability with a smaller number of items.

True Variance and Item Intercorrelation

An alternative way of expressing the relationship of item intercorrelation to reliability is here given for its illustrative value. The true variance can be expressed in terms of the number of items, their common standard deviation, and the average item intercorrelation. The test variance may be written:

$$\sigma_t^2 = n\sigma_i^2 + n(n-1)\,\bar{r}_{ik}\,\sigma_i^2\,,$$

which may be simplified to

$$\sigma_t^2 = n\sigma_i^2[1 + (n-1)\,\bar{r}_{ik}]\,. \tag{13}$$

Equation (13) is simply another way of writing equation (5).

Since the true variance is given by

$$\sigma_\infty{}^2 = \mathrm{R}\sigma_t^2\,, \tag{14}$$

we obtain by substituting in equation (14) the estimates of R and σ_t^2 from (10) and (13) respectively,

$$\sigma_\infty{}^2 = \frac{n\,\bar{r}_{ik}}{1 + (n-1)\,\bar{r}_{ik}} \cdot n\sigma_i^2\left[1 + (n-1)\,\bar{r}_{ik}\right]\cdot$$

This can be simplified to

$$\sigma_{\infty}^{2} = n^{2}\sigma_{i}^{2}\bar{r}_{ik} \,. \tag{15}$$

The conclusion is that:

For tests of homogeneous difficulty and constant length, the true variance is proportional to the average item intercorrelation.

Empirical Verification

It is hardly necessary to verify equation (7), since the verification must consist essentially of numerical substitution into each of two cognate algebraic formulas. Nevertheless, the following data are presented. Twenty-five objective items were selected from a long achievement test, in a completely random manner, except that they were of approximately the same difficulty. Table I gives the difficulty distribution of the items.

TABLE I

Percentage of correct answers	Number of items
35	1
36	6
37	6
38	6
39	5
40	1

The mean score of the 100 subjects on the 25 item test was 9.36; the standard deviation was 4.24. The item-test correlations were computed by use of the formula for the point bi-serial coefficient (the Pearson r) $r = \frac{M_p - M_q}{\sigma} \cdot \sqrt{pq}$, where M_p is the mean score of those passing the item, M_q is the mean score of those failing the item, σ is the standard deviation of the distribution of scores, p and q are the percentage of correct and incorrect answers, respectively. (7).

The item intercorrelations were computed according to the formula

$$r = \frac{p_{12} - p_1 p_2}{\sqrt{p_1 q_1 p_2 q_2}} \,,$$

where $p_1 =$ the percentage of population who give correct response on the first item,

$p_2 =$ the percentage of correct response on the second item.

$q_1 = 1 - p_1$,

$q_2 = 1 - p_2$,

$p_{12} =$ percentage of the population who give the correct response to both items.

Table II displays in parallel columns the two independently computed values of the item-test coefficients of correlation.

TABLE II

Item Number	Item-test Correlation: Computed by the formula $r = \frac{M_p - M_q}{\sigma} \cdot \sqrt{pq}$	Item-test Correlation: Computed by equation (7)
1	.424	.424
2	.510	.517
3	.289	.287
4	.373	.376
5	.157	.181
6	.370	.385
7	.285	.285
8	.144	.148
9	.262	.254
10	.189	.202
11	.456	.454
12	.080	.079
13	.564	.561
14	.328	.326
15	.436	.438
16	.515	.514
17	.214	.218
18	.388	.387
19	.416	.421
20	.280	.284
21	.412	.410
22	.481	.477
23	.312	.309
24	.274	.272
25	.559	.556

Average discrepancy = 1.31 per cent of first computed value.

Summary

The foregoing development indicates that the reliability of a test may be improved by the use of the procedures of item analysis. Furthermore, such procedures will tend to make the test more pure or homogeneous, in the sense of conserving those items which have the largest intercorrelations. This is the only sense in which it may be said that the conserved items are more "valid" than the rejected items. (8, 10).

The use of item analysis procedures of the type described does not necessarily select items whose sums will give the best prediction of an external criterion; Horst's Method of Successive Residuals is a solution of this problem. (3).

BIBLIOGRAPHY

1. Anderson, John E., The Effect of Item Analysis upon the Discriminative Power of an Examination, *J. Appl. Psychol.*, 1935, 19, 237–244.
2. Brownell, Wm. A., On the Accuracy with which Reliability May Be Measured by Correlating Test Halves, *J. Exper. Educ.*, 1933, 1, 204–215.
3. Horst, Paul, Item Analysis by the Method of Successive Residuals, *J. Exper. Educ.*, 1934, 2, 254–263.
4. Lentz, T. F., Hirshstein, Bertha, and Finch, J. H., Evaluation of Methods of Evaluating Test Items, *J. Educ. Psychol.*, 1932, 23, 344–350.
5. Lindquist, E. F., and Cook, W. W., Experimental Procedures in Test Evaluation, *J. Exper. Educ.*, 1933, 1, 163–185.
6. Long, John A., and Sandiford, Peter, and others: The Validation of Test Items, *Bull. Dept. Educ. Res. Ontario Coll. Educ.*, 1935, No. 3, pp. 126.
7. Richardson, M. W., and Stalnaker, J. M., A Note on the Use of Biserial *r* in Test Research, *J. Gen. Psychol.*, 1933, 8, 463–465.
8. Smith, Max, The Relationship between Item Validity and Test Validity, *Teach, Coll. Contrib. Educ.*, 1934, No. 621. pp. vii + 40.
9. Thurstone, L. L., The Vectors of Mind, Chicago: Univ. Chicago Press, 1935. pp. xv + 266.
10. Zubin, J., The Method of Internal Consistency for Selecting Test Items, *J. Educ. Psychol.*, 1934, 25, 345–356.

36. Criticisms of Commonly Used Methods of Validating Achievement Test Items

OSCAR K. BUROS

Dr. Buros, in this brief article, identifies four methods of item validation that he believes should be abandoned, and suggests three other approaches that should receive increased attention. The author presents his suggestions ". . . with the hope of provoking discussion and thought. . . ." They are

Buros, O. K. Criticisms of commonly used methods of validating achievement test items. *Proceedings of the 1948 Invitational Conference on Testing Problems, Educational Testing Service,* 1949, 18–20. Reprinted with the permission of the publisher and author.

reprinted here for the same reason and not because the editors of this volume agree with all of the recommendations made.

With the hope of provoking discussion and thought regarding the adequacy of many of our practices in the construction of achievement test items, I should like to make several suggestions. Since my time is very short, I shall present each suggestion rather briefly and somewhat dogmatically. If you wish me to elaborate upon any of these points during the discussion period, I shall be glad to do so.

1. *The practice of validating achievement test items by selecting only those items which are answered correctly by an increasing percentage of students in successive grades should be abandoned.* This procedure was, to my knowledge, first used in the construction of a school achievement test by three of our most distinguished testing specialists—Truman L. Kelley, the late Giles M. Ruch, and Lewis M. Terman—when they prepared the Stanford Achievement Test over twenty-five years ago. Practically all achievement batteries today use the same procedure of item validation; e.g., this was done in the recently revised *Metropolitan Achievement Tests* and the recently published *Coordinated Scales of Attainment*. This criterion begs the question and results in emasculated tests of questionable validity. No test validated in such a manner can be used to determine differences in grade achievement. The tests which result exaggerate differences in grade achievements, conceal areas in which little or no learning has taken place, and cover up areas in which there have been actual decreases in student attainments.

2. *The practice of validating achievement test items by selecting only those items which are most closely correlated with the total score should be discontinued.* This criterion also begs the question and results in emasculated tests of questionable validity. No test validated in such a manner can be used to determine differences in the performance of the so-called poor and good students. The tests which result exaggerate differences in student achievements, give a lopsided emphasis to those factors represented most heavily in the total score, and fail to give information about growth or lack of growth toward certain desired learning outcomes.

3. *The practice of considering "measurement" and "differentiation" as synonymous terms should be abandoned.* A test may be an excellent measuring instrument and yet not differentiate among individuals within a given group. Our objective should be primarily to measure with a given degree of accuracy—differentiation may or may not follow.

4. *The practice of discarding items merely because they are passed or failed by all examinees in a tryout group should be abandoned.* If the items have curricular validity, they should be retained both for purposes of measurement and for purposes of motivation. Under no

circumstances should items be omitted solely on the grounds that only chance scores were obtained in a tryout group.

5. *We should give more attention to subjective procedures for evaluating test items.* In most cases, the best way to determine item validity is to study carefully the nature of the response which the item elicits and then to decide whether the response would give any useful evidence concerning growth or lack of growth toward the particular objectives which the test is designed to measure. Unfortunately, this procedure will call for much more work and ability than our present cut-and-dried methods of item validation by the statistical methods which I mentioned earlier. Additional procedures which might well be used to validate individual test items would be the use of a free response or short essay question covering the same ground and the use of individual interviews in which the examinee is probed to ascertain his understanding of the concept covered by the question. It also should be remembered that checks on the validity of test items must be repeated at intervals in order to determine whether changes in the learning situation may have diminished or destroyed the original validity of the test. For example, coaching exercises designed to help students pass reading tests have certainly vitiated to a large extent the validity of many of our reading tests.

6. *We should enlist the cooperation of specialists in subject matter, teaching, and curriculum construction.* This cooperation must not be of the kind which has characterized most of the test construction work to date. At present there is too much of a tendency to enlist the support of only those subject-matter and curriculum specialists who will go along with the test technician in his erudite methods of statistical validation. The specialists in other areas should be invited to cooperate as coequals and not be intimidated by technical jargon which makes no sense to them.

7. *Test authors and publishers should be impelled to present a great deal more data than they now do concerning the methods which they used to secure a valid test.* Vague statements such as, "The customary methods of curricular and statistical validation of test items have been used to ensure the best possible test," are useless and misleading. If an analysis of textbooks was made, a detailed description of the analysis and the results should be reported in order that others may judge the study and the use made of it. In any equally as detailed manner, all other aspects of test construction should be described. I should like to suggest that test authors and publishers go further. Let them point out common objectives not measured by their tests; let them suggest ways in which the tests may be supplemented locally in order to have a reasonably well-rounded evaluation program. I am confident that the publication of much more detailed data regarding test validity will result in criticism which will force test makers to construct better tests.

37. Efficiency of Multiple-Choice Tests as a Function of Spread of Item Difficulties*

LEE J. CRONBACH
WILLARD G. WARRINGTON

The preceding articles in this section of the book have dealt primarily with item discrimination. Item difficulty has been mentioned mainly in connection with its presumed influence on item discrimination. But in some situations the effectiveness of a test may be affected directly by the distribution (or spread) of item difficulty values.

Many test specialists have turned their attention to this problem. They discovered long ago the fallacy in the simplistic notion that because examinees differ in ability, test items must differ correspondingly in difficulty. They discovered that for the kinds of tests ordinarily used in education, uniform item difficulty at some middle level gave greatest overall validity. But they also discovered that these principles need to be qualified in some special situations.

In the following article Cronbach and Warrington present a thorough analysis of the problem and arrive at a number of practical recommendations. Other articles related to this issue are Richardson (1936), Gulliksen (1945), Lord (1952), and Myers (1962).

The validity of a univocal multiple-choice test is determined for varying distributions of item difficulty and varying degrees of item precision. Validity is a function of $\sigma_d^2 + \sigma_y^2$, where σ_d measures item unreliability and σ_y measures the spread of item difficulties. When this variance is very small, validity is high for one optimum cutting score, but the test gives relatively little valid information for other cutting scores. As this variance increases, eta increases up to a certain point, and then begins to decrease. Screening validity at the optimum cutting score declines as this variance increases, but the test becomes much more flexible, maintaining the same validity for a wide range of cutting scores. For items of the type ordinarily used in psychological tests, the test with uniform item difficulty gives greater over-all validity, and superior validity for most cutting scores, compared to a test with a range of item difficulties. When a multiple-choice test is intended to reject the poorest *F* per cent of the men tested, items should on the average be located at or above the threshold for men whose true ability is at the *F*th percentile.

Cronbach, L. J., and Warrington, W. G. Efficiency of multiple-choice tests as a function of spread of item difficulties. *Psychometrika,* 1952, *17,* 127–147. Reprinted with the permission of the publisher and authors.

* This research was performed under contract Nop 536 with the Bureau of Naval Personnel, and received additional support from the Bureau of Research and Service, College of Education, University of Illinois.

Psychometric literature contains many articles which imply, directly or indirectly, that the efficiency of a test may be increased by using items more homogeneous in difficulty. Particularly when a test is to be used for dividing a group of persons being processed into accepted and rejected candidates, a test is desired which will discriminate the poorest acceptable men from the best of the rejected group, and no premium is placed on ability of the test to discriminate *within* the subgroups. Hence it has been suggested that for tests designed to identify the best x per cent of applicants, items should be placed close to the level where just x per cent can pass each item.

At the time this study was undertaken, the most definitive contribution on the subject had been made by Gulliksen (3). His rationale leads to the conclusion that test reliability and variance are maximized when items are at the same difficulty level, and he noted that this recommendation conflicts with the conventional practice of spreading items widely in difficulty. His solution is specifically limited to the free-response case, where students have no probability of passing items by chance. Gulliksen evaluates test efficiency in terms of a reliability coefficient of the product-moment type.

While working at the Naval Electronics Laboratory, the senior author applied Gulliksen's suggestion, along with several other design changes, to the classification test used to measure pitch discrimination in potential sonarmen. The results of preliminary experiments confirmed the expectation that screening efficiency would be improved by using nearly uniform item difficulty throughout the test. At this point, the late E. G. Brundage suggested that more definitive studies were needed before adopting the recommendation to use peaked (uniform difficulty) tests. In particular, while a test designed to pass just 45 per cent of recruits might be ideal for screening at that level, if a change in the manpower supply made it necessary to lower the standard, taking from the top 60 per cent, or permitted raising the cutting point to take only 30 per cent, the test peaked at the 45-per cent point might be inferior to a test of conventional design. As work progressed on this problem, it became equally important to examine the effect of multiple-choice "do-guess" directions upon the recommendation, which had previously been applied only to the free-response case. Moreover, careful consideration was given to selecting the best function for evaluating test efficiency.

This study is restricted to three-choice items on which the following limitations are imposed:

1. All items in any test measure the same underlying ability with equal saturation. The tetrachoric correlation between items after correction for chance success (2) is uniform for all item-pairs.

2. The underlying ability is normally distributed in the population tested.

3. For persons whose true ability is far below the level required to pass any item, the probability of selecting the correct alternative for the item is one-third.
4. The person's performance on any item is experimentally independent of his performance on any other item.
5. The probability that a person will succeed on an item is a function of his ability, and this function is described by the integral of the normal curve, an ogive asymptotic to $y = 1.00$ and $y = 1/3$.
6. The test score is the sum of the number of items passed.

Our study investigates how the screening efficiency of a test varies with changes in the spread of item difficulty, for various degrees of item reliability. Minor analyses indicate the effect of change in test length and of level of item difficulty on the efficiency. Attention is also directed to the question, what level of item difficulty offers maximum screening validity for multiple-choice tests?

While this study was in progress, the fundamental investigation by F. M. Lord became available (4). This thesis, influenced in part by the suggestions of Gulliksen and Tucker, attempts a rational analysis of the problem of item difficulty and test validity. Save for restricting himself to the free-response case, his assumptions are identical to ours and his conclusions are in general accord with ours. Pending the publication of his attempts at rational treatment of the multiple-choice case, we have only the present empirical findings to guide test construction of this type, since the generalizations from the free-response case require alteration when guessing is possible. Because of our concern with the flexibility of a test as cutting scores are changed, we have used a different function than Lord's to evaluate validity, and this introduces minor differences into the results. Lord's conclusions which relate most closely to ours are as follows:

4. Maximum discrimination at a given ability level, as defined by the discrimination index developed here, is provided by a test composed of items all of equal difficulty such that examinees at the given ability level will have a fifty per cent chance of answering each item correctly.
5. There are strong indications, provided the item intercorrelations are not extraordinarily high, that a test composed entirely of items of fifty per cent difficulty will be more discriminating for practically all examinees in the group tested than will any test characterized by a spread of item difficulties. If the examinees have a normal distribution of ability, for example, the former test will be the most discriminating for all examinees except those who are more than, say, two-and-a-half standard deviations from the mean.

6. The shape of the frequency distribution of test scores or of true scores does not necessarily reflect the shape of the frequency distribution of ability. Sufficiently high tetrachoric item intercorrelations (.50 or higher) will produce rectangular or *U*-shaped distributions of test scores and of true scores even for groups having a normal distribution of ability. (The construction of tests that will produce rectangular or U-shaped score distributions has been urged more than once in the recent literature; this goal can be approached, but its actual achievement, when the examinees have a normal distribution of ability, requires higher item intercorrelations than are at present usually obtained with most types of test items.)

"The foregoing conclusions have here been derived only for the case where the test items cannot be answered correctly by guessing" (4, p. 75).

Our study may also be compared to the pioneer rational treatment of the problem by Richardson (5). Our theoretical model adopts the ideas Richardson used, save that we are concerned with three-choice items. Our question differs from his in that he was concerned with the effect of changing the level of item difficulty whereas we have been concerned with changing the range of item difficulty. Our approach permits consideration of a range of item reliabilities. These extensions, while allowing our work to confirm the majority of his findings, introduces some modifications into the implications of his work. In particular, it will be seen that our findings stress the flexibility of peaked tests, under ordinary conditions, even when the cutting level shifts quite a bit from the difficulty level of the items.

PROCEDURE

The method we employ is neither rational analysis nor the empirical treatment of actual data. We make an empirical study using hypothetical data designed to meet our conditions and to represent the type of item used in the Navy pitch test. We define the following variables:

x_p The true ability of persons on the underlying variable of our test. x is normally distributed, with a mean of zero and an s.d. of 1. x constitutes our criterion.

y_i The scale-value of item i, expressed on the same scale of ability as x. 67 per cent of the persons whose true ability is y_i pass the item (50 per cent after correction for chance).

σ_d The standard deviation of the normal curve whose integral is the ogive that defines $p_{i \cdot x}$ as a function of x. $p_{i \cdot x}$ is the probability that a person with true ability x will pass item i. h, the psychophysical measure of precision, is $\sqrt{2}/2\sigma_d$. σ_d expresses that error of measurement which results from lack of precision in a single observation, apart from guessing.

Our steps are as follows:

Step 1. The ogive $p_{i \cdot x} = f(y_i - x)$ is determined for five values of σ_d, namely 0, 0.2, 0.5, 1.0, and 2.0. Because guessing as well as lack of precision lowers the item intercorrelation, σ_d is related to item reliability as indicated in Table 1. In practice, it should be realized, item correlations are ordinarily low. Hence σ_d will rarely be less than 0.5.

TABLE 1. Relation of σ_d to Item Reliability

σ_d	Correlation with similar item if probability of chance success by guessing is zero		Correlation with similar item if probability of chance success by guessing is one-third	
	r_{tet}	phi*	r_{tet}*	phi*
0	1.00	1.00	.70	.50
.2	.94	.80	.55	.37
.5	.82	.60	.40	.27
1.0	.50	.34	.25	.17
2.0	.23	.13	.12	.07

* Values in these columns will vary according to item difficulty. These computations are based on items where $y = 0$. Our computational procedure was to determine the probability that a person with a given criterion score would pass both, one only, or neither, of two items with the same precision and $y = 0$. These conditional probabilities were multiplied by the probability of each x value, and summed to form a four-fold table from which the coefficients could be determined.

The following steps use one value of σ_d at a time.

Step 2. The conditional probability $p_{i \cdot x}$ is known from Step 1, for any value of $y - x$. The conditional probability that the person will earn any score s from zero to n on a test of n items of uniform difficulty is obtained by the binomial theorem.

Step 3. The expected relative frequency of any score x is known from the normal curve. Multiplying the conditional probability of any score $p_{s \cdot x}$ by p_x gives the joint probability p_{sx}. Arraying these against s and x gives the bivariate distribution of score and criterion.

Step 4. The validity coefficient (see below) is determined for each cutting score.

Step 5. To study tests not uniform in difficulty, short component tests were constructed in which y was held constant (Step 2). The conditional probability matrices for these components were then multiplied to get the conditional probability of any desired combination. Then Steps 3 and 4 were followed. For example, one thirty-item test was constructed by multiplying matrices for five six-item peaked tests.

Table 2 lists the patterns examined. In choosing patterns of item difficulty for study, an attempt was made to include a wide variety without

TABLE 2. Test Patterns Studied, Described in Terms of Number of Items at Each Scale Position

Length of Test	Scale Value (y)	Pattern A	Pattern B	Pattern C	Pattern D
	+ 2.5				3
	+ 2.0				3
	+ 1.5				3
	+ 1.0			6	3
	+ 0.5		6	6	3
30	0	30	18	6	3
	− 0.5		6	6	3
	− 1.0			6	3
	− 1.5				3
	− 2.0				3
	+ 0.5			6	
18	0	18		6	
	− 0.5			6	
	+ 0.5			6	
12	0	12			
	− 0.5			6	
6	0*	6			

* 6-item tests were also studied for scale values $y = +1.0, +0.5, -0\ 5$, and -1.0.

unduly increasing computation. Pattern A, the "peaked" test, is examined at all lengths and values of σ_d. Pattern B is moderately peaked, Pattern C less so, and Pattern D has virtually a flat distribution of item scale values. It is perhaps more common to think of item difficulty in terms of p_i. After correction for chance success, p_i has a non-linear relation to y_i ; where $\sigma_d = 0$, the relation is as follows:

y	+3	+2	+1	0	−1	− 2	−3
p	0.1	2	16	50	84	98	99.9

For less precise items (σ_d larger) p is smaller than these values when $y < 0$ and greater when $y > 0$. Thus for Pattern C, $\sigma_d = 0$, the distribution of item p's is U-shaped, with many very hard and very easy items. It happened that the pitch test, based on a physical scale, had items spaced according to scale units rather than item p's. In any case our patterns are sufficiently consecutive that inferences regarding intermediate patterns are not hard to make.

Evaluation function. To judge the screening efficiency of a test, one thinks first of the phi coefficient and biserial r. Men are to be dichotomized, and errors of classification are to be avoided. Where the scores are to be used in no other manner, there is no need to discriminate among men well above or below the point of cut. Suppose F per cent of the men are to be eliminated. Phi might be determined by dividing the x scale at that point above which F per cent of the men fall, dividing the score scale similarly, and computing from the four-fold. Biserial r would use the continuous x scale with the dichotomized s scale. The difference is that biserial r weights errors of classification according to their distance from the point of intended cut (i.e., their "seriousness"). Phi is closely related to the number of misses and false positives, being the ratio of actual "hits in excess of chance expectancy" to possible "hits in excess of chance." Preliminary studies showed that conclusions for phi and for r_{bis} differ negligibly.

Unlike product-moment r, r_{bis} is independent of the test score metric. Our results are therefore invariant as test scores are transformed to other scales. It was thought possible that transformations of the test score distribution would seriously alter the product-moment correlation of the test with a normally distributed criterion. As another part of our inquiry, we have determined validity in terms of η. Lord uses as his evaluation function an index which is not invariant under transformation of scores but which, unlike our functions, is independent of the range of ability in the population tested.

The reader should note that we have used a sort of index of reliability, the correlation of test score with normalized true score, as a validity coefficient. This is legitimate for a test of pitch, a very pure function, where true threshold is a good criterion. In the case of a test where items contain a common factor other than the criterion factor, which is ruled out by our assumption (1), it would not be correct to regard our r_{bis} as a validity coefficient.

RESULTS: SCREENING VALIDITY

Figures 1 and 2 present the results of our computations for thirty-item tests with varying patterns and varying σ_d. Each curve shows the screening validity at each possible cutting score, for one test. For a test having a limited number of items, validity is lower when a cut is made at any percentile point not falling midway between two items. This would give our curves a "scalloped" effect, and has not been shown in these charts as we are concerned with main effects. In Figure 4 an unsmoothed curve showing these dips is plotted.

In Figure 1, we see that validity of the peaked test varies considerably with change in cutting score. Thinking of the validity curve in relation to the marginal curve showing distribution shape, we see that screening validity is high if a cut is made at the trough of the bimodal distribution. But half the people, whose ability is below the scale value of the items, pass items only by chance, and any cut which chooses among the lower half of the cases does so only by chance. Hence this peaked test with

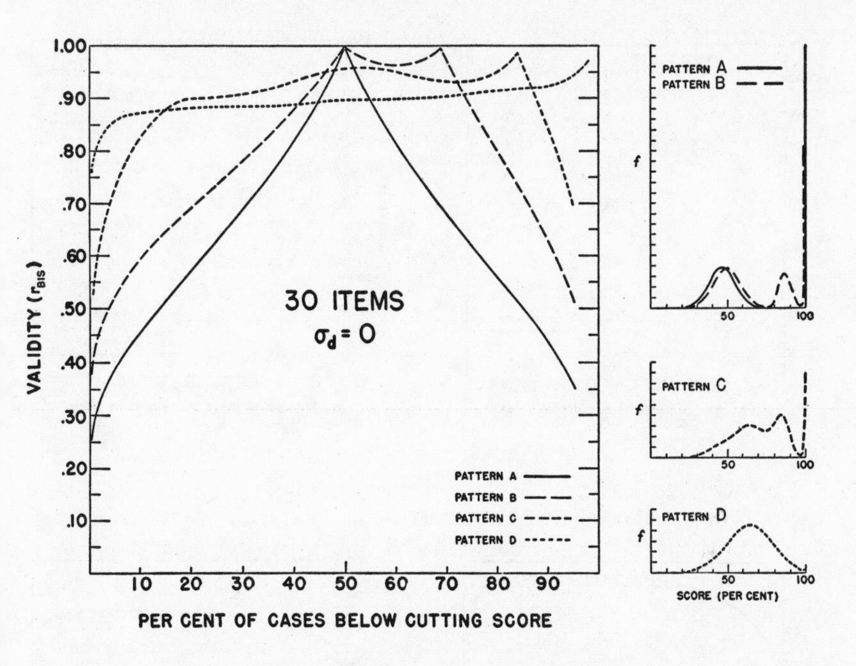

FIGURE 1. Validity curves for various patterns.

perfectly reliable items (except for the effect of chance) is inflexible, and unsuitable for a situation where the selection ratio may change. As the items vary more in difficulty, the maximum validity begins to drop but the validity stays nearly constant over an increasingly wide range of selection ratios.

Considering now the additional facts offered by Figure 2, we have these generalizations:

1. For tests of at least moderate length, the distribution of scores is bimodal for very precise items of uniform difficulty. An increase in either σ_d or σ_y (or both) causes the distribution to become unimodal and ultimately normal. (The distributions demonstrating this conclusion are assembled in Figure 6.)

2. The validity curve for a more peaked test rises above the validity curve for any less peaked test for some selection ratios in the middle of the scale, but falls below for very high or low selection ratios. This suggests that we examine the "range of advantage" of one test over the other, as we do in Table 3.

3. The range of advantage of the highly peaked test over other patterns is very small for precise items but increases as σ_d increases. *For values of* σ_d *expected in practice, the sharply-peaked test A is superior*

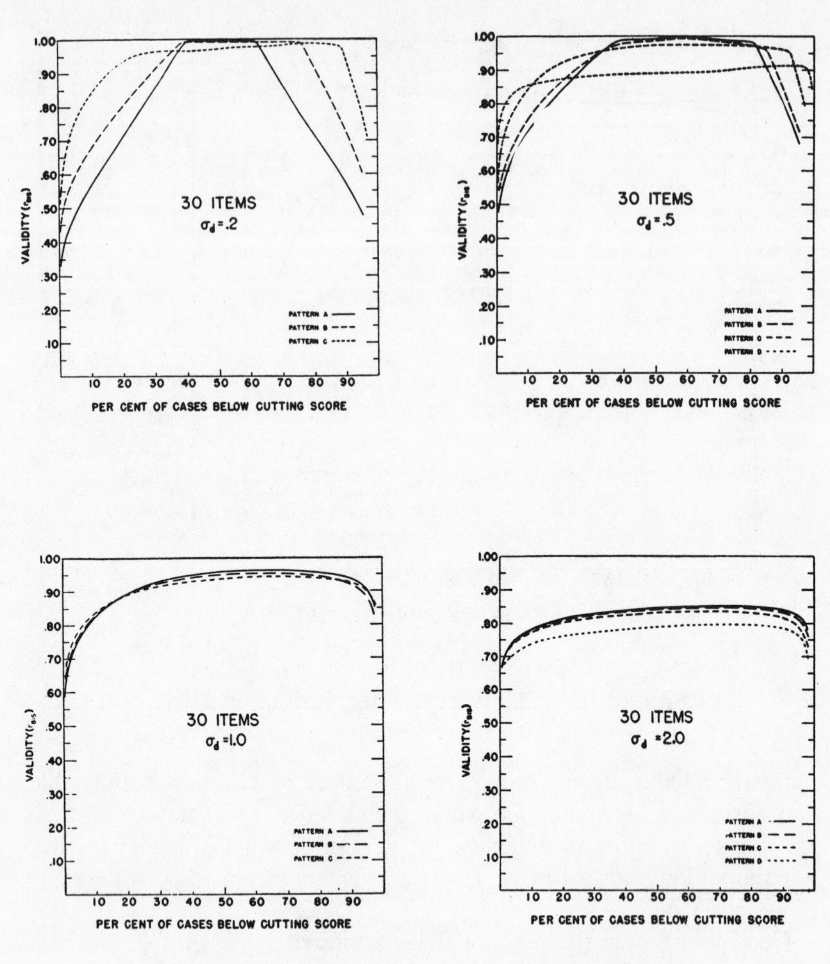

FIGURE 2. Validity curves for various patterns.

TABLE 3. Superiority of Peaked Test A over Pattern B and Pattern C, for Five Degrees of Item Precision

σ_d	Range of Advantage of A over B*	Range of Advantage of A over C*
0	50	50
.2	40 to 62	38 to 63
.5	34 to 82	34 to 82
1.0	19 to 99 (or 100)	19 to 96
2.0	02 to 99 (or 100)	02 to 99 (or 100)

* Percentage-of-men-rejected for which biserial validity for A is better than for less peaked test.

to the other patterns over a wide range of selection ratios. Hence the peaked test is not inflexible for practical utility.

4. The magnitude of the gain in validity at the maximum, as a result of reducing the range of items, is much greater for highly reliable items than for unreliable ones. While decreasing the range of item difficulty increases validity at most cutting scores when $\sigma_d \geqq 1.0$, the increase is very slight in amount.

These results completely confirm Lord's conclusions 5 and 6. Results for η will be discussed in a later section.

Validity and test length. In Figures 3 and 4 we present the validity functions for a few shorter tests. These results indicate that the conclusions advanced above are in no way dependent on test length. We note the interesting fact (Figure 4) that increasing the length of a peaked test where $\sigma_d = 0$ does not raise reliability or validity noticeably after the test distribution is separated into two portions. The validity curve for 30 items would fall almost identically on the six-item curve in Figure 4.

Validity related to item precision. Figure 5 shows validity curves for varying σ_d, pattern being constant in any chart. The results resemble in some ways the curves that come from varying pattern: the tests with greater precision are most valid for intermediate selection ratios but have inferior validity at the extremes. The chart for Pattern D seems to contradict this, but only because the curves are incomplete at the very ends. Markedly increasing item precision reduces the flexibility of a test for screening without any appreciable gain in validity at the point of greatest efficiency. This conclusion, which agrees with Tucker's (6), we shall discuss further below.

It is strange that improving individual items should lower validity. The explanation of our paradox is this: If an item has perfect precision, it gives no information about which of the men whose criterion score is below y_i are best. All of these men will have the same score (zero) on a group of perfectly precise free-response items, if guessing is impossible. If each item allows two or more choices, the scores will vary but the differences will not be related to ability. Since the obtained scores are equal or differ only by chance, the test does not discriminate among low-ability men having different criterion scores. Likewise the peaked test gives no information about individual differences within the high-ability group, whose thresholds are above the scale position of the items. In a less precise item, the proportion passing is a sloping function of criterion score, and a man whose ability falls slightly below the scale position of the item will tend to earn a higher score than the man who is far below the scale position. Each item contributes information along the whole scale. Hence in the peaked test, less precise items do discriminate better than precise items at all cutting scores except where the precise item has maximum validity.

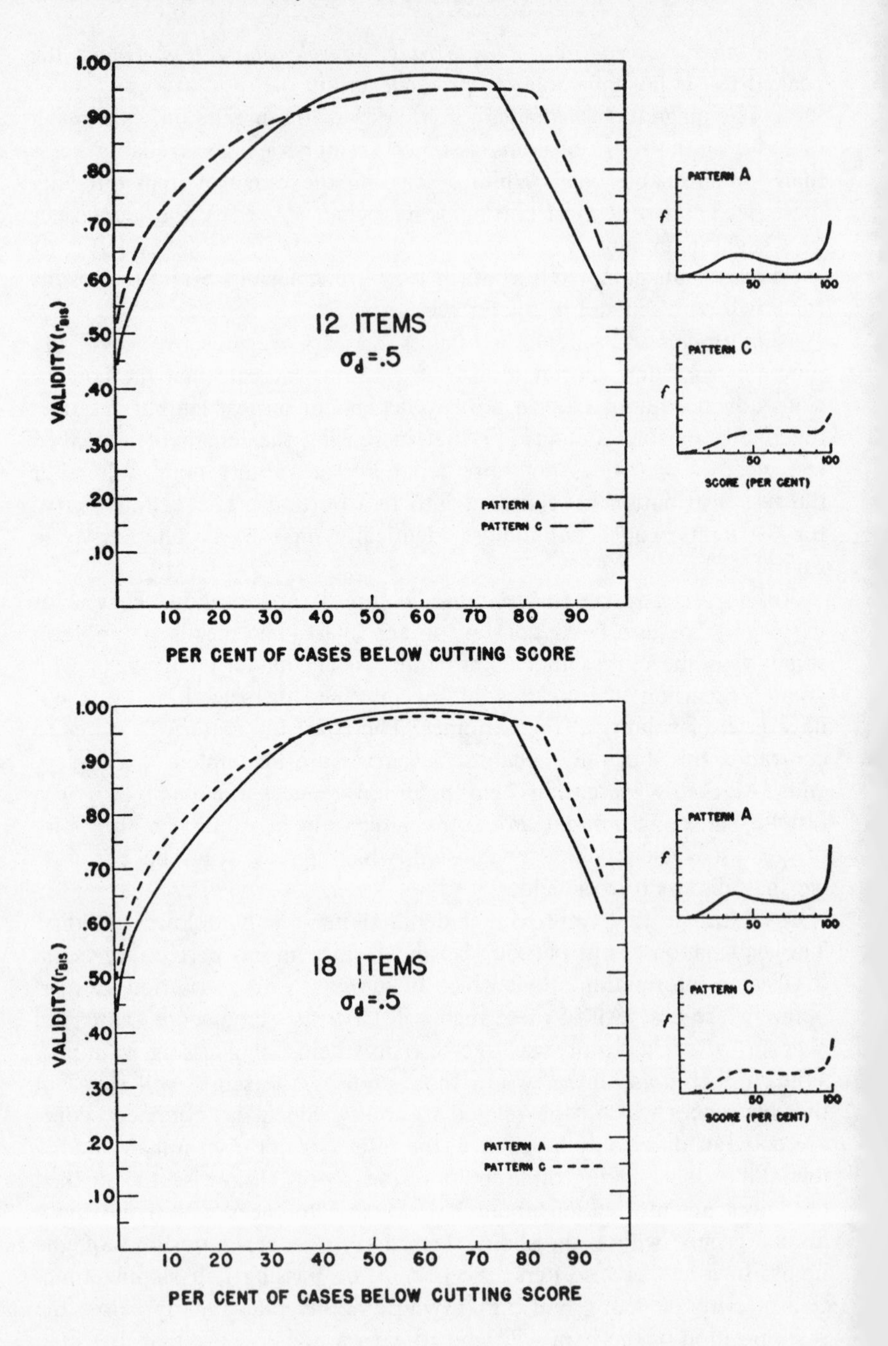

FIGURE 3. Validity curves for shorter tests, Pattern A *vs.* Pattern C.

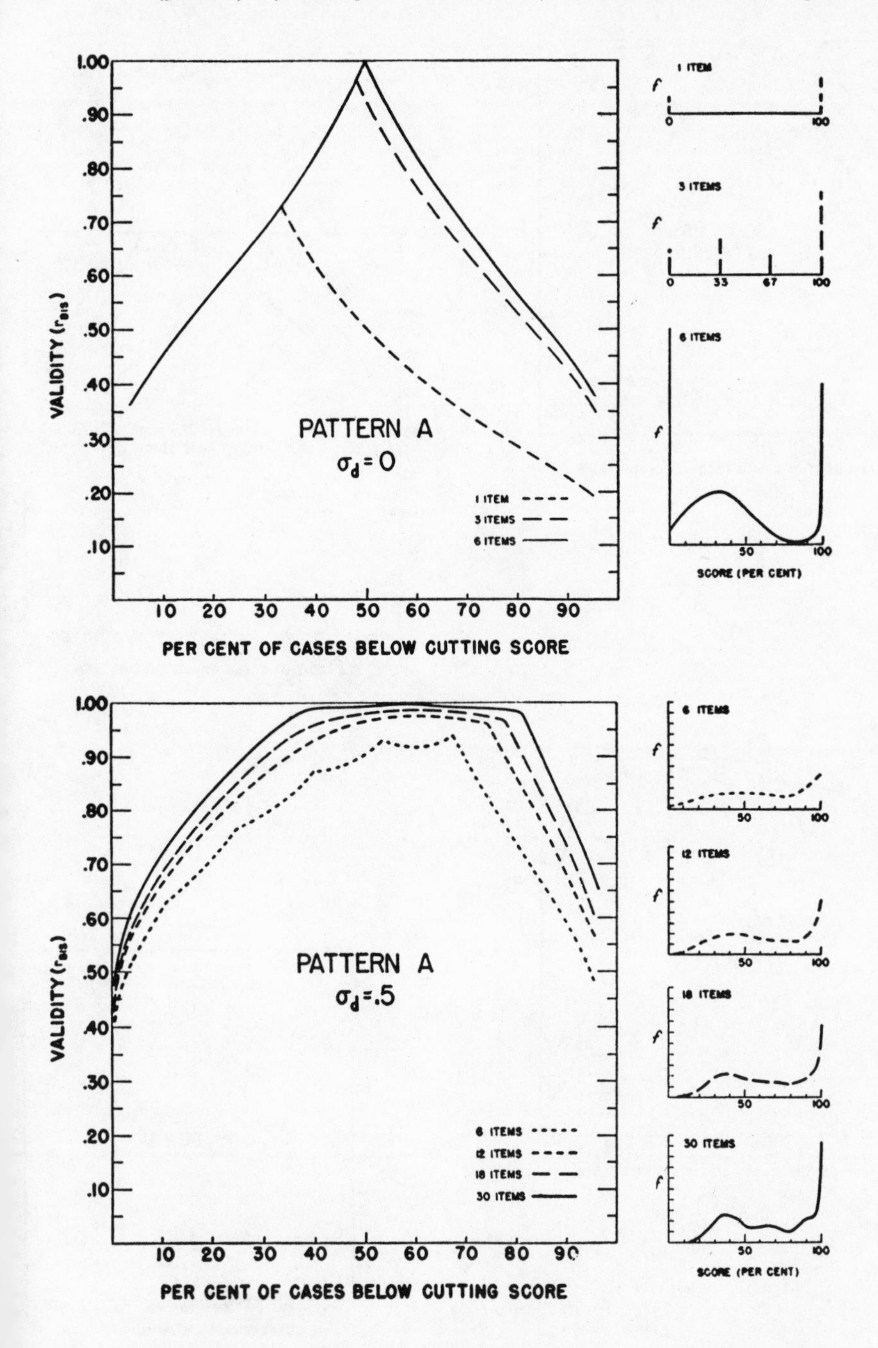

FIGURE 4. Changes in validity curve of peaked test with increasing length.

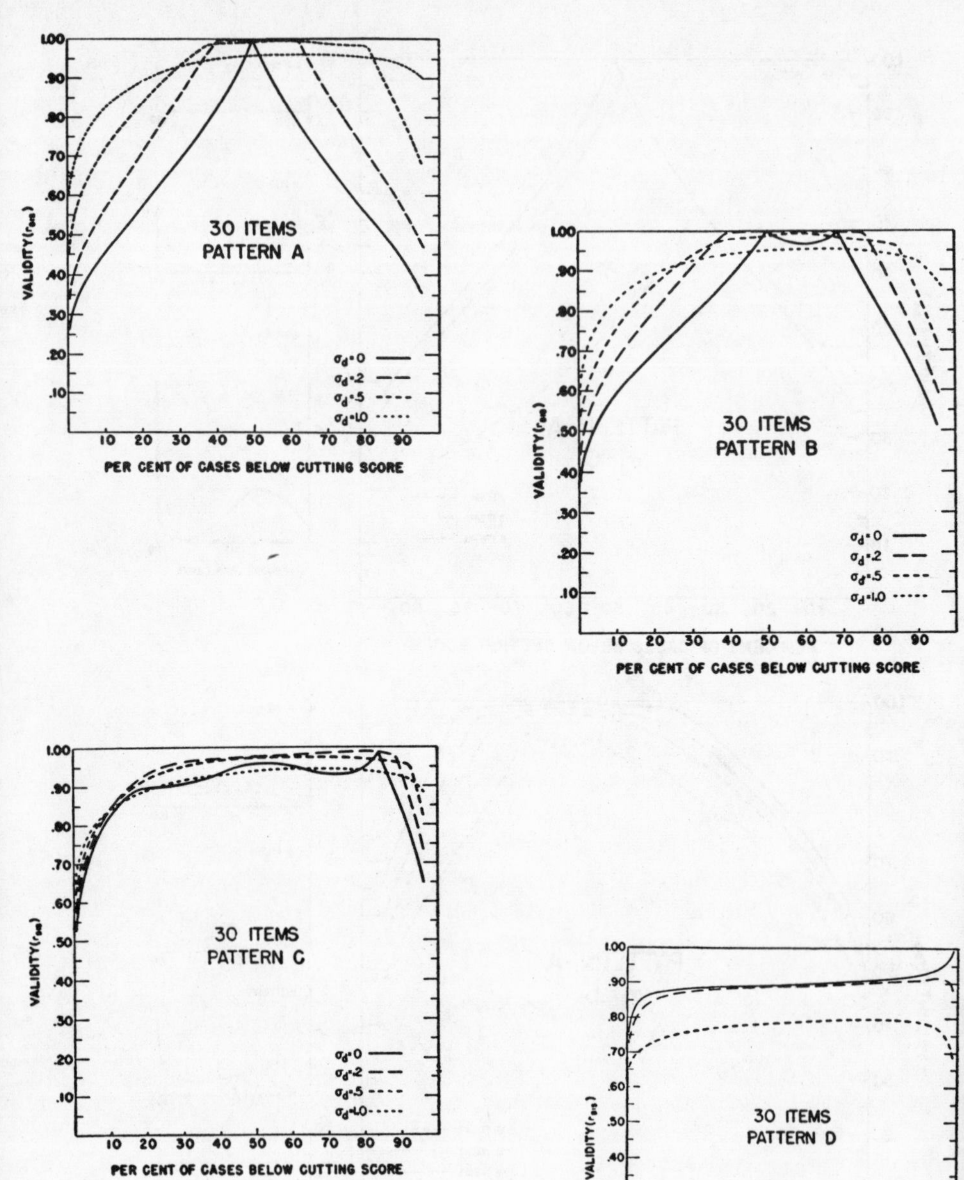

FIGURE 5. Validity curves for varying item precision.

As Table 4 indicates, validity of a test at extreme cutting scores may be increased by *increasing* either σ_d or σ_y up to a certain point. It appears that when we have inaccurate items we gain validity *over nearly the whole range* by peaking the item difficulty distribution. When we have very accurate items, greatest validity over the range is obtained with a spread of item difficulties.

TABLE 4. Validity at Two Cutting Scores as a Function of Precision and Pattern

Cut to eliminate poorest 50%					Cut to eliminate poorest 90%				
σ_d	A	B	C	D	σ_d	A	B	C	D
0	*1.00*	1.00	.96	.895	0	.44	.63	.84	*.93*
.2	*1.00*	1.00	.98		.2	.57	.73	*.95*	
.5	*.99*	.985	.975	.89	.5	.80	.84	*.96*	.91
1.0	*.96*	.95	.94		1.0	*.93*	.92	.92	
2.0	*.845*	.84	.83	.79	2.0	*.84*	.83	.82	.79

The highest validity in each row is italicized.

A comprehensive interpretation. Several of our results indicate that σ_d and σ_y have much the same effect on score distribution and validity. This effect would be even more striking if we had not, for ease of computation, used a discontinuous pattern of y's while letting error of measurement be continuous. As it is, in Figure 5, the curve for Pattern *A*, $\sigma_d = .5$ ($\sigma_y = 0$), falls exactly between the curves for Pattern *B*, $\sigma_d = 0$($\sigma_y = .3$), and Pattern *C*, $\sigma_d = 0$($\sigma_y = .7$). We are indebted to Dr. R. S. Gales for putting us on the track of an explanation for this relation.

When $\sigma_d > 0$, a single person sometimes passes an item, sometimes fails it. This may be regarded as sheer inconsistency, but in looking for deeper causes we can describe it as a variation in the person's instantaneous threshold. In the pitch test, the person's threshold presumably varies as a result of fluctuations in the physical or electrical states of his ear and brain, of fluctuations in alertness, and so on. His "internal noise level" changes. In effect, the difference between signal (test item) and noise level (threshold) changes just as it would if his ability remained perfectly stable and the stimulus changed in discriminability. Another source of unreliability might be variation in signal received, where items are supposed to be equally difficult. A noise made by a neighbor, a momentary distraction, or a variation in turntable speed would cause an item to be harder than others of supposedly equal scale value. These variations, too, alter the difference between momentary item scale value and momentary threshold. The effect of this shift in $y_{it} - x_{pt}$ (the t indicating value at a particular time) is to shift the ogive $p_i = f(y - x)$ to right or left. There is no operation by which we can distinguish, for a single person, between changes in scale value of item presented, in scale value of item received, and in threshold of the person. Hence on any test we would expect identical probability of passing any item or attaining any score, and consequent identical validity, whichever of these varies by a given amount.

An increase in σ_y (variation in true item difficulty) has the same consequences as an increase in σ_d (variation in performance from trial to trial), so long as we are dealing with homogeneous items. Therefore we may seek generalizations in terms of these interrelated phenomena.

When $\sigma_y = 0$ and $\sigma_d = 0$, we have a test which is highly precise and highly specific. It gives perfect information as to the classification of persons around a single cutting score (as soon as enough items are used to separate scores attained by chance from earned scores). It gives no valid discrimination within either the superior or the inferior group. Such a test measures, not pitch-threshold on a continuous scale, but ability to pass a particular level as an all-or-none quality. There is no advantage in lengthening such a test beyond a small number of items.

When total variance in relative threshold ($\sigma_d^2 + \sigma_y^2$) increases, the test becomes gradually less specific and less precise. In the usual testing situation the quality of items is hard to improve after care has been used in preparing them, and σ_d may therefore be regarded as given. This fixes the upper limit of specificity and the upper limit of validity for the best cutting score and given test length. Considering Figure 2, $\sigma_d = .5$, as an example, the curve for Pattern A ($\sigma_y = 0$) shows the maximum validity for this type of item, and shows that validity holds up well for cutting scores which reject from 35 to 80 per cent of the group. If such flexibility is enough for one's purposes, he can do no better than to use the peaked pattern. If he must have greater flexibility, he can increase σ_y and so obtain validity at more extreme cutting scores, thereby sacrificing to a greater or less degree the validity at the point of greatest efficiency.

This rationale suggests that we can clarify our generalizations by examining the data in terms of the variance of relative thresholds within persons. This is $\sigma_d^2 + \sigma_y^2$, the variance of the difference between the person's momentary threshold and the item scale value over all items and over many trials. Applying the concept to our materials, we present in Table 5 the variances for each of the thirty-item patterns of this study.

In Figure 6, we have arranged the relative score distributions for eight tests, selected to show a regular increment in $\sigma_d^2 + \sigma_y^2$ from .00 to 6.06. It is seen that the curves progress regularly from a bimodal distribution through a relatively flat distribution toward a normal distribution. Any departure from the regular trend arises because changes in item difficulty were discontinuous, whereas errors of measurement were normally distributed at all times.

TABLE 5. Variance in Relative Threshold for Various Test Characteristics

σ_d	Pattern A $\sigma_y = 0$	Pattern B $\sigma_y = .3$	Pattern C $\sigma_y = .7$	Pattern D $\sigma_y = 1.4$
0	0	.10	.50	2.06
0.2	0.04	.14	.54	2.10
0.5	0.25	.35	.75	2.31
1.0	1.00	1.10	1.50	3.06
2.0	4.00	4.10	4.50	6.06

When we examine the validity curves of Figures 1 and 2 in order of variance in relative threshold we find a regular progression over the entire series of twenty curves (two not actually computed). The progression shows the curves to form a single family, save for discrepancies introduced by the discontinuity of item scale values. We can now state our major generalization as follows: For three-choice items representing a single ability in a test of fixed length and fixed average item difficulty, as $\sigma_d^2 + \sigma_y^2$ increases,

1. the validity of the test at its point of greatest efficiency decreases;
2. the validity has nearly the maximum value over an increasing range of selection ratios (i.e., the test is more adaptable to new selection ratios).

For relatively unreliable items such as are normally encountered in practice, sufficient flexibility is guaranteed by the magnitude of σ_d, *and uniform item difficulty is advisable in order to minimize* $\sigma_d^2 + \sigma_y^2$ *and thereby maintain validity as high as possible.*

OPTIMUM ITEM DIFFICULTY FOR A GIVEN SELECTION RATIO

Where chance is not a factor, a test is expected to be most efficient at a selection ratio which corresponds to the proportion passing the items. For the three-choice test, however, the maximum validity is usually found to the *right* of the mean scale position of the test items. In the tests so far discussed the mean y has been 0*, which corresponds to a selection ratio that fails 50 per cent of the men. The rightward displacement cannot be determined accurately for the flat-topped curves, but it is seen, for example, that Pattern A when $\sigma_d = .5$ has its maximum validity when about 57 per cent of the men are rejected. (Cf. Lord's conclusion 4.)

This rightward displacement is shown especially by the series of curves in Figure 7 where five peaked tests, each six items long, are

* Except for 30-item Pattern D, where the mean y is +0.25.

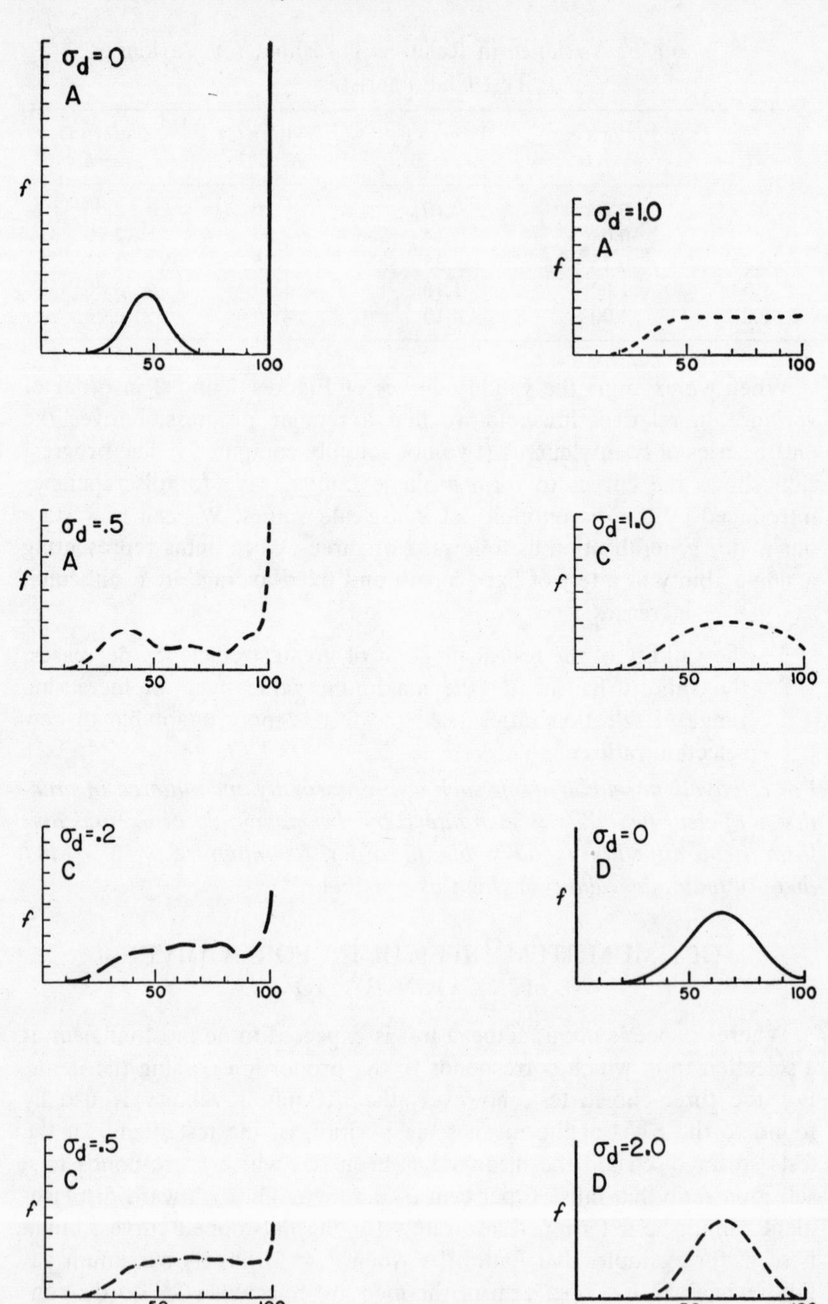

FIGURE 6. Distributions of scores, expressed as per cent of possible score, for patterns representing increasing variance of relative threshold.

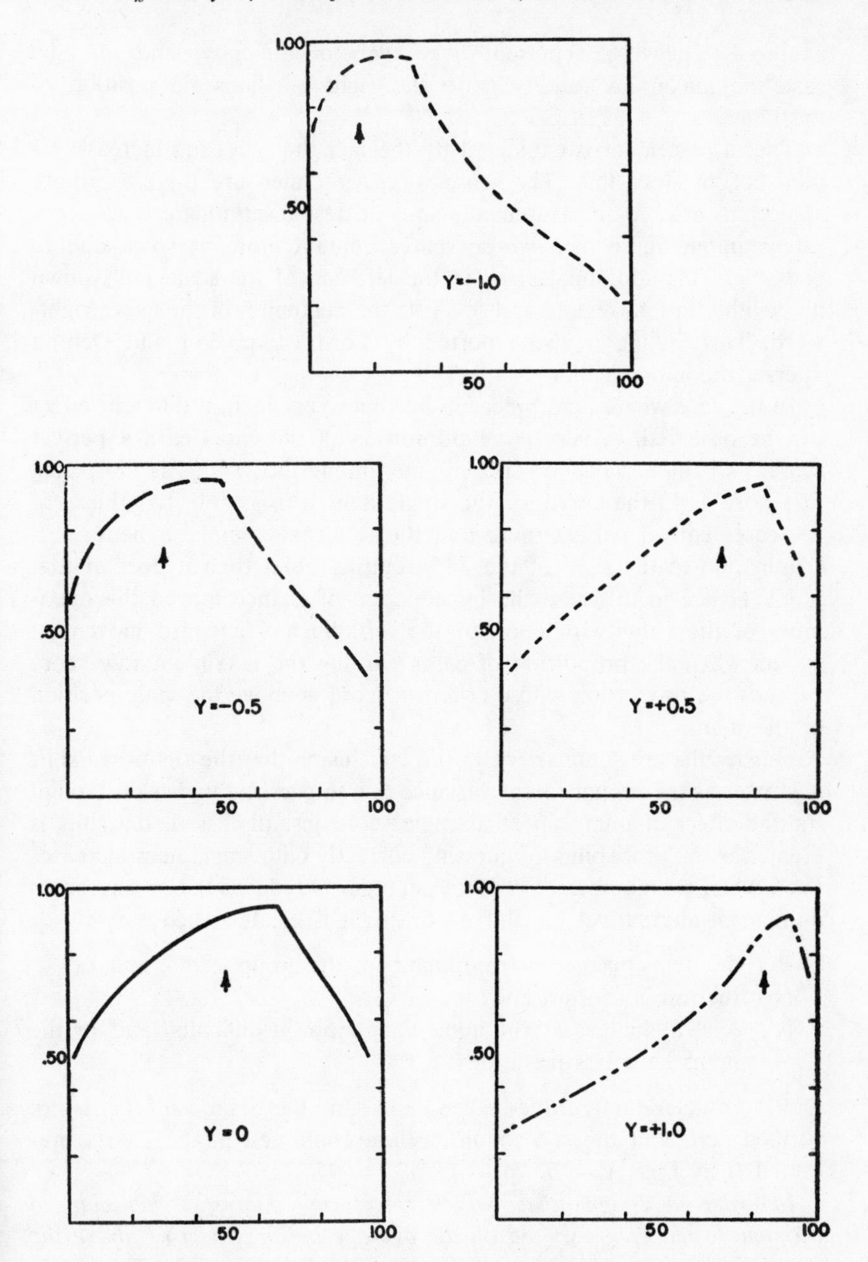

FIGURE 7. Validity curves for peaked tests of varying difficulty. Each test is based on six items, Pattern A, $\sigma_d = .5$. Horizontal axis shows selection ratio (per cent failed). Vertical axis shows biserial *r*. Arrow indicates scale value at which test is peaked.

analyzed. The tests represent five levels of difficulty, and in each case the maximum validity is to the right of the scale position of the items.

The displacement is explained by the fact that guessing increases as men become less able. The scores of poorer men are therefore more subject to error of measurement, and the test discriminates less accurately among these men whose scores contain more variance due to guessing. This additional error at the left end of the scale pulls down the validity in that region, and so shifts the maximum of the curve rightward. This finding is also reported by Lord (4, p. 35) and Denton (personal communication).

In the case where item precision becomes very high, a different effect can be observed. A very large proportion of the cases earn a perfect score, and the test cannot discriminate among them. This is illustrated in Figure 4. In the curve for the single item with $\sigma_d = 0$, two-thirds of the cases earn a perfect score and the test cannot make a better discrimination to the right of the 33% cutting point than it does at that point. Hence in this case the introduction of chance moved the maximum of the validity function to the *left*. Such a leftward movement occurs when the proportion of cases earning the maximum raw score exceeds the proportion whose criterion score is above the scale position of the items.

Our results are summarized in the conclusion that the rightward shift is greater as the proportion of variance due to guessing increases. Except for the effect of piling up at a single score just discussed, the shift is greater as the probability of guessing correctly on a single item increases (i.e., when the number of choices per item is reduced). For any given number of alternatives the shift to the right is greater when

(a) the items become more difficult for the group tested, and/or
(b) the test is shorter, and/or
(c) $\sigma_d^2 + \sigma_y^2$ increases (the items vary more in difficulty, and/or the items have less precision).

Our data include only three-choice items, and the basic condition is not verified here, but the sub-conditions are confirmed in the charts presented (esp. Figs. 1, 4, 5, 7).

In order to design a test which rejects the poorest F *per cent of the men tested, items should on the average be located at or above the threshold for men whose true ability is at the* F*th percentile.* These men are at the borderline on the criterion. Then according to our results these borderline men should have a fifty per cent, or more than a fifty per cent, chance of passing the mean test item, after correction for chance. That is, test items should ordinarily be easier than items at the threshold of these borderline men. Just how much easier depends upon the factors listed in the preceding paragraph. An exception is the case where many men pile up at a single score as discussed above.

This recommendation departs from the published view that the proportion passing an item should correspond exactly to the proportion intended to be selected. Our rightward shift, which dictates use of items easier than the threshold for borderline men, results from our use of three-choice items. Previous theory has always been qualified with the comment that it applies only to free-response items where chance success is not allowed. Lord has pointed out another factor, however, which casts doubt on the published generalization in the free-response case (4, p. 33–35).

RESULTS: OVER-ALL VALIDITY

While our study was designed to resolve questions regarding screening validity, it is also of interest to evaluate the over-all correlation of scores with criterion. η, which is substantially the same as the correlation of normalized test scores with the normal criterion, indicates how much the test can contribute in prediction and in multiple correlation. Our data were not in a form which permitted accurate computation of η for some tests, because of use of broad categories. For this reason, two of the entries in Table 6 are uncertain.

TABLE 6. Correlation (η) of Test with Criterion

σ_d	Pattern			
	A	B	C	D
0	.80	*	**	.90
.2	.87	.91	.94	
.5	.92	.92	.93	.88
1.0	.92	.91	.91	
2.0	.82	.82	.81	.77

* Computed as greater than .86; probably near to .91.
** Computed as greater than .91; probably near to .94.

As in Tucker's study of a peaked test (6), validity is seen to increase and decrease as item precision rises. Insofar as we can compare the present data with Tucker's, the introduction of fixed responses and resultant guessing lowers validity for higher values of σ_d. Apparently use of η rather than *r* had no substantial effect on validities, but a firm conclusion on this cannot be offered.

When data in Table 6 are organized according to $\sigma_d^2 + \sigma_y^2$, a clear functional relation exists:

$\sigma_d^2 + \sigma_y^2$	.00	.04	.14	.25	.54	1.00	1.50	2.06	4.00	6.06
η	.80	.87	.91	.92	.94	.92	.91	.90	.82	.77

Because the extremely peaked test of precise items does not discriminate along the entire scale, for any given length of test there is a value of $\sigma_d^2 + \sigma_y^2$ which gives maximum validity. For the thirty-item test, this maximizing value is about .50. Hence if items have low to moderate precision so that $\sigma_d^2 > .50$, the peaked test will have greater validity than any other pattern. Insofar as we can judge from these and Tucker's results, the peaked test has superior validity for even lower values of σ_d (higher r_{ij}) when the test is longer than thirty items.

When σ_d^2 is less than the maximizing value, there is a value of σ_y which maximizes η, i.e., an ideal degree of peaking for the given item precision and number of items. The curve of validity as a function of $\sigma_d^2 + \sigma_y^2$ has a very small slope, which implies that precise determination of the maximum is of little importance.

SUMMARY AND CONCLUSIONS

We have examined the validity (r_{bis} and η) of a univocal test in which each item has three alternatives. Our findings, in general, apply also to tests of the free-response type, but further evidence is needed regarding tests where items contain a factor other than the criterion factor.

Validity is found to depend on the quantity $\sigma_d^2 + \sigma_y^2$, where σ_d is a measure of item precision and σ_y reports the spread of item difficulties. As this variance increases,

1. validity (η) increases up to a maximum value and then declines. For a thirty-item test, the maximizing variance is about .50.
2. the distribution of scores becomes more nearly normal.
3. the screening validity (r_{bis}) of the test at the selection ratio where it has maximum efficiency decreases.
4. the screening validity has nearly the maximum value over an increasing range of selection ratios.

The selection ratio at which a test is most efficient depends on the difficulty of items. In order to design a test which rejects the poorest F per cent of the men tested, items should on the average be located at or above the threshold for men whose true ability is at the Fth percentile.

In view of the fact that items ordinarily used in mental tests have rather low intercorrelations, so that σ_d is usually greater than .5, we conclude that narrowing the range of item difficulty will generally have beneficial effects on the validity of tests. This will maximize η (unless the test is very short or the items unusually precise), and will allow increased validity at the best cutting score without greatly sacrificing validity at most other cutting scores. Constructors of educational and psychological tests would be wise to make item difficulty constant in most of their tests, since this lowers validity only for persons having extremely high or low ability.

REFERENCES

1. Brogden, H. E. Variation in test validity with variance in the distribution of item difficulties, number of items, and degree of their intercorrelation. *Psychometrika*, 1946, 11, 197–214.
2. Carroll, J. B. The effect of difficulty and chance success on correlations between items or between tests. *Psychometrika*, 1945, 10, 1–19.
3. Gulliksen, H. The relation of item difficulty and interitem correlation to test variance and reliability. *Psychometrika*, 1945, 10, 79–91.
4. Lord, F. M. A theory of test scores and their relation to the trait measured. *Res. Bull.* 51–13, Educational Testing Service, 1951. See also A theory of test scores. Psychometric Monograph No. 7, 1952.
5. Richardson, M. W. The relation between the difficulty and the differential validity of a test. *Psychometrika,* 1936, 1, 33–49.
6. Tucker, L. R. Maximum validity of a test with equivalent items. *Psychometrika*, 1946, 11, 1–13.

UNIT FIVE: ITEM ANALYSIS AND SELECTION ADDITIONAL READINGS

Adams, J. F. Test item difficulty and the reliability of item analysis methods. *Journal of Psychology*, 1960, *49*, 255–262.

Baker, F. B. An intersection of test score interpretation and item analysis. *Journal of Educational Measurement*, 1964, *1*, 23–28.

Das, R. S. Item analysis by profit and fractile graphical methods. *British Journal of Statistical Psychology*, 1964, *17*, 51–64.

Davis, F. B. Notes on test construction: The reliability of item analysis data. *Journal of Educational Psychology*, 1946, *37*, 385–390.

Davis, F. B. Item analysis in relation to educational and psychological testing. *Psychological Bulletin*, 1952, *49*, 97–122.

Ferguson, G. A. On the theory of test discrimination. *Psychometrika*, 1949, *14*, 61–68.

Gulliksen, H. O. The relation of item difficulty and interitem correlation to test variance and reliability. *Psychometrika*, 1945, *10*, 79–91.

Gulliksen, H. O. Item selection to maximize test validity. *Proceedings of the 1948 Invitational Conference on Testing Problems, Educational Testing Service*, 1949, 13–17.

Kelley, T. L. The selection of upper and lower groups for the validation of test items. *Journal of Educational Psychology*, 1939, *30*, 17–24.

Lord, F. M. The relation of the reliability of multiple-choice tests to the distribution of item difficulties. *Psychometrika*, 1952, *17*, 181–194.

Mosier, C. I. A note on item analysis and the criterion of internal consistency. *Psychometrika*, 1936, *1*, 275–282.

Myers, C. T. The relationship between item difficulty and test validity and reliability. *Educational and Psychological Measurement*, 1962, *22*, 565–571.

Richardson, M. W. The relation of difficulty to the differential validity of a test. *Psychometrika*, 1936, *1*, 33–49.

Richardson, M. W., and Adkins, Dorothy C. A rapid method of selecting test items. *Journal of Educational Psychology*, 1938, *29*, 547–552.

Swineford, Frances. Some relations between test scores and item statistics. *Journal of Educational Psychology*, 1959, *50*, 26–30.

Symonds, P. M. Choice of items for a test on the basis of difficulty. *Journal of Educational Psychology*, 1929, *20*, 481–493.

Travers, R. M. W. A note on the value of customary measures of item validity. *Journal of Applied Psychology*, 1942, *26*, 625–632.

Vernon, P. E. Indices of item consistency and validity. *British Journal of Psychology, Statistical Section*, 1948, *1*, 152–166.

EPILOGUE

You have studied some of the very best articles in the field of measurement. Unless a field of knowledge is very, very narrow (psychometrics isn't) and static (psychometrics isn't) it is quite impossible to cover more than a very limited amount of it in one book. We would like to borrow the last sentence from Stanley's basic measurement book and use it here.

"We wish you continued growth in knowledge of measurement and evaluation."[1]

[1] Stanley, J. C. *Measurement in Today's Schools,* 4th edition. Englewood Cliffs, N. J.: Prentice-Hall, 1964, 414 pp.

INDEX

PRINTED IN U.S.A